SECOND EDITION

ETHICS

and the

LEGAL
PROFESSION

SECOND EDITION

ETHICS

and the

LEGAL
PROFESSION

EDITED BY

Elliot D. Cohen & Michael Davis
with Frederick A. Elliston

 **Prometheus Books**

59 John Glenn Drive
Amherst, New York 14228-2119

Published 2009 by Prometheus Books

Inquiries should be addressed to
Prometheus Books
59 John Glenn Drive
Amherst, New York 14228–2119
VOICE: 716–691–0133, ext. 210
FAX: 716–691–0317
WWW.PROMETHEUSBOOKS.COM

13 12 11 10 09   5 4 3 2 1

Library of Congress Cataloging-in-Publication Data

Ethics and the legal profession / edited by Elliot D. Cohen and Michael Davis
with Frederick A. Elliston. – 2nd ed.

p. cm.

Includes bibliographical references.

ISBN 978-1-59102-621-1 (pbk. : alk. paper)
1. Legal ethics—United States. I. Cohen, Elliot D. II. Davis, Michael, 1943–
III. Elliston, Frederick.

KF306.E84 2009
174'.30973--dc22

2009014442

Printed in the United States on acid-free paper

CONTENTS

PART II: THE MORAL CRITIQUE OF THE LEGAL PROFESSION

PART III: THE ADVERSARY SYSTEM

PART IV: CONFLICT OF INTEREST AND PROFESSIONAL JUDGMENT

PART V: PERJURY AND CONFIDENTIALITY

PART VI: MAKING LEGAL ASSISTANCE AVAILABLE

INTRODUCTION

There are two general approaches to teaching "legal ethics," "professional integrity," "lawyer professionalism," or "the professional responsibility of lawyers" (all these terms naming the same subject more or less): the *legal* (or compliance) and the *ethical* (or philosophical). The legal approach asks, "What must a lawyer do to stay within the rules? How does a lawyer stay out of (serious) trouble?" The legal approach treats the ABA's *Model Rules of Professional Conduct* as just another statute or regulation, a constraint others have imposed as a condition of practicing law, or a close relative of the criminal law or, at least, of consumer protection (such as the truth-in-lending law). Naturally, a rational person would want to know how close she can get to that limit without getting on the wrong side of it. The ethical approach, in contrast, asks, "What must a lawyer do to be both a good lawyer and a good person? How should a lawyer contribute to 'the practice of law'?" The ethical approach treats the *Model Rules* as a standard voluntarily accepted to achieve a purpose all lawyers share, earning a living in a morally praiseworthy way. Lawyering is to be a "noble undertaking." One should aim for the target's center (to be as good a lawyer as one can be), not the target's edge (to be as poor a lawyer as one can get away with being).

While most texts in legal ethics seem to take the legal approach, this volume takes the ethical. Legal ethics is, we assume, not a mere side-constraint on the practice of law, itself a merely technical manipulation of language; legal ethics is essential to understanding what lawyers do, to understanding it not as theoretical knowledge, language game, or mere occupation, but as a profession. We do not discount the importance of rules in defining the practice of law. But we do assume that lawyers are much more likely to follow the rules competently if they interpret them as part of a common attempt to serve a certain moral ideal (justice within the bounds of the law) in a morally permissible way.

FALL AND RISE OF LEGAL ETHICS

The term "professional ethics" has been connected with lawyering in America at least since the publication of George Sharswood's 1854 essay, *Professional Ethics*.[1] Sharswood, then dean of the University of Pennsylvania's law school (and before that a judge for two decades), wanted to help young lawyers to start their legal career in the right way. His essay was originally published about seven years after the American Medical Association adopted its first code of ethics and more than a half century after the English physician Thomas Percival published a similar essay for physicians (with a similar title), *Medical Ethics*. Professional ethics was, it seems, already "in the air." It would, however, be another half century before lawyers—or engineers or any other non-medical occupation—adopted a formal code of ethics.

Sharswood's essay, like others, was not a code of ethics, though some writings on ethics on the same subject did serve as law school texts or handbooks for practitioners. The purpose of such essays was, as Sharswood put it, "to attempt to arrive at accurate and intelligible rules of action, by which to square the conduct of professional life."[2] The early books on professional ethics were like the contemporaneous guides to Christian gentlemen, which they much resembled. They gave the young lawyer a high-minded interpretation of legal requirements (statute, oath, and various customs) under which he was to practice.

Perhaps that was what legal ethics remained until the 1930s or 1940s. Then something changed and law schools began to drop the subject. By the late 1950s, formal instruction in legal ethics had disappeared from American law schools almost completely. The same trend was evident in medicine, nursing, engineering, teaching, and most other professions. Ethics was no longer "in the air."[3]

The air changed again in the 1960s, beginning with medicine. For lawyers, the Watergate scandals of the early 1970s seem to have been decisive. Many of those involved, including President Nixon and Vice President Agnew (both of whom resigned in disgrace), were lawyers. In response, the American Bar Association required law schools to provide all candidates for a professional degree "with instruction in the duties and responsibilities of the legal profession."[4] The most common approach to providing this instruction was (and remains) a required course. In most of these, the *Model Rules of Professional Conduct*, supported by a casebook, is the primary text. The course is much like any other "code course" (e.g., Commercial Transactions) except that, owing to a shortage of good cases, it often strikes students as intellectually thin.[5]

While the embarrassments of the 1970s seem to have been the main reason why law schools began to teach legal ethics again, there may have been two other reasons as well. One is the low regard almost everyone seemed to have—and still seems to have—for the honesty of lawyers. Gallup regularly polls Americans on their attitude toward a range of occupations. Only a fifth of interviewees rate lawyers' honesty as "high" or "very high." Lawyers in fact rank *below* "business executives" (and not comfortably above "used car salesmen"). In contrast, three-quarters of those polled rank the honesty of nurses, pharmacists, and military officers high or very high. About 50 percent rank clergy, college teachers, and even police that high.[6] Even lawyers seemed to have a low opinion of lawyers. In 1978, Warren Burger, then chief justice of the US Supreme Court, criticized the bar for incivility, incompetence, and lack of preparation.[7]

Another reason for the return of legal ethics to law schools may have been that legal ethics, tracking professional ethics generally, had become a different—and intellectually more attractive—subject. Philosophers, especially philosopher-lawyers, were bringing conceptual and moral analysis to questions of legal ethics. They substituted for Sharswood's sermons a systematic attempt to understand legal ethics as a rational undertaking. They provided legal ethics with intellectual resources not available before, a resource courses in legal ethics have been slow to use. Legal ethics, though an active field of legal scholarship, remains a difficult course to teach.[8] What can a course in legal ethics achieve?

ETHICS AND THE PRACTICE OF LAW

Answering this question presupposes an answer to another question: What is ethics? While "ethics" can be a simple synonym for ordinary morality, it is used here to name a discipline (and course of study). That discipline studies morality. There are, however, at least two ways to study morality: (1) as an observer and (2) as a participant. An observer, for example, a sociologist, seeks to describe (rather than assess) the particular moral views of a given group. Such groups can include not only communities of language users related by nationality, race, ethnicity, religion, but also those defined by a certain way of earning a living. Lawyers constitute such a group. And so, for an observer of morality, legal ethics would be the study of the moral views of lawyers as expressed in what they do, including what is written in codes of ethics, ethics opinions, case law, and statute. The legal approach to legal ethics (as discussed earlier) tends to use "ethics" in this descriptive sense.

In contrast, the study of morality from the perspective of participants (that is, moral agents) attempts to put their sense of what they are doing, in order, that is, to understand morality (or some part of it) as a rational activity. It is, in this respect, philosophical. As a philosophical discipline, legal ethics would not only describe what, for example, the

ABA's *Model Rules* say or mean, but would also ask whether a moral agent can rationally endorse the rule (and, if he can, why). Philosophical ethics is, in this respect at least, prescriptive.

When legal ethics is understood in this second way, it amounts to a kind of "applied" (or "practical") philosophy, a discipline concerned with understanding—and helping to resolve—certain moral problems arising in a practice. Insofar as legal ethics is taught as a philosophical discipline, it affords students an opportunity to see the practice of law in relation to more abstract, philosophical questions. For example, what is the relationship between legal ethics and ordinary morality? Can ethical theories—such as Kantianism and Utilitarianism—help lawyers solve their ethical problems? What is the nature of a profession? What is the relationship between the adversary system and truth? Is the adversary system really the best system of justice? How should a lawyer proceed when one duty conflicts with another? Can a good lawyer be a good person? Do lawyers who work for government have special obligations (or duties) to the public?

There is nothing revolutionary about seeing legal ethics in this way. That is how the preamble to the ABA *Model Rules* understands it:

> Virtually all difficult ethical problems arise from conflict between a lawyer's responsibilities to clients, to the legal system and to the lawyer's own interest in remaining an ethical person while earning a satisfactory living. The *Rules of Professional Conduct* often prescribe terms for resolving such conflicts. Within the framework of these Rules, however, many difficult issues of professional discretion can arise. Such issues must be resolved through the exercise of sensitive professional and moral judgment guided by the basic principles underlying the Rules....

Any code of ethics, regulation, or statute provides a framework for the exercise of moral judgment without necessarily providing a clear directive. Because lawyers are always (primarily) participants in the legal system, not mere observers, the philosophical approach to legal ethics should always be a part of a course in legal ethics. For easy questions, a description of what the *Code* says or what lawyers do may provide a reasonable guide to what a lawyer should do. For the harder questions, however, there is no substitute for the philosophical approach. This book accordingly takes a philosophical approach, but not without providing enough description to provide a context for decision.

WHAT CAN LEGAL ETHICS TEACH?

A course in legal ethics that takes such an approach can teach ethics in at least four ways: (1) sensitizing students to ethical problems; (2) providing knowledge helpful in the solution of those problems; (3) improving ethical judgment and (4) increasing ethical commitment. How can such a course in legal ethics accomplish all these things, indeed, any of them?

Teaching ethical sensitivity is much like teaching sensitivity to legal issues. A first-year law student may begin class not seeing most of the legal issues that arise, say, when he buys a theater ticket. But as he reads cases in which issues arise, is posed hypotheticals in which similar issues are hidden, and is given rules of thumb to guide him in his search for issues, he eventually begins to see the issues—without even trying. A certain kind of looking becomes "second nature." In the same way, lawyers can learn to see issues of legal ethics in what they do. This book includes a large collection of "problems" requiring the identification of such issues. The readings are meant to help prepare students to identify issues in the problems.

Ethical knowledge is whatever knowledge is relevant to resolving issues of legal ethics. Some of that ethical knowledge is legal or quasi-legal, a state's regulations governing legal practice or the *Model Rules*. Some is psychological, for example, the difference in likely effect of just telling a client "No way, never" and explaining in detail what is wrong with a certain course of conduct. And some is institutional, for example, the avenues open within an organization or the legal profession for getting advice on how to deal with an ethical issue. It is therefore important in discussing the problems not only to identify ethical issues but to pass on to students enough ethical knowledge to make a reasonable solution to the problem possible. Many of the readings include ideas for how to solve specific problems. Sometimes the solution is individual, saying this rather than that, or using this procedure rather than that. Sometimes it is institutional, for example, changing some provision of the *Model Rules* or the federal rules of evidence.

Judgment tends to improve with practice, especially with practice that includes defending one's decision by reasoned argument in the face of reasoned criticism. The Socratic method, moot court, and legal clinics are all standard means by which law school seeks to teach legal judgment. The same means may be used to teach the specifically ethical part of the good judgment a good lawyer must have.

Students who have enhanced their ethical sensitivity, knowledge, and judgment in some such ways as this may be expected to have had their commitment to ethical practice enhanced as well—where "commitment" is measured by a willingness to act on one's ethical judgment. There are at least two reasons why teaching legal ethics should increase ethical commitment. First, experience of openly discussing ethical issues should give students confidence in their own ethical judgment, making them more likely to act on it than they would without that experience. Second, the open discussion of legal ethics should help students distinguish the few controversial questions from the large body of settled matters. Students who believe that lawyers (generally) do certain things in certain ways (for good reason) will be more likely to do the same than lawyers who view that way of doing things as a mere arbitrary imposition.

WHAT IS A PROFESSION?

Since Sharswood, legal ethics has been understood to be "*professional* ethics." What then is a "profession"? And what does profession have to do with ethics? Unfortunately, "profession" seems to be as ambiguous as "ethics." The term can be a mere synonym for "occupation"—an occupation being any typically full-time activity defined in part by an easily recognizable body of knowledge, skill, and judgment (a "discipline") by which one can (and people typically do) earn a living. It is in this sense that we may, without irony or metaphor, speak of someone being a "professional thief," "professional beggar," or "professional athlete," provided the person in question makes a living by the activity in question. While law certainly is a profession in this sense ("the second oldest," as a joke has it), this is not a sense having anything to do with legal ethics.

"Profession" can also have the more limited sense (also common in English) of honest occupation: "Plumbing is a profession; prostitution is not." This is, however, still not the sense that allows us to say (as lawyers often do), "Law is a profession; plumbing is not." A profession (in the relevant sense) seems to be a special kind of honest occupation, one that we can compare to other similar occupations such as medicine, engineering, architecture, and so on.

There are at least two approaches to conceptualizing profession in this special-kind-of-honest-occupation sense. One, the philosophical, will be a focus in the readings to follow. For now, it is important to explain why the other, "the sociological," should be ignored here. The sociological approach has its origin in the social sciences (as the name suggests). Its language tends to be statistical. The statement of the conception, a definition of sorts, does not purport to give necessary or sufficient conditions for some occupation to be a profession but merely what is true of "most professions," "the most important professions," "the most developed professions," or the like. Every sociologist concerned with professions seems to have a list of professions that the definition must capture. Law and medicine are always on the list; the clergy, often; and other occupations commonly acknowledged as professions, such as engineering, sometimes.[9]

We may distinguish three traditions in the sociology of professions (what we may call): the economic, the political, and the anthropological. Though individual sociologists often mix their elements, distinguishing them as "ideal types" should help us to think about them more clearly, even in their less ideal (that is, mixed) forms. What is wrong with all three ideal types, a failure to understand how central ethics is to profession, remains even when the types mix.

The economic tradition interprets professions as primarily a means of controlling market forces for the benefit of the professionals themselves, that is, as a form of monopoly, guild, or labor union. The economic tradition has two branches: Marxist and free market. For sociologists in the economic tradition (whether Marxist or free market), it is the would-be members of a profession who, by acting together under favorable conditions, create their monopoly. Successful professions have high income, workplace autonomy, control of who can join, and so on; less successful professions lack some or most of these powers (more or less). Morality, if relevant at all, is relevant merely as a means to monopoly, a way of making a "trademark" (the profession's name) more attractive to potential employers. The success in question may be independent of what participants in events sought. The economic tradition likes to discover "the invisible hand" at work, for example, attempts to serve one's own interest that in fact serve the public interest instead. Like the monopoly itself, signs of the profession's success may be embedded in law, but need not be. What matters for the economic tradition are market arrangements ("economic realities"), not (mere) law.

For the political tradition, however, the law is crucial. Often associated with Max Weber, the political tradition interprets profession as primarily a legal condition, a matter of (reasonably effective) laws that set standards of (advanced) education, require a license to practice, and impose discipline upon practitioners through formal (governmental) structures. "Professional ethics"—and, indeed, even ordinary moral standards—are, if distinguished at all, treated as just another form of regulation. To be a profession is to be an occupation bureaucratized in a certain way. For the political approach, it is the society (the government) that creates professions out of occupations, and the society (the public) that benefits (whoever else may benefit as well). The political approach substitutes society's very visible hands for the invisible hand of economics. The members of the profession have little or no part in the making of their profession.

The anthropological tradition, often associated with Emile Durkheim or Talcott Parsons, interprets professions as primarily cultural facts, the natural expression of a certain social function under certain conditions. Neither the professionals nor society can have much to say about whether a certain occupation will be a profession. Professions are a function of special knowledge used in a certain way, a community created by a common occupation requiring advanced study. Its ethics are as much a natural product of that community as anything else about it.

Distinguishing these three traditions helps to make the point that the sociological approach has not yet yielded a single definition of profession and, more important, is unlikely to. Sociology's way of developing definitions, that is, abstracting from a (short) list of clear cases something common to most or all, is unlikely to yield a single definition—or, at least, is unlikely to yield one until sociologists agree on a list of clear cases sufficiently long to exclude most candidate definitions. Today, only two professions appear on all sociological lists (medicine and law). That is much too few to derive a widely accepted definition. Whatever the utility of a particular sociological definition for a particular line of social research, no such definition is likely to seem definitive to more than a minority of sociologists.

What should concern us is that few, if any, of these definitions would rule out an immoral profession, for example, a profession of torturers. Let us assume that there is enough employment for torturers for them to form an occupation. Nothing in the *economic* conception of profession as such rules out the grant to certain persons of a monopoly on torture—with resulting high income, workplace autonomy, control of who can join them, and so on. Similarly, nothing in the *political* conception as such rules out laws requiring torturers to be educated in certain ways, to pass certain tests, to be licensed, and to be subject to having their license revoked should they prove incompetent, careless, or otherwise unsatisfactory. Last, there is nothing in the *anthropological* conception as such to rule out special knowledge of how to torture that defines an occupational community—a profession of torturers. Because there is nothing in the sociological approach as such to require professions to be moral undertakings, there is nothing in it to rule out a profession of torturers. Individual sociologists are, of course, free to define profession to exclude torturers (since none of the usual lists of clear cases includes any profession that routinely tortures).

The sociological approach provides many possibilities, but little help with choosing among them. So, for example, sociologists have long equated professions with consulting occupations (sometimes also called "free professions" or "liberal professions"), excluding from professional status most engineers, journalists, nurses, teachers, and others who work as employees in large organizations. When physicians and lawyers in the United States recently began to be absorbed into large organizations, much was written about their "de-professionalization," though these professions otherwise continued much as before. The sociological approach to professions seems to lead away from the concern with "honesty" that seems to be embodied in such terms as "professional ethics" or "professional responsibility."

ETHICS AND THE LEGAL PROFESSION

This book explores the main topics of legal ethics through a dialogue between philosophers, legal scholars, and lawyer-philosophers. Part I sketches law as a profession: its history, regulation, sociology, and future. Part II introduces the critique of the legal profession. Drawing on the information provided in part I, how is the role of the lawyer to be understood? What is—or should be—the relationship of legal practice to ordinary human decency? What does profession have to do with the answer to that question? In America, answers to these questions often refer to "the adversary system." Accordingly, part III examines the adversary system in some detail.

Part IV shifts from these general questions toward specific issues in ethics, both pure and applied. Part IV deals with conflict of interest—and the role of judgment in lawyering. If what a lawyer mainly offers clients is not knowledge but legal judgment, how is that judgment to be protected?

Part V raises the familiar problem of what to do when a client lies, or is about to lie. Client perjury has long been a way for lawyers to evaluate theories of their profession. The lawyer's response also seems to have shaped the public image of the lawyer as perhaps no other aspect of legal practice has.

Part VI takes up three now "hot" issues related to making legal services available. When should a lawyer volunteer legal services to someone in need? What limits should a lawyer impose on an international practice? And what should a lawyer not help a client do?

It is impossible to treat the full range of ethical problems that arise in the practice of law. Because good materials are readily available on topics like plea-bargaining, we have not included those topics here, nor have we dealt with such important concerns as prosecutorial discretion, advertising, and specialized practices like public interest law. Instead, we have sought central or defining issues for which there were engaging and informative materials available.

At the end of each part, "hypothetical cases" (all drawn from experience) have been provided to facilitate classroom discussion. We have also appended a few "Suggested Readings" to assist students with assignments, or to help them start to explore a given issue in more depth without being overwhelmed by the huge haul a search of a legal index would generate.

We hope that this book will encourage philosophers to test the principles and prescriptions of ethical theories against the realities of professional life. We hope that it will aid the legal profession in its own examination of the practice of law and the place of lawyers in contemporary American society. We hope students, both professional and undergraduate, will find much to engage them.

Elliot Cohen Michael Davis
Ft. Pierce, Florida Chicago, Illinois

NOTES

1. David Hoffman's earlier work on legal ethics (1836) may be ignored here (though important elsewhere) because its title was *Professional Deportment*, suggesting less of a connection with ethics than Sharswood's.

2. George Sharswood, *Professional Ethics: Compend of Lectures on the Aims and Duties of the Profession of the Law* (Philadelphia: T. & J.W. Johnson, 1854), p. 10.

3. Michael Davis, "The Ethics Boom: What and Why," *Centennial Review* 34 (Spring 1990): 163–86.

4. "ABA Approval of Law Schools," *ABA Standards and Rules of Procedure*, Section 302(a)(iii)(1979).

5. Michael J. Kelly, *Legal Ethics and Legal Education* (Hastings Center, NY: Hastings-on-the-Hudson, 1980), p. 68.

6. Compare Gallup, "Honesty and Ethical Standards," *The Gallup Poll. Public Opinion 1972–1977*, pp. 1196–97, with the most recent available (2006): Gallup News Service, USATODAY.com (accessed July 22, 2007).

7. See, for example, Chief Justice Warren Burger, "The Role of the Law School in the Teaching of Legal Ethics," *Cleveland State Law Review* 29 (1980): 377–95.

8. More than two thousand titles come up when "lawyer ethics" is entered into amazon.com's search engine (July 24, 2007).

9. For more on the enormous variety of sociological definitions, see John Kultgen, *Ethics and Professionalism* (Philadelphia: University of Pennsylvania Press, 1988), especially, pp. 60–62. See also the recent exchange between: David Sciulli, "Continental Sociology of Professions Today: Conceptual Contributions," *Current Sociology* 53 (November 2005): 915–42; and Rolf Torstendahl, "The Need for a Definition of 'Profession,'" *Current Sociology* 53 (November 2005): 947–51.

PART I:

HISTORY AND ORGANIZATION OF THE PROFESSION IN THE UNITED STATES

INTRODUCTION TO PART I

ETHICS AND LEGAL ETHICS

Legal ethics is concerned with how a community should have its legal business done (assuming lawyers do it). Thus, broadly speaking, legal ethics is as much a part of political philosophy (i.e., the study of the proper role of social institutions) as of ethics. The title of this book is *Ethics and the Legal Profession,* however, and not *Legal Ethics.* Including "profession" in the title stresses the centrality of profession to the ethics of lawyering. Legal ethics is today professional ethics. Indeed, among lawyers "professional responsibility" is just another name for legal ethics.

"Ethics" here has two familiar uses. First, as "moral philosophy" (that is, the systematic attempt to understand morality as a rational undertaking), ethics is concerned with what makes acts right or wrong, good or bad, virtuous or vicious, and with reasons properly offered to justify conduct. Ethics makes explicit our understanding of standards of conduct, opening them to criticism and revision. Although ethics cannot make people good, it can help people to see better what the good is (and why being good makes sense). Legal ethics assumes no more knowledge of *ethics* (understood in this way) than one may reasonably expect of any educated person.

Unfortunately, the knowledge of an ordinary educated person is nevertheless not enough to understand legal ethics. Even if ethics is no more than the application of ordinary standards of conduct to lawyering (and even that is controversial), ordinary persons could not apply those standards without more knowledge of lawyering than they are likely to have. One cannot understand, for example, why lawyers consider "commingling of funds" to be a serious breach of legal ethics until one understands the importance they attach to avoiding even the appearance of wrongdoing. (What, after all, is wrong with putting your client's money in an account with yours if you have no intention of embezzling it?) That lawyers think of themselves as members of something they call "a profession" influences the way they think about what they should do. For them, legal ethics is primarily about special standards of conduct, another familiar sense of "ethics." Because few nonlawyers have a sense for how much history, organization, and controversy rustle beneath the surface when lawyers talk of *their* profession, the study of legal ethics must begin with that history and organization and the controversy surrounding them. We must learn something of them to understand what lawyers mean when they describe themselves as a profession—and the relation of that description to "ethics" in both senses.

PROFESSIONS AND PROFESSIONALISM

When lawyers describe law as a profession, they mean in part to associate it with such vocations as medicine, engineering, and accounting and to distinguish it from others—for example, carpentry, selling used cars, or running a corporation. *Profession* is a term of respect, as are *professional* and *professionalism,* but the respect they show is not the same. Professionalism is the style of a professional, usually cool and effective. To describe someone as a "professional" (or a "real pro") is to say that she exhibits the competence one would expect of a member of a profession. Though "professional" in "professional sports" now denotes only that athletes earn their living by playing sports, it still connotes relatively high competence (that is, more than one would expect of an "amateur"). The contrast between the respect invited by "professional" and by "profession" is therefore great. A profession is not just a group of professionals, however competent. Football is not a profession even for professional players, and so we hear nothing of "football ethics." ("Good sportsmanship" is not equivalent, since that virtue is at least as appropriate to amateurs as to professionals.) To be a member of a profession seems somehow better than being a mere professional. What then is a profession? What makes being a member of a profession so good? And why is law a profession?

According to the conception that seems standard among lawyers, a certain number of persons constitute a profession if, and only if, (1) they are all engaged in the same learned art, (2) that engagement is more or less full-time, (3) the art itself is helpful to others in some important way, (4) the persons so engaged form an organization governing how they practice their art, and (5) the governance so imposed is primarily for the public good rather than for the good of those so organized. This definition is complex. Let us look at its main points again.

The members of a profession must practice an "art." Unskilled workers cannot, according to this definition, form a profession because what they practice is not an "art," that is, an activity requiring long training to develop even minimal competence. Carpentry or professional football, though certainly an art, is, however, not the right sort of art to be a profession. The art must be "learned," that is, one depending heavily on books (a "liberal art" rather than a "manual art"). Though one can be a carpenter or football player without being able to read, one cannot be a doctor, an engineer, or an accountant without reading a good deal.

But even "book learning" is not enough to make an art a profession. The art must be one that a person can practice more or less full-time; otherwise the art could only have amateur practitioners. (A lawyer who works only part-time is often said to be partially retired from the profession.) The art must also be helpful to others in an important way. Thus, medicine can be a profession because it cures the sick, comforts the dying, and helps to keep the rest of us well. In contrast, solving crossword puzzles, though a learned art and one a few practice full-time, cannot be a profession. It is "just a game."

Those engaged in a learned art must, according to this conception, be organized as well. Without organization, practitioners of even the most learned and helpful art would not be a profession but simply so many individuals practicing the same art (a collection of experts). The organization need not be self-governing. The Anglican ministry is no less a profession because the Church of England is organized as part of the state apparatus. But even a self-governing organization of practi-tioners of the most learned and helpful art might be no more than a trade association or union. Indeed, some professions (for example, teaching) seem to have both a professional organization and unions.

To practice a profession is, lawyers often say, not to pursue a "mere money-making calling" (as, for example, MBAs do). To organize as a profession is to undertake more than serving oneself. There must, in addition (or instead), be a commitment to the good of others—clients, patients, students, or the like—even when carrying out that commit-ment does not benefit those who practice the art. Physicians, for example, must be ready to help those who cannot afford to pay. A lawyer who, though working full-time, never accepts payment, is no less a member of the profession than one who usually exacts high fees.

To organize as a profession is to impose upon the members a disci-pline they would otherwise not be subject to—a discipline beyond what morality, law, market, and public opinion would otherwise impose—"a higher standard." Professional organizations may maintain such disci-pline by promulgating special standards, including an express "code of ethics," by following such standards themselves, by limiting member-ship in the organization to those likely to satisfy the standards, by encouraging each other to maintain those standards, by supporting others when they try to meet the standards, and by censuring, sus-pending, or expelling members whose conduct is "unprofessional" (that is, falls well short of meeting the profession's standards). To be a member of a profession is—according to this conception—to declare oneself to be someone to whom a certain higher standard of conduct applies (to "profess" oneself someone who follows those standards).

LAW AS A PROFESSION

Is law a profession in this sense? Certainly, it is now. Law is a learned art. Lawyers must have an advanced degree and pass a difficult competency examination. Lawyers spend much of their time providing an important service to others. By himself, the typical client would be helpless to offer a competent defense in a criminal case, to collect damages for a serious injury, or even to prepare a complicated contract. Lawyers have organized themselves into national, state, county, and city associations. Among the purposes of such associations are maintaining the integrity and competence of lawyers, making legal counsel available to all who need it, and improving the legal system. More important, lawyers generally view themselves as sharing with other lawyers—whether or not members of any formal association of lawyers—a common undertaking that goes beyond merely competing in the same business or occupation.

Though law is now a profession in this strict sense, it has not always been, nor will it necessarily always remain so. David R. Papke's history of lawyering in the United States reports two periods in which law was not a profession (as well as two when it was). This history may be read as a series of experiments with the provision of legal services.

The early colonial period was an experiment in amateur lawyering. Lawyers were few. Most were unskilled "pettifoggers," whose conduct sometimes led to the practice of law (as a business) being banned outright. More often the practice of law was so regulated that making a living at the bar was almost impossible (as making a living as a notary public still is). But during the later colonial period, groups similar to the modern bar association appeared in commercial centers such as Boston, New York, and Philadelphia. This was America's first experiment with (something like) a profession of law.

The American Revolution brought on a long period of decline in legal organization. Lawyers became increasingly important but bar associations almost disappeared. Lawyers were subject to no special discipline but that provided by the formal supervision of courts (which usually was quite lax) and the informal judgment of peers, public opinion, or the market. Some states abolished all educational requirements for admission to practice. Society treated law as just one business among many. Only after the Civil War did this process reverse. The reemergence of an organized bar was contemporaneous with the rise of trade associations, unions, and giant corporations. But, unlike these (and like contemporaneous organizations of physicians, engineers, dentists, and so on), the declared purpose of the bar associations was public service rather than the advantage of their members.

Though Papke seems to take a jaundiced view of much that the bar associations accomplished (echoing sociological approaches to profession discussed in this book's introduction), does the definition of "profession" itself suggest another instead? Might these associations have been trying to do nothing more objectionable than create a profession of law?

Papke's history provides a natural orientation to the contemporary problems of legal ethics. Of special importance is the conflict between (what we may call) "client-centered" conceptions of professional responsibility (associated by Papke with Sharswood's famous manual) and "justice-centered" conceptions (associated with Geneva's code of ethics). Under a client-centered conception, a lawyer is an "agent" whose public service is primarily (or even exclusively) helping clients to do what they want within the bounds of the law. Lawyers serve the public by serving clients. On the justice-centered conception, in contrast, the lawyer's public service is to help clients get justice within the bounds of the law. The profession bars lawyers from appearing in unjust causes. They are to serve the public by serving justice. They are "officers of the court." Papke suggests that the client-centered conception has won a complete victory over the justice-centered conception.

But is that so? Consider Fred C. Zacharias's description of the ABA's recent search for a "perfect code." While explaining some of the complexities of legal (and professional) regulation of lawyers, he describes a debate that seems to fall somewhere between the client-centered and the justice-centered poles. Lawyers are to serve both their client's interest (within limits) and the interest of justice (within limits). He also argues that, since no regulation will be perfect, lawyers will always have to think carefully about the purpose of professional regulation to choose the right conduct in a particular situation.

Frederick Elliston's paper is concerned with admission to the bar. Nonlawyers are usually surprised to learn that one cannot be admitted to the practice of law without passing a test for "character and fitness." There seems to be something quaint (if not positively Victorian) about would-be lawyers having to present letters from the dean of their law school, a member of the bar, and others attesting to their good character and their fitness to practice law. More surprising perhaps is that would-be lawyers must also provide addresses of all the places they have lived or worked, information about their parents, spouses, children, and other relatives, and access to their credit records, academic records, and so on. But most surprising may be the gravity with which the bar seems to consider the question of character and fitness. There may be a special committee (all unpaid volunteers) to meet with each prospective lawyer, to question her, and then to make a recommendation. Though the work of such committees often seems pro forma, it is not. An applicant discovered to have cheated on a college examination may, for example, be denied admission to the bar if she cannot convince the committee that she has reformed. Character and fitness committees seem to be especially hard on offenses that suggest to other lawyers that the would-be lawyer is not trustworthy.

Elliston's paper covers almost every aspect of the character and fitness test. His criticism raises sobering doubts about even the possibility of such tests. What is good moral character? How can we tell whether someone's character is good (apart from seeing how his life turns out)? What is fitness to practice law (apart from possessing knowledge sufficient to pass the bar exam)? How is a committee of lawyers to tell whether such "fitness" exists? Elliston also suggests alternatives. Why not treat past wrongdoing not as a sign of bad character justifying flat (and permanent) rejection but as a crime to be punished by a certain period of nonadmission? Why can't punishment change character? Perhaps the profession should give up the character and fitness test altogether as a requirement for admission and instead try a regular "moral audit" after admission? Is that not a better way to change character? Elliston even wonders whether we really want lawyers to be moral.

Ted Schneyer concludes this part with an attempt to describe lawyering in 2050. His method is to take trends visible in 1990 and follow them to their logical outcome. Because history is seldom logical, many of his predictions will doubtless turn out false. Yet some, such as the increasingly large percentage of lawyers working in large organizations, have already come true. And even the ones that will turn out to be false, or have already, raise important questions about how to organize lawyering in a world increasingly dominated by large organizations crossing national boundaries, indeed, having large components on several continents that rely on legal systems and "lawyers" quite different from those American lawyers commonly work with. Are we entering a period of legal practice as different from what came before as the isolated practice of pre–Civil War America was from what came after? Are lawyers soon to form one worldwide profession? How would that change legal ethics?

DILEMMA FOR THE ETHICS COMMITTEE

In addition to the committees already mentioned, many bar associations have an "ethics committee" (not always separate from the "grievance committee" that responds to wrongdoing). The purpose of an ethics committee is to answer questions about the professional responsibilities of lawyers. The following letter poses the sort of question an ethics committee might be asked. How would you answer it now? As you read the essays in this and subsequent parts, consider this letter again and see whether your answer has changed (that is, whether your knowledge of the legal *profession* has affected your sense of what it is right to do as a lawyer). You *might also* want to consult the ABA's *Model Rules of Professional Conduct.*

DEAR ETHICS COMMITTEE:

I am in a partnership with L. L is a good negotiator, but sharp in his practices. Last week we had a client who owed $1000 for furniture to a local store. The store was threatening to put our client, a working woman in her mid-thirties, into collection. The furniture had been lost in a fire a month after delivery. The store had not insured the loan, and our client had not been insured against loss by fire. She did not want her credit ruined, needed every cent she could earn to replace what she had lost in the fire, and could not pay $1000. She had savings of $400. She wanted to settle with the store. When she had personally inquired about settling, she had been told no. (She was not even given a chance to suggest a settlement amount.)

Our fee for arranging the settlement was $100. L negotiated the settlement in this way: He asked the client to bring her remaining $300 in savings in small bills. He put $100 of the $300 into his own wallet (having removed all other money). He then accompanied the client to the credit office of the store, met with the credit manager, and explained the situation: the fire, inability to pay in full, and the wish to settle. There was the usual probing and parrying, but when the credit manager asked "How much?" L asked the client to produce her money. He then said, "This is all she has now, $200." The credit manager hesitated, the amount apparently too small for him. L then said, "Look, I think you ought to show some compassion under the circumstances." The credit manager still hesitated. L continued: "Look," reaching for his wallet, "I'll even add to her money out of my own pocket," opening his wallet and throwing the $100 onto the table. The credit manager counted the money, thought for a moment, and then agreed to settle.

Did L act unethically? If so, do I have an obligation to report him to the Grievance Committee? Do I have an obligation to do something else instead?

Sincerely, etc.

David Ray Papke

THE LEGAL PROFESSION AND ITS ETHICAL RESPONSIBILITIES: A HISTORY

W hile one might study certain areas of law by focusing only on contemporary doctrine, the study of the legal profession's ethics can profit greatly from a historical perspective. As the American nation evolved from traditional communities into a complex, bureaucratic society, the legal profession itself developed different social practices and self-impressions. In the context of this evolution, the profession gradually began to direct its attention to the conduct of American lawyers. In each period, the central and often inherently difficult questions of an attorney's ethical responsibility toward clients, social groups, and the society in general took on new meanings and received new answers. These changes set the stage for the sometimes disillusioning issues of professional ethics, which have emerged in the first decade of the twenty-first century.

Reprinted by permission of the author.

THE COLONIAL BAR'S STRUGGLE FOR SOCIAL ACCEPTANCE

The American colonies, operating independently of one another with different principles and goals, constituted a varied patchwork. From New England to the Carolina plantations, colonial legal practice was precarious and lacking in uniformity. For a century following the founding of the first colonies, traditional elites dominated the largely agrarian social structures: these dominant groups periodically refused to sanction legal practice. Few in number, poorly trained, and unorganized as a profession, lawyers practiced in communities where the value of their work was suspect. Was the practice of law ethical? Not until the last half of the eighteenth century did the colonies answer this question in the affirmative. Only then, with social acceptance contributing to professional confidence and autonomy, could lawyers begin dealing with the more specific questions pertinent to their professional responsibilities.

Definitive histories of the assorted colonial legal professions remain to be written, but modern scholars have collected intriguing information concerning the practice of law in two socially and ideologically different colonies—Virginia and Massachusetts. In Virginia, the founders were proud Englishmen, but they were not determined to bring all of England's trappings to the New World. The founders adopted English Common Law as the general basis for jurisprudence, but their 1606 charter urged a civil justice that resembled the English Chancery, geared to "naturall right and equity" rather than "the niceness and lettre of the lawe."[1] Once the colony was established, landed gentry supplied the most prominent citizens, judges, and legislators. This planter class believed that the law should support rather than threaten the social structure, which they directed and controlled. From the perspective of this Virginia elite, an independent legal profession seemed a factious, fracturing nuisance.

Seventeenth-century Virginia legislation regarding the practice of law illustrates how ominous the legal profession seemed to men who attempted to maintain a stratified farming community.[2] Most pointedly, a 1645 act of the Virginia House of Burgesses ordered all attorneys practicing for a fee to be expelled from office. The act proved awkward and difficult to enforce, but after briefly tempering its terms, the legislature decreed again in 1656 that no one could accept reward or profit for pleading a case in the courts or for giving legal advice. In keeping with the dominant economy of the period, the penalty for violating this act was five thousand pounds of tobacco. Throughout the late seventeenth century, Virginia leaders perceived lawyers as troublesome encouragers of needless legal suits, as men more interested in fees than in the good of their community.

Royal nullification of anti-lawyer legislation during this period was partly responsible for Virginia's reluctant acceptance of the roughly forty lawyers practicing in the colony. Yet this step was cautious, and well into the eighteenth century, Virginia attempted to restrict legal practice to "gentlemen" who were likely to have a particular perspective on the social role of attorneys. With appropriate preparatory education, gentlemen could study at the English Inns of Court, the sanctioned form of legal education. With ties to the planter elite, they could honestly take the colony's professional oath to foment neither strife nor lawsuits. As men of financial means, the gentry could still prosper even though the colony's courts set lawyers' fees at low levels. Most importantly, gentlemen lawyers were likely to appreciate and respect Virginia's stratified social structure.

In the Massachusetts Bay Colony, Puritan magistrates and ministers rather than landed gentry led early efforts to suppress lawyers. The colony's courts recognized English law, but the Scriptures were also made a part of their jurisprudential framework. This natural law, the word of God, was crucial for Puritan courts. Surely one did not need a legal education to comprehend it; indeed, too much legal education might prevent one from seeing clearly the everlasting meaning of God's divine words. More generally, the dominant ministry's utopian community, a "City on the Hill," theoretically precluded the sort of disagreement conducive to legal work. In a predominantly agrarian community united by faith, the early Puritan ministry questioned the usefulness of lawyers.[3]

Given the power of a Puritan jurisprudence and world view in the Massachusetts Bay Colony's social life, it should come as no surprise that the colony's earliest lawyers encountered difficulties practicing.[4] None of the sixty-five male founders actively practiced law, although John Winthrop and Emanuel Downing had studied at the Inns of Court and had practiced law prior to their immigration.[5] Thomas Morton, perhaps the first practicing lawyer in the colony, claimed to have studied at the distinguished Clifford's Inn, but critics alleged that he was a mere Chancery pettifogger. After exhausting Puritan tolerance with his Maypole, secular songs, and commercial trade with the Indians—just the type of conduct one might expect from a lawyer—Morton found himself rudely expelled from the colony.[6] Morton was followed at the bar by Thomas Lechford, a gentleman of Clifford's Inn, who practiced in Boston in the late 1630s. In 1639, after Lechford had sought to influence a jury out of court, Puritan magistrates reprimanded and temporarily disbarred him. At the time, Lechford acknowledged that "he had overshot himselfe, and was sorry for it," but in 1642, after his return to England, he asserted more grumpily that New England Puritans did not respect the Common Law or the lawyers who understood it.[7] In addition to the individual cases of Morton and Lechford, the Massachusetts Bay Colony completely banned the practice of law by professional pleaders during several periods of social unrest.[8]

Puritan hostility toward lawyers continued, but by the end of the seventeenth century the colony had implicitly acknowledged the legitimacy of its legal profession. In 1689, in fact, Edward Randolph, secretary to Governor Andros, wrote to England requesting "two, or three honest attorneys, (if any such thing in nature),"[9] and the new royal charter of 1691 also led to an expanded role for lawyers. Yet this acknowledgment of lawyers' legitimacy hardly gave the profession full reign. As was the case in early eighteenth-century Virginia, courts determined who was eligible to take the lawyers' oath, how much lawyers could charge, and how they could practice. Lawyer Daniel Ela, for example, was ordered whipped for charging what the courts considered excessive fees.[10]

The controlling opinion concerning lawyers in early eighteenth-century Massachusetts can be gauged by considering a 1710 address of Cotton Mather. One of the most prominent ministers in Puritan New England, Mather, addressed lawyers as a group, beginning with assurances that he found them to be liberally educated gentlemen and scholars. As such, Mather continued, lawyers had the responsibility to "shun all those indirect ways of making haste to be rich, in which a man cannot be innocent." Mather urged attorneys to keep a Court of Chancery always in their breasts and to "abhor . . . to appear in a dirty cause." A learned man, accustomed to respect, Mather conceived of colonial society as communal and unified. Lawyers, he thought, should not approach their work as experts for hire but rather as men devoted to fairness and justice. By being loyal to truth rather than victory, by thinking of the social community rather than individual clients, lawyers could respect the God who looked over the affairs of men.[11]

It was not until the mid-eighteenth century that the legal profession in Massachusetts, Virginia, and the rest of the colonies began to achieve the professional security that is taken for granted today. In rural areas the profession remained small. As late as 1760, Massachusetts' counties in what is now Maine had only four lawyers.[12] Even lawyers in the cities lacked complete occupational differentiation; they provided clerical, copying, and bookkeeping services as well as legal advice. But, in general, by 1750 lawyers were sufficiently numerous and distinct as legal workers to feel confident of their social activities. In addition, planter and ministerial elites had lost their firm grip on colonial affairs, and particularly in the larger settlements a more commercial economy began to emerge. Although merchants, like the landed gentry and Puritan ministers before them, were not always enamored of the legal profession, they were forced to turn more and more frequently to lawyers as commerce expanded. The growth of towns brought with it the first glimmerings of a diversified society and an individualistic world view; social security for lawyers inevitably accompanied these developments.

As the history of Massachusetts illustrates, security enabled lawyers to elaborate their professional identity.[13] In the words of John

Adams, himself a member of the bar, lawyers in mid-eighteenth-century Massachusetts had begun to "swarm and multiply."[14] In 1758, Boston lawyers formed the Suffolk County Bar Association, and ten years later lawyers in nearby Essex County also organized. A professional subculture began to flower in rituals, reading groups, and folklore. As lawyers developed shared perspectives and presumptions, they became, more than ever before, a self-conscious professional group.

In the context of these developments, attorneys began addressing matters of professional qualifications, conduct, and ethics. In particular, the Suffolk County Bar Association drafted formal apprenticeship and training requirements and appointed committees to examine would-be lawyers. Members of the Massachusetts associations also agreed not to enter, argue, or assist in actions brought by self-trained practitioners. In Essex County, the bar association introduced a minimum fee schedule for its members. Prior to the American Revolution, Massachusetts bar associations were voluntary. They could not enforce their rules on all practitioners, but association admission requirements and fee schedules were steps in that direction.

The Revolutionary War stalled the growth of the organized bar, but the political prominence of lawyers during the conflict indicated how far the profession had come since the founding of the colonies. Strong ties and loyalties to the English government led one-quarter of the profession to return to England when the war began. But on the patriots' side, revolutionary leaders such as John Adams, William Byrd, Thomas Lee, Patrick Henry, and Thomas Jefferson were lawyers. When fifty-six delegates signed the Declaration of Independence, twenty-five were lawyers, and thirty-one of the fifty-five members of the Constitutional Convention were also lawyers. Indeed, several of the core documents of the Revolution demonstrated the legal training of their authors. Made bold by their new security and respectability, lawyers by the late 1700s were prepared to comment not only on the ethics of their legal practice but also on that of revolution and nationhood.

ANTEBELLUM PROFESSIONALISM AND THE PRIMACY OF RESPONSIBILITIES TO THE CLIENT

During the years that separated the American Revolution and the Civil War, the practice of law grew as rapidly as America's cities and its entrepreneurial economy. Often embodying the initiative and enterprise of their period, lawyers scurried to make their fortunes. The profession's formal organization remained rudimentary, but changes in society and in the social roles of attorneys brought a new conception of the profession. In particular, a new ethical presumption appeared, one that would remain a central feature of the profession's thinking for more than a century.

The legal profession's development during the early nineteenth century was not always in step with other sectors of the rapidly changing society. Throughout the period, popular hostility toward lawyers was common, but to a large extent this hostility reflected unique concerns. At the turn of the century, for example, animosity toward British Common Law, hopes for a utopian republic, and the work of lawyers as postwar debt collectors fueled a dislike for the practice of law. Boston merchant Benjamin Austin, writing as "Honestus," called for the abolition of the profession, while other critics demanded a small profession paid by the state and a greater reliance on lay arbiters.[15] This early-nineteenth-century hostility toward lawyers also assumed a more general character, for lawyers were doing the type of work that was certain to displease assorted clients, litigants, and observers.[16]

While popular commentators railed against pettifoggery, lawyers, according to an 1818 *Niles Register*, became "as plentiful as blackberries."[17] In the rural South and West, a few attorneys became sophisticated practitioners, but most depended far more on the speed of a good horse than on Lord Blackstone. Whether riding circuit or stationed in a clapboard office, frontier lawyers primarily did criminal, probate, collection, and land transfer work.[18] In the East, where cities were growing rapidly, some lawyers provided low-skilled legal services comparable to those supplied by their rural brethren, while others won the confidence of larger commercial interests.[19] Daniel Webster, the dignified lawyer-politician who could bring tears to the eyes of Supreme Court justices with pleas on behalf of beloved Dartmouth College, represented sophisticated commercial interests during his years of greatest prominence.[20] When the French political observer Alexis de Tocqueville surveyed the American republic in the 1830s, the elite eastern bar rather than the scrambling generalists inspired his belief that the profession could effectively bridle democratic excesses.[21]

While a diversified American legal profession thrived in the entrepreneurial frenzy of early nineteenth-century America, it achieved only limited organization. Private and university-based law schools of the antebellum period trained hundreds of lawyers, but the majority of practitioners learned their calling through informal office apprenticeships. John Livingston's American Legal Association became a nationwide legal referral service, but bar associations, lawyers' clubs, and "moots" atrophied. The profession's eastern elite commanded fees that were ten or fifteen times higher than general practitioners, but attempts to follow the English model of a formally established and graded profession ended in failure. For certain traditional historians, the overall picture of professional organization during the period was one of tragic disintegration. One historian has described the early nineteenth-century legal profession as "an undifferentiated mass."[22] Most recent scholarly work has tempered these appraisals, but it nevertheless remains clear that the legal profession did not constitute a cohesive guild.[23]

Given the unstructured state of the profession, its limited role in self-management during this period was hardly surprising. In general, legislatures and courts rather than the profession made decisions regarding legal training requirements and admissions to the bar. In keeping with the growing demand for legal services and a belief in social mobility, state legislatures required less and less preparation for the practice of law. Apprenticeship periods were shortened and, in a few cases, completely abolished. Judges, themselves increasingly subject to popular election, did little to hinder men who sought admission to their courts. Court-administered entrance examinations were perfunctory at best. Would-be lawyers passed routinely, and admission to one court enabled a lawyer to practice before other courts in the same state, and before the courts of other states as well.

State codes regarding professional conduct provided a framework for lawyers' discipline, but the codes were short and vague. Sometimes, as in the case of a Tennessee code that threatened to disbar any lawyer who gambled, the codes reflected specialized concerns. But more commonly, the codes stressed lawyers' punctuality and merely prohibited unauthorized holding of client funds and the buying up of notes and confused land titles. With imprecise standards of practice and with lawyers and their clients frequently on the move, courts only rarely initiated formal disciplinary procedings.[24]

Even though legislatures and courts rather than the profession dealt formally with questions of legal ethics, individual lawyers still offered their opinions regarding ethical issues. Lawyers' statements were often reactions to the allegations that the profession consisted of usurers and sharpers, snakes and sharks. J. F. Jackson, one of the many lawyers who contributed to *The Knickerbocker*, argued that the popular attack on lawyers represented a "vulgar and mistaken notion" and "the bitter feelings of an ignorant rabble." In Jackson's opinion, the profession of advocate could be "consistent with perfect integrity."[25] More generally, the comments made by lawyers with respect to legal ethics were part of their changing view of social life and professionalism. As the Civil War approached, lawyers, like many other Americans, abandoned visions of a unified, Christian community and endorsed instead an open society of action and mobility. Lawyers increasingly understood themselves not as benevolent practitioners serving the community but rather as businessmen with specialized knowledge.

The presumptions of legal ethics also changed, as lawyers began to discuss their relative responsibilities to the society and to the individual client. For centuries, as the words of Cotton Mather illustrated, the lawyer's larger responsibility to the society and its values had been primary. This presumption constrained lawyers from representing criminal defendants whom they knew to be guilty, or civil clients whose causes they considered unjust. In the antebellum period, however, lawyers began to assert that the morality of human conduct was difficult to appraise and that justice was impossible unless defendants and clients were fully represented. As early as the 1830s, some lawyers argued that the profession's primary ethical responsibility was loyalty to the will of clients. Editors of. *The Law Reporter* posited a "somber truth": "the more mercenary our profession is, the more it will deserve respect." Influential Philadelphia lawyer, judge, and law teacher George Sharswood, about whom more remains to be said, told his colleagues and students that professional morality was entirely compatible with arguing any and every case.[26]

THE BAR ASSOCIATION MOVEMENT AND THE CODIFICATION OF LAWYERS' ETHICS

The Civil War acutely convulsed American society, but after several years of postwar adjustment, the country and its legal profession resumed the transformation that had begun in the antebellum years. Industrial capital accumulated, particularly in the steel and farm equipment industries, and with the help of federal subsidies, railroads crisscrossed the continent. National markets developed for commodities and labor, and as bloody strikes suggested, industrial laborers sometimes tried to organize unions. Cities burgeoned, with several in the Midwest surpassing in size some of the great cities of the East. The legal profession grew from 22,000 practitioners in 1850 to 60,000 in 1880, and 114,000 in 1900.[27]

The actual practice of law between 1865 and 1915 was more diverse and stratified than ever before. In less settled areas, small-town lawyers had a great variety of clients. Courtroom criminal work remained a staple, as did debt collection, but particularly on the Great Plains and in the West, rural lawyers also turned to land speculation and money brokerage for their livelihood.[28] In the larger cities, the bar differentiated in ways that belied notions of a profession of equals. On the bottom rung were thousands of solo practitioners doing probate, criminal, and personal injury work for low rates. Like Attorney Charles Guiteau, the assassin of President Garfield, these solo practitioners often jumped from city to city hoping to catch a break.[29] In the final years of the century, Irish, Jewish, Italian, and Polish immigrants entered this professional sector and constituted the so-called "ethnic bar." Looking down on them from more lucrative perches were legal specialists: the in-house lawyers of railroads and insurance companies, the first generation of Wall Street corporate lawyers, and firms of criminal law specialists, such as New York's notorious Howe & Hummel.[30] While intra-professional stratification had begun during the antebellum period, the profession's divisions grew more rigid and permanent as the nation's economy became more complex.

After fading away during the middle of the century, bar associations reappeared and lent the profession increased organizational stability. Some of the bar associations counted reform among their chief goals, as in the case of the Association of the Bar of New York City, which was founded in 1870 by prominent lawyers concerned about the self-interested behavior of the city's ethnic machine.[31] Others were primarily interested in professional contacts and restricting competition. These various associations came eventually to be affiliated with the American Bar Association (ABA).

Founded in 1878, the ABA held annual meetings in Saratoga and offered membership only to well-established practitioners.[32] Country lawyers could rise to prominence in the bar associations of rural states, but in general urban lawyers, with the resources and types of practices that could facilitate conventioneering and organized bar work, were the leaders of the bar associations. Influential in state legislatures and courts, bar associations of the late nineteenth century successfully championed written comprehensive bar examinations and state boards of bar examiners. Through these mechanisms and others bar associations hoped to control the practice of law.

New developments in the training of lawyers meshed with the emergence of elite bar associations. In 1870 only one-quarter of the men entering the profession were law school graduates, but by 1910 the proportion had jumped to two-thirds.[33] State legislatures did not require law degrees for admission to the profession, but as lawyers festooned their office walls with diplomas, the public came to expect them. Small private law schools, offering part-time instruction and night classes, were a haven for upwardly mobile men who often held full-time jobs while earning law degrees.[34] State schools, such as the University of Wisconsin, envisioned themselves as university-based, teaching law offices and sent their graduates to all sectors of the profession.[35] Elite eastern law schools, most notably Harvard under Dean Christopher Columbus Langdell, hired full-time faculty, raised admission standards, pioneered the case method, and sent their graduates to prestigious law firms.[36] Particularly intriguing was the insistence of professors at prestigious schools that law could be scientific. Oliver Wendell Holmes and other legal theorists questioned this argument, but in adopting the pretensions of scientific inquiry, elite law schools echoed the ideological assumptions of the profession's upper crust. Secure in a sense of themselves as objective scientists, graduates of the schools could ignore the social and economic implications of their jobs in large law firms.

The pronouncements of the elite bar associations and law schools commingled with the "new judicialism" or "creative conservatism," which one scholar found prevalent in late nineteenth-century America. In national politics, this attitude became prominent in the 1890s when, after the populist conventions and the Homestead and Pullman strikes, government leaders called for national policies more supportive of industrialists and owners of capital.[37] In professional circles, the new attitude included demands for improved professional ethics and greater surveillance of lawyers' conduct. During the last decade of the century, twenty state bar associations adopted formal codes of professional responsibility, sometimes appending curious canons from the Swiss Canton of Geneva. In addition, George R. Peck, president of the American Bar Association, appointed a committee to consider a nationwide code of ethics. The committee included prominent lawyers such as Francis L. Stetson of New York and Henry St. George Tucker of Virginia and judges Alton P. Parker and Thomas Goode Jones. In 1906 it reported that the adoption of a code of ethics was advisable. In 1908, the association accepted the committee's draft of the *Canons of Professional Ethics*, a step hailed by the majority of state bar associations.[38] If lawyers had taken this step during the early colonial years or during the antebellum period, it would have provoked protests from those enamored, respectively, with visions of communal unity or open-ended individual enterprise. But in the context of early twentieth-century America, the legal profession's new boldness regarding the management of its own affairs hardly seemed out of place. As the fluid, entrepreneurial economy of the early nineteenth century gave way to an integrated, industrial economy, many organized groups with shared occupational and social perspectives garnered control over their particular sectors. The legal profession was but one group that assumed responsibility for its affairs.[39]

Since the adoption of the *Canons of Professional Ethics* constitutes an important benchmark in lawyers' ethics, we should carefully consider its inspiration, dimensions, and normative thrust. It was not a modern time-motion study or progressive tract that most inspired the codifiers of ethics; rather, it was a slim 1854 volume titled *An Essay on Professional Ethics*. George Sharswood, the author of the volume, was a graduate of the University of Pennsylvania who read law in the Philadelphia office of Joseph Ingersoll, at one time American Minister to Great Britain. After his clerkship, Sharswood became a prominent lawyer and judge. In 1850, at a time when elite Philadelphia lawyers still controlled admission to the local bar through mandatory clerkships in their offices, Sharswood accepted appointment as head of the University of Pennsylvania's new law department. His lectures to students formed the basis of *An Essay on Professional Ethics*.[40]

For today's reader, Sharswood's volume seems old-fashioned and even stuffy. The author's vision of the profession was august, stressing the dignity and importance of lawyers and casting them as God's helpmates in earthly society. Lawyers, he felt, should never be speculators or higglers, men imbued with a commercial lust; they should be men with prudence, restraint, and a taste for fine literature. They should avoid pertness or flippancy before the court and disdain tricking their professional brethren. Pleasing one's brethren, Sharswood admitted, might cause hardship for the beginning lawyer, but "Sooner or later, the real public—the business men of the community, who have important lawsuits, and are valuable clients—endorse the estimate of a man entertained by his associates of the Bar."[41]

While Sharswood acknowledged that lawyers had responsibilities not only to clients but also to courts, other lawyers, and society, he insisted that the attorney's primary responsibility was to the client. Devoting most of his volume to this concern, Sharswood argued that the lawyer was not responsible for the social utility of the cause he represented. If the lawyer began judging cases on his own, he would be usurping the powers of judge and jury who, more than lawyers, carried a responsibility to the public at large.

How consoling Sharswood's notions must have been to elite lawyers in 1908! A lawyers' code could sanction fierce loyalty to individual clients and in the process contribute to fairness. Lost in the shuffle was a realistic appraisal of the specialization and stratification of the legal profession. The 1908 code, which expanded on Sharswood's text, endorsed loyalty to the client while at the same time making it difficult to provide full representation to certain classes of clients.

According to the drafters of the *Canons of Professional Ethics*, those lawyers most likely to represent clients improperly were metropolitan solo practitioners serving working-class people. Occupying the lowest rung in the profession's hierarchy, these lawyers went largely unrepresented on bar association committees. To the chagrin of these lawyers, the newly approved *Canons* most severely affected their practice. One canon prohibited lawyers from publicly claiming a specialty. It hardly affected members of large firms with well-known corporate specialties, but it did hinder the solo practitioner who specialized in criminal or negligence work. The canon prohibiting advertising had little impact on the prominent lawyer whose membership in professional clubs and participation in the management of charities, universities, and hospitals kept his name before the public. It did restrict practitioners whose working-class clients did not know if they had a legal claim or, for that matter, what to make of a dignified business card, the only sanctioned form of advertising. A canon prohibiting solicitation restricted the personal injury lawyer, the much-demeaned "ambulance chaser," who alerted the injured to their rights and offered to represent them. The *Canons*, it seems, would have different meaning for lawyers with differing clienteles.[42]

Only the canon pertaining to contingency fees provoked manifest disagreement in bar association circles. Sharswood had argued that the use of contingency fees tended "to corrupt and degrade the character of the profession,"[43] and most elite lawyers agreed with him. Yet, a growing number of work and transportation-related accidents had made such fees an increasingly common arrangement between lawyers and injured clients. Certain mercenary practitioners used contingency fees to promote lawsuits and reap unduly large payments, but such fees also enabled some injured workers and travelers to pursue otherwise unaffordable legal actions.

Although contingency fees had been deemed "beyond legal controversy" by the Supreme Court in 1877,[44] the framers of the proposed canon concerning such fees cast them as immoral and urged close court supervision of their utilization. Some lawyers protested, noting both the canon's impact on solo practitioners who depended on contingency fees and also the general undesirability of any court control of fees. In the end, the framers of the Canons left the matter to state jurisdictions, a stance respectful of states' rights and peculiarities among local bar associations. Some state bars in turn adopted a provision more stringent than even the original American Bar Association proposal.[45]

The dispute over the contingency fee canon did not impede the adoption of the whole code, and by the beginning of World War I, three-quarters of all state bar associations had adopted the *Canons*. As organizations with selected memberships, state bar associations had no power to enact legislation for all lawyers within the state, but state legislatures commonly welcomed the profession's new articulation of purpose and ethics. In most states, a complaint regarding a lawyer's misconduct was heard first by a bar association committee whose members made a preliminary finding after referring to the *Canons*, a finding that could then be appealed to a court. Both bar association committees and courts were aided by advisory opinions of the American Bar Association Committee on Professional Ethics and Grievances, which was established shortly after the original drafting of the *Canons*.[46]

By the time President Wilson reluctantly led the United States into war, the profession had achieved virtually complete self-direction in ethical matters. In particular, primary control of the profession's ethics had passed from the legislatures and courts to bar associations and elite sections of the profession. Inspired by nostalgic pronouncements and sure of the rectitude of their own practices, the elite sectors endorsed the antebellum assumption that the legal profession's primary ethical responsibility was to represent fully the individual client. The elite sectors then elaborated this assumption in ways detrimental to the practices of ethnic solo practitioners. Expanded by bar committees, the *Canons* would guide professional conduct for the next fifty years.

TWENTIETH-CENTURY CHALLENGES TO ETHICAL STANDARDS

Between World War I and the 1970s, American bureaucracies grew rapidly, and while old beliefs in individual enterprise lived on, a new ideology emphasizing efficiency and expertise emerged. The American legal profession found its place within the new social structure and its values, but as critics recognized the problems of white-collar society, they also noted the failures of the legal profession. In the 1960s, critics alleged that the profession grossly underserved important groups of Americans. In the early 1970s, they wondered if the profession's normal practices might not leave its members particularly prone to immorality. In both decades, conservative defenders of the profession responded to the critics, but by the time the Reagan Administration took the country's reins in 1981, the profession faced an avalanche of questions regarding the very rules and codes that purportedly defined its ethics.

The most striking social change in the twentieth-century legal profession was bureaucratization. Private law firms with dozens and even hundreds of lawyers spread not only from Wall Street to midtown Manhattan, but also from New York to every other large city. Any corporation worth its stock market citation boasted an in-house legal staff, and even local companies brought salaried lawyers on board. In the public sphere, prosecutorial and public defenders' staffs expanded, and commissions, agencies, and departments on the state and federal level employed thousands of lawyers in both political and civil service positions. In the context of this large-scale bureaucratization of legal practice the attorney's most typical work shifted from courtroom pleading to drafting, negotiating, and counseling. Roughly one-half of the nation's lawyers continued to practice on their own or in two- and three-person firms, but the rapid growth, economic power, and professional prestige of bureaucratic legal practices made the solo practitioner seem a marginal member of the legal fraternity.

Various interpreters and enforcers of the *Canons* encountered little difficulty using them through the 1950s and into the 1960s. In general these rules of conduct maintained most of their 1908 language and form. Admiralty lawyers garnered a special dispensation from restrictions on specialty designations, but if Henry St. George Tucker, Alton Parker, or any of the framers could have reviewed the *Canons* in the immediate post-World War II decades, they would have recognized their work. They also would have observed that the *Canons* continued to have the greatest impact on solo practitioners representing working-class clients. The great majority of lawyers appearing before bar disciplinary committees had advertised or solicited legal work in ways that elite lawyers considered improper.[47]

With the *Canons* palatable for burgeoning legal bureaucracies and suitable for controlling commercially rambunctious solo practitioners, the profession's ethics and professional responsibility committees turned from the conduct of members to their qualifications. A special American Bar Association committee chaired by Elihu Root asserted something should be done to "purify the stream at its source."[48] In the 1920s, bar associations supported more stringent admission standards for the profession. The associations pressured state legislatures to require two or three years of college for applicants to the bar and to add character and fitness examinations to the traditional bar examinations. The state legislatures, where lawyers had become the largest occupational group, were at first slow to act, but when the Depression left many lawyers at short ends, pressure for more stringent admission standards mounted. By 1940, most states had adopted the bar association proposals.[49]

During the same period, the American Bar Association and the Association of American Law Schools also promoted improvements in legal education. Although some states still allowed would-be lawyers to study law in apprenticeships, legal education outside of law school had almost disappeared. Among the law schools, meanwhile, the hierarchy that had emerged in the late nineteenth century hardened, in large part due to the American Bar Association and the Association of American Law Schools' new practice of accrediting law schools. Accreditation standards, which stressed professor-student ratios and library size, greatly favored three-year, full-time law schools with university affiliations. University law schools seemed to bar the association and association leaders to be ideal institutions for the education of twentieth-century lawyers. State legislatures, prodded by state bars and universities, gradually accepted the accreditation standards and made graduation from an accredited school a prerequisite for taking the state bar examination.[50] Only in California did unaccredited law schools continue to prosper; the state's so-called "Lincoln laws" allowed graduates of unaccredited law schools to take bar examinations.[51]

Law school enrollments soared after World War II. The profession's stream had been "purified at its source," as almost all beginning lawyers counted both college and three-year law degrees to their credit. Bar examinations grew more comprehensive, customarily including standardized multi-state sections, and character and fitness examinations often enabled bar examiners to exclude the morally unfit. The *Canons of Professional Ethics*, buoyed by hundreds of opinions rendered by the American Bar Association Committee on Professional Ethics and Grievances, functioned as a guide to legal conduct. Institutions, which taught and spoke for the profession's ethics, were socially and ideologically synchronized with twentieth-century American society.

But if the synchronization seemed perfect, contradictions within the profession and within the society as a whole soon jarred the gears. Aggressive professional self-criticism, which had begun with the left-leaning National Lawyers' Guild during the 1930s, revived in the 1960s. Civil rights lawyers traveled south to fight for racial equality, and in the process they attacked the profession for its failure to represent African Americans. The decade's counterculture spawned legal communes in Cambridge, New York, and San Francisco. The legal workers in communes and radical lawyers such as William Kunstler and Charles Garry argued that the profession as a whole was too greatly concerned with making money. Closer to the mainstream but still critical of the profession, "public interest" lawyers led and inspired by Ralph Nader sought to prevent federal agencies from giving large corporations preferential treatment. Large corporate entities had an abundance of forceful lawyers, but who, the public interest lawyers asked, represented American consumers?

In general, critics of the profession had little power in bar association committees, and indeed, William Kunstler and other radical lawyers found themselves before bar disciplinary panels.[52] Yet, critics of the profession did prove persuasive outside of the profession. In particular, Robert F. Kennedy, Sargent Shriver, and other members of the Kennedy and Johnson administrations championed a drive for federally funded legal services for the poor. Once established in the Office of Economic Opportunity, the legal services program grew in a few years to over 2,000 lawyers. Its legal staff not only represented individual indigent clients but also vigorously spoke out in the courts and before administrative panels on behalf of all the poor. The program, participants agreed, could begin correcting the legal profession's long-standing failure to serve the poor.[53]

If the initial success of the legal services program indicated the reformers' power, the program's fate illustrated that more traditional forces within the profession were ready for a fight. Local lawyers, some fearing a loss of business to the government's "storefront lawyers," argued that the latter's class actions disregarded the profession's primary responsibility to individuals. County bar associations, consisting primarily of local solo practitioners, agreed, as did Spiro Agnew. A former solo practitioner himself, the Vice-President claimed in the *American Bar Association Journal* that storefront lawyers were stirring up litigation.[54] Leaders of the American Bar Association, although publicly supporting legal services, remained skeptical of the new legal institution's impact on professional norms and authority. Behind the scenes, the association urged restrictions on the program's size and power.[55]

Responsive to these arguments, members of Congress and the Nixon Administration worked to reshape the program. First, federal legal service lawyers lost the power to represent criminal defendants. Then, in 1973, the whole program itself was moved from the supportive environment of the federal anti-poverty agency to a newly constituted non-profit corporation. With a charter prohibiting legal work in politically sensitive areas and with an appointed board of directors, the National Legal Services Corporation had much in common with other modern bureaucracies.[56]

Meanwhile, bar associations were feebly attempting to reset the profession's ethical controls. Several state bar associations began requiring lawyers to enroll in classes concerning recent developments in the law. The responsible lawyer, they argued, kept abreast of legal change. Other associations loosened their restrictions on specialty designations, asserting that the public would be better served if it could locate legal specialists.[57] Most importantly, the American Bar Association in 1969 replaced the *Canons of Professional Ethics* with the new *Code of Professional Responsibility.*

Unlike the outdated *Canons*, the *Code* articulated the profession's responsibility to make legal services available to all Americans; it also specified "ethical considerations" for all lawyers. The framers of the

Code balked, however, at sanctioning group legal services by salaried attorneys, and restricted lawyers' advertising to "reputable" law lists approved by the American Bar Association.[58] Despite large-scale bureaucratization in the profession and mounting evidence that many Americans were underserved, the framers of the *Code* reasserted the responsibility of individual lawyers to individual clients. Established ethical assumptions died hard.

The new *Code* briefly quieted controversy regarding the profession's ethical responsibilities, but an unforeseen development brought the controversy into the open. As the ugly saga of Watergate played on the country's television screens during 1973 and 1974, most of the major perjurers and obstructers of justice turned out to be lawyers. For some commentators, the crimes of the administration lawyers, the Attorney General, the Vice-President, and even the President himself seemed merely acute misconduct. But in some bar associations and lay circles, observers wondered if modern legal practice might invite a fundamental abandonment of morality. Particularly troubling was the fact that the Nixon lawyers had worked in the type of bureaucratic setting that dominated the profession. Like their brethren in other private and public bureaucracies, the Nixon lawyers were primarily advisers and negotiators rather than courtroom pleaders. They believed in efficiency, good management, and expertise. Yet the work settings, practices, and professional ethical rules of the Watergate participants had apparently not translated into ethical conduct.

Even though the American Bar Association's *Code of Professional Responsibility* was less than a decade old, the Watergate scandal and general questioning of lawyers' ethics led to another effort to recast the profession's rules. Much of the work fell on the Association's Commission on the Evaluation of Professional Standards, formed in 1977 and chaired by Robert J. Kutak, the head of a large multi-city law firm. Kutak and his colleagues drafted the *Model Rules of Professional Conduct*.

The ink was hardly dry on the draft before criticism was heard. The National Association of Criminal Defense Lawyers and the American Trial Lawyers' Association, among other groups, urged rejection of the *Model Rules*, and one influential commentator said, "The controversy over the *Rules* poses the most serious threat to the unity of the American legal profession since the beginning of the bar association movement in the 1870s."[59] What made the Model rules so controversial? Media coverage stressed debates during the final stages of the approval process concerning a lawyer's responsibility to disclose a client's ongoing illegal activities, but earlier the controversy involved the more fundamental question of the lawyer's responsibilities to the client and to society. Original drafts of the rules did not assume that contemporary society was integrated or communal; the contradictory social relations of modern life precluded such nostalgia. The drafts recognized that bureaucratization and specialization of contemporary practice often isolated lawyers from larger social issues and perspectives. More pointedly, early drafts of the rules required lawyers to serve charities, public service groups, and the poor and to report annually the manner in which they had served the public.[60]

Proposals of this sort prompted hostile reactions from commentators who believed that the rules dangerously underestimated the social value of traditional loyalty to specific clients. In a symposium in the *Connecticut Bar Journal*, only one of several symposia to appear in print, one author charged the Kutak Commission with embracing an "essentially totalitarian view." Referring to the assumption that became dominant in the early nineteenth century well before the complexly interlocking modern society was in place, the author insisted, "Our duty to the legal system is, in the last analysis, our duty to the clients whom we represent."[61] Another symposium participant suggested that the corporate lawyers who dominated the Kutak Commission were unaccustomed to articulating a reasoned basis for loyalty to the client. They, as a result, took "the public relations route of seeking to appease their attackers by change where change was not necessary or desirable, but would look better."[62]

In the end, the American Bar Association approved the Model Rules but only after they had been "vitiated at a series of ABA meetings."[63] What were the true bases of lawyers' ethics? As the short life of the *Code of Professional Responsibility* and the controversy regarding the Model Rules of Professional Conduct suggest, the legal profession entered modern times uncertain of the answers.

CHARTING A COURSE FOR THE TWENTY-FIRST CENTURY

While the United States remained the home of the world's premier market economy during the final decades of the twentieth century, the economy de-industrialized while at the same time expanding and diversifying its service sector. Members of the legal profession, of course, sell and otherwise provide a service, and the legal profession not surprisingly grew rapidly, counting over one million active members as the twenty-first century began. Specific ethical issues were evident in various sectors of the profession, but the legal profession of the twenty-first century also faced the disheartening popular sense that the practice of law was generally unethical.

The contemporary legal profession, in the words of legal historian Lawrence M. Friedman, is "breeding like rabbits."[64] The increase in the overall number of lawyers was predictable, but the growth in lawyers per capita was perhaps more noteworthy. The puckish Friedman was able to identify only two groups whose growth in size and percentage of the population were comparable—computer programmers and people in prison.[65]

Lawyers became not only more numerous but also more visible to the public. The United States Supreme Court had ruled in 1977 that two Arizona lawyers had a First Amendment right to advertise their low-cost legal services.[66] This led to the gradual elimination of the prohibition of lawyer advertising. By the 1990s, the faces of smiling lawyers were common in newspapers and magazines and both daytime and late-night television. Often the advertisements described legal services, showed lawyers' offices, and even introduced eager-to-please support staff.

One might conclude from the advertisements that most lawyers practiced on their own or in small firms, but that is decidedly not the case. Even more than in earlier decades, solo practitioners seemed to be living on borrowed time. By 2000, men and women practicing on their own constituted less than a quarter of the profession. The numbers and percentages of lawyers working as in-house counsel for businesses and corporations and also for various branches of government grew, and the most noticeable growth sector in the profession was private practice in law firms. The first 1000-person law firms appeared in the 1990s,[67] and the biggest firms had offices in both a range of American cities and in foreign cities as well. While firms liked to boast of "casual Fridays" and democratic ways, there was nevertheless no denying that work in these firms was often highly bureaucratic and almost always undertaken in the context of elaborate hierarchies. While personal injury lawyers continued to receive a percentage of what they obtained for their clients—the so-called "contingency fee"—the bills from most law-firm attorneys were based on the "billable hour." Attorneys were expected to bill for large numbers of hours, and practices designed to increase the number of billable hours were widely known and condoned within the profession.[68] One perhaps apocryphal story involved an ambitious associate in a large New York City firm who managed to bill for 27 hours of work in a 24-hour day by working around the clock and also flying from the east coast to the west coast in the midst of it all.[69]

Manipulations of billable hours in large law firms notwithstanding, the public's complaints about unethical conduct remained focused on the conduct of solo practitioners or lawyers in small partnerships. "The kinds of misbehavior that cause lawyers to be disbarred mostly involve thefts from client trust funds, neglecting or ignoring clients, severe forms of malpractice, or gross forms of ambulance chasing. In many cases, these lapses are traceable to drug or alcohol addiction."[70] Many bar associations mounted special programs and counseling options for lawyers fighting to overcome their addictions, and in some states bar associations articulated special rules for particular types of lawyers. For example, after the American Bar Association's National Discipline Databank reported that more complaints were filed against divorce lawyers than any other kind, some bars instituted special rules prohibiting divorce lawyers from having sex with their clients or from demanding non-refundable retainers.[71] Lawyers in this branch of the legal profession, not coincidentally, tend to practice either on their own or in small partnerships.

While divorce lawyers, among others, had special reasons to be careful of their practices, the contemporary legal profession as a whole must carry on in a "period of heightened anti-lawyerism."[72] As this essay has suggested, earlier periods of American history also knew significant degrees of lawyer-bashing. However, in the present, hostility toward lawyers appears especially widespread and pointed. A dozen volumes of jokes about lawyers have appeared since 1990, and the jokes routinely compare lawyers to vultures, snakes, and rats—hardly the most-loved members of the animal kingdom. According to a Gallup poll of 1994, only 17 percent rated lawyers' ethics and honesty better than average, while 47 percent rated lawyers' ethics below average.[73] Things grew so nasty that after a disgruntled and perhaps deranged client shot eight people in a California law office, California's nervous bar association president called for an end to hostility toward lawyers.[74]

How might we explain the contemporary hostility toward lawyers? To a minor extent, lawyers have actually earned it with their conniving and misconduct, but in general the reasons for the hostility are more systemic than acute. American society has grown increasingly legalized, and virtually every aspect of life is touched by law and legal proceedings.[75] Since Americans turn more frequently to lawyers, they have more opportunities to perceive lawyers as failing to serve them adequately or blocking the achievement of their goals. Even more generally, contemporary lawyers provide a vehicle for indirectly airing views about the contradictions of modern life. We ask lawyers to represent us as individuals and to maximize our self-interest while simultaneously hoping lawyers can embody common values and a sense of justice. When lawyers are unable to achieve both goals, we are collectively displeased and forced to recognize the contradictions. We hate lawyers, the scholar Robert C. Post has written, "because they are our own dark reflection."[76]

Contemporary lawyers have little choice but to ride out the storm of anti-lawyerism. In earlier eras, it was possible to address concerns about legal ethics by improving the way lawyers were educated, changing the standards for admission to the bar, or revising the rules regarding professional conduct and responsibility. But in the present none of these steps offer particular promise. At best, lawyers and non-lawyers alike might reflect on how the practice of law and ethical norms have shifted over time and, more generally, on how the past has spawned the present. Seeing the legal profession and its ethics in historical perspective puts us in a better position to chart its future.

NOTES

1. Quoted in Charles Warren, *A History of the American Bar* (Boston: Little, Brown, 1911), p. 40.

2. For discussions of the legal profession in colonial Virginia, see Anton-Hermann Chroust, *The Rise of the Legal Profession in America* (Norman: University of Oklahoma Press, 1965), vol. I, pp. 262–63; Warren, *History of the American Bar*, pp. 39–48.

3. For an excellent study of the interplay of tradition and design in early Massachusetts law, see George L. Haskins, *Law and Authority in Early Massachusetts* (New York: Macmillan, 1960).

4. For discussions of the legal profession in early Massachusetts, see Chroust, vol. I, *The Rise of the Legal Profession*, pp. 55–108 and Warren, *History of the American Bar*, pp. 59–89.

5. Winthrop had served during the 1620s as common attorney at the Royal Court of Wards and Liveries, and the corruption he observed contributed to his disillusionment with English law. Edmund S. Morgan, *The Puritan Dilemma* (Boston: Little, Brown, 1958), pp. 22–44.

6. Chroust, vol. I, *The Rise of the Legal Profession*, p. 72; Warren, *History of the American Bar*, pp. 67–68.

7. Edwin Powers, *Crime and Punishment in Early Massachusetts, 1620–1692* (Boston: Beacon Press, 1966), pp. 435–37. For a treatment of Lechford's exploits, see Angela Fernandez, "Record-Keeping and Other Troublemaking:

Thomas Lechford and Law Reform in Colonial Massachusetts," *Law and History Review* 23, no. 2 (Summer 2005): 236–77.

8. Gerard W. Gawalt, *The Promise of Power: The Emergence of the Legal Profession in Massachusetts, 1760–1840* (Westport: Greenwood Press, 1979), p. 8.

9. Warren, *History of the American Bar*, p. 73.

10. Powers, *Crime and Punishment*, p. 438.

11. Cotton Mather, "Officials and Lawyers," in *Bonifacius, An Essay upon the Good* (Cambridge, MA: Belknap Press, 1966), pp. 120–31.

12. Gawalt, *The Promise of Power*, p. 25.

13. For a discussion of the legal profession in prewar Massachusetts, see Gawalt, *The Promise of Power*, pp. 36–80.

14. John Adams, *Diary and Autobiography of John Adams*, ed. L. H. Butterfield (New York: Athenaeum, 1964), vol. I (1755–1770), p. 316.

15. For discussions of hostility toward lawyers during the 1790s, see Chroust, vol. II, *The Rise of the Legal Profession*, pp. 281–83 and Warren, *History of the American Bar*, pp. 211–39.

16. Maxwell Bloomfield, *American Lawyers in a Changing Society, 1776–1876* (Cambridge, MA: Harvard University Press, 1976), pp. 32–58.

17. Quoted in Warren, *History of the American Bar*, p. 301. The Massachusetts bar grew from only 71 practitioners in 1776 to 493 in 1810. Gawalt, *The Promise of Power*, p. 118.

18. For discussions of early nineteenth-century frontier lawyers, see Elizabeth G. Brown, "The Bar on a Frontier: Wayne County, 1796–1836," *American Journal of Legal History* 14 (1970): 136–56; Daniel H. Calhoun, "Branding Iron and Retrospect: Lawyers in the Cumberland River Country," in *Professional Lives in America: Structure and Aspiration, 1750–1850* (Cambridge, MA: Harvard University Press, 1965), pp. 59–87; Chroust, vol. II, *The Rise of the Legal Profession*, pp. 92–128; Lawrence Friedman, *A History of American Law* (New York: Simon and Schuster, 1973), pp. 265–75.

19. Morton Horwitz, *The Transformation of American Law, 1780–1860* (Cambridge, MA: Harvard University Press, 1977), pp. 140–60.

20. R. Kent Newmeyer, "Daniel Webster as Tocqueville's Lawyer; The Dartmouth College Case Again," *American Journal of Legal History* 11 (1967): 127–47.

21. Alexis de Tocqueville, *Democracy in America*, trans. Henry Reeve (New York: Schocken Books, 1961), I, pp. 321, 328.

22. Friedman, *History of American Law*, p. 276.

23. For traditional interpretations stressing the decline of the early nineteenth-century bar, see Chroust, vol. II, *The Rise of the Legal Profession*; Warren, *History of the American Bar*; and Roscoe Pound, *The Lawyer from Antiquity to Modern Times with Reference to the Development of Bar Associations in the United States* (St. Paul: West Publishing, 1953). For challenges to these interpretations, see Bloomfield, *American Lawyers in a Changing Society*; Brown, "The Bar on a Frontier"; and Gawalt, *The Promise of Power*.

24. For a state by state review of early-nineteenth-century legislation regarding lawyers, see Chroust, vol. II, *The Rise of the Legal Profession*, pp. 224–80.

25. J. F. Jackson, "Is the Profession of the Advocate Consistent with Perfect Integrity?" *Knickerbocker* 28 (1846): 377–83.

26. These lawyers' opinions regarding their ethical responsibilities are collected by Perry Miller in *The Life of the Mind in America* (New York: Harcourt, Brace & World, 1965), pp. 203–205. Miller was at work on the volume at the time of his death, and the volume lacks citations for quoted material.

27. Friedman, *History of American Law*, p. 549.

28. Ibid., pp. 557–60.

29. For a sketch of Charles Guiteau's legal career, see Charles E. Rosenberg, *The Trial of the Assassin Guiteau* (Chicago: University of Chicago Press, 1968), pp. 27–31.

30. For discussions of late nineteenth-century in-house counsel, Wall Street lawyers, and criminal law specialists, see, respectively, Morton Keller, *The Life Insurance Enterprise, 1885–1910* (Cambridge, MA: Belknap, 1963); Robert T. Swaine, *The Cravath Firm and Its Predecessors, 1819–1948* (New York: private printing, 1946), vol. I (1819–1906); and Richard Rovere, *The Magnificent Shysters: The True and Scandalous History of Howe & Hummel* (New York: Grosset and Dunlop, 1947).

31. Friedman, *History of American Law*, pp. 561–62.

32. Ibid., p. 563.

33. Jerold S. Auerbach, *Unequal Justice: Lawyers and Social Changes in Modern America* (New York: Oxford University Press, 1976), p. 94.

34. Robert Stevens, "Two Cheers for 1870: The American Law School," *Perspectives in American History* 5 (1970): 428–30.

35. William R. Johnson, *Schooled Lawyers: A Study in the Clash of Professional Cultures* (New York: New York University Press, 1978).

36. Auerbach, *Unequal Justice*, pp. 74–102; Stevens, *Perspectives in American History*, pp. 424–41.

37. Arnold M. Paul, *Conservative Crisis and the Rule of Law: Attitudes of the Bar and Bench, 1887–1895* (Ithaca: Cornell University Press, 1960).

38. Henry S. Drinker, *Legal Ethics* (New York: Columbia University Press, 1953), pp. 23–26.

39. For provocative discussions of professionalization in late nineteenth-century America, see Burton J. Bledstein, *The Culture of Professionalism: The Middle Class and the Development of Higher Education in America* (New York: W. W. Norton, 1976); Corinne Gilb, *Hidden Hierarchies: The Professions and Government* (New York: Harper & Row, 1966); and Magali Sarfatti Larson, *The Rise of Professionalism: A Sociological Analysis* (Berkeley: University of California Press, 1977).

40. Gary B. Nash, "The Philadelphia Bench and Bar," *Comparative Studies in Society and History* 7 (1965): 207–208.

41. George Sharswood, *An Essay on Professional Ethics* (Philadelphia: T. & J. W. Johnson, 1907), p. 75.

42. Auerbach, *Unequal Justice*, pp. 41–52; Drinker, *Legal Ethics*, pp. 215–24.

43. Sharswood, *An Essay on Professional Ethics*, p. 159.

44. *Stanton v. Embry*, 93 U.S. 548 (1877).

45. Auerbach, *Unequal Justice*, p. 47.

46. Drinker, *Legal Ethics*, pp. 30–41.

47. Jerome E. Carlin, *Lawyers' Ethics: A Survey of the New York City Bar* (New York: Russell Sage Foundation, 1966).

48. Quoted in Auerbach, *Unequal Justice*, p. 113.

49. Stevens, *Perspectives in American History*, pp. 501–504.

50. Ibid., pp. 464, 494, 501–504.

51. David R. Papke, "The Last Gasp of the Unaccredited Law Schools," *Juris Doctor* 3 (1973): 30–37.

52. Auerbach, *Unequal Justice*, pp. 289–92.

53. Ibid., pp. 269–75.

54. Spiro T. Agnew, "What's Wrong with the Legal Services Program," *American Bar Association Journal* 58 (1972): 930–32; William R. Klaus, "Legal Services Programs: Reply to Vice-President Agnew," *American Bar Association Journal* 58 (1972): 1178–81.

55. Auerbach, *Unequal Justice*, pp. 271–72.

56. Abortion, school desegregation, and the draft were three areas in which legal service lawyers were prohibited from working. Auerbach, *Unequal Justice*, pp. 272–80.

57. Jerome A. Hochberg, "The Drive to Specialization," in *Verdicts on Lawyers*, ed. Ralph Nader and Mark Green (New York: Thomas Y. Crowell, 1976), pp. 118–28.

58. Auerbach, *Unequal Justice*, pp. 285–88.

59. Edward J. Imwinkelried, "A Sociological Approach to Legal Ethics," *American University Law Review* 30 (1981): 350.

60. Some lawyers actually felt this requirement was too weak and unsuccessfully urged that lawyers be required to contribute a fixed number of hours to public service. Robert J. Kutak, "Coming: The New Modern Rules of Professional Conduct," *American Bar Association Journal* 66 (1980): 49.

61. Theodore I. Koskoff," Proposed New Code of Professional Responsibility: 1984 Is Now!" *Connecticut Bar Journal* 54 (1980): 263.

62. Ralph Gregory Elliot, "The Proposed Model Rules of Professional Conduct: Invention Not Mothered by Necessity?" *Connecticut Bar Journal* 54 (1980): 269.

63. Marc Galanter, *Lowering the Bar: Lawyer Jokes and Legal Culture* (Madison: University of Wisconsin Press, 2005), p. 8.

64. Lawrence M. Friedman, *American Law in the 20th Century* (New Haven: Yale University Press, 2002), p. 457.

65. Ibid.

66. *Bates v. State Bar of Arizona*, 433 U.S. 350 (1977).

67. Marc Galanter and Thomas Palay, *Tournament of Lawyers: The Transformation of the Big Law Firm* (Chicago: University of Chicago Press, 1991), p. 46.

68. An excellent study of billing by law firms is William E. Ross, *The Honest Hour: The Ethics of Time-Based Billing by Attorneys* (Durham: Carolina Academic Press, 1996).

69. Stephanie B. Goldberg, "Then and Now: 75 Years of Change," *American Bar Association Journal* 76 (1990): 60.

70. Michael Asimow, "Embodiment of Evil: Law Firms in the Movies," *UCLA Law Review* 48 (2001): 1383.

71. Stephen Labaton, "Are Divorce Lawyers Really the Sleaziest?" *New York Times*, September 5, 1993, p. E5.

72. Galanter, *Lowering the Bar*, p. 5.

73. Ibid., p. 6.

74. Ibid., p. 15.

75. "The legal order has penetrated deep into the bowels of the culture. . . . No aspect of American life remained untouched." Friedman, *American Law in the 20th Century*, p. 595.

76. Robert C. Post," "On the Popular Image of the Lawyer: Reflections in a Dark Glass," *California Law Review* 75 (1987): 386.

Fred C. Zacharias

THE QUEST FOR A PERFECT CODE

The regulation of the legal profession is a modern phenomenon. Alabama adopted the first American legal ethics code in 1887. The American Bar Association (ABA) promulgated its first model code, the *Canons of Professional Ethics*, in 1908. These early efforts to regulate the bar, however, consisted largely of general principles of conduct that did little to govern actual behavior. It was not until 1969, with the advent of the *Model Code of Professional Responsibility*, that American jurisdictions began to take the function of regulating lawyers seriously.

The publication of the *Model Code of Professional Responsibility* was the watershed event beginning a flood of ethics regulation that has yet to subside. Most American jurisdictions adopted the *Model Code*. Yet within a few years of the *Model Code's* promulgation, dissatisfaction with its terms surfaced. The ABA responded promptly, proposing fleshed-out standards to govern the conduct of the criminal bar. By 1983, the ABA had developed a complete alternative regulatory model, the *Model Rules of Professional Conduct*. Hardly had the ink dried on the *Model Rules* when the American Law Institute (ALI) embarked on an ambitious project to restate the "law governing lawyers"—a project that, in practice, reexamines many of the same issues addressed by the *Model Code* and *Model Rules*. Even before the

From *Georgetown Journal of Legal Ethics* 11 (1998). © 1998 *Georgetown Journal of Legal Ethics*. Reprinted with permission of the publisher.

scheduled completion date for the *Restatement*, the ABA announced "Ethics 2000," a new project that will reevaluate existing regulation of legal ethics.

The failure to achieve consensus regarding appropriate regulation of legal ethics reflects the complexity of the task. Professional regulation serves numerous functions, ranging from controlling lawyer misconduct, to providing guidance, to establishing fraternal norms that enable the legal system to operate. Professional regulation takes account of a variety of sometimes conflicting values, including the interests of clients, third parties, courts, the legal system, and lawyers themselves. Reasonable persons differ as to the weight that professional codes should assign to these different functions and values. With each regulatory compromise, the drafters disappoint some constituency.

Conceptualizing the various redrafting projects as steps in a process of finding the perfect code tends to mislead the bar. By celebrating each incarnation of legal ethics regulation as the elusive "model" code, proponents of reform suggest the existence of a simple response to the complicated array of moral issues that lawyers face. Law students and untutored lawyers hope and expect professional rules to provide all the answers. The articles [discussed here] expose the fallacy of this attitude.

For example, when professional regulation purports to legislate—to provide clear rules governing lawyer behavior—it encourages lawyers to accept the rules as definitive. Yet rarely are regulatory principles as absolute as they appear. Professor David Luban, in "Rediscovering Fuller's Legal Ethics," reconsiders Lon Fuller's original vision of lawyering, which was the driving intellectual force behind the modern codes.

Professor Luban suggests that modern ethicists misstate, or overstate, the extent to which Fuller's vision demanded complete partisanship on the part of lawyer-advocates: "what Fuller envisions is far from adversary advocacy as common-law lawyers understand and practice it."[1] Of course, the more one moderates reliance on a partisanship model, the more one is willing to moderate client-centered professional norms such as attorney-client confidentiality.

Conversely, when professional regulation emphasizes guidance over legislation, the rules become less absolute and less enforceable. In the hands of financially-driven lawyers, discretion-laden rules provide opportunities for lucrative amoral behavior. In "Using Legal Ethics to Screw Your Enemies and Clients," Professor John Leubsdorf describes some of the many ways in which lawyers can misuse the codes as weapons to injure clients and third parties for the lawyers' personal advantage.[2]

Moreover, the balancing of values that most codes engage in inevitably leads to inconclusive or misplaced mandates. When professional regulation purports to integrate the needs of all parties interested in the legal system, but fails to produce a perfect balance, the regulation undermines the values it underemphasizes. Professor David Wilkins's provocative "Do Clients Have Obligations to Lawyers? Some Lessons from the Diversity Wars," for example, suggests that the modern emphasis on client rights leads both the bar and consumers of legal services to ignore the possibility that clients themselves owe lawyers, and perhaps society, some duties in exchange for the lawyers' services.[3] Professor Wilkins notes that modern ethical regulation is premised on two basic models of the attorney-client relationship: the "agency" model and the "officer of the court" model. In a world of increasing client control of lawyer action, Professor Wilkins offers what may be a more accurate alternative—a "joint venture" model. This conceptualization, in practice, would impose on clients more responsibility for the consequences of their lawyers' actions.

In the same vein, my own article, "Limited Performance Agreements: Should Clients Get What They Pay For?" suggests that modern code drafters have forgotten that the terms of retainer agreements, rather than the codes, typically define lawyer and client obligations.[4] As a result, general prescriptions in the codes that lawyers must provide full performance and zeal to all clients often send incorrect and misunderstood messages to lawyers. The reactions of the bar have adverse implications for who provides and who receives appropriate representation.

Professor Deborah Rhode's "Too Much Law, Too Little Justice: Too Much Rhetoric, Too Little Reform" illustrates the same problem on a more global level. Professor Rhode focuses on the needs of unprotected and underrepresented members of society. Professor Rhode does not discuss lawyer regulation *per se*.[5] But the background to her analysis is the notion that professional regulation purports to provide a full definition of the rights and obligations of lawyers in providing legal services to the poor and middle class. Professor Rhode points out that the status quo ignores the unsatisfied demand for legal services in a litigation-oriented American society. She urges a new regulatory structure that provides less protection for lawyers against lay providers of competing services and more protection for consumers in terms of the quality of legal services they receive.

Professor Rhode's and Professor Luban's Articles, and to some extent my own, highlight an additional problem with relying on codes written at varying levels of generality. In some respects, the bar's quest for the perfect code has led drafters to include aspirational principles that guide and inspire well-intentioned lawyers. The original 1908 *Canons* consisted almost entirely of such generalizations. Generalized regulation can cover more conduct, but it also risks pontificating–often with serious consequences. Thus, for example, Professor Rhode's debunking of popular rhetoric regarding the overuse of legal services implicitly suggests that codes which urge lawyers to "meet" society's needs for legal services create the false impression that lawyers can, and do, satisfy these needs. Professor Rhode counters the claims that there are "too many lawyers" and that there is "too much law" in American society with the empirical reality that "the law" and lawyers do not fulfill the basic legal requirements of many potential users of legal services. Likewise, Professor Luban suggests that regulators' misperceptions of Fuller's theoretical model of the adversary system has led them to presuppose the answers to dilemmas arising from conflicts between clients and third party interests.

At root, the almost religious search for the holy code leads drafters and the bar to expect perfect regulation. The products of regulatory efforts in the second half of this century try to incorporate all relevant values and resolve, or help lawyers resolve, all moral issues. This grand ambition often has caused the drafters to avoid addressing particular dilemmas, except to note that a conflict of values exists. Because reasonable persons would resolve the dilemmas in different ways in different situations, the drafters simply cannot satisfy everyone. It turns out that the "perfect codes" do not provide perfect answers.

Does this mean that efforts to draft improved regulation are meaningless? Hardly. But the dangers resulting from overambitious expectations do suggest that regulators should identify more carefully the ends that they are trying to accomplish. I am not arguing that codes need be specific in every regard. However, regulators can reduce a code's negative by-products by noting, in some manner, the respects in which a code or code provision is designed to legislate, guide, identify ideals, or accomplish some other end.

To understand the ramifications of failing to identify a code's or rule's purpose, consider California Rule of Professional Conduct 3.310(c), California's parallel to *Model Rule* 1.7. Unlike *Model Rule* 1.7, California purports to permit concurrent clients to consent to continued representation in *every* conflict situation, even those in which a lawyer may find himself on opposite sides of the same case.

Presumably, Rule 3.310(c)'s unlimited waiver aspect is designed to honor client autonomy. To the extent that a client makes an informed decision that the benefits of joint representation justify the concomitant risks, consent governs. Unfortunately, in addressing the question of whether clients should be allowed to waive a particular conflict, the provision also appears to resolve the issue of how lawyers who find themselves in the conflict situation should act. A reasonable lawyer reading Rule 3.310(c) might conclude that if he can obtain the concurrent clients' consent, joint representation is appropriate, even if unwise.

This interpretation assumes that Rule 3.310(c) is designed to guide lawyers as well as to set the limits on joint representation. A better interpretation, however—and one more in line with the California courts' view of appropriate behavior—is that the rule says nothing about what lawyers *should* do. Arguably, lawyers who look after their clients' interests should do everything in their power to discourage any waiver that would be detrimental to their clients. Moreover, lawyers are not required to accept clients' willingness to allow joint representation.

Indeed, lawyers often should refuse a case involving even a potential conflict, both for the sake of the clients and of the legal system.

By failing to clarify that Rule 3.310(c) is not intended to guide the conduct of lawyers in obtaining waivers, its drafters have contributed to the rule's misinterpretation. A lawyer can "inform" clients about the waiver decision in various ways. There is a significant difference between telling a client that, "In theory, I might be tempted to take action that benefits the other client to your disadvantage, but I do not anticipate that happening," and saying, "Every time I give you advice, I will have to consider its negative effect on the other client. I do not think it would be wise to have me represent both of you at the same time." As written, Rule 3.310(c) may encourage lawyers to implement their incentives by persuading clients to accept joint representation.

My point here is a simple one. For regulation to present a proper balance between the rights of clients, the duties of lawyers, and the needs of the legal system, the regulation must clearly articulate its goals. In situations like that presented by California's Rule 3.310(c), drafters may need to write separate rules to effectuate separate purposes—such as guiding lawyers and defining what lawyers may do without penalty if clients insist on particular conduct. Professor Leubsdorf's Article brings home the many ways in which lawyers, in practice, abuse well-intentioned but inadequately defined rules.

The new *Restatement of the Law Governing Lawyers* provides the most recent example of ambiguously drafted rules. The *Restatement* states that it does not purport to advise lawyers on appropriate or ethical conduct but, rather, addresses only the legal ramifications of lawyer behavior. However, in attempting to "restate" the *entire* law governing lawyers, the *Restatement* addresses areas in which the main existing laws *are* the professional codes. In these situations, of course, the codes may have proposed rules precisely in order to guide lawyers in determining morally appropriate conduct, given the constraints and needs of the legal system. Instead of simply avoiding the subject matter or identifying alternative approaches, the *Restatement* treats the codes like any other "law" and selects the view that the drafters believe to be the "best" approach. The *Restatement*, thus, may contribute to the attitude that "legal" behavior also is correct behavior. As illustrated by the example of California's Rule 3.310(c), this attitude may be inaccurate. Again, the quest for a perfect body of material regulating the profession has led the drafters to profess too much.

How, then, should regulators and the bar deal with the problems inherent in the search for a perfect code? Perhaps the only safeguard is for the profession to maintain a healthy skepticism. The problems associated with ambiguous regulation are reduced when commentators persistently analyze the regulation from unorthodox perspectives and examine, question, and note flaws in the regulation's underlying assumptions.

NOTES

1. David Luban, "Rediscovering Fuller's Legal Ethics," *Georgetown Journal of Legal Ethics* 11 (1998): 801.

2. John Leubsdorf, "Using Legal Ethics to Screw Your Enemies and Clients," *Georgetown Journal of Legal Ethics* 11 (1998): 831 n22 Id.

3. David Wilkins, "Do Clients Have Ethical Obligations to Lawyers? Some Lessons from the Diversity Wars," *Georgetown Journal of Legal Ethics* 11 (1998): 855.

4. Fred C. Zacharias, "Limited Performance Agreements: Should Clients Get What They Pay For?" *Georgetown Journal of Legal Ethics* 11 (1998): 915.

5. Deborah L. Rhode, "Too Much Law, Too Little Justice: Too Much Rhetoric, Too Little Reform," *Georgetown Journal of Legal Ethics* 11 (1998): 989.

Frederick A. Elliston

THE ETHICS OF ETHICS: TESTS FOR LAWYERS[1]

CONTROLLING THE PROFESSIONS

According to sociologists, one of the distinguishing characteristics of professionals is their possession of "dangerous knowledge." A doctor has the means to cure you or kill you. A nuclear scientist can light a city or build a bomb that levels it. A mechanical engineer can build a bridge to transport you or a prison to trap you. As Sir Francis Bacon remarked, knowledge is power; in the case of professionals, their specialized knowledge gives them power over our lives.

For this reason society is rightly concerned that the power of professionals be used properly. It requires not only that they be competent in order to reduce the probability of accidents, but that some mechanisms be in place to ensure that their power will not be abused.

In the case of lawyers, two mechanisms exist for regulating their conduct: a fitness test, whereby a candidate who is otherwise competent to practice law can be denied admission to the bar; and disciplinary proceedings, through which a lawyer who has already been admitted to the bar can be disbarred.

From *Bar Examiner* 51, no. 3 (August 1982). Reprinted with permission.

The power to set standards for admission to the bar resides in the courts and in the state legislatures, who in turn have delegated it to a board or committee of bar examiners. Though the decisions of bar examiners are not final, they are rarely overturned.

Despite variations in the specific standards and provisions, across states, one requirement remains constant: the candidate must demonstrate that he or she has "good moral character." In effect, to be admitted to the bar a lawyer must pass an ethics test.

As a profession, law is not unique in testing candidates for ethics. The National Board of Medical Examiners and the American Board of Internal Medicine have introduced ethics questions into their examinations.[2] Most of the discussions of ethics tests for lawyers have been written by lawyers and legal scholars. Their questions focus on whether ethics tests violate provisions of the constitution, particularly First Amendment rights to freedom of speech and privacy . But my purpose is to examine these character and fitness tests from what Baier terms "the moral point of view."[3] Are ethics tests themselves ethical? Is there any good reason to believe that they violate the moral rights of candidates?

MORALITY, MORALS, AND MORES

What is a "good moral character?" Unless this question can be answered clearly and convincingly, the very basis for moral fitness tests is undermined. In one sense, the question is easy—too easy—for almost everyone has a conception of what a good person is. The problem, to put it succinctly, is not that we have no answer, but that we have too many. Whose morality, or whose conception of morality, should prevail? Supreme Court Justice Hugo Black broached just such a question when he characterized this "unusually ambiguous" term, "easily adapted to fit personal views and predilections," as a potentially "dangerous instrument for arbitrary and discriminatory denial of the right to practice law."[4]

THE ENFORCEMENT OF MORALS

When a board of bar examiners interviews a candidate, are they testing that person's morals against morality itself, someone else's morals, or the mores of community? According to one member of a fitness board, the test "is applying contemporary community standards of morality and character to those who seek to practice law."[5] But there are difficulties in appealing to community mores, or what Lord Patrick Devlin refers to as positive or public morality,[6] as H. L. A. Hart[7] and Devlin's other critics[8] have argued persuasively.

First, any appeal to the morality of the community presupposes that the community is one group with one coherent set of values that remain relatively constant over time. However, if the community is made up of several different groups—ethnic, economic, and political— then this assumption is overly simplistic. On a pluralistic model of society, there is no single set of values to use as a standard. The Fitness Board Members, then, must choose one group and elevate its morality to a privileged status. But what is the moral justification for the selection of this group? Certainly there can be various historical and political explanations for the preeminence of white, middle-class male values. But any appeal to that group's morality as a basis for its special treatment would beg the question. Furthermore, circularity cannot be avoided by appealing to a principle of morality beyond that of the group. If we were to do so, then that very principle, rather than the group's morality, would function as the ultimate source of moral justification. The community mores, whether they agree or disagree with these objective principles, will be of no account.

Second, the values of individuals, groups, and communities shift over time, and these shifts generate inequities when Fitness Boards appeal to community mores. The various discussions of homosexual applicants or those who cohabitate illustrate this problem.

In the past, many communities regarded homosexuality as unnatural and perverted.[9] Understandably, Fitness Boards, whose decisions are based on community mores, excluded applicants who were practicing homosexuals. In doing so they were simply reflecting the moral values operative in their community at the time. And insofar as their actions were supposed to be based on community mores, they were right.

But sexual mores change, and many communities today regard private homosexual acts as permissible conduct, provided they are restricted to informed consenting adults. Such changes in community mores generate a moral paradox. On the one hand, if the community was mistaken in its earlier belief that homosexuality was wrong, then it was equally mistaken in denying applicants admission to the bar because they were homosexuals. If, on the other hand, the community was not mistaken at that time, then it must be mistaken now. Either way, some applicants for admission to the bar will be treated unfairly.

Third, the current procedures for applying community standards generate moral anomalies similar to the moral paradox just described. In practice they take state lines as the boundaries of the community. Consequently, an applicant can be rejected from the bar in Virginia because of cohabitation but admitted in Georgia. But if cohabitation is indeed sufficiently serious to justify disqualification, as the Virginia Bar believes, then the admission practice in Georgia is wrong. If cohabitation is not sufficiently serious to justify disqualification, as the Georgia Bar believes, then the practice in Virginia is wrong. In either case some candidates for admission to the bar will be wronged. Such moral mistakes are inevitable if admission practices are based on the moral beliefs of communities that do not agree.

The fourth and final objection can be elicited by an analogy. Suppose we substitute interracial marriage for cohabitation and, in addition, change the time frame to the period when blacks were considered inferior. Under these conditions, a black candidate would be denied admission to the bar; even though from a moral point of view such a denial is blatantly wrong because it betrays an obvious racist bias. But if one is appealing to the morality of the community, and the community is sexist or racist, then one's admission practices are racist or sexist.

Though community mores may serve as a point of departure, they cannot as such serve as a final court of appeal without perpetuating injustices. Before making the community's moral beliefs the basis for law or legal practice, we must subject them to careful scrutiny. Fundamental principles of ethics and social justice must be invoked to appraise shifting conventional values. It is not the community's moral beliefs, but the logical force of the arguments used to sustain them, that should shape the legal profession's policy. Failure to appreciate this distinction between the beliefs and their rationale can easily lead to the enthronement of social biases and shared prejudices.

Do Fitness Boards in fact apply community standards? One survey suggests that they do not: "Bar Examiners and the general, though informed public, while responding with identical criteria, arrived at recommendations that were uniformly opposed."[10] When we look at the actual decisions of Fitness Boards, we find that the board members from the legal profession do not always agree with the public's evaluation of some candidates. In view of this discrepancy, the ideology that claims a preeminence of community standards is suspect.

Moreover, if Fitness Boards were serious in their intention to apply community standards, they would need to conduct systematic surveys to discover just what the community's standards are. But such surveys could place them in the difficult situation of having to decide what to do when their own evaluations are at odds with that of the public. Wisely, Fitness Boards forego community surveys.

One solution is to substitute the Board's decisions for the community's morality, which is thereby relegated to a secondary status. Indeed, this is the solution of many boards. This substitution is typical in the life of any organization, though initially deriving its authority from without, it can all too easily become a power unto itself.

One consequence of this displacement of authority is illustrated by the Board's response to lack of candor from applicants who fail to disclose fully all the information the Board requested. Withholding information threatens the operation of the Board, and is therefore taken seriously by its members. Lack of candor is itself a serious transgression—indeed sometimes more serious than the wrong-doing the applicant sought to conceal. Candidates are rejected for failure to provide

information that, upon disclosure, would not have been a bar to omis-
sion. For example, refusal to answer a question about one's membership
in a communist party has been grounds for dismissal, despite pleas that
such a question violates the applicant's constitutional rights. Such
Board actions are more a reflection of operational need than principles
of justice.

ALTERNATIVE IDEOLOGIES

The Purpose of the Test

Perhaps we can get a firmer grip on the question "Whose morality
should prevail?" if we consider the purposes of moral fitness tests.
Their ostensible purpose has already been identified: to protect the
public. Given this purpose, the public's morality should prevail, rather
than that of the legal profession.

But ethics tests serve a less visible but equally important second
purpose: to protect the public image of the legal profession. Members
of the bar want to be held in esteem by the community, a particularly
urgent demand after the high involvement of lawyers in the Watergate
scandal. Accordingly, prospective new members must exhibit high standards of personal conduct. Do such standards reflect principles of fairness, or the social aspirations of lawyers? Even putting aside questions
of effectiveness, one can ask: Do these standards visit the sins of their
predecessors on the next generation of lawyers?

To these two purposes—protecting the public and protecting the
public image of lawyers—I would add two others. First, ethics tests are
designed to protect prospective clients. Since businessmen with financial problems would not want to compound them by hiring an
unscrupulous attorney who had been convicted of embezzlement,
candidates for the bar who have been convicted of such a crime are
disqualified. More generally, disqualifying applicants with felony convictions protects clients. But disqualification is not the only means of

protection. Such applicants could be restricted in the kind of practice they could undertake—e.g., prohibiting them from practicing corporate law, handling bankruptcy cases, or being hired to process real estate closings. Admittedly it would be difficult to monitor compliance, but the machinery might be no more complicated than that set up for fitness tests. Or, one could require that the lawyer reveal his past crimes to prospective clients who are then free to determine for themselves the attorney's fitness to represent them. Some clients might believe that an embezzler is just the kind of shrewd lawyer they want!

The disqualification of a schizophrenic applicant is an example of the fourth purpose—to protect the applicant. If the stress of a courtroom situation may induce a schizophrenic attack, then disqualifying such an applicant averts it. Disqualification on this basis is obviously paternalistic: the Board is implicitly asserting that it knows better than the applicants what is in their best interests and how to achieve it. As an empirical thesis, such a paternalistic presumption is problematic. Boards know comparatively little about applicants, much less what is in their best interest. As an ideological thesis, paternalism is a crude tool for shaping adult behavior, especially compared to alternatives like educating, advising, and counseling.

But again, one can ask if disqualification is the fairest or most effective way to protect candidates. If the candidate has no intention of becoming a courtroom lawyer, disqualification is unnecessary. If he or she does have this inspiration, disqualification is extreme: the candidate could be admitted with the stipulation (or recommendation) that he or she select a less stressful type of practice.

The general point I am trying to make with these examples is that denying someone access to his or her chosen profession is a severe action that should not be undertaken unless equally effective, less drastic, and more equitable means can not be found. Moreover, since preventing people from pursuing their careers is blatantly harmful, the burden of proof is on those who defend such a measure. It will be difficult to provide this proof until the alternatives have been much more fully explored.

AN IMMODEST PROPOSAL

What are the alternatives? There are many, a few of which I have mentioned in passing. Greater disclosure of the attorney's background would allow a client to make an informed choice about the kind of lawyer he or she wants. More restrictions on the attorney's choice of practice may help protect both the lawyer and the client. I would like to suggest an ethical audit as one of the most promising alternatives.

Some businesses, in order to accommodate the demand for greater social accountability, have undertaken a social audit. One member of their senior management team has the task of appraising the company's contribution to the community. In so doing, the manager has an opportunity to take stock of what the company has done, both the good and the bad, as a measure of its contribution to and its status in the community.

Private law firms could undertake a similar ethical audit to determine how their senior and junior partners are measuring up to their social responsibilities. They could undertake their own assessment of the extent to which the standards of the *Code of Professional Conduct* are being met. Lawyers in small private practices could be randomly subject to an ethical audit. Such an investigation carried out by the State Bar Ethics Committee, would be comparable to a random tax audit: it would serve to determine how well lawyers are fulfilling professional responsibilities. The virtue of making such audits random is that they would serve as a deterrent to questionable conduct and provide each lawyer with an incentive to meet all minimal disciplinary standards.

If the legal profession seriously believes that lawyers should be honest and truthful, it could ask a random sample of recent clients whether their attorneys displayed a lack of candor in professional dealings with them, whether important information was ever withheld or if they were misled in any way. The clients' assessment of their lawyers' moral characters, filtered through an informed and critical committee of peers, would provide a more significant and reliable measure of the moral status of practicing lawyers than preadmission reviews or tests. Of course, complaints from clients, like complaints from patients, do not always indicate that something is wrong. But they are a starting point for a profession trying to regulate itself, and could prove to be an effective way to maintain high standards of professional responsibility.

REHABILITATION

Suppose the candidate fails the moral fitness test. Must he or she be excluded from the practice of law forever? In an effort to treat candidates more humanely, boards are increasingly willing to answer in the negative. Over time, rejected candidates may mend their ways and therefore deserve reconsideration. As their rationale, Fitness Boards have invoked a rehabilitative ideology. Though they are doing the right thing, they are doing so for the wrong reason.

Until recently, this rehabilitative ideology permeated penal policy. But over the past decade it has been widely discredited by criminologists. It is ironic to find such a view creeping into the legal profession after its failure to achieve widespread support in the courts and prisons. There are several problems with it.

First, the track record of rehabilitative programs in prisons raises serious doubts that anything works. They are largely ineffective because people cannot be forced to mend their ways. When it is a matter of a person's character or way of life, there is little that others can do to force change. If prisoners cannot be forced to change their ways when they are almost totally in the power of those who are euphemistically called "correctional authorities," then it is highly unlikely that prospective lawyers will be forced to change their ways by threatening to deny them access to their chosen career.

Second, it is almost impossible to tell when a person is rehabilitated. Correctional personnel are able to monitor an individual's behavior twenty-four hours a day, seven days a week for months on end. And yet, as the discouraging statistics on recidivism prove, mistakes are frequently made. How, then, is a Fitness Board, having far less information and time with which to base its decision, to determine when a person has been rehabilitated? The task is more than difficult, it is next to impossible.

Boards correctly realize that the lack of a subsequent similar offense on an individual's record over a fixed period of time does not mean that another such offense will not be committed. Perhaps the opportunity never presented itself. Since the Board cannot distinguish between lack of opportunity and lack of desire, it cannot distinguish between the rehabilitated and the "deprived."

One solution for the Fitness Board is to follow the courts and corrections in abandoning the principle of rehabilitation in favor of a principle of "just deserts."[11] Guided by this principle the Board could delay consideration of an application for a period of time proportional to the seriousness of the offense. If an embezzlement conviction makes a person unfit to practice law, then defer reconsideration for a fixed period of time (say, equal to the minimum sentence for embezzlement). This deferral would constitute a fair penalty, and when the time had been "served" the individual could reapply. There would be no question of whether the person was rehabilitated, but there would be a question of whether any offenses had been committed in the interim. If so, these would be the basis for a further deferral, again proportional to the seriousness of the new offense.

THE MENTAL HEALTH ISSUE

In addition to moral fitness, Boards are charged with the responsibility of assessing an applicant's mental health. The question of whether an applicant is emotionally and psychologically fit to practice law is, at one level, a straight-forward empirical one, to be answered by mental health specialists. Yet difficult problems of confidentiality and equity underlie this question.[12]

How might a Board of Bar Examiners learn that an applicant is emotionally unstable? There are three sources from whom such information can be obtained: a professional counselor, the applicant, or someone who knows the applicants situation. Yet there are moral hurdles in using any one of these sources.

THE PSYCHIATRIST'S NEW CODE OF CONDUCT

Consider first professional psychiatrists or psychologists. Insofar as they offer a professional judgment, it falls under their own professional code of ethics. Typically, under such codes, a judgment about a patient's mental condition should not be made public except in extreme cases such as an immediate threat to someone's life. Whatever threats a candidate for the bar may pose to the public, the "danger" is not usually immediate. Accordingly, the psychiatrist's disclosure often violates a professional commitment of confidentiality. For this reason, it would be morally unjustifiable and wrong for lawyers to request such information.

The request from lawyers to psychiatrists for information about patients is ironic: lawyers are themselves strictly enjoined by their own code of ethics to safeguard the confidences—indeed the secrets—of their own clients. They cannot secure privileged information from psychiatrists, psychologists, and therapists without at the same time violating a principle of their own profession. Consistency in the application of principles governing disclosures precludes lawyers asking other professionals to provide information when they are forbidden to do so themselves. Both the disclosure and the request for the disclosure are morally proscribed by a principle of confidentiality in professional ethics.

SELF DISCLOSURE

Is it right to require applicants to disclose this information themselves? Several have challenged this request on the grounds that it violates constitutional guarantees against intrusion into one's personal and most intimate self. The relevant moral principle is that of the right to privacy. Everyone has a right not to be required to reveal information about their innermost life. As a corollary, they have a moral right not to be forced to reveal information that would harm them. This moral right underlies the Fifth Amendment guarantee against self-incrimination. The legal parallel is telling: requiring applicants to furnish information about their past, information that may be used to deny them admission to the bar, is like requiring witnesses to testify against themselves. In both legal and moral contexts, such intrusions have been properly condemned. Moreover, a troublesome irony is that the applicants most willing to admit personal problems are often less disturbed than those who refuse to acknowledge them.

OTHER SOURCES OF INFORMATION

Another source of information is third parties who are knowledgeable about the applicant's mental condition. Typically they would come by such knowledge as the result of the applicant's decision to seek help from them—e.g., support groups, counselors, or friends. The problem with using this source of information is ably identified by Dr. Kaslow's question: What about the applicant who never sought such help and for whom consequently no such source of information is available?[13] These people, who may be more emotionally unstable, would be admitted to the bar. Their willingness to seek help is an important first step on the road to mental health. Yet, to disqualify persons who take this step while admitting those who do not is surely wrongheaded, and it would be a weak defense of such a policy simply to say that nothing can be done about those who do not seek help. If we are to be fair, we must abandon a procedure that discriminates against those who seek help and in favor of those who do not.

I have tried to show that the conventional avenues for obtaining information about mental or psychological fitness are blocked. If I have succeeded, then we should drop any effort to test the mental health of applicants to the bar. Some may fear that the result would be to diminish the stature of the bar by admitting "crazies." I doubt such fears are warranted. The teaching profession does not screen applicants for mental fitness and yet universities are not populated by academics with mental disorders. The main reason for this is not hard to find: a doctoral program is so demanding that those who are mentally unfit are unlikely to complete it. Similarly, the law school program is sufficiently demanding that those who are emotionally unstable are unlikely to see it through. Until the data can be generated to demonstrate that the sanity of lawyers is a serious problem, I would not fear the consequence of abandoning mental health screening.

GOOD LAYWERS AND GOOD PEOPLE

Underlying moral fitness tests is the assumption that to be a good lawyer one must be a morally good person. I shall call this the principle of identity for it identifies a good lawyer with a good person. From this principle it follows logically that if one is not a morally good person, one will not be a good lawyer. On the basis of this inference the various boards of bar examiners disqualify individuals who are not morally good people.

What makes someone a morally good person, and how does one decide: Does a homosexual orientation, membership in a communist organization, political dissent,[14] a declaration of bankruptcy to avoid paying student loans,[15] a series of convictions for drunk driving or for brewing beer[16] constitute ample grounds for disqualification as a morally good person, and hence justify exclusion from the legal profession? All these questions are beside the point, however, if it is not necessary to be a morally good person in order to be a good lawyer. If indeed it is sometimes a hindrance, then moral fitness tests are pointless. I believe that the identity principle is false, and in its place I shall offer two others. The first is that a good lawyer sometimes does otherwise immoral actions for good ends. The second is that a good lawyer is amoral, i.e., simply the instrument of the client's will.

A PHILOSOPHICAL CHALLENGE

The work of Allan Goldman provides a theoretical challenge to the simplistic view that standard moral principles "apply" uniformly across all professions. [17] He argues that moral principles must be worked out within the context of a professional role and he goes on to distinguish two types. A professional role is strongly differentiated if it requires unique and distinctive moral principles different from those of morality generally. A role is weakly differentiated if the moral principles are qualified by the institutional context but not violated. In the case of the former, actions which would otherwise be wrong could, for a certain profession, be permissible or obligatory.

For example, it is ordinarily wrong to shoot people except in self defense. But the police regularly shoot offenders who pose no threat to the officer's life in order to prevent their escape and to apprehend them. Similarly, in order to uphold the rule of law, judges must defer to legal precedent when it violates their own moral sensibilities or challenges those of the community at large. The role of these criminal justice officials is, according to Goldman, strongly differentiated.

What these two examples show, along with the arguments Goldman develops to defend them, is that one cannot without further ado move from general moral principles to an evaluation of the conduct of professionals. The relation between ethics and the professions is more complicated—and must be worked out for each profession. Until it has been worked out, moral fitness tests are a problematic and perhaps unwarranted procedure.

CHALLENGES FROM THE PROFESSION

The recent literature on the professional responsibilities of lawyers attempts to work out a professional ethic for lawyers. In so doing many legal scholars have challenged the assumption that a good lawyer is a good person. Perhaps the most famous (or infamous) example of this is Monroe Freedman.[18] In a ground-breaking article, he argued that lawyers must put clients on the stand even when the lawyer knows that there is intent to commit perjury. By ordinary moral standards, it is wrong to lie or to help others lie. Yet Freedman's lawyers would permit and, perhaps through their silence, facilitate the client's lying.

Similarly, it is ordinarily wrong to prevent others from discovering the truth. Yet in the celebrated Garrow case, the lawyer, who knew where the two bodies were buried and deliberately did not tell, has been defended by writers and exonerated by the New York State Bar.[19]

Ordinarily it is wrong to harm innocent people. But if a defense attorney can discredit a truthful rape victim's testimony, because she is emotionally distraught, the Code of Professional Conduct would allow such cross examination.

These examples can be multiplied, qualified, and questioned. But the fact that actions ordinarily judged wrong are defended by legal scholars challenges the testing of candidates for their adherence to ordinary moral principles.

No doubt many would like to dismiss these examples as aberrations, exceptions to the rule that good lawyers are good people. But I do not think they are. The roots of lawyers' moral obligations are planted in their duty to represent client interests zealously within the limits of the law. However one quibbles over the qualification "zealously," the point remains that the primary constraint on the actions of attorneys is the law and not morality—certainly not their own morality, the community's morality, or any general or ordinary morality, except insofar as these have been enacted into law.

If an action is legal and will help a client, then a lawyer is obliged to so act. If the action is legal and immoral but will nonetheless help a client, then a lawyer is still enjoined or at least allowed to do it. Lawyers are agents of and advocates for client interests; they are bound to pursue these interests, and morality plays no role.

In helping a client do something legal but wrong, the action of lawyers can be judged in two ways. First we might say that it is wrong to help others to do wrong, i.e., the sins of the client are to be visited on the lawyer. Alternatively, we can treat lawyers as mere tools of their clients: their actions are not so much immoral as amoral. On this second interpretation the moral neutrality of lawyers is stressed; they are treated not as persons but as things.

But whether the lawyers are regarded as occasionally immoral or basically amoral, a paradox arises at the heart of the legal profession today. When it is a matter of entry, prospective lawyers are required to be morally good persons. Yet once admitted, they are required to be immoral, if not amoral. It is inconsistent and self-defeating to test people for qualities they must have to be admitted to a profession if they are subsequently required to abjure those same qualities in order to function within it.

I have painted this paradox in bold strokes in order to emphasize the contrast. One can propose various measures to mediate the conflict between these opposing demands. The most common means proposed is to give lawyers the option of withdrawing when the actions of clients violate personal moral codes. But this provision displaces the problem without solving it. As long as everyone is entitled to representation, some lawyers will need to assist persons in legal but immoral acts. There are only two solutions if the system is to be made consistent: the first is to drop the demand that prospective lawyers be moral persons: the second is to deny individuals the opportunity to use the law to achieve ends. The first entails the abolition of moral fitness tests. The second calls for far-reaching reforms in law as it is currently practiced.

NOTES

1. This essay was originally published as "Character and Fitness Tests: An Ethical Perspective," *Bar Examiner* 51, no. 3 (August 1982): 8–16.

2. See the symposium "Ethics Tests for Medical Boards: The State of the Question," *Center Report* 13 (June 1983): 20–33.

3. Kurt Baier, *Moral Point of View* (New York: Random House, 1965).

4. *Koenigsburg v. State Bar*, 353 U.S. 252, 263 (1957).

5. Lawrence B. Custer, "Georgia's Board to Determine Fitness of Bar Applicants," *Bar Examiner* 51, no. 3 (August 1982): 17–21.

6. Lord Patrick Devlin. *The Enforcement of Morals* (New York: Oxford University Press, 1965), chapter 1.

7. H. L. A. Hart, *Law, Liberty, and Morality* (Stanford, CA: Stanford University Press, 1963).

8. Excerpts from Lord Devlin's essay and the responses of several critics are gathered together in Richard Wasserstrom's useful little collection *Morality and the Law* (Belmont, CA: Wadsworth Publishing Co., 1971).

9. Ibid., p. 3.

10. Ms. Susan Robinson.

11. For an early and popular discussion of this philosophy as applied to sentencing, see Andrew Von Hirsch, *Doing Justice* (New York: Hill and Wang, 1976). Richard D. Singer offers a scholarly appraisal of the retributivist philosophy in his *Just Desserts* (Cambridge, MA: Ballinger Publishers, 1979).

12. Florence W. Kaslow, "Moral, Emotional and Physical Fitness for the Bar: Pondering (seeming) Imponderables," *Bar Examiner* 51, no. 3 (August 1982): 38–48.

13. Ibid.

14. Donald Weckstein, "Recent Developments in the Character and Fitness Qualifications Practice of Law: The Law School Role; the Political Dissident," *Bar Examiner* 40 (January 1971): 17–24.

15. The case is the *Florida Board of Bar Examiners re G. W. L.*, 364 So. 2d 164 (Fla. 1978). For a discussion of it, see Michael D. White's "Good Moral Character and Admission to the Bar: Constitutionally Invalid Standard?" *Cincinnati Law Review* 48 (1979): 876.

16. An attorney was disbarred for three years simply because he brewed beer. See *Barton v. Nebraska*, 19 F 2d 722 (1927).

17. See Alan Goldman's *The Moral Foundations of Professional Ethics* (Totowa, NJ: Littlefield Adams, 1980).

18. Monroe Freedman, "Professional Responsibility of the Criminal Defense Lawyer: The Three Hardest Questions," *Michigan Law Review* 64 (1966): 1469–84.

19. Frank H. Armani, "The Obligation of Confidentiality," *Juris* (March 1975): 3–5; Jeffrey F. Chamberlain, "Legal Ethics: Confidentiality and the Case of Garrow's Lawyers," *Buffalo Law Review* 25 (1975): 211–39.

Ted Schneyer

PROFESSIONAL DISCIPLINE IN 2050: A LOOK BACK

Beginning with the ABA's Clark Report in 1970, and especially after the McKay Report in 1991, the philosophy of lawyer discipline changed.[1] The old emphasis had been on "cleansing the profession," removing the few bad apples who committed serious offenses. This was cheap; annual spending on discipline in the United States as late as 1975 was only $18 per lawyer. But "cleansing," for all its attention to the honor of the legal profession, was not responsive to most of the public's concerns about lawyers.

And so, it gave way to a philosophy of deterrence and rehabilitation, a philosophy supported by the aggressive new breed of bar counsel who were increasingly making careers of investigating and prosecuting disciplinary cases. The disciplinary process in this period became user-friendly, with intake personnel helping clients prepare complaints. It also began to respond even to minor grievances. As a result, the number of lawyers sanctioned during the 1990s rose considerably faster than did bar membership, though disbarments and suspensions—the traditional "cleansing" sanctions—dwindled in favor of public censure, restitution, probation, and eventually fines.

The more responsive the disciplinary process became, the more grievances it received. The expense of processing every grievance in a

From *Fordham Law Review* 60 (1991). Reprinted with permission of the publisher.

timely fashion became enormous, despite the creation of a "fast track" for minor offenses and the diversion of many cases to fee and malpractice arbitration panels or to special counseling programs for lawyers afflicted with poor office management skills, substance abuse problems, or what came to be called "incivility syndrome." By 1996, led by developments in California before the Big Quake, the average annual disciplinary outlay per lawyer swelled to $1000.

Lacking any general taxing power, the state supreme courts had to cover this expense by charging lawyers ever-higher annual license fees, though some courts generated modest additional revenues by making fines a disciplinary sanction. The license fees squared nicely with the benefit principle of public finance—the principle that providers and their clients rather than the general public should pay for professional regulation. But as the financial burden grew, many lawyers began to argue that all citizens, not just lawyers and clients, had an interest in the quality of the legal system and thus benefitted from the disciplinary process. This implied that license fees should be supplemented by general appropriations from state legislatures. Some state legislatures began to make appropriations, thereby reducing the financial burden on the bar. They insisted, however, on satisfying themselves that their appropriations were well spent. By 2005, state legislatures were as involved as the courts in overseeing lawyer discipline.

As late as 1950, a majority of American lawyers practiced alone and even the lawyers who practiced in firms were by our standards only loosely organized. Today, of course, the sole practitioner is as extinct as the bald eagle. And thanks to the mergers and internal growth that accelerated so dramatically after 1980, nearly 90% of today's [2050] lawyers practice in entities employing at least 200 professionals. These entities include prosecutors' and defenders' offices, legal services programs, law departments in corporations, government agencies, LMO's [Legal Maintenance Organization, the legal equivalent of an HMO], and, of course, law firms.

As practice entities grew to their present size, they began to look and behave like the large corporations that some of them actually became.

Most legal tasks were assigned to teams. Entity governance became a matter of departments, committees, formal rules, policy manuals, standard operating procedures, long chains of command, and lay administrators. Many ethically sensitive tasks—fee setting, file maintenance, billing, public relations, calendaring, handling of client funds and property, and avoiding conflicts of interest—came to be performed by central staff, not by the lawyers who directly serviced clients. In short, the delivery of legal services became highly bureaucratized. In this climate, ethical lawyering seemed to depend more on the culture, structure, policies, and procedures of an entity than on the values of individual lawyers.

Policymakers began to dimly perceive the disciplinary implications of all this in the 1970s and 80s. Though the disciplinary agencies of the period only had jurisdiction over individuals, a few curious provisions in the old ABA *Code of Professional Responsibility* were addressed to law firms as well as lawyers. An example was DR 9-102(A), requiring lawyers *and* law firms to keep client funds in trust accounts. In 1983, the *Model Rules of Professional Conduct* went further and began to turn issues of entity governance into ethical issues. Most notably, *Model Rules* 5.1(a) and 5.3 imposed on managing lawyers a duty to ensure that all lawyers and employees in their offices behaved ethically.

These governance provisions in the *Model Rules*, along with pressure from malpractice insurers, propelled us into the era of law office "monitoring." By 1998, for example, all but the smallest firms used new business committees and sophisticated databases to avoid conflicts, and maintained ethics committees to decide other sensitive questions. In retrospect, we can see that the development of such monitoring techniques took longer than it should have because the governance provisions of the *Model Rules* could at first be enforced only against individual lawyers. The trouble was that disciplinary authorities never knew which lawyers to blame when, for example, a firm became embroiled in a conflict because it lacked an appropriate intake procedure. Only a firm collectively, and not specific individuals, could be blamed for a structural or policy defect of this sort, but the agencies had no authority to proceed against firms.

Pointing out the problem, a seminal article in *Cornell Law Review* in 1991 called for expanding disciplinary jurisdiction to include law firms and other practice entities. Drawing an analogy to the federal regulation of corporate crime, the article suggested that practice entities be subject to discipline not just for collective monitoring failures, but vicariously for the misconduct of the individuals working within them, even when complainants and disciplinary authorities could not show exactly just which lawyers had misbehaved, something that became harder to show once the bulk of legal work was done in teams. By proceeding against a firm, the article noted, disciplinary agencies could avoid scapegoating a particular lawyer for sins that might just as easily have been committed by others in the firm. A disciplined entity, the article added, could generally decide for itself whether to adopt new monitoring procedures and whether to discipline specific providers internally.

Entity discipline found its way into the law by the year 2000. The *Model Rules* were amended to address entities as well as individuals. At first, the state supreme courts gained jurisdiction over practice entities simply by requiring licensed individuals to work only for organizations that made themselves amenable to the disciplinary process. The modern focus on entities as disciplinary targets has, of course, affected the mix of disciplinary sanctions. Firm dissolution, the analogy to disbarment, is almost unheard of; it makes no sense except in response to a chronic and pervasive pattern of institutional wrongdoing. On the other hand, fines are common, because law firms as such have proven more attentive to their bottom lines and better able to pay than individual lawyers. Public censure has also proven to be an effective sanction, since well-known practice entities have a huge stake in preserving their institutional reputations; firms with good ethical track records find it much easier than others to hold onto good lawyers and clients alike. Some firms are placed on "preventive" probation until they adopt the monitoring or hiring practices that NDCLAP [National Disciplinary Commission for Lawyers and Allied Professionals—radical change from today's state disciplinary system] considers essential to prevent further wrongdoing. Often, a combination of these sanctions is imposed, typically after negotiations between NDCLAP and firm management, as in the Skadden, Gibson case.

To maximize detection and minimize administrative expense, NDCLAP rules call for a substantial reduction in discipline whenever a practice entity comes forward and reports its own ethical violations. This carrot has proven much more effective than the twentieth-century stick of requiring lawyers to report violations. It has even encouraged practice entities to form their own ethical compliance offices, which in turn help to prevent wrongdoing. Sanctions are also reduced whenever an accused firm can show that it had appropriate monitoring procedures in place at the time of an underlying infraction by a "rogue" lawyer.

All these developments in entity discipline were presaged by the US Sentencing Commission's treatment in 1991 of an analogous subject—criminal sanctions for organizational offenders. Ironically, the Sentencing Commission's guidelines for organizational sanctions had a greater impact on the evolution of lawyer discipline in the United States than the ABA's McKay Commission, whose report was published the very same year.

NOTE

1. "Report to the House of Delegates," *ABA Commission on Evaluation of Professional Enforcement* (1991) (this report is commonly named for the original chair of the commission, legal educator Robert McKay).

PROBLEM SET I

SLICK SLIPS UP

You are the attorney for Breed D. Fastbucks, who died only yesterday along with his wife. He is survived by two nasty children, by his sister, retired from a factory job and living on Social Security, and by her son, a widower, who manages a small convenience store and supports three children of his own. Fastbucks, Jr., has brought you all of his father's legal papers, including a will.

Fastbucks's estate is now worth at least $500,000, but the will under which it is to be administered was drawn up in 1970 at a cost of $10 and, it seems, the document is not worth even that. The will was drafted by Lawton Slick, then an attorney fresh out of law school who has since achieved fame as a criminal defense lawyer. Fastbucks never bothered to get a new will made because, as he so often put it, "I haven't changed how I want my money distributed after I die, so why should I pay you $1,000 to do the work I already paid another lawyer $10 to do?" He never even let you see the will.

Fastbucks was a good businessman, but sometimes he was too frugal for his good. The will he left is a good example of what can happen when one is too frugal. The intent of the will is clear. The money is to go to the poor children of Fastbucks's sister. His own children, who are well-to-do in their own right, will receive nothing. Unfortunately, the will is irretrievably flawed in a way that most first-year law students would recognize and every competent attorney should be on guard against. Slick violated the rule against perpetuities. For all practical purposes, Fastbucks has died without a will. His children inherit everything.

You roll back into your chair and think of Slick's expensive suits, his Mercedes, and his eighteen-room house in the country. You also think of his brilliant courtroom tactics, his eloquence, his reputation for doing all he can for people he defends. When all of this is set against the $10 will on your desk you conclude that, forty years ago, Slick either did not know enough to draft a will or he did not spend the time required to do it right. The $10 fee suggests that Slick was cutting corners, a cut-rate job for a cut-rate price. But you cannot be sure. Anyway, that was a very long time ago. The will tells you nothing about Slick now.

You wonder: Did Slick do something unethical when he drafted that will? Should he be disciplined for it now so many years after the fact? Do you have a professional obligation to say anything to him about what he has done; to ask whether he wrote any other wills; to ask whether he wants to make some compensation to the children of Fastbucks's sister? Do you have a professional obligation to report Slick to the grievance committee of your local bar association? You are reasonably sure that, if you do nothing, the local probate judge will also do nothing. Fastbucks's sister is unlikely to seek legal assistance, much less to file a grievance or pursue a malpractice action. What should you do? Although you have met Slick at social functions, you and he are not friends.

FALSE ANSWER IN A GOOD CAUSE

Your client is a poor old widow who lives in a house for which she has long since paid the mortgage. She has $900 in outstanding debts from repairs made on her roof approximately one year ago. A finance company is now seeking payment of the debt. The repair work was done satisfactorily, and the price, although a little high, is not unreasonable.

She paid $400 in advance and $50 per month for four months, but inflation and various unexpected medical bills have rendered her unable to continue the payments. Faced with the choice of meeting basic needs or not making the monthly payments, she stopped making payments. The finance company, after sending letters for six months, is now seeking a judgment against her, with the forced sale of her house as a possibility.

The ailing widow does not expect to live much longer, and would like to spend her remaining years in the house her husband left her. She can afford no more than $50 for legal help.

After reviewing the facts, you see no grounds for resisting payment (and no hope of working out a compromise with the finance company). But, given the congestion of the courts, you could delay any action against the widow for up to eighteen months, simply by filing a general denial. This move might force the finance company to give up trying to collect, since the debt is not sufficiently large to make it economical for the creditor to pursue further action. There is one "technical" hitch, however. While filing a denial solely for the purpose of delay is "common," it is contrary to court rules of procedure (and you must file a form along with the denial affirming that the arguments made are in "good faith"). Should you file the denial or just tell the widow there is nothing you can do?

THIS FEE MEANS "NO"

Bob Blackard, a regular client, has been sued for $22,000. He admits to owing the plaintiff, a box company, $16,000. Blackard contends that the plaintiff treated him poorly, first billing him for more boxes than he received and, when Blackard refused to pay, notifying other suppliers of his refusal.

Blackard is not a particularly agreeable fellow. He refused to pay anything toward the debt because he felt that the company should have taken his word about the number of boxes delivered rather than asking for documentation. He also refused to negotiate with the box company for the same reason. Blackard is willing to pay the $16,000 "eventually" but he wants to make the plaintiff "sweat" for the money. He wants you to delay the litigation as long as possible.

The court backlog would provide an automatic delay of almost a year, even if you did nothing but file a denial. The fact that the plaintiff notified other suppliers offers some ground for a counterclaim, which allows for additional delay. The counterclaim is not strong, however, since there were only two other suppliers, the brother-in-law and an uncle of the owner of the box company, and communication between them might well have been as innocent as it was natural.

Basically, Blackard wants you to delay for the sake of delay. It is purely fortuitous that you can make good-faith arguments in support of the denial that would be filed on his behalf. You can't bring yourself to take the case, but you don't want to lose Blackard as a client. Should you offer to do what he asks but at a fee so high he will not want to proceed? Or should you do something else?

SUGGESTED READINGS

Michael Bayles, *Professional Ethics* 2 (Belmont, CA: Wadsworth, 1988).

Michael Burrage, *Revolution and the Making of the Contemporary Legal Profession: England, France, and the United States* (New York: Oxford, 2006).

Michael Davis, *Profession, Code, and Ethics* (Aldershot, England: Ashgate 2002).

Stephen Gillers, *Regulation of Lawyers: Problems of Law and Ethics* (New York: Aspen Publishers, 2005).

Daryl Koehn, *The Ground of Professional Ethics* (London: Routledge, 1994).

Anthony T. Kronman, *The Lost Lawyer: Failing Ideals of the Legal Profession* (New York: Belknap Press, 2007).

Deborah L. Rhode, *Ethics in Practice: Lawyers' Roles, Responsibilities, and Regulation* (New York: Oxford University Press, 2003).

PART II:
THE MORAL CRITIQUE OF THE LEGAL PROFESSION

INTRODUCTION TO PART II

THE NEED FOR A MORAL CRITIQUE OF THE LEGAL PROFESSION

A "critique" is a judicious separating out and weighing, a judgment defended by careful analysis of a subject. A critique may be favorable or unfavorable, but it must be searching. *A moral* critique is a critique based on moral considerations (the application of standards we, at our rational best, would want everyone else to follow even if that meant we had to do the same). A profession is, as noted in part I, a way of carrying on an occupation according to special standards designed to serve a certain moral ideal ("public service"). The conception of professional standards among lawyers does not make clear what the relation of those standards is to ordinary morality. Must they be consistent with ordinary morality? Are they morally obliging? What is the justification of that moral obligation, if it exists?—the lawyer's role, the command of society, the lawyer's oath, a contract between the profession and society, a contract among members of the profession, or some combination of these or other morally significant factors? Each of the three essays in this chapter offers a conception of lawyering that answers these questions at least in part.

Why is such a critique necessary? Having been introduced to the profession of law in part I, we are likely to want to move immediately to particular problems of legal ethics. That move is premature. There may be a moral problem about becoming a lawyer at all and, if there is, there will be no problems of professional ethics. No "profession" is morally permissible by virtue of merely existing as an organized occupation (or even satisfying all five conditions in part I). Part of being a profession—as distinct from immoral conspiracy—is operating under morally permissible standards. An occupation indifferent to morality cannot be a profession. So, for example, there can be no profession of torturers. Even if torturing were as learned an occupation as law or medicine (and as dedicated to the public good), it could not be a profession. That is why questions of "torturer's ethics" (e.g., "When, if *ever*, may one torture an infant to get a parent to talk?") sound like grim jokes, not subjects of serious moral concern. The ideal torturer's service cannot make what they do morally permissible. To enter such an occupation would be morally bad, something no morally decent person could do—and professions, according to those who know most about them, their members, are supposed to be morally decent undertakings. Discussion of legal *ethics* (or *professional* responsibility) thus presupposes that lawyering is organized in a morally permissible way—or, in other words, that the moral critique has turned out favorably.

There are at least three features of lawyering that worry lawyers, philosophers, and other critics of the legal profession. First, there is the question of accepting clients. When, if ever, may a lawyer refuse a case? Must a lawyer serve every client who comes in the door? Or only every such client who can pay? May a lawyer refuse a case because the client, though legally right, is morally wrong? Should a lawyer refuse such a case? Second, once a lawyer accepts a client, he is generally supposed to have entered a special relation, one that sometimes justifies—indeed, requires—doing for the client what the lawyer would otherwise think morally wrong to do (helping to keep an admitted rapist out of prison). Does the role of lawyer require that one abandon ordinary moral decency? And, if it does, how can a morally decent person be a lawyer?

Underlying these two questions is the third. There seems to be a fundamental tension between the end the profession of law claims to serve (legal justice, justice within the law, or the like) and the means lawyers use. Lawyers must work for a client (whether paid by the client or an employer), not for justice as such. Sometimes they represent a client (acting as advocate or business agent). Sometimes they advise a client. But whatever role they take, they are supposed to be on the client's side, not a neutral agent (as a judge is supposed to be). Lawyering seems inevitably to involve identification with the ends the client seeks and the means used to achieve it. Law is an adversary calling, a taking of a side in order to earn a living. Such mechanical partiality seems to threaten moral autonomy.

Charles Fried, US Solicitor General 1985–89, offers a conception of the lawyer's role that, he argues, allows a morally decent person to be a lawyer; indeed, a role that makes being a good lawyer a morally good thing to be. Fried begins with the role of parent—but with a difference. No reasonable morality, Fried argues, could ask us to look at ourselves as a mere resource to benefit others. We are free, within certain limits, to bestow our energies as we wish. Thus, a person needs no special reason to put his own child through college rather than a poor neighbor's, even though the neighbor's child is plainly more deserving in every (objective) way. The parent's biological or social relationship with the child is reason enough. Morality does, of course, set bounds on such partiality. I may not kill another child to save my own.

There are, Fried thinks, many relationships permitting *such* special preference. Friendship, like parenthood, is one, but friendship rather than parenthood seems to be the most apt analogy for lawyering. The lawyer is a "special purpose friend," someone who will make the client's legal interests his own. Just as there is nothing wrong with showing special preference for the interests of a friend, there is nothing wrong with a lawyer showing special preference for the interests of his client.

This leaves Fried with the question of whether it is morally permissible to be *anyone's* legal friend. His answer seems to be that it is, within the bounds set by relatively just laws. Helping someone with a legal problem is, for example, always to perform a morally worthy function. A lawyer cannot be faulted for bestowing his services on the rich rather than on the poor because even the rich need a legal friend (and the lawyer should not be treated like a scarce resource to be dispatched where needed most). He should be free to do good where he will. A lawyer also cannot be faulted for helping the guilty go free, defeating a just debt by pleading the statute of limitations, or otherwise helping a client to work the levers of the law that he cannot work for himself. Giving help does for a client what he would do for himself had he the legal knowledge. The lawyer thus contributes to the client's moral autonomy, and that is certainly morally good, even when it does not serve justice.

Much of Fried's essay is devoted to showing that the analogies between friendship and the lawyer-client relationship are more important than the disanalogies. But the paper concludes by trying to give rough definition to the limits of a lawyer's legal friendship. Fried's "moral universe" turns out not to be all that simple. The means that a lawyer uses must not, according to Fried, be immoral. Lying, stealing, degrading, cruelty, and the like are "personal relations" governed by ordinary moral constraints. Pleading the statute of limitations is, in contrast, an "institutional relation," not subject to ordinary moral restraints. The lawyer may plead the statute of limitations to defeat a just debt, but may not lie, steal, or otherwise mistreat another for any client.

Fried's response to the three worries noted above is to point to a familiar relationship in which similar tensions are not so worrisome. Morality allows us to choose our friends for almost any reason and to be partial to them. This gives such an appealing interpretation of lawyering that the first half of Robert J. Condlin's paper must come as a shock. He summarizes a series of important papers, mostly by lawyers, rejecting Fried's analogy for one reason or another, the most important of these reasons being that ordinary friendship is reciprocal. I cannot really be your friend if you are not also mine. Legal friendship, in contrast, is one-sided. Lawyers do not expect clients to show any sort of partiality, only to be reasonably truthful, to recognize good service when provided, and to pay the bill. Condlin therefore proposes a less dramatic way to think about the lawyer—as "friendly role." A fiduciary is someone who has responsibility for looking after the interests of another, a responsibility that must meet the highest standard of care. "Fiduciary" is, of course, a legal term, not a moral one. Its use leaves two questions unanswered. First, why must lawyers be fiduciaries rather than something else? And, second, why is being a fiduciary a good thing when the fiduciary does what lawyers do? While perhaps catching the complexity of the lawyer's role (and the emotional distance, the coolness, typical of a professional) better than Fried, Condlin seems to have failed, as Fried did not, to connect the lawyer's role with a moral good.

Michael Davis seems to accept something like Condlin's description of the lawyer's role. He certainly recognizes both the role's complexity and the historical contingency of much of it. He nonetheless makes three claims that directly connect the lawyer's role, however contingent, with morality. First, the public service lawyers provide is a morally good thing. That is not because lawyers must serve the client's moral autonomy (or any other single good) but because lawyers have designed the role to be morally good. Serving a client's moral autonomy is one moral good but serving justice instead is another. Second, lawyers have tried to design their role, their standards of conduct, so that the means available to lawyers are morally permissible. When lawyers identify a conflict between their role as defined and morality as they understand it, they try to redesign the role to satisfy morality. The hard problems of legal ethics are those where the conflict has been identified but there is no obvious general solution. Third, the resulting standards of conduct bind lawyers morally because they define a cooperative practice, the legal profession, which lawyers enter voluntarily and from which they benefit.

As you read the essays in this section, consider what each author would say about accepting the following case (and what each might advise you to say to the client if you decided to decline it):

George Thomas has provided you with two successful and lucrative personal injury suits. In each case, the injury he sustained was one that most people would have shrugged off. George, however, is someone who likes to stand on his rights. He is, in short, instinctively litigious.

Today George has come to you with another case. As with the others, he is legally right in a way likely to make some money for both of you. George bought a used car from Happy Sam's on the installment plan. The price was, by George's own admission, fair; and, in your opinion, more than fair. The interest rate was a little lower than the going rate.

George nevertheless has a case. He reads the financial section of the evening newspaper religiously. Several days ago he read about the truth-in-lending law. Upon examining his contract with Sam (who finances his own cars), George determined that Sam had not filled in the contract properly. He had left several lines blank, thus committing a clear but technical violation of the law. (Though the purpose of the law is to assure that borrowers are not tricked into signing unfair loan agreements, the law itself does not require that one demonstrate an intention to trick, because such intention is usually hard to prove and the requirement made earlier legislation ineffective.) Under the law, George is entitled to both double the interest charge and the cost of suing.

Suing Sam would be lawful—and profitable for both you and your client. But, Sam is an old man, running a small used-car lot without the usual deceit and thievery. He did not harm George. You therefore wonder whether it would be morally permissible to use the technicalities of the law in this way. Or should you instead tell George to forget this one and explain why? Should you just refuse to take the case and send George elsewhere? Or do you have a professional obligation to proceed with the suit?

Charles Fried

THE LAWYER as FRIEND

Can a good lawyer be a good person? The question troubles lawyers and law students alike. They are troubled by the demands of loyalty to one's client and by the fact that one can win approval as a good, maybe even great, lawyer even though that loyalty is engrossed by overprivileged or positively distasteful clients. How, they ask, is such loyalty compatible with that devotion to the common good characteristic of high moral principles? And whatever their views of the common good, they are troubled because the willingness of lawyers to help their clients use the law to the prejudice of the weak or the innocent seems morally corrupt. The lawyer is conventionally seen as a professional devoted to his client's interests and as authorized, if not in fact required, to do some things (though not anything) for that client which he would not do for himself. In this essay I consider the compatibility between this traditional conception of the lawyer's role and the ideal of moral purity—the ideal that one's life should be lived in fulfillment of the most demanding moral principles, and not just barely within the law. So I shall not be particularly concerned with the precise limits imposed on the lawyer's conduct by positive rules of law and by the American Bar Association's *Code of Professional Responsibility* except as these provide a background. I assume that the lawyer observes these scrupulously. My

From *Yale Law Review* 85 (1975): 1060–1069. Copyright © 1975 by Charles Fried. Reprinted by permission of the author, the Yale Law Journal Company, and Fred B. Rothman & Company.

inquiry is one of morals: Does the lawyer whose conduct and choices are governed on by the traditional conception of the lawyer's role, which these positive rules reflect, lead a professional life worthy of moral approbation, worthy of respect—ours and his own?

THE CHALLENGE TO THE TRADITIONAL CONCEPTION

The Two Criticisms

Two frequent criticisms of the traditional conception of the lawyer's role attack both its ends and its means. First, it is said that the ideal of professional loyalty to one's client permits, even demands, an allocation of the lawyer's time, passion, resources in ways that are not always maximally conducive to the greatest good of the greatest number. Interestingly, this criticism is leveled increasingly at doctors as well as lawyers. Both professions affirm the principle that the professional's primary loyalty is to his client, his patient. A "good" lawyer will lavish energy and resources on his existing client, even if it can be shown that others could derive greater benefit from them. The professional ideal authorizes care for the client and the patient which exceeds what the efficient distribution a scarce social resource (the professional's time) would dictate.

That same professional ideal has little or nothing to say about the initial choice of clients or patients. Certainly it is laudable if the doctor and lawyer seek their clients among the poorest or sickest or most dramatically threatened, but the professional ideal does not require this kind of choice in any systematic way—the choice of client remains largely a matter of fortuity or arbitrary choice. But once the client has been chosen, the professional ideal requires primary loyalty to the client whatever his need or situation. Critics contend that it is wasteful and immoral that some of the finest talent in the legal profession is devoted to the intricacies of, say, corporate finance or elaborate estate plans, while important public and private needs for legal services go unmet. The immorality of this waste is seen to be compounded when the clients who are the beneficiaries of this lavish attention use it to avoid their obligations in justice (if not in law) to society and to perpetuate their (legal) domination of the very groups whose greater needs these lawyers should be meeting.

The second criticism applies particularly to the lawyer. It addresses not the misallocation of scarce resources, which the lawyer's exclusive concern with his client's interests permits, but the means which this loyalty appears to authorize, tactics which procure advantages for the client at the direct expense of some identified opposing party. Examples are discrediting a nervous but probably truthful complaining witness or taking advantage of the need or ignorance of an adversary in a negotiation. This second criticism is, of course, related to the first, but there is a difference. The first criticism focuses on a social harm: the waste of scarce resources implicit in a doctor caring for the hearts of the sedentary managerial classes or a lawyer tending to the estates and marital difficulties of the rich. The professional is accused of failing to confer benefits wisely and efficiently. By the second criticism the lawyer is accused not of failing to benefit the appropriate, though usually unidentified, persons, but of harming his identified adversary.

Examples

Consider a number of cases which illustrate the first criticism: A doctor is said to have a duty of loyalty to his patient, but how is he to react if doing his very best for his patient would deplete the resources of the patient's family, as in the case of a severely deformed baby who can only be kept alive through extraordinarily expensive means? Should a doctor prescribe every test of distinct but marginal utility for every patient on public assistance, even if he knows that in the aggregate such a policy will put the medical care system under intolerable burdens? Should he subject his patients to prudent testing of new remedies because he knows that only in this way can medicine make the strides that it has in the past?

These problems are analogous to problems which are faced by the lawyer. The lawyer who advises a client how to avoid the effects of a tax or a form of regulation, though it is a fair tax or a regulation in the public interest, is facing the same dilemma and resolving it in favor of his client. So does the public defender who accedes to his client's demands and takes a "losing" case to trial, thereby wasting court time and depleting the limited resources of his organization. We tolerate and indeed may applaud the decision of a lawyer who vigorously defends a criminal whom he believes to be guilty and dangerous. And I for one think that a lawyer who arranges the estate of a disagreeable dowager or represents one of the parties in a bitter matrimonial dispute must be as assiduous and single-minded in fulfilling his obligation to that client as the lawyer who is defending the civil liberties case of the century.

Illustrative of the second criticism (doing things which are offensive to a particular person) are familiar situations such as the following; In a negotiation it becomes clear to the lawyer for the seller that the buyer and his lawyer mistakenly believe that somebody else has already offered a handsome price for the property. The buyer asks the seller if this is true, and the seller's lawyer hears his client give an ambiguous but clearly encouraging response. Another classic case is the interposition of a technical defense, such as the running of the statute of limitations to defeat a debt that the client admits he owes.[1]

There is another class of cases which does not so ambiguously involve the lawyer's furthering of his client's interests at the direct expense of some equally identified, concrete individual, but where furthering those interests does require the lawyer to do things which are personally offensive to him. The conventional paradigms in the casuistic literature deal with criminal defense lawyers who are asked improper questions by the trial judge ("Your client doesn't have a criminal record, does he?" or "Your client hasn't offered to plead guilty to a lesser offense, has he?"), a truthful answer to which would be damningly prejudicial to the client, but which the lawyer cannot even refuse to answer without running the risk of creating the same prejudice. There are those who say that the lawyer must lie in defense of his client's interests even though lying is personally and professionally offensive to him. The defense lawyer who cross-examines a complaining rape victim (whom he knows to be telling the truth) about her chastity or lack thereof in order to discredit her accusing testimony faces a similar moral difficulty. In some respects these cases might be taken to illustrate both principal criticisms of the traditional conception. On the one hand, there is harm to society in making the choice to favor the client's interests: a dangerous criminal may escape punishment or an appropriately heavy sentence. On the other hand, this social harm is accomplished by means of acting toward another human—the judge, the complaining witness—in ways that seem demeaning and dishonorable.

THE LAWYER AS FRIEND

The Thesis

In this essay I will consider the moral status of the traditional conception of the professional. The two criticisms of this traditional conception, if left unanswered, will not put the lawyer in jail, but they will leave him without a moral basis for his acts. The real question is whether, in the face of these two criticisms, a decent and morally sensitive person can conduct himself according to the traditional conception of professional loyalty and still believe that what he is doing is morally worthwhile.

It might be said that anyone whose conscience is so tender that he cannot fulfill the prescribed obligations of a professional should not undertake those obligations. He should not allow his moral scruples to operate as a trap for those who are told by the law that they may expect something more. But of course this suggestion merely pushes the inquiry back a step. We must ask, not how a decent lawyer may behave, but whether a decent, ethical person can ever be a lawyer. Are the assurances implicit in assuming the role of lawyer such that an honorable person would not give them and thus would not enter the profession? And, indeed, this is a general point about an argument from obligation: It may be that the internal logic of a particular obligation demands forms of conduct (e.g., honor among thieves), but the question remains whether it is just and moral to contract such obligations.

I will argue in this essay that it is not only legally but also morally right that a lawyer adopt as his dominant purpose the furthering of his client's interests—that it is right that a professional put the interests of his client above some idea, however valid, of the collective interest. I maintain that the traditional concept of the professional role expresses a morally valid conception of human conduct and human relationships, that one who acts according to that conception is to that extent a good person. Indeed, it is my view that, far from a mere creature of positive law, the traditional conception is so far mandated by moral right that any advanced legal system which did not sanction this conception would be unjust.

The general problem raised by the two criticisms is this: How can it be that it is not only permissible, but indeed morally right, to favor the interests of a particular person in a way which we can be fairly sure is either harmful to another particular individual or not maximally conducive to the welfare of society as a whole?

The resolution of this problem is aided, I think, if set in a larger perspective.

Charles Curtis made the perspicacious remark that a lawyer may be privileged to lie for his client in a way that one might lie to save one's friends or close relatives.[2] I do not want to underwrite the notion that it is justifiable to lie even in those situations, but there is a great deal to the point that in those relations—friendship, kinship—we recognize an authorization to take the interests of particular concrete persons more seriously and to give them priority over the interests of the wider collectivity. One who provides an expensive education for his own children surely cannot be blamed because he does not use these resources to alleviate famine or to save lives in some distant land. Nor does he blame himself. Indeed, our intuition that an individual is authorized to prefer identified persons standing close to him over the abstract interests of humanity finds sharpest expression in our sense that an individual is entitled to act with something less than impartiality to that person who stands closest to him—the person that he is. There is such a thing as selfishness to be sure, yet no reasonable morality asks us to look upon ourselves as merely plausible candidates for distribution of the attention and resources which we command, plausible candidates whose entitlement to our own concern is no greater in principle than that of the other human being. Such a doctrine may seem edifying, but on reflection, it strikes us as merely fanatical.

This suggests an interesting way to look at the situation of the lawyer. As a professional person one has a special care for the interests of those accepted clients, just as his friends, his family, and he himself have a very general claim of his special concern. But I concede this does no more than widen the problem. It merely shows that in claiming this authorization to have a special care for clients I am doing something which I do in other contexts as well.

THE UTILITARIAN EXPLANATION

I consider first an argument to account for fidelity to role, for obligation, made most elaborately by the classical utilitarians, Mill and Sidgwick.[3] They argue that our propensity to prefer the interests of those who are close to us is in fact perfectly reasonable because we are more likely to be able to benefit those people. Thus, if everyone is mainly concerned with those closest to him, the distribution of social energies will be most efficient and the greatest good of the greatest number will be achieved. The idea is that the efforts I expend for my friend or my relative are more likely to be effective because I am more likely to know what needs to be done. I am more likely to be sure that the good I intend is in fact accomplished. One might say that there is less overhead, fewer administrative costs, in benefiting those nearest to us. I would not want to ridicule this argument, but it does not seem to me to go far enough. Because if that were the sole basis for the preference, then it would be my duty to determine whether my efforts might not be more efficiently spent on the collectivity, on the distant, anonymous beneficiary. But it is just my point that *this* is an inquiry we are not required, indeed sometimes not even authorized, to make. When we decide to favor our children, to assure our own comforts, to fulfill our obligations to clients or patients, we do not do so as a result of a cost-benefit inquiry that takes into account the ease of producing a good result for our friends and relations.

Might it not be said, however, that the best means of favoring the abstract collectivity is in certain cases not to try to favor it directly but to concentrate on those to whom one has a special relation? This does not involve tricking oneself, only recognizing the limitations of what an individual can do and know. But it seems to me, that is just Mill's and Sidgwick's argument all over again. There is no trickery involved, but this is still a kind of deliberate limitation of our moral horizon which leaves us uncomfortable. Do I know in a particular case whether sticking to the narrow definition of my role will in that case further the good of all? If I know that it will not further the general good, then why am I acting as the role demands? Is it to avoid setting a bad example? But for whom? I need not tell others—whether I tell or not could enter into my calculation. For myself then? But that begs the question, since if short-circuiting the role-definition of my obligation and going straight for the general good is the best thing to do in that case, then the example I set myself is not a bad example, but a good one. In short, I do not see how one can at the same time admit that the general good is one's only moral standard, while steadfastly hewing to obligations to friends, family, and clients. What we must look for is an argument that shows that giving some degree of special consideration to myself, my friends, my clients is not merely instrumentally justified (as the utilitarians would argue) but to some degree intrinsically so.[4]

I think such an argument can be made. Instead of speaking the language of maximization of value over all of humanity, it will speak the language of rights. The stubborn ethical datum affirming such a preference grows out of the profoundest springs of morality: the concepts of personality, identity, and liberty.

SELF, FRIENDSHIP, AND JUSTICE

Consider for a moment the picture of the human person that would emerge if the utilitarian claim were in fact correct. It would mean that in all my choices I must consider the well-being of all humanity—actual and potential—as the range of my concern. Moreover, every actual or potential human being is absolutely equal in his claims upon me. Indeed, I myself am to myself only as one of an innumerable multitude. And that is the clue to what is wrong with the utilitarian vision. Before there is morality there must be the person. We must attain and maintain in our morality a concept of personality such that it makes sense to posit choosing, valuing entities—free, moral beings. But the picture of the universe in which my own interests disappear and are merged into the interests of the totality of humanity is incompatible with that, because one wishes to develop a conception of a responsible, valuable, and valuing agent, and such an agent must first of all be dear to himself. It is from the kernel in individuality that the other things we value radiate. The Gospel says we must love our neighbor as ourselves, and this implies that any concern for others which is a *human* concern must presuppose a concern for ourselves.

The human concern which we then show others is a concern which first of all recognizes the concrete individuality of that other person just as we recognize our own.

It might be objected that the picture I sketch does not show that each individual, in order to maintain the integral sense of himself as an individual is justified in attributing a greater value to his most essential interests than he ascribes to the most essential interests of all other persons. Should not the individual generalize and attribute in equal degree to all persons the value which he naturally attributes to himself? I agree with those who hold that it is the essence of morality for reason to push us beyond inclination to the fair conclusion of our premises. It *is* a fair conclusion that as my experience as a judging, valuing, choosing entity is crucial to me, I must also conclude that for other persons their own lives and desires are the center of their universes. If morality is transcendent, it must somehow transcend particularity to take account of this general fact. I do not wish to deny this. On the contrary, my claim is that the kind of preference which an individual gives himself and concrete others is a preference which he would in exactly this universalizing spirit allow others to exhibit as well. It is not that I callously overlook the claim of the abstract individual, but, indeed, I would understand and approve were I myself to be prejudiced because some person to whom I stood in a similar situation of abstraction preferred his own concrete dimensions.

Finally, the concreteness which is the starting point of my own moral sensibility, the sense of myself, is not just a historical, biographical fact. It continues to enter into and condition my moral judgments because the effects which I can produce upon people who are close to me are qualitatively different from those produced upon abstract, unknown persons. My own concreteness is important not only because it establishes a basis for understanding what I and what all other human beings might be, but because in engaging that aspect of myself with the concrete aspects of others, I realize special values for both of us. Quite simply, the individualized relations of love and friendship (and perhaps also their opposites, hatred and enmity) have a different, more intense aspect than do the cooler, more abstract relations of love and service to humanity in general. The impulse I describe, therefore, is not in any sense a selfish impulse. But it does begin with the sense of self as a concrete entity. Those who object to my thesis by saying that we must generalize it are not wholly wrong; they merely exaggerate. Truly, I must be ready to generalize outward all the way. That is what justice consists of. But justice is not all of morality; there remains a circle of intensity which, through its emphasis on the particular and the concrete, continues to reflect what I have identified as the source of all sense of value—our sense of self.

Therefore, it is not only consonant with, but also required by, an ethics for human beings that one be entitled first of all to reserve an area of concern for oneself and then to move out freely from that area if one wishes to lavish that concern on others to whom one stands in concrete, personal relations. Similarly, a person is entitled to enjoy this extra measure of care from those who choose to bestow it upon him without having to justify this grace as either just or efficient. We may choose the individuals to whom we will stand in this special relation, or they may be thrust upon us, as in family ties. Perhaps we recognize family ties because, after all, there often has been an element of choice, but also because—by some kind of atavism or superstition—we identify with those who share a part of our biological natures.

In explicating the lawyer's relation to his client, my analogy shall be to friendship, where the freedom to choose and to be chosen expresses our freedom to hold something of ourselves in reserve, in reserve even from the universalizing claims of morality. These personal ties and the claims they engender may be all-consuming, as with a close friend or family member, or they may be limited, all-purpose claims, as in the case of the client or patient.[5] The special-purpose claim is one in which the beneficiary, the client, is entitled to all the special consideration *within* the limits of the relationship which we accord to a friend or a loved one. It is not that the claims of the client are less intense or demanding; they are only more limited in their scope. After all, the ordinary concept of friendship provides only an analogy, and it is to the development of this analogy that I turn.

SPECIAL-PURPOSE FRIENDS

How does a professional fit into the concept of personal relations at all? He is, I suggested, a limited-purpose friend. A lawyer is a friend in regard to the legal system. He is someone who enters into a personal relation with you—not an abstract relation as under the concept of justice. That means that, like a friend he acts in your interests, not his own;

or rather he adopts your interests as his own. I would call this the classic definition of friendship. To be sure, the lawyer's range of concern is sharply limited. But within that limited domain the intensity of identification with the client's interests is the same. It is not the specialized focus of the relationship which may make the metaphor inapposite, but the way in which the relation of legal friendship comes about and the one-sided nature of the ensuing "friendship." But I do insist upon the analogy, for in overcoming the arguments that the analogy is false, I think the true moral foundations of the lawyer's special role are illuminated and the utilitarian objections to the traditional conception of that role are overthrown.

THE PROFESSIONAL ROLE AS SOCIALLY DEFINED: THE CONTENT OF THE RELATION

The claims that are made on the doctor or lawyer are made within a social context and are defined, at least in part, by social expectations. Most strikingly, in talking about friendship the focus of the inquiry is quite naturally upon the free gift of the donor; yet in professional relationships it is the recipient's need for medical or legal aid which defines the relationship. So the source of the relationship seems to be located at the other end, that of the recipient. To put this disquiet another way, we might ask how recognizing the special claims of friendship in any way compels society to allow the doctor or the lawyer to define his role on the analogy of those claims. Why are these people not like other social actors designated to purvey certain, perhaps necessary, goods? Would we say that one's grocer, tailor, or landlord should be viewed as a limited-purpose friend? Special considerations must be brought forward for doctors and lawyers.[6]

A special argument is at hand in both cases. The doctor does not minister to just any need, but to health. He helps maintain the very integrity which is the concrete substratum of individuality. To be sure, so does a grocer or landlord. But illness wears a special guise: it appears as a critical assault on one's person. The needs to which the doctor ministers usually are implicated in crises going to one's concreteness and individuality, and therefore what one looks for is a kind of ministration which is particularly concrete, personal, and individualized. Thus, it is not difficult to see why I claim that a doctor is a friend, though a special-purpose friend, the purpose being defined by the special needs of illness and crisis to which he tends.

But what, then, of the lawyer? Friendship and kinship are natural relations existing within, but not defined by, complex social institutions. Illness, too, is more a natural than social phenomenon. The response here requires an additional step. True, the special situations—legal relations or disputes—in which the lawyer acts as a limited-purpose friend are themselves a product of social institutions. But it does not follow that the role of the lawyer, which is created to help us deal with these social institutions, is defined by and is wholly at mercy of the social good. We need only concede that at the very least the law must leave us a measure of autonomy, whether or not it is in the social interest to do so. Individuals have rights over and against the collectivity. The moral capital arising out of individuals' concrete situations is one way of expressing that structure of rights of individuals that the law must also create and support the specific role of legal friend. For the social nexus—the web of perhaps entirely just institutions—has become so complex that without the assistance of an expert adviser an ordinary layman cannot exercise that autonomy which the system must allow him. Without such an adviser, the law would impose constraints on the lay citizen (unequally at that) which it is not entitled to impose explicitly. Thus, the need which the lawyer serves in his special-purpose friendship may not be, as in the case of the doctor, natural or pre-social. Yet it is a need which has a moral grounding analogous to the need which the physician serves: the need to maintain one's integrity as a person. When I say the lawyer is his client's legal friend, I mean the lawyer makes his client's interests his own insofar as this is necessary to preserve and foster the client's autonomy within the law.

This argument does not require us to assume that the law is hostile to the client's rights. All we need to assume is that even a system of law which is perfectly sensitive to personal rights would not work unless the client could claim a professional's assistance in realizing that autonomy which the law recognizes.

THE ASYMMETRY OF MOTIVE AND DUTY: THE FORM OF THE RELATION

The institutional origin of the lawyer-client relationship is not its only characteristic which suggests that the analogy to natural friendship is vulnerable. In natural friendship the ideal relation is reciprocal; in legal friendship it is not. The lawyer is said to be the client's friend insofar as he is devoted to his client's interests but it is no part of the ideal that the client should have any reciprocal devotion to the interests of his lawyer. Furthermore, I have argued that our right to be a friend to whomever we choose is a product of our individual autonomy. But in legal friendship the emphasis has been on the autonomy of client, and it is the client who chooses the lawyer; yet it is the lawyer who is a friend in the relation. And as a final contrast to natural friendship, the motive for agreeing or refusing to provide legal services is money. Indeed, when we speak of the lawyer's right to represent whomever he wishes, we are defending his moral title to represent whoever pays.

But recall that the concept of legal friendship was introduced to answer the argument that the lawyer is morally reprehensible to the extent that he lavishes concern on some particular person. The concept of friendship explains how it can be that a particular person may right-fully receive more than his share of care from another: he can receive that care if he receives it as an act of friendship. Although in natural friendship I emphasized the freedom to bestow, surely, that freedom must imply a freedom to receive that extra measure of care. And it is right of the client to receive such an extra measure of care (without regard, that is, to considerations of efficiency or fairness) as much as the lawyer's right to give it; that I have been trying to explicate. Thus, the fact that the care in friendship systematically runs all one way does not impair the argument.

Yet the unease persists. Is it that while I have shown that the lawyer has a right to help the "unworthy" client, I have not shown that whenever the lawyer exercises this right he does something which is morally worthy, entitling him to self-respect? I may have shown that the law is obliged to allow the "unworthy" client to seek legal help and the lawyer to give it. But have I also shown that the lawyer who avails himself of this legal right (his and the client's legal right) performs a *morally worthy* function? Can a good lawyer be a good person?

The lawyer acts morally because he helps to preserve and express the autonomy of his client vis-à-vis the legal system. It is not just that the lawyer helps the client accomplish a particular lawful purpose. Pornography may be legal, but it hardly follows that I perform a morally worthy function if I lend money or artistic talent to help the pornographer flourish in the exercise of this right. What is special about legal counsel is that whatever else may stop the pornographer's enterprise, he should not be stopped because he mistakenly believes there is a legal impediment. There is no wrong if a venture fails for lack of talent or lack of money—no one's rights have been violated. But rights are violated if, through ignorance or misinformation about the law, an individual refrains from pursuing a wholly lawful purpose. Therefore, to assist others in understanding and realizing their legal rights is always morally worthy. Moreover, the legal system, by instituting the role of the legal friend, not only assures what it in justice must—the due liberty of each citizen before the law—but does it by creating an institution which exemplifies, at least in a unilateral sense, the idea of personal relations of trust and personal care which (as in natural friendships) are good in themselves.

Perhaps the unease has another source. The lawyer does work for pay. Is there not something odd about analogizing the lawyer's role to friendship when in fact his so-called friendship must usually be bought?

If the lawyer is a public purveyor of goods, is not the lawyer-client relationship like that underlying any commercial transaction? My answer is no. The lawyer and doctor have obligations to the client or patient beyond those of other economic agents. A grocer may refuse to give food to a customer when it becomes apparent that the customer does not have the money to pay for it. But the lawyer and doctor may not refuse to give additional care to an individual who cannot pay for it if withdrawal of their services would prejudice that individual. Their duty to the client or patient to whom they have made an initial commitment transcends the conventional quid pro quo of the marketplace. It is undeniable that money is usually what cements the lawyer-client relationship. But the content of that relation is determined by the client's needs, just as friendship is a response to another's needs. It is not determined, as are simple economic relationships, by the mere coincidence of a willingness to sell and a willingness to buy. So, the fact that the lawyer works for pay does not seriously undermine the friendship analogy.

INSTITUTIONAL CLIENTS

Another possible objection to my analysis concerns the lawyer in government or the lawyer for a corporation. My model posits a duty of exclusive concern (within the law) for the interests of the client. This might be said to be inappropriate in the corporate area because larger economic power entails larger social obligations, and because the idea of friendship, even legal friendship, seems peculiarly far-fetched in such an impersonal context. After all, corporations and other institutions, unlike persons, are creatures of the state. Thus, the pursuit of their interests would seem to be especially subject to the claims of the public good. But corporations and other institutions are only formal arrangements of real persons pursuing their real existence. If the law allows real persons to pursue their interests in these complex forms, then why are they not entitled to loyal legal assistance, "legal friendship," in this exercise of their autonomy just as if they pursued their interests in simple arrangements and associations? The real problem in these cases is that the definition of the client is complicated and elusive. The fundamental concepts remain the same, but we must answer a question which so far we could treat as straight-forward: Who is the client? It is the corporation. But because the corporation is an institutional entity, institutional considerations enter into both the definition of the entity to whom the loyalty is owed and the substance of that loyalty. This is dramatically the case of a government lawyer, since his client might be thought to be the government of the United States, or the people of the United States, mediated by an intricate political and institutional framework. So it is said that a United States attorney is interested (unlike any ordinary lawyer) not only in winning his case but also in seeing that "justice is done," because his client's interests are served only if justice is done. Since more and more lawyers have only institutional clients, the introduction of institutional concerns into the definition of the representational obligation is virtually pervasive. From this, some would conclude that my argument is inappropriate or at least anachronistic. I insist that my analogy is the correct one, that it is applicable to the institutional client, but it must be combined in a complicated though wholly coherent way with arguments about who one's client is and how that client's interests are to be identified.

THE TWO CRITICISMS AND THE FRIENDSHIP ANALOGY

Choice of Clients: The Question of Distribution

It is time to apply the concept of legal friendship to the first of the two criticisms with which this essay began: that the lawyer's ethic of loyalty to his client and willingness to pick clients for any and every reason (usually, however, for money) result in a maldistribution of a scarce resource, the aid of counsel. It is this criticism which the lawyer shares with the doctor. The preceding sections demonstrated at least this much: that legal counsel—like medical care—must be considered a service, and that he who provides it does a useful thing. But this first criticism in no way questions that conclusion. On the contrary, precisely because medical care and legal counsel are benefits to those who receive them, the critic blames the individual doctor or lawyer for not bestowing his skills in the way which best meets the social need. The notion of legal friendship helps us respond to his criticism.

The lawyer-client relation is a personal relation, and legal counsel is a personal service. This explains directly why, *once the relation has been contracted,* considerations of efficiency or fair distribution cannot be allowed to weaken it. The relation itself is not a creature of social expediency (though social circumstances provide the occasion for it); it is the creature of moral rights and therefore expediency may not compromise the nature of the relation. This is true in medicine because the human need creates a relation of dependence which it would be a betrayal to compromise. In the lawyer-client relation, the argument is more complex but supports the same conclusion. The relation must exist in order to realize the client's rights against society, to preserve that measure of autonomy which social regulation must allow the individual. But to allow considerations—even social regulations—to limit and compromise what by hypothesis is an entailment of the original grant of right to the individual is to take away with the left hand what was given with the right. Once the relation has been taken up, it is the client's needs which hold the reins—legally and morally.

If I have a client with legal needs, then neither another person with greater needs nor a court should be able to compel or morally oblige me to compromise my care for those needs. To hold differently would apply the concept of battlefield emergency care (*triage*) to the area of regular legal service. But doctors do not operate that way and neither should lawyers. For it is just the point of emergencies and wars that they create special, brutal, and depersonalized conditions which civilization, by its very essence, must keep from becoming the general rule of social life.

So much for the integrity of the relation once it has taken hold. But what about the initial choice of client? Must we not give some thought to efficiency and relative need at least at the outset, and does this not run counter to the picture of purely discretionary choice implicit in the notion of friendship? The question is difficult, but before considering its difficulties we should note that the preceding argumentation has surely limited its impact. We can now affirm that, whatever the answer to this question, the individual lawyer does a morally worthy thing for whomever he serves and, moreover, is bound to follow through once he has begun to serve. In this he is like the doctor. So if there is fault it is a limited fault. What would be required for a lawyer to immunize himself more fully from criticism that he is unjust in his allocation of care? Each would have to consider at the outset of his career and during that career where the greatest need for his particular legal talents lies. He would then have to allocate himself to that area of greatest need. Surely there is nothing wrong with doing this (so long as loyalty to relations already undertaken is not compromised); but is a lawyer morally at fault if he does not lead his life in this way? It is at this point too that the metaphor of friendship and the concept of self as developed above suggest the response. But this time they will be viewed from another perspective—the lawyer's as opposed to the client's rights and liberties.

Must the lawyer expend his efforts where they will do the most good, rather than where they will draw the largest fee, provide the most excitement, prove most flattering to his vanity, whatever? Why must he? If the answer is that he must because it will produce the most good, then we are saying that he is merely a scarce resource. But a person is not a resource. He is not bound to lead his life as if he were managing a business on behalf of an impersonal body of stockholders called human society. It is this monstrous conception against which I argued earlier. Justice is not all; we are entitled to reserve a portion of our concern and bestow it where we will. We may bestow it entirely at our discretion as in the case of friendship, or we may bestow it at what I would call "constrained discretion" in the choice and exercise of a profession. That every exercise of the profession is morally worthwhile is already a great deal to the lawyer's credit. Just as the principle of liberty leaves one morally free to choose a profession according to inclination, so within the profession it leaves one free to organize his life according to inclination. The lawyer's liberty to take up what kind of practice he chooses and to take up or decline what clients he will is an aspect of the moral liberty of self to enter into personal relations freely.

I would not carry this idea through to the bitter end. It has always been accepted, for instance, that a court may appoint an available lawyer to represent a criminal defendant who cannot otherwise find counsel. Indeed, I would be happy to acknowledge the existence of some moral duty to represent any client whose needs fit one's particular capacities and who cannot otherwise find counsel. This is not a large qualification to the general liberty I proclaim. The obligation is, and must remain, exceptional; it cannot become a kind of general obligation of the particular lawyer involved. And the obligation cannot compromise duties to existing clients. Furthermore, I would argue that this kind of representation should always be compensated—the duty to the client who cannot afford representation is initially a duty of society, not of the individual lawyer. I go this far for a number of reasons. If the representation is properly compensated, then the very need to appoint a lawyer will be exceptional, an anomaly arising in one of two ways: a fortuitous perturbation in the law of supply and demand or a general, if not concerted, professional boycott of this particular client. If the first is the reason, then the lifetime imposition on any one lawyer will be slight indeed. If it is the second, then the assertion of a duty, oddly enough, serves to express and strengthen the principle of the lawyer's independence. For the moral position of the lawyer rests on the claim that he takes up his client's interests irrespective of their merits. By accepting from time to time the duty to represent the undesirable, he affirms this independence.

But surely I must admit that the need for legal representation far exceeds what an unstructured, largely individualistic system could supply. Are there vast numbers of needy people with a variety of legal problems who will never seek us out, but must be sought out? And what of the general responsibility that just laws be passed and justly administered? These are the obligations which the traditional conception of the lawyer, with his overriding loyalty to the client, is thought to leave unmet. At this point I yield no further. If the lawyer is really to be impressed to serve these admitted social needs, then his independence and discretion disappear, and he does indeed become a public resource cut up and disposed of by the public's needs. There would be no justice to such a conception. If there are really not enough lawyers to care for the needs of the poor, then it is grossly unfair to conscript the legal profession to fill the needs. If the obligation is one of justice, it is an obligation of society as a whole. It is cheap and hypocritical for society to be unwilling to pay the necessary lawyers from the tax revenues of all, and then to claim that individual lawyers are morally at fault for not choosing to work for free. In fact, as provision of legal services has come to be seen as necessary to ensure justice, society has indeed hired lawyers in an effort to meet that need.

Finally, I agree that the lawyer has a moral obligation to work for establishment of just institutions generally, but the entirely wrong kind of conclusions have been drawn from this. Some of the more ecstatic critics have put forward the lawyer as some kind of anointed priest of justice—a high priest whose cleaving to the traditional conception of the lawyer's role opens him to the charge of apostasy. But this is wrong. In a democratic society, justice has no anointed priests. Every citizen has the same duty to work for the establishment of just institutions, and the lawyer has no special moral responsibility in that regard. To be sure, the lawyer like any citizen must use all his knowledge and talent to fulfill that general duty of citizenship, and this may mean that there are special perspectives and opportunities for him.

The Choice of Means

More difficult problems are posed by the conflict between the interests of the client and the interests of some other concrete and specified person to whom the client stands in opposition. How does my friendship analogy help to resolve the conflict which a lawyer must feel if his client asks him to lie, to oppress, to conceal—to do something which is either illegal or felt by the lawyer be immoral?

Staying within the Law

I have defined the lawyer as a client's legal friend, as the person whose role it is to insure the client's autonomy within the law. Although I have indicated that the exercise of that autonomy is not always consonant with the public interest, it does not at all follow that the exercise of that autonomy, therefore, must violate the law. If the legal system is itself sensitive to moral claims, sensitive to the rights of individuals, it must at times allow that autonomy to be exercised in ways that do not further the public interest. Thus, the principle that the lawyer must scrupulously contain his assistance and advocacy within the dictates of the law seems to me perfectly consistent with my view of the lawyer as the client's friend, who maintains the client's interests even against the interests of society.

To be sure, there may have been and may still be situations where the law grossly violates what morality defines as individual rights; and there have been lawyers who have stood ready to defy such laws in order to further their client rights—the rights which the law should, but did not, recognize. Whatever might be said about these cases, the lawyer's conduct in them travels outside the bounds of legal friendship and becomes political friendship, political agitation, friendship *tout court*. But that is not the case I am examining. The moral claim which a client has on his lawyer can be fully exhausted though that lawyer contains his advocacy strictly within the limits of the law.

A critic who fails to see the importance of the lawyer's moral status in assisting the autonomy of his client may also be inclined to complain that the constraints of the law restrain his advocacy of truly just causes too much. Such a critic has things wrong at both ends. Just as it is false to argue that the lawyer is morally reprehensible if he furthers the interests of some clients and not others or some purposes and not others, so it is false to assume that the lawyer fails to have the proper zeal if he does for his client only what the law allows. The line between the role of the lawyer as a personal adviser and that of the lawyer as a citizen and member of the community should be quite clear. It is by controlling what the law is and by varying the interests that clients may lawfully pursue that social policy should be effectuated; it is not by deforming the role of lawyer as the client's legal friend and asking him to curb his advocacy in that relationship.

This explains why in a reasonably just system which properly commands the lawyer's loyalty, he must confine his advocacy to what the rules of advocacy permit.

He may not counsel his client to commit a crime, nor to destroy evidence, nor to perjure himself on the witness stand. Of course, here as elsewhere there will be borderline problems. It may not be a crime to lie to the judge who asked the improper and prejudicial question of the defense attorney, but the implicit or quasi-official rules defining the limits of the lawyer's advocacy may nonetheless forbid this. Nothing in my model should discourage the lawyer from observing such limits scrupulously.

A very difficult question would arise if the law imposed upon the lawyer an obligation first to seek and then to betray his client's trust, an obligation to do that which seems outrageous and unjust. I do not mean to say that the resolution of this question would be easy, but my analysis at least clearly locates the area in which a resolution should be sought. For such laws, if they are to be opposed, ought to be opposed as are other unjust laws, and not because the lawyer is in general entitled to travel outside the constraints of the law in protecting his client's interests. Maybe in such a dilemma a conscientious lawyer would keep the client's confidence as would a priest or a natural friend, but if conscientiousness requires this, it requires it as an act of disobedience and resistance to unjust law, rather than as a necessary entailment of some extreme view of the lawyer's general role.

IMMORAL MEANS

I come to what seems to me one of the most difficult dilemmas of the lawyer's role. It is illustrated by the lawyer who is asked to press the unfair claim, to humiliate a witness, to participate in a distasteful or dishonorable scheme. I am assuming that in none of these situations does the lawyer do anything which is illegal or which violates the ethical canons of his profession; the dilemma arises if he acts in a way which seems to him personally dishonorable, but there are no sanctions— legal or professional—which he need fear.

This set of issues is difficult because it calls on the same principles which provide the justification for the lawyer's or the friend's exertions on behalf of persons with whom he maintains a personal relation. Only now the personal relation is one not of benefit but of harm. In meeting the first criticism, I was able to insist on the right of the lawyer as friend to give this extra weight to the interests of his client when the only competing claims were the general claims of the abstract collectivity. But here we have a specific victim as well as a specific beneficiary. The relation to the person whom we deceive or abuse is just as concrete and human, just as personal, as to the friend whom we help.

It is not open to us to justify this kind of harm by claiming that personal relations must be chosen, not thrust upon us. Personal relations are indeed typically chosen. If mere proximity could place on us the obligations of friendship, then there would soon be nothing left of our freedom to bestow an extra measure of care over and above what humanity can justly claim. But there is a personal relation when we inflict intentional harm; the fact that it is intention that reaches out and particularizes the victim. "Who is my neighbor?" is a legitimate question when affirmative aid is in question; it is quite out of order in respect the injunction "Do not harm your neighbor." Lying, stealing, degrading, inflicting pain and injury are personal relations too. They are not like failing to benefit, and for that reason they are laid under a correspondingly stricter regime than abstract harms to the collectivity. If I claim respect for my own conscious particularity, I must accord that respect to others. Therefore, what pinches here is the fact that the lawyer's personal engagement with the client is urging him to do that to his adversary which the very principles of personal engagement urge that he not do to anyone.

It is not wrong, but somewhat lame to argue that the lawyer like the doctor has autonomy. From this argument it follows that the lawyer who is asked to do something personally distasteful or immoral (though perfectly legal) should be free either to decline to enter into the relationship of "legal friendship" or to terminate it. And if the client can find a lawyer to do the morally nasty but legally permissible thing for him, then all is well—the complexities of the law have not succeeded in thwarting an exercise of autonomy which the law was not entitled to thwart. So long as the first lawyer is reasonably convinced that another lawyer can be found, I cannot see why he is less free to decline a morally repugnant case than he is a boring or poorly paid case. True, but lame, for one wants to know not whether one *may* refuse to do the dirty deed, but whether one is *morally bound* to refuse—bound to refuse even if he is the last lawyer in town and no one else will bail him out of his moral conundrum.

If personal integrity lies at the foundation of the lawyer's right to treat his client as a friend, then surely consideration for personal integrity—his own and others'—must limit what he can do in friendship. Consideration for personal integrity forbids me to lie, cheat, or humiliate, whether in my own interests or of a friend, so surely they prohibit such conduct on behalf of a client, one's legal friend. This is the general truth, but it must be made more particular if it is to do service here. For there is an opposing consideration. Remember, the lawyer's special kind of friendship is occasioned by the right of the client to exercise his full measure of autonomy within the law. This suggests that one must not transfer uncritically the whole range of personal moral scruples into the arena of legal friendship. After all, not only would I not lie or steal for myself or my friends, I probably also would not pursue socially noxious schemes, foreclose on widows or orphans, or assist in the avoidance of just punishment. So we must be careful lest the whole argument unravel on us at this point.

Balance and structure are restored if we distinguish between kinds of moral scruples. Think of the soldier. If he is a citizen of a just state, where foreign policy decisions are made in a democratic way, he may well believe that it is not up to him to question whether the war he fights is a just war. But he is personally bound not to fire dum-dum bullets, not to inflict intentional injury on civilians, and not to abuse prisoners. These are personal wrongs, wrongs by his person to the person of the victim.[7] So also, the lawyer must distinguish between wrongs that a reasonably just legal system permits to be done by its rules and wrongs which the lawyer personally commits. I do not offer this as a rule which is tight enough to resolve all borderline questions of judgment. We must recognize that the border is precisely the place of friction between competing moral principles. Indeed, it is unreasonable to expect moral arguments to dispense wholly with the need for prudence and judgment.

Consider the difference between humiliating a witness or lying to the judge, on one hand, and, on the other hand asserting the statute of limitations or the lack of a written memorandum to defeat what you know to be a just claim against your client. In the latter case, if an injustice is worked, it is worked because the legal system not only permits it, but also defines the terms and modes of operation. Legal institutions have created the occasion for your act. What you do is not personal; it is a formal, legally-defined act. But the moral quality of lying or abuse contains both without and within the context of the law. Therefore, my general notion is that a lawyer is morally entitled to act in this formal, representative way even if the result is an injustice, because the legal system which authorizes both the justice (*e.g.*, the result following the plea of the statute of limitations) and the formal gesture for working it insulates him from personal moral responsibility. I would distinguish between the lawyer's own wrong and the wrong of the system used to advantage by the client.

The clearest case is a lawyer who calls to the attention of the court a controlling legal precedent or statute which establishes his client's position even though that position is an unjust one. (I assume throughout, however, that this unjust law is part of a generally just and decent system. I am not considering at all the moral dilemmas of a lawyer in Nazi Germany or Soviet Russia.) Why are we inclined to absolve him of personal moral responsibility for the result he accomplishes? I assert it is because the wrong is wholly institutional; it is a wrong which does not exist and has no meaning outside the legal frame-work. The only thing preventing the client from doing this for himself is his lack knowledge of the law or his lack of authority to operate the levers of the law in official proceedings. It is to supply that lack of knowledge or of formal capacity that the lawyer is in general author-ized to act, and the levers he pulls are all legal levers.

Now contrast this to the lawyer who lies to an opposing party in a negotiation. I assume that (except in extreme cases akin to self-defense) an important lie with harmful consequences is an offense to the victim's integrity as a rational moral being, and thus the liar affirms a principle which denigrates is own moral status. Every speech set invites belief, and so every lie is a betrayal. How may a lawyer lie in his representa-tive capacity? It is precisely my point that a man cannot lie just in his representative capacity; it is like stabbing someone in the back just in a representative capacity. The injury and betrayal are worked not by the legal process, but by an act which is generally harmful apart from the legal context in which it occurs.

There is an important class of cases which might be termed "lying in a representative capacity." An example is the lawyer presenting to the court a statement by another that he knows to be a lie, as when he puts a perjurious client defendant on the stand. There is dispute as to whether and when the positive law of professional responsibility per-mits this,[8] but clearly in such instances it is not the lawyer who is lying. He is like a letter carrier who delivers the falsehood. Whether he is free to do that is more a matter of legal than personal ethics.

A test that might make the distinction I offer more palpable is this: How would it be if it were known in advance that lawyers would balk at the practice under consideration? Would it not be intolerable if it were known that lawyers would not plead the defense of the Statute of Frauds or of the statute of limitations? And would it not be quite all right if it were known in advance that you cannot get a lawyer to lie for you, though he may perhaps put you on the stand to lie in your own defense?

A more difficult case to locate in the moral landscape is abusive and demeaning cross-examination of a complaining witness. Presumably, positive law and the canons of ethics restrict this type of conduct, but enforcement may be lax or interpretation by a trial judge permissive. So the question arises: what is the lawyer *morally* to do? Here again I urge the distinction between exposing a witness to the skepticism and scrutiny envisaged by the law and engaging in a personal attack on the witness. The latter is a harm which the lawyer happens to inflict in court, but it is a harm quite apart from the institutional legal context. It is perhaps just a matter of style or tone, but the crucial point is that the probing must not imply that the lawyer believes the witness is unworthy of respect.

The lawyer is not morally entitled, therefore, to engage his own person in doing personal harm to another, though he may exploit the system for his client even if the system consequently works injustice. He may, but must he? This is the final issue to confront. Since he may, he also need not if there is anyone else who will do it. Only if there is no one else does the agony become acute. If there is an obligation in that case, it is an institutional obligation that has devolved upon him to take up a case, to make arguments when it is morally permissible but personally repugnant to him to do so. Once again, the iniquity is moral, for if the law enjoins an obligation against conscience, a lawyer, like any conscientious person, must refuse and pay the price.

The obligation of an available lawyer to accept appointment to defend an accused is clear. Any moral scruples about the proposition that no man should be accused and punished without counsel are not morally well-founded. The proposition is intended to enhance the autonomy of individuals within the law. But if you are the last lawyer in town, is there a moral obligation to help the company foreclose on the widow's refrigerator? If the client pursues the foreclosure in order to establish a legal right of some significance, I do not flinch from the conclusion that the lawyer is bound to urge this right. So also if the finance company cannot foreclose because of an ideological boycott by the local bar. But if all the other lawyers happen to be on vacation and the case means no more to the finance company than the resale value of one more used refrigerator, common sense says the lawyer can say no. One should be able to distinguish between establishing a legal right and being a cog in a routine, repetitive business transaction, part of which just happens to play itself out in court.

CONCLUSION

I do not imagine that what I have said provides an algorithm for resolving some of these perennial difficulties. Rather, what I am proposing is a general way of looking at the problem, a way of understanding not so much the difficult borderline cases as the central and clear ones, in the hope that the principles we can there discern will illuminate our necessarily approximate and prudential quest for resolution on the borderline. The notion of the lawyer as the client's legal friend, whatever its limitations and difficulties, does account for a kind of callousness toward society and exclusivity in the service of the client which otherwise seem quite mysterious. It justifies a kind of scheming which we would deplore on the part of a lay person dealing with another lay person—even if he were acting on behalf of a friend.

But these special indulgences apply only as a lawyer assists his client in his legal business. I do not owe my client my political assistance. I do not have to espouse his cause when I act as a citizen. Indeed, it is one of the most repellent features of the American legal profession—one against which the barrister-solicitor split has to some extent guarded the English profession—that many lawyers really feel that they are totally bought by their clients, that they must identify with their clients' interests far beyond the special purpose of advising them and operating the legal system for them. The defendants' antitrust law or defendants' food and drug lawyer, who writes articles, gives speeches, pontificates generally about the evils of regulation may believe these things, but too often he does so because it is good for business or because he thinks such conduct is what good representation requires. In general, I think it deplorable that lawyers have specialized not only in terms of subject matter—that may or may not be a good thing—but in terms of plaintiffs or defendants, in terms of the position that they represent.

There is a related point which cuts very much in the opposite direction. It is no part of my thesis that the *client* is not morally bound to avoid lying to the court, to pay a just debt even though it is barred by the statute of limitations, to treat an opposite party in a negotiation with humanity and consideration for his needs and vulnerability, or to help the effectuation of policies aimed at common good. Further, it is no part of my argument to hold that a lawyer may assume that the client is not a decent, moral person, who has no desire to fulfill moral obligations, and is asking only what the minimum is that he must do to stay within the law. On the contrary, to assume this about anyone is itself a form of immorality because it is a form of disrespect between persons. Thus, in very many situations a lawyer will be advising a client who wants to effectuate his purposes within the law, to be sure, but who also wants to behave as a decent, moral person. It would be absurd to contend that the lawyer may abstain from giving advice that takes account of the client's moral duties and presumed desire to fulfill them. Indeed, in these situations the lawyer experiences the very special satisfaction of assisting the client not only to realize his autonomy within the law, but also to realize his status as a moral being. I want to make very clear that my conception of the lawyer's role in no way disentitles a lawyer from experiencing this satisfaction. Rather, it has been my purpose to explicate the less obvious point that there is a vocation and a satisfaction even in helping Shylock obtain his pound of flesh or in bringing about the acquittal of a guilty man.

Finally, I would like to return to the charge that the morality of role and personal relationship I offer here is almost certain to lead to the diversion of legal services from areas of greatest need. It is just my point, of course, when we fulfill the office of friend—legal, medical, or friend *tout court*—we do right, and thus it would be a great wrong to place us under a general regime of always doing what will "do the most good." What I affirm, therefore, is the moral liberty of a lawyer to make his life out of what personal scraps and shards of motivation his inclination and character suggest: idealism, greed, curiosity, love of luxury, love of travel, a need for adventure or repose; only so long as these lead him to give wise and faithful counsel. It is the task of the social system as a whole, and of all its citizens, to work for the conditions under which everyone will benefit in fair measure from the performance of doctors, lawyers, and musicians. But I would not see the integrity of these roles undermined in order that the next millennium might come sooner. After all, it may never come and then what would we be left with?

NOTES

1. For a striking example, see *Zabella v. Pakel*, 242 F.2d 452 (7th Cir. 1957), where debtor asserting the technical defenses was a savings and loan association president, and the creditor was a man who had worked for him as a carpenter and had lent him money in earlier, less fortunate days.

2. Charles Curtis, "The Ethics of Advocacy," *Stanford Law Review* 4 (1951): 3.

3. Mill, "Utilitarianism," in *The Philosophy of John Stuart Mill*, ed. M. Cohen (1961) p. 321; H. Sidgwick, *The Methods of Ethics* 7 (1907): 252.

4. See generally D. Lyons, *Forms and Limits of Utilitarianism* (1965); J. Smart and B. Williams, *Utilitarianism: For and Against* (1973); Harrod, "Utilitarianism Revised," *Mind* 45: 1936–37; Mabbott, "Punishment," *Mind* 48 (1936): 152.

5. This argument is, of course, just a fragment which must be fitted into a larger theory. This larger theory would have to explain, among other things, what the precise contents of the various personal roles might be and how conflicts between personal roles are to be resolved. My discussion of permissible and impermissible tactics in legal representation deals with this in one context. A complete theory would also have to spell out the relation between personal roles and duties to the larger collectivity. These latter duties to man in the abstract as opposed to concrete persons are the subject of principles of justice. I have no doubt that such duties exist and that they can be very demanding. Roughly, I would adopt something like the principles put forward in J. Rawls, *A Theory of Justice* (1971), pp. 54–117. I would require, however, that these principles of justice leave sufficient scope for the free definition and inviolability of personal relations—to a greater extent perhaps than Rawls allows. These systematic concerns are the subject of a larger work from which the

present essay is drawn. The relation of principles of justice to other aspects of right and wrong is a principal concern of that larger work.

6. This question might be more troubling in a socialist system in which the profit motive is theoretically subordinated to the service of the general good. But my argument is that the needs for which lawyers and doctors provide are significantly different in kind from those met by other economic agents. Therefore, my argument about doctors and lawyers should be general enough to apply in either a free enterprise or a socialist system.

7. See Nagel, "War and Massacre," *Philosophy & Public Affairs* 1 (1972): 123–44.

8. Compare M. Freedman, supra note 7, at pp. 27–41 with Noonan, "The Purposes of Advocacy and the Limits of Confidentiality," *Michigan Law Review* 64 (1966): 64.

Robert J. Condlin

WHAT'S LOVE GOT TO DO WITH IT? THE LAWYER AS FRIENDLY FIDUCIARY

C harles Fried argued, in full-blown and unapologetic fashion, that lawyers ought to be thought of as their clients' friends (or at least friends for purposes of using the legal system), and as such be entitled, on moral grounds, to do for clients the legal equivalent of what social friends are entitled to do for one another.[1]

Fried did not try to dissuade lawyers from giving moral advice to clients, or ask lawyers to assume that clients are interested only in complying minimally with the law, and have no desire to fulfill their moral obligations to others. On the contrary, as he said, to make such an assumption "is itself a form of immorality because it is a form of disrespect between persons."[2] Instead, he proposed a general way of looking at the "central and clear" cases in the problem of legal representation that "account[s] for a kind of callousness toward society and exclusivity in the service of the client which otherwise [would] seem quite mysterious." It was his purpose to show that "there is a vocation and a satisfaction even in helping Shylock obtain his pound of flesh or in bringing about the acquittal of a guilty man," because such actions affirm the

---

From *Nebraska Law Review* 82 (2003): 211–311. Reprinted with permission of the publisher.

moral liberty of a lawyer to make his life out of what personal scraps and shards of motivation his inclination and character suggest: idealism, greed, curiosity, love of luxury, love of travel, a need for adventure or repose; only so long as these lead him to give wise and faithful counsel.[3]

"It is the task of the social system as a whole," as Fried saw it, and not individual lawyers, to create the "conditions under which everyone will benefit in fair measure from the performance of . . . lawyers" and law.[4]

If the power of an argument exists in proportion to the stature of its critics and the intensity of their criticism, then Fried's argument was powerful indeed, since highly-respected commentators jumped all over it immediately upon its publication. Professors Edward Dauer and Arthur Leff, both then of the Yale Law School, were the first to respond. In the issue of the *Yale Law Journal* next following Fried's, and in the form of a letter to the Editors (and, *a fortiori,* to Fried), they took Fried to task on a number of counts.[5] While not disagreeing with the basic claim that a good lawyer can be a good person, they objected to the "route" by which Fried arrived at that conclusion, and to the lack of qualification or nuance in his description of the obligations of friendship. "Assum[ing] for [a] moment that grounding an ethical system on what people in fact believe and do [is] not [mere] twaddle," they stated, then it is no doubt intuitively correct "to some extent," to say that one is permitted to "favor oneself and one's friends . . . *more than* abstract others." But the difficult issues, they continued, are "in what ways, and how much," "[f]or almost no one believes that totally individualistic selfishness is 'good' either," and on these issues Fried does not have much of anything to say.[6] Moreover, Dauer and Leff argued, the concept of friendship does not, by itself, help determine who is qualified to be a friend, and being able to make this determination correctly is central to the legitimacy of Fried's entire scheme.

The criticism that seemed to sting Fried the most, however, was the charge that he resorted to quasi-utilitarian props for a tottering non-utilitarian argument.[7] Fried had rejected a utilitarian defense of the legal friend theory in "The Lawyer As Friend" article, one will recall, arguing that the right to prefer friends is based on reasons inherent in the "concepts of personality, identity, and liberty," and not on the idea that we have a better understanding of "what needs to be done" in the case of friends. Yet, as Dauer and Leff pointed out, in Fried's world, lawyers are entitled (if not obligated) to get clients "what they want in any way that is not illegal," because the

> system of law is fundamentally just, and if it provides that persons in the clutches of that system be fully represented, then it is not unjust (or morally bad) to do the representing, even if some of the things one must do in the course of that representation look not only not socially optimal, but downright nasty. . . .[8]

This answer is interesting, said Dauer and Leff, because it is so obviously "the ordinary rule-utilitarian lawyer-defending argument after all."[9] The good effects produced by the legal system as a whole excuse individual bad lawyer acts. But what if, on rule-utilitarian grounds, asked Dauer and Leff, "the system—the rule—. . . is more unjust than it needs to be? Is it still 'good' to serve a bad system within its own rules?"[10] Fried apparently thought so, they concluded, because when a lawyer harms others on behalf of a client it is "the legal system which authorizes . . . the injustice . . . and the formal gesture [of] working it insulates [the lawyer] from personal moral responsibility."[11] The utility of following the rule wipes out the disutility of harming discrete others. But if this is what Fried meant to say, concluded Dauer and Leff, then his "argument against the 'utilitarian' critique of lawyering was at least partly disingenuous."[12]

Dauer and Leff also criticized the friendship analogy directly,[13] denying that a client is like a friend. There is at least one point of overlap between the two, they admitted—both a lawyer and a friend adopt others' interests as their own—but even that similarity comes about mostly because Fried defines friendship in terms of that one quality. For Fried, they argued, "a lawyer is like a friend . . . because . . . a friend is like a lawyer." But most of the time in real life, they suggested, there are more differences than similarities between the "affective commitment to friends' causes and the espousal of [the causes] of clients." For example, when one prefers a friend to others, one

> has typically injured others only in the sense that he has withheld from [them] what they may never have had to begin with. But when one acts as lawyer, he is often in the position of . . . tak[ing] away from some other person something which that other person already "has," or giv[ing] as little as possible [for it] in return.[14]

This suggests, advised Dauer and Leff, that "lawyers should sometimes be *more* constrained in pursuing their friendship[s] than others need to be,"[15] but Fried does not consider this possibility.

In addition, said Dauer and Leff, "except in reasonably rare circumstances, if the attorney finds espousing his client's cause too morally 'costly,' both the formal and unwritten standards of the profession permit [the lawyer] to get rid of the client."[16] Moreover, "when there is a flat conflict between the attorney and his client, the same rules allow the attorney to be loyal to himself, even if that involves using the client's confidences against him."[17] And "[s]till further, insofar as an attorney can predict [a conflict in advance], he is almost perfectly free to refuse to take on that client in the first place." Given all of this, argued Dauer and Leff, "whatever the actual contingency and chilliness of the lawyer's relationship to his client, it is firm, wholehearted, and ardent compared to the client's reciprocal feelings" for the lawyer.[18] As Fried sees it, Dauer and Leff said,

> A lawyer is a person who, without expecting any reciprocal activity or inclination thereto, will attempt to forward or protect the interests of a client, within the rules of a legal system, so long as he is paid a sufficient amount to do so, and so long as doing so does not inflict any material unforeseen personal costs.[19]

"That's 'friendship'?"[20] they asked.

For all the difficulties it created, one wonders why Fried bothered with the friendship analogy in the first place. Why not just argue for a lawyer's right to prefer clients directly, or as Dauer and Leff asked, "[s]ince it was so easy to define a friend as good, why not just do the same for the lawyer?" The answer writes itself. Since "[l]awyers frequently do feel guilty about what they do for a living, and the public pretty thoroughly agrees that they ought to," Fried's move of "declaring human opinion to be the measure of goodness," will not work nearly as well if he begins his argument by asserting that we know intuitively that lawyers are entitled to prefer clients. In fact, argued Dauer and Leff, proceeding in this way would make the "callow prestidigitation of the original friendship-justifying move too painfully obvious."[21] Fried's metaphorical opening is an "absolute necessity," they explained, "for [Fried] must say that while human opinion and intuition defines the good, in [the case of lawyers] it happens to be wrong ... [H]e must convince people to change their views. And for persuasion there's nothing like [a] metaphor."[22]

These criticisms, strong as they were, did not shake Fried's faith in the friendship analogy. On the contrary, in his reply to Dauer and Leff, he still found the analogy "fruitful,"[23] and continued to defend it. But it turned out that the criticism was just beginning. Other commentators, following up on Dauer and Leff's initiative, made new objections, or restated familiar ones, usually in stronger language.

William Simon,[24] for example, found Fried's definition of friendship "clearly an error."[25] "The classical definition of friendship," said Simon, "emphasizes, not the adoption by one person of another's ends, but rather the sharing by two people of common ends . . . [It also] includes a number of other qualities foreign to the relation Fried describes . . . [such as] affection, admiration, intimacy, and vulnerability."[26] Moreover, continued Simon, "if Fried's definition is amplified to reflect the qualification . . . that the lawyer adopts the client's interests *for money*, it becomes apparent that Fried has described the classical notion, not of friendship, but of prostitution."[27] "Fried's lawyer," added Simon, "is a friend in the same sense that your Sunoco dealer is 'very friendly' or that Canada Dry Ginger Ale 'tastes like love.'"[28]

The friendship analogy, charged Simon, was an example of one of those "self-validating, analytical propositions" Herbert Marcuse criticized for closing the universe of discourse.[29] As Marcuse explained:

> The unification of opposites which characterizes the commercial and political style is one of the many ways in which discourse and communication make themselves immune against the expression of protest and refusal. How can such protest and refusal find the right word when the organs of the established order admit and advertise that peace is really the brink of war, that the ultimate weapons carry their profitable price tags, and that the bomb shelter may spell coziness? In exhibiting its contradictions as the token of its truth, this universe of discourse closes itself against any other discourse which is not on its own terms.[30]

Discourse of this sort flattens out personality rather than respects it, argued Simon, and evidence of this can be found in Fried's discussion. For example, "Fried celebrates the [frankly] exploitative alliances of convenience between desperate, selfish little men . . . [and] explicitly strives to infuse with pathos and dignity the financial problems of the tax chiseler and the 'disagreeable dowager.' By collapsing traditional moral categories," said Simon, "[Fried's] rhetoric reflects the homogenization of previously distinct personal characteristics. Fried can assert that the lawyer affirms the client's individuality because . . . Fried's clients have almost no individuality."[31]

David Luban, a moral philosopher by training, and a prolific and highly respected commentator on legal ethics as well, also took issue with Fried's view.[32] In one of the best discussions of the legitimacy of the American adversary system anywhere in the literature,[33] Luban reviewed the justifications typically offered for adversary justice. Among the "intrinsic justifications," he included Fried's argument for "enhancing . . . client autonomy and individuality . . . [as] an intrinsic moral good."[34] Luban admitted that Fried's system of "concentric-circles morality" captured, "albeit in a distorted form," some of the legitimacy in the idea of "professionals as devoted by the nature of their calling to the service of their clients."[35] In other words, said Luban, "Fried's analogy contains a grain of truth."[36] But it does not excuse lawyers from being morally accountable for actions they take on behalf of clients, he continued, because "we are *not*—except for Nietzsche's Teutons and G. Gordon Liddy—willing to do grossly immoral things to help our friends, nor should we be."[37] And Fried's method for saving his argument, the distinction between personal wrongs and institutional wrongs, said Luban, "has not been very popular since World War II."[38]

The problem, argued Luban, "is that Fried takes the lawyer to be the mere occasion rather than the agent of morally-bad-but-legally-legitimate outcomes."[39] It was as if he believed that when bad things happened it was because "[t]he system did it; it 'was just one of those things difficult to pre-visualize—like a cow, say, getting hit by lightning."[40] This is false in three respects, argued Luban. First, "it discounts the extent to which the lawyer has . . . a creative hand in [influencing] . . . outcome, at times even reversing the law . . . Second, [a legal system] is not an abstract structure of propositions but a social structure of interacting human beings, so that the actions of its agents *are* the system. [And] [t]hird . . . [a] lawyer is indeed acting *in propria persona* by 'pulling the levers of the legal machinery.'"[41] Fried's view, said Luban, "seems to trade on a Rube Goldberg insight: if the apparatus is complex enough, then the lever-puller doesn't really look like the agent. But that cannot be," he continued, because "I chop the broccoli, whether I do it with a knife or merely push the button on the blender. The legal levers are pulled by the lawyer: no one else can do it."[42]

Even some of Fried's philosophical fellow travelers, those with views on the lawyer-client relationship substantively similar if not identical to Fried's, disagreed with the use of the friendship analogy. Alan Donagan, for example, now deceased but formerly a Professor of Philosophy at the University of Chicago and one of the world's leading Kantian philosophers, found the friendship overlay a kind of non-consequentialist gilding of the lily.[43] Thinking of a lawyer as a friend, he said, "will no doubt be . . . funny [to] anybody who has recently paid a lawyer's bill. For while it is true that the lawyer and the client may be friends, like the butcher and the baker, what they do for each other for the sake of money are not offices of friendship."[44] The "lawyer as friend" analogy, said Donagan, "was as unnecessary [to Fried's argument] as it is misleading. If [Fried] had contented himself with likening lawyers to other hired professionals, his argument would have been clearer and would have appeared less ridiculous."[45] Fried's argument for the right to prefer friends, in Donagan's view, should have gone (and did go, properly understood) something like this:

> A society fails to respect the human dignity of those within its jurisdiction if it denies them a fair opportunity to raise questions about what is due to them under the law before properly constituted courts, and to defend themselves against claims upon themselves or charges against themselves. It would so fail if it denied them the opportunity to hire legal advisers whose professional obligation would be to advise them how best to do these things and to represent them in doing them. This justification demands that lawyers be willing to suspend their own beliefs about the merits of their clients' aims or the truth of what they attest, provided that the morality of their aims be rationally defensible and that what they attest be possibly true.[46]

Donagan agreed that there are limits on what lawyers may do for clients. For example, "[i]f a client's testimony is inconsistent or irreconcilable with physical or documentary evidence," or if disbelief in it "can be suspended only at the price of calling into question beliefs ... about physical nature or about how certain kinds of documents are produced," then "no intelligent attorney can treat it as possibly true."[47] Similarly, "if the only principles on which a client's claim can be morally defended appear to the lawyer to be morally pernicious, the lawyer cannot treat the client's position as rationally defensible."[48] On the other hand, "[i]f a lawyer's personal disagreement with a client's moral position depends on complex deductions from moral principles the lawyer considers established, especially if those deductions turn on disputed premises about matters of fact, the lawyer will as a rule be justified in treating the client's position as defensible."[49] Fried recognized all of this, said Donagan, and did not intend the friendship principle to be interpreted to "entail[] every remote consequence" that could be drawn from it. In his (i.e. Fried's) own formulation and application of the principle, continued Donagan, "in no case [did] he fail to specify that it has to do with a client's autonomy."[50]

Donagan agreed with Fried's claim that "a lawyer . . . may act to bring about a wrong to a third party that the legal system permits without thereby committing a personal wrong," and saw this as a "morally significant" distinction."[51] In drawing attention to what the law requires in a client's case, even though it injures a third party," said Donagan echoing Fried, "a lawyer merely sets the judicial system in motion; in lying in a negotiation or legal proceeding he or she does more, by introducing into that negotiation or proceeding an injurious factor for which the legal system is in no way responsible."[52] While approving of the "wrongs of the person-wrongs of the system" distinction, therefore, Donagan also thought that it needed to be refined, because even in generally just and decent legal systems, a lawyer acting as the system permits may do morally intolerable things if the laws of that system enjoin or permit violations of morality.[53] With these limited qualifications, however, Donagan thought Fried's understanding of the lawyer's role was just about right.

Others found fault with the lawyer-as-friend argument as well. Jerrold Auerbach thought the idea of a "limited-purpose friend" was a "limited-purpose analogy,"[54] and Thomas Shaffer and Robert Cochran saw it as just a sophisticated version of the "hired gun" view[55]—but the above criticisms give one a pretty complete sense of the range of objections made to Fried's argument. One of the most important themes in these criticisms is the diminished, if not almost non-existent, role accorded mutuality and reciprocity in Fried's view of friendship. A Friedian friend is not a "best enemy" in the Nietzschean sense, someone who is equal in character, has a shared sense of ends, and is free to criticize one's projects when they do not do justice, and free to be criticized on the same grounds in return. These are important omissions. Mutuality and reciprocity have always been part of the understanding of friendship in the Western literary and philosophical tradition, and their absence in Fried's view is a major flaw in his understanding of the subject. . . .

THE LAWYER AS FRIENDLY FIDUCIARY AND AGENT

If lawyers are not their clients' friends, what are they? What social or work world analogy best describes the relationship between the two, and thus provides the best guide for defining the nature of lawyer role? Consider the possibility that this might not be the right question to ask. The lawyer-client relationship has a number of dimensions, each one of which is analogous to a different type of social or work world relationship, and it is difficult, if not impossible, to understand lawyer-client relations in all of their complexity if, at the same time, one must confine the lawyer role to the boundaries of some single, all-encompassing metaphor, such as friend, hired gun, or even free-lance bureaucrat. A better course would be to accept the lawyer-client relationship for the complex social and political phenomenon that it is, recognize its idiosyncratic combination of qualities and dimensions, and devise a correspondingly complex conception of lawyer role for operating within it. Any other approach, of necessity, must oversimplify reality and obscure what is really going on between lawyer and client, and it is always a mistake to make the world conform to one's analytical categories, rather than the other way around. . . . At the most basic level, lawyers are purveyors of goods and services in the same fashion as all other commercial actors. They sell retail, in other words, and as such, have an obligation to be sociable to the same extent as do merchants generally. They should be courteous, pleasant, interested in what clients (customers) have to say, respectful of different values and belief systems, considerate of others' particular circumstances and constraints, kind, compassionate (and passionate), and generally in command of the social skills needed to be friendly and likeable. They should be pleasant to deal with rather than difficult, and make people want to come back to them rather than avoid them at all costs. It also would help if they liked people generally and took a genuine satisfaction in helping them realize their goals, by making the interaction with the stressful, complicated, and often frightening world of law as tolerable as possible. Think of all of this as the duty of sociability or friendliness (but not friendship) owed by merchants to customers and, in a sense (although this is more controversial), by persons to strangers. It is not so much a special obligation of lawyers as it is one of citizenship, or social relations generally, and it is an important one at that.

Lawyers also are their clients' fiduciaries. Clients have no choice but to depend upon lawyers if they are to use the legal system to enforce their rights. It is not just that lawyers know substantive law and legal procedure and clients do not, but also that clients must tell lawyers their innermost thoughts and feelings (insofar as they relate to the representation), even if they are embarrassing or painful, if lawyers are to use their expertise to protect client rights. Clients must become unilaterally vulnerable to lawyers, in other words, with no expectation that lawyers will do the same in return. When one is coerced into being dependent and vulnerable as a condition of using a public system such as law, agents of that system should minimize the risk inherent in such dependence and vulnerability by adhering to a heightened standard of honesty and fair dealing in return. This means that lawyers must be truthful with clients, and not hold back information selectively, or for self-interested or paternalistic reasons. They must not take advantage of information they learn from clients to make better-than-market deals for themselves, with clients or others. They must be candid about where their own interests lie, and put client interests ahead of their own whenever there is the possibility that the two will conflict. They must provide clients with the information needed to make fully informed decisions about their cases (with respect to issues assigned to clients by law and the profession's ethical codes), and give them the opportunity to consider that information freely and without pressure. Finally, they must not judge clients or client projects unfairly or harshly simply because they disagree with them, or pull punches in the advancement of those projects as a consequence of this disagreement, by failing to take actions that would be effective but also personally distasteful. This cluster of obligations is best captured in the familiar and longstanding concept of lawyer as client fiduciary.

Lawyers also are their clients' agents, in the sense that they are the instruments of their clients' wills. They have an obligation to put client plans into effect successfully insofar as that is possible, but, at a minimum, in a manner that gives those plans their greatest possibility of being realized. This means that lawyers must be aware of and use the full range of skills available to competent practitioners working in the field, be imaginative and clever in the use of these skills, pursue client objectives diligently, and also have the courage to use methods that step outside of conventional or preferred ways of doing things when something out of the ordinary is needed, even if it entails some risk to the lawyers' reputations or personal interests. The only limit on this instrumental dimension of lawyer role is the familiar one of positive law, that is, in protecting client rights lawyers always must operate "within the bounds of law."

Finally, lawyers are persons in their own right, with moral principles and limits of their own. They are entitled to act in accordance with these principles by placing restrictions on whom they represent and what they will do for persons they choose to represent. For the most part, however, they should honor these principles by avoiding relationships in which the principles are likely to be compromised, rather than by refusing to do things for persons they already have agreed to help. Extreme cases excepted, they should not withdraw from or compromise representation when what clients ask conflicts with the lawyers' own sense of what is right. While they can and should argue about moral and political issues with clients, they should not coerce clients, explicitly or *sub rosa*, into changing their minds about what to do when they (the lawyers) lose these arguments. Lawyers are agents, not principals, and their primary responsibility is to make the public good of the legal system available to citizens generally. As such, they are a form of public good themselves, and public goods cannot be denied for purely private reasons.

When the foregoing obligations of sociability, fiduciary loyalty, instrumental competence, and personal integrity are combined, the image of the lawyer's role that emerges, if one needs a single image, is that of friendly fiduciary, so to speak. This is an unremarkable, even commonplace, conception of the lawyer's role, not at all catchy or emotionally evocative, and without any ring of moral or political novelty about it. But when understood properly, it includes all of the qualities commentators like Fried demand in a conception of the lawyer's role, and it has the added advantage of being compatible with what positive law and the legal profession's ethics codes demand of lawyers as well. It does not liberate lawyers from the constraints of ordinary morality, a *sub rosa* goal of some efforts to construct an independent conception of the lawyer's role . . . Most important, this particular combination of faithfulness and friendliness does not require that lawyers be their clients' friends, since obligations in the relationship run in only one direction. Lawyers must do all of the above whether clients reciprocate or not.

It is a mistake to try to convert every kind of social connection into a deep or intimate relationship. Intimate relationships are based on love, and love is a rare quality in work, notwithstanding the fact that the language of modern marketing professes to find it in all sorts of chance or fleeting encounters, with both people and things. The idea of intimacy loses all meaning, however, as Samuel Johnson reminds us, when one "spreads his arms to humankind, and makes every man, without distinction, a denizen of his bosom."[56] While this quality "may be useful to the community, and pass through the world with the reputation of good purposes and uncorrupted morals . . . [it is] unfit for close and tender intimacies."[57] To make every relationship a love relationship is to destroy rather than enrich the notion of love. As Dworkin explains, "[i]f we felt nothing more for lovers or friends or colleagues than [we do for] fellow citizens [i.e., clients], this would mean the extinction not the universality of love."[58] It is just wrong to believe that one can and should care deeply for everyone. Most relationships in life, of necessity, are superficial and fleeting, but that does not mean that they cannot have an integrity of their own. The genuine expression of a "lesser" emotion, such as respect, tolerance, understanding, concern, compassion, sympathy, or the like, is a perfectly fine basis on which to ground a relationship and a much better one than the pretend expression of a "greater" emotion, such as love. Genuine feeling, whatever its nature, has integrity, and integrity is a precondition of all social relationships worthy of the name.

NOTES

1. Charles Fried, "The Lawyer as Friend," this text, pp. 111–42.

2. Ibid., p. 140.

3. Ibid., p. 141.

4. Ibid., p. 141.

5. Edward A. Dauer and Arthur Allen Leff, "Correspondence: The Lawyer as Friend," *Yale Law Journal* 18 (1977): 573.

6. Ibid., p. 575.

7. Dauer and Leff, "Correspondence," pp. 574–75 n. 11.

8. Ibid., p. 579.

9. Ibid., p. 576 n. 17.

10. Ibid., p. 580.

11. Ibid., p. 1084.

12. Ibid., p. 579.

13. Ibid., pp. 577–79.

14. Ibid., p. 577 n. 23.

15. Ibid.

16. Ibid., p. 578.

17. Ibid.

18. Ibid., p. 579.

19. Ibid.

20. Ibid.

21. Ibid., p. 577 n. 22.

22. Ibid.

23. Ibid., p. 586.

24. William H. Simon, "The Ideology of Advocacy: Procedural Justice and Professional Ethics," *Wisconsin Law Review* 29 (1978): 107.

25. Ibid., p. 108.

26. Ibid.

27. Ibid.

28. Ibid., p. 109.

29. Ibid.

30. Herbert Marcuse, *One-Dimensional Man: Studies in the Ideology of Advanced Industrial Society* (1964), pp. 88, 90.

31. Simon, "The Ideology of Advocacy," p. 109.

32. David Luban, "The Adversary System Excuse," in *The Good Lawyer: Lawyers' Roles and Lawyers' Ethics*, ed. David Luban (1983), pp. 83, 84.

33. Ibid., p. 83.

34. Ibid., p. 105.

35. Ibid., p. 106.

36. Ibid.

37. Ibid.

38. Ibid., p. 107.

39. Ibid.

40. Ibid.

41. Ibid.

42. Ibid., pp. 107–108.

43. Alan Donagan, "Justifying Legal Practice in the Adversary System," in *The Good Lawyer: Lawyers' Roles and Lawyers' Ethics*, ed. David Luban (1983).

44. Ibid., pp. 129, 128.

45. Ibid.

46. Ibid., p. 133.

47. Ibid., pp. 131–32.

48. Ibid., p. 133.

49. Ibid., p. 132.

50. Ibid., p. 129.

51. Ibid., pp. 137–38.

52. Ibid., p. 138.

53. Ibid., pp. 125–26.

54. See Jerold S. Auerbach, "What Has the Teaching of Law to Do with Justice?" *New York University Law Review* 53 (1978): 457, 468.

55. Thomas L. Shaffer and Robert F. Cochran Jr., *Lawyers, Clients, and Moral Responsibility* (1994).

56. Robert Demaria Jr., *The Life of Samuel Johnson* (1993), p. 71.

57. Ibid., p. 70.

58. Ronald Dworkin, *Law's Empire* (1986), p. 215.

Michael Davis

PROFESSIONALISM MEANS PUTTING YOUR PROFESSION FIRST

Ask a lawyer what "professionalism" means and you are likely to hear that professionalism means *putting your client first* or *acting as an officer of the court*. Only rarely will a lawyer say that professionalism means *putting justice first*. Never, I think, will a lawyer even suggest that professionalism means *putting your profession first*. Yet that is my thesis: *Professionalism means putting your profession first*. While one article—indeed, even a whole book—is unlikely to enter this thesis into the common wisdom of professionals, it may serve to get it a fair hearing, which it deserves. Though perhaps never explicitly stated before, much less defended, the thesis seems to me fundamental to professionalism as we know it.

When lawyers say "first," do they mean first? Do they mean that family, religion, country, and even simple human decency come "second"? While most lawyers don't seem to have thought through what they mean by "first," some have. So, for example, some lawyers still quote *approvingly* what Henry Brougham (later, Lord Brougham) said in 1820 about their obligations (while speaking in Parliament in defense of Queen Caroline):

From *Georgetown Journal of Legal Ethics* 2, no. 1 (1998): 341–57. © *Georgetown Journal of Legal Ethics*. Reprinted with permission of the publisher.

[An] advocate, in the discharge of his duty, knows but one person in all the world, and that person is his client. To save that client by all means and expedients, and at all hazards and costs to other persons, and, amongst them, to himself, is his first and only duty; and, in performing this duty he must not regard the alarm, the torments, the destruction which he may bring upon others. Separating the duty of a patriot from that of an advocate, he must go on reckless of consequences, though it should be his unhappy fate to involve his country in confusion.[1]

When I say "professionalism means putting your profession first," I do not mean by "first" anything this extreme. But I shall have to explain not only what the limits of professionalism are but why professionalism must be so limited.

This article has three parts. Section I makes certain distinctions necessary to prevent misunderstanding my thesis. Sections II and III develop the thesis into a conception of professionalism. Sections IV and V use that conception to help with that most difficult of undertakings, justifying discipline to someone convicted of professional misconduct that harmed neither client nor identifiable third-party.

I. THE PROFESSION IN "PROFESSIONALISM"

Professionalism means putting your profession first, but only on a certain understanding of profession. We sometimes use "profession" to mean *the members of a certain occupational group.* According to this usage, lawyers are the legal profession and a lawyer would put profession first by putting the interests of lawyers ahead of everyone else's. Needless to say, that is not how I understand "profession."

In a more common usage, "profession" means an occupational group organized to use the characteristic knowledge, skill, and judgment of its members to serve a moral ideal. "Profession" in this sense distinguishes certain occupational groups (those organized to serve a certain moral ideal) from similar organizations with somewhat different purposes (for example, protecting members from exploitation, making a profit, or recreation). This second sense of "profession" is also not what I now have in mind. The profession to be put first is not an occupational group, however organized.

The profession that should be put first is what the professional professes, the standard of conduct she commits herself to simply by being a member of the profession. For example, the lawyer's profession is what she invites the public to expect of her when she declares herself to be a lawyer. To declare yourself to be a member of a certain profession is to hold yourself out as one who satisfies all the requirements members of that profession are supposed to satisfy. To declare yourself a lawyer is to profess more than knowledge or experience of legal work. It is, in effect, to claim that you have the education lawyers are supposed to have, that you have passed the tests lawyers are supposed to pass, and that you have made the commitments lawyers are supposed to make. Among those commitments is the commitment to act in accordance with a code of ethics—for lawyers today, *The Model Rules of Professional Conduct*, *The Model Code of Professional Responsibility*, or some similar code (depending on where the lawyer practices).

For a lawyer, then, professionalism can only mean putting the client first when that is part of what lawyers are supposed to do. If, however, the profession's code of ethics requires something else, for example, revealing a damaging precedent, professionalism means that the client's interests must yield to the judge's interest in discovering the law. The concept of professionalism does not, as such, give the client (or anyone else) priority in a lawyer's work. The concept of professionalism leaves such matters to the profession's standards of practice. If the client receives no priority in the standards, professionalism does not require it.

What I have said so far may suggest that the content of professionalism is arbitrary. Whatever a profession puts into its standard of conduct is what professionalism requires. There is no "natural profession" of lawyering or anything else. Professionalism means doing as you profess, whatever you happen to profess. In fact, that is not quite what I mean. As I understand professionalism, its content, while largely arbitrary, is not altogether so. Those constituting a profession have wide latitude, but they cannot make just anything professionalism.

The claim of professionalism is primarily a moral claim. To be a professional is to have obligations one would not otherwise have. These are not mere legal obligations (though they may be legal obligations too). They are obligations that one is in honor, in conscience, and in decency, bound to respect. Professionalism would not be worth the praise commonly given it if it were no more than what a lawyer must do to keep meal-ticket and freedom. Since the claim of professionalism is primarily moral, morality must limit the content of professionalism. Professionalism can never require anything immoral (though professionalism can require us to do what, but for our commitment to the profession, we should not do). The "professionalism" of a contract killer must always remain in scare quotes. Such "professionalism" is to true professionalism what impersonators are to the persons impersonated.

Since morality limits what professionalism can require, there is a sense in which professionalism means putting morality first. Since morality requires us, at the very least, to "regard the alarm, the torments, the destruction which [we] may bring upon others," professionalism (as we have understood it) rules out Brougham's fanaticism. What else it may rule out we shall soon consider.

The claim of professionalism is, however, not simply a moral claim. To be a professional is (truthfully) to profess membership in a certain group, a profession. To be a profession, an occupational group must be organized (in large part at least) to serve a moral ideal. This is a conceptual truth, neither more nor less. In the same way, a trade union remains a trade union while its primary purpose is improving the conditions under which its members work. Though professions do not necessarily do more good than other occupational organizations, they are distinguished from the others by what they do (or, at least, by what they profess to do). Morality does not require occupations to organize, much less to organize for any particular purpose (though it may require small groups within the occupation to organize their work in a way avoiding undue risk to others). So, by definition, professionalism includes a commitment beyond what ordinary morality requires. The organization's purpose must not be a mere "paper purpose," one the acts of the organization regularly belie. To be a profession rather than a counterfeit one, an occupational group must really be organized in a way likely to achieve its stated purpose. Because the members of any large organization will ordinarily be rational, experienced, and serious, such an organization can be counted upon to act more or less as its purpose requires. And because relatively few people are hypocrites, the purpose of such an organization may as readily be read from its statements as from its acts.

We should, however, not read the acts of a human organization too closely. Humans are fallible. Even an organization of the educated may now and then adopt a practice at odds with its purpose, or leave a once-defensible practice in place long after its defense has collapsed. More common, though, are practices in place because of disagreement among people of good will. Suppose, for example, that everyone in a certain profession agrees that a certain practice should be changed, but no alternative so far proposed seems clearly superior to more than a minority. Unsatisfactory as the practice might be, it would survive. But that survival would not be evidence against the organization's professional status. Indeed, we can easily imagine its survival to be part of the evidence *for* the organization's professional status. For example, suppose that the debate over alternatives is largely in terms of how this or that alternative would serve the public interest better than any other. A debate in such terms is just what we would expect of a profession. Consider, for example, the long-standing debate among lawyers concerning "public service." Almost all lawyers seem to agree that there is such an obligation; the disagreement seems to concern how much public service is required and whether the code should require it.

So, an organization's status as a profession should not be made to depend on a perfect fit between the moral ideal it undertakes to serve and what it in fact does. An organization will be a profession if, on the whole, it seems reasonably well designed to serve its moral ideal—if, that is, its standards of admission appear reasonably well designed to assure competence, its code of ethics forbids many abuses that might otherwise occur, its enforcement procedures seem equal to the task of maintaining substantial compliance with its professed standards, and so on.

II. MORAL IDEAL AND SELF-INTEREST

Lawyers (and other professionals) are often mocked for suggesting that their motives are better than those of ordinary people. Yet, on my analysis, there is a clear sense in which their motives are better. The (moral) obligations of any decent person are among his motives. (Like fear, love, or interest, obligation may move him to act.) Ordinary people, however decent, do not have any specific obligation of public service (for example, an obligation to provide free to the poor who need it the service they make their living selling). All lawyers have that obligation—because, and only because, it is part of what they profess. The obligation of public service is not only a morally good motive but a morally better one than simply making a living. Hence, all else equal, lawyers have better motives than ordinary people do.

Having better motives because one has special obligations does not, however, make one a better person. A lawyer who satisfied all her obligations, including her professional ones, is (all else equal) no better than a nonprofessional who satisfied all his. Both have done exactly what morality requires. The lawyer may, however, be morally worse than the nonprofessional, even if she does everything required of a nonprofessional. The lawyer can fail to live up to her professional obligations, something an ordinary person cannot fail to do. I have heard lawyers complain bitterly that they are blamed for doing what passes without comment in a business person. My response is: "If you want to be held to no higher standard than business people are, renounce the law and go into business." Indeed, one function of professions seems to be to assure that professionals need not be better than ordinary people even though they have better motives.

Fulfilling one's (moral) obligations is, as we have seen, morally the same, all else equal, whatever one's obligations. Only if professional obligations were, all things considered, a heavier burden than the obligations of ordinary people would fulfilling one's obligations as a professional make one morally better. But, in fact, professions generally enable their members to do *at no cost to themselves* what an ordinary person could do only with significant sacrifice. Consider, for example, the grocer who (as an individual) gives food to the poor. He must take his gift out of his profits and live less well than his competitors, or figure the gift into the price of his goods and put himself at a competitive disadvantage. He bears the cost of his good deed and, therefore, deserves praise for it. But a lawyer who does a certain amount of *pro bono* work when other lawyers do the same, can help the poor without sacrifice. Her good deed will be a normal cost of legal business. Whatever little praise a lawyer deserves for it will be what we give those who simply live up to their obligations.

Lawyers can, I think, claim to be better than ordinary people only insofar as they enter their line of work with motives better than those with which ordinary people enter theirs, or fulfill their obligations better than ordinary people fulfill theirs. The lawyer who enters the law only to make money, satisfy ambition, or have a good time is morally no better (and no worse) than someone who sells cars for the same reason. Each simply accepts certain obligations to obtain certain benefits.

People entering the law primarily from a motive of service to others are probably as rare as saints. The law does not require saints. Indeed, it should not. Those who want only saints to serve them will generally have to do without. This fact, so plain that it is often overlooked, puts substantial limits on the content of professionalism. For example, the *Model Rules* allow lawyers to breach a confidence in order to collect a fee. Such a provision cannot be justified directly by the profession's concern for justice, the client, or the public. Its justification is necessity. A legal profession dependent on fees would be impossible or, at least, far less attractive, if lawyers either had to collect their fees in advance or risk being barred by lawyer-client confidentiality from going into court to force payment. The better organized the profession, the less often self-interest and moral obligation are at odds.

While those organized into a profession may, *as individuals*, be no better (and no worse) than those not so organized, they will, *as an organ-*

ization, generally be not only different but better—for two reasons. First, they will be better because, as an organization, they will have a commitment to a moral ideal that unions, businesses, trade associations, other organizations of self-interest, and even most individuals do not. Second, they will be better because, as an organization, they will have a power to do good the unorganized do not. Those not organized to serve some moral ideal must do what good they do in an unorganized way, if at all, much as a crowd might respond to a purse snatching among them. Some may stare, some freeze, some start to help. A few may actually be able to do something useful, for example, comfort the victim or call the police—but even this will happen almost by chance. A profession, in contrast, responds in an organized way, much as a well-trained squad of soldiers might, each soldier knowing what he is supposed to do and being able to act with reasonable assurance that others in the squad will do what they are supposed to do. If a thief sneaks up to steal from the squad, the sergeant will issue orders, each subordinate will respond accordingly, and the thief will be overwhelmed in a few seconds.

III. PROFESSION, COOPERATION, AND FAIRNESS

The good that a professional organization does is done by coordinating the conduct of its members. A profession is a cooperative undertaking. In exchange for putting herself under an obligation to do as those in her profession are doing, each member of the profession receives the benefits of being identified as a member of that profession. The benefits are not extrinsic to the exchange. For example, the trust people place in someone they identify as a lawyer is itself a function of what they suppose lawyers to be. What they suppose lawyers to be is, in turn, in large part at least, a function of what the profession itself requires of its members (and what lawyers have been up to this moment). If, for example, one could become a lawyer without proving any knowledge of the law, being identified as a lawyer might be worth far less than it is today.

I have now explained how professional obligations can be moral obligations even though the content of professionalism is largely arbitrary. I have not had to base the morality of professional obligation on such substantive moral principles as "do no harm" or "be loyal to your friends." I am therefore not obliged to divide professional ethics into "real ethics" and "mere etiquette." Any standard of practice having a reasonable relation to the profession's purpose will be part of its professional ethics.

I have also not had to suppose any contract between the profession and society. This is important. Not all professions have the legal privileges the legal profession has. Engineering, for example, can be practiced in most American states without a license (though a license may be required to approve certain documents under certain circumstances). Certified financial analysts are entirely unlicensed (though they have a system of private certification). Journalists do not even have a system of certification. Such professions seem to lack a "contract with society" such as law has, yet they seem in all other respects as much professions as law does. One strength of my approach to professionalism, I think, is that it escapes the view that professional obligations depend primarily on any "contract with society." Of course, "negotiation with society" may explain this or that provision of a code of ethics (for example, current language on advertising). But neither such "negotiations" nor such a contract can explain the moral standing of professional obligations as such. For some professions at least, the obligations seem to exist more or less independent of society.

Those who want to assign "negotiations with society" (or "contract with society") a central place in professional ethics—or even claim that society sets the standards whatever the profession wants—must, I think, assume, however unwittingly, a relatively unappealing theory of human rights: "Profession" is a status that "society" (whether acting through government or through some less well-defined agency external to the profession itself) can grant or withhold as it sees fit, much as it can grant or withhold a license. Society can grant or withhold professional status because it has the right (and power) to decide whether members of an occupation, doing nothing morally wrong, may associate for what they take to be a good purpose, set (morally permissible) standards for themselves, and win compliance (in morally permissible ways) from those so associated. Those defending society's right to decide whether an occupation can form a profession need to be more explicit than they commonly are about how they interpret the human right to associate. Society cannot simply have the right to decide professional status because the profession affects the public. Society does not have a moral right to limit the association of individuals just because the association affects others. Society needs some further reason, for example, that the association threatens some substantial, unjustified harm. Hence, I have no reason to stress society's role in forming a profession or setting its standards.

I also have no reason to stress the lawyer-*client* relationship. This too seems to me to be a good thing. Much of what a lawyer is required to do is outside any particular lawyer-client relationship (for example, her obligation to report the misconduct of other lawyers). And some of what she is required to do, though internal to a particular lawyer-client relationship, is not necessarily in the client's interests. (Consider, for example, the obligation not to delay simply for the sake of delay, however much delay may benefit the client.) My approach invites professionals to think of their professional standards as primarily of their collective making, the outcome of negotiation *within* the profession, not as a necessary by-product of just one of the relationships into which lawyers as such enter.[2]

IV. IN RE EAGLE: THE FACTS

The discussion has so far been quite abstract. It is time to get down to cases. The case to which I shall now apply the foregoing analysis I owe to Monroe Freedman. Freedman has, of course, made a career of putting forth cases that force a rethinking of what it is to be a lawyer. The case I shall discuss is no exception.[3]

Freedman asks us to imagine Laura Eagle, a sole practitioner in a large city in an unnamed state. One evening an acquaintance of hers, a social worker, mentions over cocktails the horrible conditions he saw that day on a visit to a private nursing home—filth, poor food, neglect. One patient actually had maggots growing in her flesh. The patients are poor, elderly, bedridden, and rarely visited by anyone. The staff seems indifferent. State inspectors have probably been bribed. The social worker doubts anything could be done and ends his story with a sigh. Eagle thinks otherwise and immediately offers him $100 to return to the nursing home, explain to some of the patients about the possibility of suing on their behalf, and sign up one or more of them on a contingent fee. Eagle stresses that the social worker is not to mislead or pressure the patients in any way but simply to make sure they are as fully informed as possible about what can be done.

Eagle soon becomes attorney for the patients and, after much maneuvering and a dramatic trial, obtains both a substantial judgment against the nursing home and an order protecting the patients from further neglect. Her share in the judgment is the normal one-third. The case causes a stir in the newspapers. They report Eagle's substantial fee with considerable irony. They also report the solicitation without comment. Soon thereafter the local bar association begins disciplinary proceedings. At her hearing, Eagle admits that the fee was a significant motive for taking the case. Indeed, she emphasizes that she could not have afforded to do such a difficult and time-consuming case *pro bono*. She prefers representing the patients. But she admits that she would have been willing to represent the nursing home operator instead. "You can call me a hired gun if you like," she says, "but I believe in the English barrister practice of taking the next client in line."

Eagle's case is relatively easy to decide. Suppose the *Model Rules* are in effect in her locale. *Rule* 7.3 forbids a lawyer to "solicit professional employment from a prospective client with whom the lawyer has no family or prior professional relationship, by mail, in-person, or otherwise, when a significant motive for the lawyer's doing so is the lawyer's pecuniary gain . . ." Eagle did indeed solicit professional employment from persons she did not know and she admitted that her own pecuniary gain was a significant motive. This clear violation of the *Model Rules* is compounded by another. *Rule* 7.2(c) forbids a lawyer to "give anything of value to a person for recommending the lawyer's services . . ." Eagle gave the social worker $100 to do just that.

Freedman concludes by imagining that the local grievance committee would recommend that Eagle be disciplined and that the state's supreme court would so order. This outcome is troubling. Eagle is, in many ways, a good lawyer. She gave legal help to some who, though needing it desperately, might not have gotten it but for her. She won their case, leaving her clients far better than she found them. And she did it without sacrificing the financial well-being upon which depends her ability to do such good work again. Yet, she is guilty of unprofessional conduct under the *Model Rules* (as she would be under any predecessor). While she achieved the sort of good the legal profession aims at, she did so by means the profession has renounced.

Eagle's case is, in other words, one involving the question of whether a good end can justify an otherwise forbidden means. But it is not a classic case of that. In a classic case, the means in question is immoral in itself. It is an act like killing innocent children or torturing a prisoner. In Eagle's case, the means is not immoral in itself. Soliciting legal business "in the state of nature" (that is, absent a professional organization or legal prohibition) would be no more morally wrong than soliciting ordinary business is in most countries. Eagle's soliciting is morally wrong, *if* it is, only because it violates a professional rule. Professional rules are themselves a proper subject of moral evaluation. If the rule against solicitation were itself immoral, violating it would not be morally wrong; disciplining Eagle for violating the rule would be. But the rule against solicitation is not itself immoral. The rule merely requires lawyers not to do certain acts that, while morally good, are not morally required. What is troubling is that the rule discourages Eagle from doing just the sort of good her profession supposedly wants to do. Can discipline be justified in such a case?

I believe it can. I shall consider myself successful if, drawing on the conception of professionalism developed so far, I can provide a justification that any rational lawyer, Eagle included, should accept. To make the test as fair and dramatic as possible, I shall imagine myself to be addressing my justification to Eagle directly, as if I were the chair of her grievance committee and she a lawyer whom I regarded as a good colleague gone astray.[4]

V. WHAT EAGLE WOULD HAVE HEARD FROM ME

Ms. Eagle, you have violated two provisions of the *Model Rules*. You solicited clients, using an intermediary, and you paid the intermediary. Your only defense is that you are (and I am quoting) "a hired gun" and "believe in the English practice of taking the next client in line." That, of course, is no defense. The same code of ethics that requires the English barrister to take the next client also forbids him to stir up litigation (as you have done). You seem to expect the benefits of the English system without its burdens. You seem in addition, and inconsistently, to think yourself an individual as free as any car dealer to get business where you can. In short, you seem to misunderstand your profession. I hope what I shall say now will help you to understand it better.

Let me begin, Ms. Eagle, by pointing out that you have entered into something like a contract with other lawyers. You took an oath to obey the laws of this state, including the *Model Rules* under which you now stand convicted. Had you refused to take that oath, you would not have been admitted to the practice of law. You would not have become a lawyer able to do the good you did for those whom you solicited. Since you passed the ethics section of the bar exam, you must have taken the oath knowing what the *Model Rules* would require of you. You also underwent an investigation for character and fitness. If you had felt you could not abide by the *Model Rules* as they stood, you might have said so. You would then have given us a fair opportunity to refuse you admission. You did not. Why?

Perhaps you took the oath in good faith, changing your mind about obeying the *Model Rules* only after you found it hard to make a living practicing law as the *Rules* require. That happens.

But, by itself, such a change of mind cannot change your obligations. You have, after all, continued to claim the benefits of the contract you made. You have continued to claim to be a lawyer. Do you expect to have the benefits of being a lawyer without the obligations? But, you may say, it is no ordinary contract we are talking about. The bargaining power of the parties was very unequal. The profession could easily do without you, but you could not easily do without it. You were presented with a standardized contract and, in effect, told to take it or leave it.

True, of course; yet, standing alone, such circumstances are not enough to void the contract. You are claiming, in effect, that the contract between you and the profession was one of adhesion. A contract of adhesion is void only if its terms are demonstrably unfair to the weaker party (or, a point I shall come back to, against public policy). The terms you accepted were, on the contrary, perfectly fair.

When you graduated college, you had a wide range of careers open to you. Many of them, though potentially as lucrative as the law, would not have burdened you with obligations like those the *Model Rules* impose. You chose law. You studied hard, passed your exams, filled out long forms, and paid all the fees. You were then granted the right to practice law "with," as we say, "all the rights and obligations pertaining thereto." That was the very thing you had worked so hard to obtain. You could not have been unfairly surprised. Indeed, you should not have been surprised at all.

The *Model Rules* are, it is true, not written in stone. They can be changed without your express approval. You are, in that respect, subject to a contract some terms of which you could not have known when you took the oath. Still, even this incompleteness does not make the contract unfair. On the one hand, the rules under which you are now being disciplined were in effect when you took your oath. So, you had fair notice of them. On the other hand, your oath did not subject you to anyone's *arbitrary* power. Admission to the profession made you eligible to join the state bar association and serve on committees that have the power to recommend changes in the *Model Rules*. True, the bar does not have final power to make the *Rules*, though their advice is usually followed. But you were already a member of the electorate that chooses [either directly or indirectly] those who do have final power. You will not, I gather, claim that the constitution of this state is unfair to you. You are, then, in all these respects, neither better off nor worse off than any other member of the state bar. Surely, that is fair.

But, you ask, is it fair to deny you the opportunity to find clients wherever you can, by any lawful means you can? Is it fair to lawyers to deny them opportunities to do business open to other business people? These two questions are, of course, distinct. One is about fairness to you as a lawyer; the other, about fairness to lawyers generally. Let us take them one at a time, beginning with you in particular.

How can it be unfair to you in particular to deny lawyers in general the opportunity to find clients wherever they can? Are you claiming that lawyers in general should be forbidden to do as you have done but that you, being somehow special, should not? I suppose not.

But, if you do not claim that, how can you justifiably claim that we are treating you unfairly when we treat you the same as the rest of us? You are not anyone special. You are under no formal disadvantage with respect to us. All of us are equally denied the opportunity you have usurped. Nor are you under any obvious material disadvantage as a result. If all lawyers were free to do as you have done, Ms. Eagle, you might well be trampled in the stampede for clients. What reason do you have to believe that you would do better in wide-open competition than you are doing now?

That, Ms. Eagle, brings us to the possibility that the rule against solicitation is unfair to lawyers generally. But how could it be unfair to us? What is at issue is, after all, *self-denial*, not the work of an alien power. Lawyers, in general, have approved the rule against soliciting business. When we no longer want that rule, it likely would be repealed. Indeed, the rule remains largely because lawyers have fought to keep it. Why have lawyers fought to keep it? I shall come back to that question. For now, it is enough to point out that the rule does not seem to put lawyers at a disadvantage compared to business people who are not subject to such restraint. Those who sell life insurance, aluminum siding, or flowers by direct solicitation are not, on the whole, financially better off than lawyers. They simply bear an extra burden of competition with no obvious reward.

So, Ms. Eagle, must we not conclude that the contract between you and us is fair to you in particular and to lawyers in general?

Perhaps, though, that is beside the point. Perhaps the "unfairness" you are really concerned about is not unfairness to you or to other lawyers but to those potential clients whom the *Model Rules* seem to have inadvertently doomed to lie helpless in dirty beds, maggots eating their flesh. You would then be claiming that the rule under which you have been charged is legally void because it is against public policy or at least morally void because of the unjust harm it allows. *That* claim must be treated with great respect. The legal profession is committed to the ideal that those needing a lawyer's help to seek justice within the law should have the help they need.

I must, however, admit to doubting that your chief concern was for the needy. Surely, if *they* had been your chief concern, you would at least have tried to find a lawyer to do *pro bono* what you could only do for pay. There are many lawyers who can afford the time you say you cannot. The *Model Rules* put them under an obligation (unenforceable, I admit) to devote some time to those who need a lawyer's help but cannot pay the usual fee. Perhaps, then, a few phone calls would have been all you need have done to find a lawyer to do for free what you would only do for pay. Did you make even one call? You did not.

You might also have shown your concern for the needy in other ways. You made a profit on their suffering. You might instead have taken as pay only enough to cover your costs, including time. The good you did seems much more the by-product of the profit you saw in the case than the other way around.

I say that, Ms. Eagle, not to shame you but to suggest a problem for which I think profession is the best solution. Our profession is an organization the purpose of which is to benefit the public by assuring that legal help is provided in a morally good way. A noble purpose, Ms. Eagle, but one to be accomplished, if it is to be accomplished at all, only by such human beings as you and I. *How can people whose chief, but not sole, interest is their own welfare and that of people close to them, be organized so that they can make a living, provide legal help to those who need it, and benefit the public?* That is the problem to which the legal profession offers one solution. What about another?

We may, I think, dismiss as unrealistic having all legal services performed by people drafted into lawyering the way we used to draft young men into soldiering, or by a high-paid government service like today's all-volunteer military. That leaves only one solution beside making law a profession, that is, allowing legal services to be provided in a free market the way cars are today.

A legal market may at first seem better than a legal profession. With a market, people would do legal work because they thought they were better off doing it than doing anything else. They would take particular clients because they thought they could do better serving them than serving others. A legal market would certainly give us enthusiastic legal help, just as it now gives us enthusiastic car dealers. But would it give us the kind of legal help we want?

The market is, after all, like the police, primarily a means of supervision. It works well for those items of commerce consumers have both the will and the means to control. But, for those items the virtues and faults of which are in large part concealed from all but the maker, or fall largely on third parties, the market is likely to be a poor supervisor. Deregulation of trucking seems, for example, to have forced more cost-cutting than is safe. Trucks now cause fatal accidents at a much higher rate than they did before deregulation. Yet, shippers, the actual consumers of trucking, neither have much incentive to prefer safe truckers nor are well-placed to identify them. The difference between what a good lawyer would do and what a shyster would do is often as invisible to the legal consumer as a trucker's cost-cutting is to a shipper. One weakness of a legal market is that it tends to discourage (what we might call) "invisible quality" (including in that term protection of third parties).

That, I think, is reason enough to doubt whether a legal market is better than a legal profession. But there is another. The poor are likely to suffer. Of course, where the poor have a fee-generating case such as the one you brought, Ms. Eagle, they would have a good chance of finding legal help. Indeed, their only problem would be distinguishing between the competent and the incompetent, the honest and the crooked. The sick, the old, the worn out, the ignorant, might not choose well from the crowd of profit-hungry would-be helpers likely to gather at their bedside. But, at least they would have help. Not so those other poor whose cases can generate no fee or only a fee too small to cover the work. In a pure market, they would have to do without legal help, just as now they must do without cars.

We can, of course, try to correct that market failure by penal statute (for example, by punishing lawyers for not taking a certain number of "charity cases" each year). But, doing so would introduce into the market the draft's weaknesses. The poor may, for example, end up with lawyers whose only concern is to avoid punishment while spending as little time as possible on an unprofitable case. Another way to correct that market failure would be buying legal help in a free market with money raised by tax or gift. But, doing so would still leave the problem of supervision. What incentive would such legal helpers have to do more than the minimum necessary to avoid losing business, paying too much for malpractice insurance, or the like?

So much for a legal market. Why is a legal profession better? Remember how our profession is organized. We admit into practice only people whose performance in law school and on the bar exam gives us good reason to believe they know what they should. The character and fitness investigation should exclude all those who seem disinclined to do their share in a fair practice. Those remaining are then bound by oath to practice as the *Model Rules* provide. If (as I believe) the oath requires nothing immoral and lawyers generally do as they have sworn, everyone admitted into practice will have a moral obligation to do as she has sworn.

The obligation will have a double foundation, the same two moral rules upon which the law of contract is generally supposed to rest. Though these rules are not without exceptions, the exceptions do not matter here. One rule is "Keep your promises." It applies because of the oath. The second rule is, "don't cheat"—or, if you prefer the positive, "do as required by any morally permissible cooperative practice in which you voluntarily participate." A practice is cooperative insofar as each participant's reason for acting as the defining convention requires is that he expects to benefit from so acting because the other participants will also act as the convention requires. The second rule applies to lawyering because the *Model Rules* make lawyering a practice in which each lawyer stands to benefit from practicing law as the *Model Rules* require in part at least because other lawyers can be relied on to do the same.

If that is what it is to organize law as a profession, then organizing law in that way makes conscience, rather than the market or law, the chief "supervisor" of legal work. Conscience, of course, is a cheaper method of guiding conduct than penal statute. Conscience is also able to keep watch where neither the police nor the market can.

But, Ms. Eagle, though we are entitled to expect more of lawyers than of ordinary business people (because lawyers undertake to do more), we are not entitled to expect too much. Compliance with the *Model Rules* is much like compliance with any other convention. It is an obligation only so long as there is a practice. If the practice disintegrates, the obligation vanishes. Any voluntary practice will disintegrate unless most of the participants benefit from participating. For each lawyer, it is the compliance of *other* lawyers that makes acting as the *Model Rules* require both rational and morally obligatory. So, if the *Rules* set standards so high that sufficient compliance is unlikely, each lawyer may reasonably conclude that not enough other lawyers will act as required. He would then be justified in ignoring the *Rules* himself. (Think of constructive breach in contract law.) The profession would die of its own idealism.

I have stressed that the benefits of compliance must outweigh the costs. "Benefits" should, however, not be read too narrowly. The benefits need not all be self-serving. For example, because lawyers are generally decent people, they would consider it a benefit not to have to choose between serving a client badly and going broke. If lawyers generally maintained high standards in their work, no lawyer would be at a competitive disadvantage for doing the same, even if much of the resulting good work is "invisible" to the client. High standards for legal work serve the lawyer by serving the client.

Lawyers also generally want to help the needy or oppressed now and then. So we have tried in various ways to get every lawyer to do a fair share of such good works. Our attempt to impose an enforceable obligation to do a certain amount of *pro bono* work each year was, as you know, not well received.[5] Still, the basic strategy was right. If doing a certain amount of such work were made part of practicing law, no lawyer would be at a competitive disadvantage if he did help the needy now and then.

Since lawyers are only human, we must not expect them to sacrifice very much very often. The law would probably not long remain a profession if practicing as the *Model Rules* required impoverished almost anyone who tried it. Much in the *Model Rules* that may seem out of place given their noble purpose may be understood as part of what is necessary to make it a living practice.

I admit, though, that some provisions may simply be mistaken. Lawyers are as capable of writing a bad rule as anyone else. But the burden of proof should fall on the one who claims a particular rule is bad. After all, the majority is, all else equal, more likely to be right than any minority is. Of course, should a minority carry that burden and show a particular rule to be immoral, I would refuse to enforce it. If, however, the minority could only show the rule to be less than perfectly suited to its purpose, I would still feel obliged to enforce it until a better one had been adopted or, at least until a consensus had formed in favor of one alternative. Coordinating the conduct of many thousands of lawyers (as we must do in this state) is not easy. Confusion about the rules of practice would make coordination harder. Anyone serious about professional standards must resolve reasonable doubts about her conduct in favor of the standards as they are.

Which brings us, Ms. Eagle, to the rule against solicitation. It makes sense, I think, in part because lawyers are free to solicit so long as they do not profit. Ordinarily, some lawyer or other can be expected, if asked, to help *pro bono* with a case like the one that brought you here.

The rule against solicitation also makes sense, in part, because the alternative your misconduct suggests is likely to force lawyers to choose between participating in an unseemly scramble for business at the bedside of the sick and losing out in open competition. Who would benefit in the long run if lawyers were forced to make that choice? There may, I admit, be a way around this problem. But neither you nor anyone else has yet suggested one that more than a small fraction of lawyers favor over the present rule. We are, then, committed to the present rule for now not because it is the best possible, but because it is not plainly a bad rule and it is the one upon which our profession has agreed.

So, Ms. Eagle, what can we conclude? You are not in any way distinguishable from those lawyers who, though perhaps as hard up, do not solicit as you have. If we made a practice of letting lawyers profit from doing as you have done, solicitation like yours might soon become common and the advantages of the rule against it would be lost. Preserving the practice from which you unfairly benefited seems to require taking the profit out of what you did. So, Ms. Eagle, are we not justified in imposing on you a penalty proportioned to the benefits you unfairly took?[6]

VI. CONCLUSION

With that rhetorical question, I yield up the chair of Eagle's grievance committee and become myself again. I have now given an example of how the understanding of profession I proposed earlier might be applied in practice. I have explained why Eagle should have put her profession, that is, the obligations she voluntarily accepted when she became a lawyer, ahead of making money by helping the poor, sick, and old. Though that explanation included a defense of the present rule against solicitation, nothing of importance depends on whether that rule is in fact defensible. So long as it is defensible-on-the-facts-as-I-have-stated-them, Eagle's case will serve my purpose. My subject is professionalism, not solicitation.[7]

NOTES

A version of the second half of the chapter was presented at the American Bar Association Conference on Professionalism, Denver, CO, June 25, 1987, under the title "Profession as a Cooperative Undertaking." I should like to thank those present, especially co-panelist Monroe Freedman, for giving me much to think about. I should also like to thank my colleague, Vivian Weil, for helpful comments on an early draft. This chapter was first published as "Professionalism Means Putting Your Profession First," *Georgetown Journal of Legal Ethics* 2 (Summer 1988): 341–57; and later reprinted, somewhat revised, as chapter 4 in *Profession, Code, and Ethics* (Ashgate: Aldershot, 2002).

1. Quoted in David Mellinkoff, *The Conscience of a Lawyer* (St. Paul, MN: West Publishing Co., 1973), p. 189.

2. This, I think, is the main advantage my approach has over that Charles Fried takes in "The Lawyer as Friend: The Moral Foundations of the Lawyer-Client Relation," *Yale Law Journal* 85 (July 1976): 1060–89 (the first reading in this part).

3. Freedman presented this case for our panel at the *American Bar Association Conference on Professionalism*, Denver, CO, June 25, 1987. Need I say that he is not responsible for the use I shall make of it?

4. Freedman actually had Eagle being disbarred for her misconduct. I cannot defend treating her so harshly. Disbarment is the most severe penalty the profession can impose on a lawyer. Disbarment should therefore be reserved for the most serious misconduct (as well as for lawyers who demonstrate absolute inability or disinclination to do as they profess). Eagle seems to be a first offender. Her misconduct, though serious, is certainly much less serious than it would have been had she also falsified evidence, taken an exorbitant fee, or the like. So, I can only defend disciplining her if the resulting penalty is near the lower end of the scale, say, censure, a thirty-day suspension, or a fine large enough to wipe out her profit from the case. (I have also changed the facts in other minor ways to sharpen the problem.)

5. After heated debate in the ABA's legislative assembly, the drafting committee's mandatory "shall" was reduced to an hortatory "should," the only "should" among the *Model Rules'* rules—and so it has remained for almost two decades now.

6. If this last question seems to invoke a retributive notion of punishment, that is because it does. Though retributivism is not necessary for anything I have said up until now, it is, I think, necessary to justify a particular penalty. For a defense of this view, see my *To Make the Punishment Fit the Crime* (Boulder, CO: Westview, 1992).

7. There is in Ms. Eagle's conduct a disdain for her friend the social worker that I do not want to pass over. Why did she think it necessary to offer her friend $100 to go back to the nursing home and solicit clients? A good social worker, concerned about his clients, should have been delighted to have a lawyer come to their aid. Ms. Eagle treated the member of another profession as a mere runner. She also turned a friend (whom Freedman styles "an acquaintance") into an employee. Why? Was it because she wanted to avoid having to explain why she couldn't just take the case as a way of helping a friend with a problem?

PROBLEM SET II

A CLIENT WHOM A LIE MIGHT HELP

You have represented Bonji Bosso for many years—indeed, until two years ago, when he was duly and legally committed to a mental hospital as a person of unsound mind. You attended the competency hearing at his request and did what you could for him there. You have no doubt about his incompetency or about the propriety of his commitment and retention. But Bosso does. In fact, he believes himself to be wholly competent and therefore illegally restrained. He consequently writes begging you to do something to get him out of the mental hospital. These letters leave you with no doubt that Bosso is not ready to get out.

A few weeks ago, one of the hospital's psychologists called you to see whether you could tell Bosso that you are working on his release. The psychologist thought that such a statement on your part might have a soothing effect on him and so make treating him easier and more likely to succeed. Since then you have also received calls from some members of Bosso's family urging you to do as the psychologist asked. You can think of no good-faith argument for Bosso's release. Should you agree to humor your former client?

NEGOTIATING WITH THE PROSECUTOR

You are sitting in the office of Fred Grim, county prosecutor. Under discussion is the case of Vinnie Krule, your client by court appointment. Krule is charged with one count of rape (six to thirty years upon conviction, with no chance of probation). You and Grim are the only ones in the room. After examining the file on his desk, Grim says: "Since your client has, as I read here, no previous criminal record, I'm willing to knock the charge down to the lesser included offense of gross sexual imposition, in return for a guilty plea. I am also prepared to recommend probation. I wouldn't do this if your client weren't a first offender. Frankly, in person he looks to me like a real masher. Is the deal okay with you?"

Gross sexual imposition means a sentence of between six months and six years, some or all of which could be served on probation. Fred has a reputation as a good prosecutor and a decent man. It is well known that he does not make a charge unless he believes he can convict. He is also known to avoid rape prosecutions except in cases of repeat offenders.

On the other hand, your client is, as Fred suggests, a *real masher*. Beside a rape conviction, his criminal record includes two rape charges (later dropped), a conviction for armed robbery, and two convictions for aggravated assault. You know this because your client admitted the rape charges and the armed robbery conviction to you, and because you thereafter verified his admissions at the Hall of Records, discovering the rape and aggravated assault convictions at the same time.

You know Fred only professionally, seeing him a couple times a year to bargain for someone like Krule. You have a general practice that seldom includes a criminal case. You know the judge will use the same file Grim has on his desk. You suppose some clerk pulled the wrong record.

What would you do? What should you do?

CRAZY JANE TAKES THE STAND

You don't usually do criminal cases. But one day you receive a call from Judge Vernolli. Your name has reached the top of the bar list, he said, and would you handle a case? You agree, having been told by the partners in your firm that the way for a young associate to get trial experience is to serve on the bar list taking those cases which legal aid for some reason cannot.

Your client is one Crazy Jane Fish, accused of assault with a deadly weapon. The person allegedly assaulted is a bartender about twice her size; the weapon seems to have been a beer bottle. The assault took place in a nearly empty bar early one Saturday morning. The only witness may well have been drunk. The first time you talk to Crazy Jane, you ask her why she is called *Crazy* Jane. She says, "Because I'm crazy, don't you know."

Jane refuses to plea bargain, even though, as you have already told her, you probably can get her a short probation in return for a plea of simple assault. But you're happy with her refusal, since you took the case for the trial practice. Nonetheless, you carefully explain the risks of trial. She responds that it's okay to take the risks because she is innocent. You again explain, adding that, if the facts are as she claims them to be, she is guilty of assault *at least* and, if the prosecutor can convince the judge of that, she will be found guilty of assault and perhaps of assault with a deadly weapon. She again says it's okay, adding that "the assault was justified."

Jane probably did commit an assault, though not assault with a *deadly* weapon. From all you know, the prosecutor will have trouble getting a conviction even on the simple assault. Crazy Jane is, after all, half the size of the man assaulted, she succeeded in doing him no visible harm, and there is only one witness against her (in addition to the bartender) and he is probably unreliable.

The only thing that could convict Crazy Jane is her taking the stand and telling her side of the story. Her reason for wanting to do it does not concern the merits of the case. "I want the judge to know what I did and why. I don't care if I go to jail. The bartender made fun of my religion. He deserved to have his lousy face bashed in. And I would have done it too, if I hadn't slipped. I want everybody to know that."

Should you prevent her from taking the stand? If so, how? If not, should you continue as her attorney? After all, she seems to want to use the court for non-legal purposes.

SUGGESTED READINGS

Michael D. Bayles, "The Professional-Client Relationship," *Professional Ethics* (Belmont, CA: Wadsworth Publishing Co,. 1981), pp. 60–70.

Elliot D. Cohen, "Pure Legal Advocates and Moral Agents: Two Concepts of a Lawyer in an Adversary System," *Criminal Justice Ethics* (Winter/Spring, 1985): 38–59.

Michael Davis, "Professional Responsibility: Just Following the Rules?" *Business and Professional Ethics Journal* 18 (Spring 1999): 65–87.

Alan H. Goldman, *Moral Foundations of Professional Ethics* (New York: Rowman and Littlefield Publishers, 1980)

Richard Wasserstrom, "Lawyers as Professionals: Some Moral Issues," *Human Rights Quarterly* 5, vol.1 (February 1975): 105–28.

Daniel E. Wueste, "The Realist Challenge in Professional Ethics: Taking Some Cues from Legal Philosophy," *Professional Ethics* 7 (1999): 3–22.

PART III:
THE ADVERSARY SYSTEM

INTRODUCTION TO PART III

THREE SENSES OF "ADVERSARY SYSTEM"

Lawyers sometimes do for their clients what they would not do for anyone else: for example, ask a stranger humiliating questions in front of a crowded courtroom, evict a poor widow from her home of fifty years, or fail to reveal that a corporation is poisoning the local drinking water. Lawyers often justify (or, at least, excuse) such acts by pointing to their role in the "adversary system." The critique of the legal profession has already suggested that the adversary system might be much of what makes lawyering in the United States more troubling morally than, say, teaching or medicine. In this section, we take a closer look at that "system" and proposals to change it in small or large ways.

What is the "adversary system"? The term has at least three senses, which are seldom clearly distinguished. In one sense, an adversary system is any system of trial that recognizes at least two (and generally only two) opposing parties ("adverse interests"). No legal system is completely adversarial in this sense. Even under Anglo-American law, some legal proceedings (for example, adoption or changing one's name) do not have adverse parties. But some systems are less adversarial than ours. In most "civil law" countries, for example, contracts are regularly drawn up by, and signed before, an impartial notary without the intervention of partisan lawyers. In Cuba under Castro, even criminal proceedings seem to be nonadversarial. While the accused may have an attorney, the attorney is not there to fight the state. The client's interests are supposed to be the same as the state's, that is, to determine whether the accused is guilty and, if he is, to determine what would be best for society to do with him. The defense attorney is there much as attorneys in our own juvenile courts used to be—to present what the client knows. Many of Carrie Menkel-Meadow's suggestions seem intended to cure defects in the "adversary system" in this sense (reducing head-to-head conflict).

In another sense of "adversary system," the term is contrasted with "inquisitorial." The common law form of trial is adversarial (or "accusatorial"); the civil law form, "inquisitorial." An adversary system is (in this sense) defined by a division of labor *at trial* rather than (as in the previous sense) by an opposition of interests. Under an adversary system, the judge is relatively passive, while the attorneys before him are relatively active. The judge does not make an independent investigation, has little to say about which witnesses are called or what they will be asked, and may even depend upon the opposed attorneys to raise relevant points of law, to brief legal points so raised, and to help draft an opinion. Under an inquisitorial system, on the other hand, the judge is relatively active. She (or, more commonly, one of a panel) will make a preliminary investigation of the case, prepare a file to put into evidence, decide who will be called as witnesses, and do most of the questioning at trial. Of course, the parties' attorneys can advise on such matters and, from time to time at trial, may ask a question or two helpful to their side. But their role, though adverse, is quite secondary until all the evidence has been presented. Each attorney ("advocate") is then permitted to argue his client's position. Under the inquisitorial system, lawyers tend to be only interpreters of evidence (and law), not (as under the adversary system) presenters as well. There are, of course, no pure inquisitorial or adversarial systems, but systems do seem to be very much one or the other. Most are inquisitorial. The common law system is confined to states formerly within the British empire (and, as in Scotland, not even all of the British empire).

"Adversary system" may also be used in a third sense to refer to a certain *style* of lawyering. (We might use Menkel-Meadow's term "adversarialism" for this sense—except that she seems to include all three senses.) In this third sense, "the adversary system" is a *style* of lawyering rather than a set of institutions. Lawyers act as if all persons but the client they are now acting for were potential (or actual) adverse litigants and all questions of law or justice should be left to be decided by trial. There is in this third sense (as in the second) a division of labor, but the division is now not confined to the courtroom. In this third sense, the adversary system can be a universal form of practice. A lawyer in a civil law country could adopt the adversary style as easily as an attorney in a common-law country. The procedures at trial do not make it much more or less reasonable to leave certain questions to be decided by trial.

This third sense of "adversary system" is also independent of the first. A lawyer might, for example, think of trial as a cooperative attempt to determine what justice requires and yet still suppose other legal relations between persons to be adversarial (in our third sense). "If I have gotten too much for my client," the lawyer may reason, "it will come out at trial and justice will be done. It's not my concern now (outside of court). My concern is to do all I legally can for my client." Yet, as Menkel-Meadow argues, lawyers who accept the adversarial style tend to create institutions emphasizing, and very likely encouraging, adverse interests.

THE DEBATE OVER THE ADVERSARY SYSTEM

The first reading in this section, a report of the Joint Conference on Professional Responsibility, is a classic example of the connection lawyers make between the idea of profession and legal ethics. In this official ABA document from 1958, Lon Fuller and John D. Randall agree that the "adversary system" represents "the chief obstacle" to lay people, law students, and even lawyers understanding the lawyer's professional responsibilities. They therefore undertake a defense of "the system" that will (they hope) make sense of what lawyers do. Their defense is not intended to show merely that what lawyers do is legal and useful to their clients. Instead, Fuller and Randall try to show that what lawyers do (within the adversary system) is a *public* service—and, therefore, positively morally good. In the courtroom, lawyers serve justice by serving their clients; outside, they serve their clients by serving justice.

Fuller and Randall seem not to see the ambiguity of the term "adversary system." Their concern is to dispel the charge that a lawyer is "nothing but a hired brain and voice" (and so, not a member of a profession at all). This charge is older than the common law, older even than the legal profession. Thus, twenty-three hundred years ago, Socrates was already describing "the lawyer" (or, at least, the sort of person who goes to court a lot) in much the same terms:

> He is always in a hurry; . . . and there is his adversary standing over him, enforcing his rights; the affidavit, which in their phraseology is termed the brief, is recited; and from this he must not deviate. He is a servant before his master, who is seated, and has the cause in his hands;. . . The consequence has been, that he has become keen and shrewd; he has learned how to flatter his master in word and indulge him in deed; but his soul is small and unrighteous. His slavish condition has deprived him of growth and uprightness and independence; dangers and fears, which were too much for his truth and honesty, came upon him in early years, when the tenderness of youth was unequal to them, and has driven him into crooked ways; from the first he has practiced deception and retaliation, and has become stunted and warped. And so he has passed out of youth into manhood, having no soundness in him; and is now, as he thinks, a master of wisdom. Such is the lawyer, Theodorus. (*Theaetetus* III: 172–73)

Though the charge of being a hired brain and voice ("a servant" or slave) is quite old, Fuller and Randall unaccountably take their problem to be defending the practice of law within the adversary system understood in our second sense, that of trial before a relatively passive judge (something relatively new and rare). Their defense is nonetheless provocative. The role of partisan advocate is, they argue, not an accident or regrettable necessity but a positive contribution to the proper ordering of affairs. Indeed, they claim that attempts to dispense with the distinct roles traditionally implied in adjudication under the common law have generally "failed" (no doubt a surprise to the Swiss, Japanese, Germans, French, and other democratic states with inquisitorial systems). The truth, it is thought, is most likely to arise from the clash of partisans before an impartial judge who has not had to invest himself in preparing the case. The partisan advocate's zeal in his client's case promotes a wise and informed decision in the best way possible. That zeal should not, of course, extend to making "muddy the headwaters of decision." For Fuller and Randall "zeal" does not include lying, fabricating evidence, or misstating the law. Does "zeal" include failing to reveal adverse facts or law, asking "leading questions," or humiliating a witness? They do not say.

The benefits of partisan advocacy appear, according to Fuller and Randall, only in the special environment of "open court." Elsewhere lawyers need not—indeed should not—behave as partisan advocates. The same lawyer who should be zealous in her defense of a guilty client should not participate *as legal adviser* in conduct that is immoral, unfair, or even of doubtful legality. She should be at pains to preserve sufficient detachment from her client's interests to be capable of sound and objective appraisal of the propriety of what the client proposes to do. Indeed, even in open court, not all lawyers are equally free to engage in partisan advocacy. The public prosecutor should not, Fuller and Randall say, take as her guide the standards of an attorney appearing on behalf of an individual. The prosecutor must recall that she occupies a dual role. She is obligated, on the one hand, to furnish the adversarial element essential for informed decision and, on the other, to see that impartial justice is done. She should not, for example, bring to trial a case she believes she can win if she also believes the accused is innocent.

Fuller and Randall thus seem to defend only a limited version of the adversary system (even in our second sense of that term). The adversary style (our third sense) is justified only in the courtroom and then only for an advocate acting for a private party. That limited defense seems odd given the advantages Fuller and Randall find in partisan advocacy. If the adversary trial is the best means for getting at the truth, why should the prosecutor not leave impartial justice to the judge instead of preempting the judge's role? Why should a lawyer not always resolve all reasonable doubts in favor of his client (so long as it is in the client's interest to do so) even when he is advising? Why should he not leave the courts to decide what is legal or just? Have Fuller and Randall in effect offered not a defense of *the* adversary system but a reminder that there are in fact many adversary systems possible, differing from each other both in the mix of kinds and of degrees of adversarial relationships and each requiring a somewhat different defense?

While in effect answering that question with an emphatic yes, Menkel-Meadow does considerably more. She challenges the assumption upon which Fuller and Randall rest their defense of the adversary system. Not only do we have no reason to believe the common law trial to be better at getting to the truth than the civil law trial (or even than many of the less well-known procedures of various tribal peoples), we are all familiar with activities where learning is more cooperative than at a common law trial. While science is, of course, the best example of cooperative learning, the American legal system itself includes many departures from an adversarial approach, what are often lumped together under the head "alternative dispute resolution." While Menkel-Meadow casts her critique of the adversary system in terms of "postmodernism," she could easily have made the same points, in other terms, in 1958—though she would have had less evidence to draw on and her audience, American lawyers, would then have been less aware of the disadvantages of American legal practice. If ideology is a view of the world more or less impervious to evidence, then the defense Fuller and Randall made for the adversary system may be an example of ideology. What would they count as evidence against their defense?

In contrast, Elliot D. Cohen's approach is to change the way the adversary system is conceptualized. Cohen has argued elsewhere[1] that there are two ways to approach the adversarial role: (1) as pure legal advocate and (2) as moral agent. According to the first, the primary obligation of a lawyer is to her client. This longstanding tradition in common law practice was clearly expressed in Canon 15 of the 1908 ABA *Canons of Professional Ethics* when it stated,

> the lawyer owes "entire devotion to the interest of the client, warm zeal in the maintenance and defense of his rights and the exertion of his utmost learning and ability," to the end that nothing be taken or be withheld from him, save by the rules of law, legally applied.

This "pure" advocacy tends to view law and morality as separate. Since the lawyer's obligation is to the law (which includes bar ethics rules), the pure legal advocate does not recognize moral constraints on what she can legally do for her client. In contrast, the moral agent approach sees morality and law as connected and therefore recognizes moral as well as legal limits to client advocacy. This concept was clearly expressed by John Noonan, long before he became a federal judge:

> a lawyer should not impose his conscience on his client; neither can he accept his client's decision and remain entirely free from all moral responsibility, subject only to the restraints of the criminal law. The framework of the adversary system provides only the first set of guidelines for a lawyer's conduct. He is also a human being and cannot submerge his humanity by playing a technician's role.[2]

In his defense of "lawyers' liberation" Cohen defends the moral agent approach to advocacy, which might well also be viewed as an extension of the critique of lawyers that Socrates made. Insofar as the lawyer leaves all decisions concerning the client's ends to the legal system, reserving to herself only decisions concerning the means for pursuing those ends, she acts as a mere servant—or, at least, as an agent who has put her own moral judgment to one side. Yet, to act "amorally," that is, in a way indifferent to morality, is not morally indifferent; it is morally wrong. Morality is not something we should ever set to one side. Whatever else we are when we act, we are always moral agents.

Cohen argues that the profession of law does not require any amorality as to ends (any more than it does amorality as to means). The ABA's *Rules of Professional Conduct* make clear provision for refusing to accept a case if the end sought is "repugnant"; a lawyer is even free to withdraw from a case if there is a fundamental disagreement about the end to pursue (provided he can withdraw without prejudice to the client). Indeed, the present *Rules* demand no more than "competence and diligence." ("Zeal"—after much debate—has been relegated to the Comments.)

Nevertheless, the *Rules* are ambiguous about the status of the lawyers' moral judgment in resolving ethical conflicts. For example, suppose a lawyer finds a prospective client's cause to be morally repugnant even though it is legal. Should the lawyer decline to represent the client only if the lawyer's repugnance is likely to interfere with her ability to represent the client? Or should the lawyer decline representation on moral grounds alone, that is, whether or not the lawyer's repugnance to the cause would impair her ability to represent the client?

Just how this question is to be answered is subject to interpretation. On the one hand, the Preamble to the *ABA Rules* seems to agree with Noonan: the Rules are to provide a "framework" in which the lawyer must, in difficult cases of ethical conflict, exercise *moral* judgment. On the other hand, some rules, such as 6.2(C) (on acceptance of public service appointments), especially in their comments, tend to favor the pure legal advocate approach.

Unfortunately (argues Cohen), the prevailing mode of interpreting ethical rules still tends to treat the lawyer as pure legal advocate. That strips the ethical rules of their moral content, leaving them mere positive law in which all reasonable doubt must be resolved in favor of the client. Cohen proposes instead interpreting ethical rules to take full account of the lawyer's status as an independent moral agent (as, of course, morality requires). Any interpretation of ethical rules should give due weight to relevant moral principles (and avoid violation of moral rules), and the *ABA Rules* should make that clear. Lawyers should cease thinking of themselves as mere skillful machines. They should recognize themselves instead as autonomous moral agents who must judge their client's legal cause just as they would judge any other cause they were asked to join. They should not be expected to leave moral decency outside the office (or courtroom) door, hoping "the system" will insulate them from the responsibility to act as autonomous, moral agents.

SOLVING THE PROBLEM BY CHANGING THE RULES

In 1974, Marvin Frankel, then a federal judge, named as the chief fault of the "adversary system" the failure of partisan advocates to cooperate in the search for truth. He proposed to cure that fault not by switching to the inquisitorial system but by adding the following provisions to the lawyer's rules of conduct:

(1) In his representation of a client, unless prevented from doing so by a privilege reasonably believed to apply, a lawyer shall:

    (a) Report to the court and opposing counsel the existence of relevant evidence or witnesses where the lawyer does not intend to offer such evidence or witnesses.

    (b) Prevent, or when prevention has proved unsuccessful, report to court and opposing counsel the making of any untrue statement by client or witness or any omission to state a material fact necessary in order to make statements made, in the light of the circumstances under which they were made, not misleading.

(c) Question witnesses with a purpose and design to elicit the whole truth, including particularly supplementary and qualifying matters that render evidence already given more accurate, intelligible, or fair than it otherwise would be.

(2) In the construction and application of the rules in subdivision (1), a lawyer shall be held to possess knowledge he actually has or, in the exercise of reasonable diligence, should have.[3]

Which sense of the "adversary system" does Frankel have in mind when he offers these rules as a way around? Would adopting Frankel's proposal improve our legal system? If so, how? Would you recommend any other changes?

NOTES

1. Elliot D. Cohen, "Pure Legal Advocates and Moral Agents: Two Concepts of a Lawyer in an Adversary System," *Criminal Justice Ethics* (Winter/Spring 1985): 38–59.

2. John T. Noonan Jr., "The Purposes of Advocacy and the Limits of Confidentiality," *Michigan Law Review* 64 (1966): 1492.

3. Marvin E. Frankel, "The Search for Truth: An Umpireal View," *University of Pennsylvania Law Review* 123 (1975): 1059.

Lon L. Fuller and John D. Randall

PROFESSIONAL RESPONSIBILITY: REPORT OF THE JOINT CONFERENCE

The Joint Conference on Professional Responsibility was established in 1952 by the American Bar Association and the Association of American Law Schools. At the first meeting of the Conference, the general problem discussed was that of bringing home to the law student, the lawyer and the public an understanding of the nature of the lawyer's professional responsibilities. All present considered that the chief obstacle to the success of this undertaking lay in "the adversary system." Those who had attempted to arrange conferences on professional ethics between lawyers, on the one side, and philosophers and theologians, on the other, observed that communication broke down at this point. Similarly, those who had attempted to teach ethical principles to law students found that the students were uneasy about the adversary system, some thinking of it as an unwholesome compromise with the combativeness of human nature, others vaguely approving of it but disturbed by their inability to articulate its proper limits. Finally, it was observed that the legal profession is itself generally not very

From *American Bar Association Journal* 44 (December 1958): 1159–1218. Reprinted in edited form with permission from the *ABA Journal*.

philosophic about this issue. Confronted by the layman's charge that he is nothing but a hired brain and voice, the lawyer often finds it difficult to convey an insight into the value of the adversary system or an understanding of the tacit restraints with which it is infused.

Accordingly, it was decided that the first need was for a reasoned statement of the lawyer's responsibilities, set in the context of the adversary system. The statement printed below is intended to meet that need. It is not expected that all lawyers will agree with every detail of the statement, particularly in matters of emphasis. It was considered, however, that the statement would largely fail of its purpose if it were confined to generalities too broad to elicit dissent, but by the same token, too broad to sharpen insight or to stimulate useful discussion.

The Conference would welcome proposals as to ways in which its statement may be put to use. It would also be grateful for suggestions of further steps that may be taken to convey to students, laymen and lawyers a better understanding of the role played by the profession and of the restraints inherent in that role.

LON L. FULLER
JOHN D. RANDALL
Co-Chairmen
of the Joint Conference on Professional Responsibility

I

A profession to be worthy of the name must inculcate in its members a strong sense of the special obligations that attach to their calling. One who undertakes the practice of a profession cannot rest content with the faithful discharge duties assigned to him by others. His work must find its direction within a larger frame. All that he does must evidence a dedication, not merely to a specific assignment, but to the enduring ideals of his vocation. Only such a dedication will enable him to reconcile fidelity to those he serves with an equal fidelity to an office that must at all times rise above the involvements of immediate interest.

The legal profession has its traditional standards of conduct, its codified Canons of Ethics. The lawyer must know and respect these rules established for the conduct of his professional life. At the same time he must realize that a letter-bound observance of the Canons is not equivalent to the practice of professional responsibility.

A true sense of professional responsibility must derive from an understanding of the reasons that lie back of specific restraints, such as those embodied in the Canons. The grounds for the lawyer's peculiar obligations are to be found in the nature of his calling. The lawyer who seeks a clear understanding of his duties will be led to reflect on the special services his profession renders society and the services it might render if its full capacities were realized. When the lawyer fully understands the nature of his office, he will then discern what restraints are necessary to keep that office wholesome and effective.

Under the conditions of modern practice it is peculiarly necessary that the lawyer should understand, not merely the established standards of professional conduct, but the reasons underlying these standards. Today the lawyer plays a changing and increasingly varied role. In many developing fields the precise contribution of the legal profession is as yet undefined. In these areas the lawyer who determines what his own contribution shall be is at the same time helping to shape the future role of the profession itself. In the duties that the lawyer must now undertake, the inherited traditions of the Bar often yield but an indirect guidance. Principles of conduct applicable to appearance in open court do not, for example, resolve the issues confronting the lawyer who must assume the delicate task of mediating among opposing interests. Where the lawyer's work is of sufficient public concern to become newsworthy, his audience is today often expanded, while at the same time the issues in controversy are less readily understood than formerly. While performance under public scrutiny may at times reinforce the sense of professional obligation, it may also create grave temptations to unprofessional conduct.

For all these reasons the lawyer stands today in special need of a clear understanding of his obligations and of the vital connection between those obligations and the role his profession plays in society.

II

In modern society the legal profession may be said to perform three major services. The most obvious of these relates to the lawyer's role as advocate and counselor. The second has to do with the lawyer as one who designs a frame that will give form and direction to collaborative effort. His third service is not to particular clients, but to the public as a whole.

Lawyer's Service in the Administration and Development of the Law

The lawyer appearing as an advocate before a tribunal presents, as persuasively as he can, the facts and the law of the case as seen from the standpoint of his client's interest. It is essential that both the lawyer and the public understand early the nature of the role thus discharged. Such an understanding is required not only to appreciate the need for an adversary presentation of issues, but also in order to perceive truly the limits partisan advocacy must impose on itself if it is to remain wholesome and useful.

In a very real sense it may be said that the integrity of the adjudicative process itself depends upon the participation of the advocate. This becomes apparent when we contemplate the nature of the task assumed by any arbiter who attempts to decide a dispute without the aid of partisan advocacy.

Such an arbiter must undertake, not only the role of judge, but that of the representative for both of the litigants. Each of these roles must be played to the full without being muted by qualifications derived from the others. When he is developing for each side the most effective statement of its case, the arbiter must put aside his neutrality and permit himself to be moved by a sympathetic identification sufficiently intense to draw from his mind all that it is capable of giving—in analysis, patience, and creative power. When he resumes his neutral position, he must be able to view with distrust the fruits of this identification and be ready to reject the products of his own best mental efforts. The difficulties of this undertaking are obvious. If it is true that a man in his time must play many parts, it is scarcely given to him to play them all at once. It is small wonder, then, that failure generally attends the attempt to dispense with the distinct roles traditionally implied in adjudication. What generally occurs in practice is that at some early point a familiar pattern will seem to emerge from the evidence; an accustomed label is waiting for the case and without awaiting further proofs, this label is promptly assigned to it. It is a mistake to suppose that this premature cataloguing must necessarily result from impatience, prejudice or mental sloth. Often it proceeds from a very understandable desire to bring the hearing into some order and coherence, for without some tentative theory of the case there is no standard of relevance by which testimony may be measured. But what starts as a preliminary diagnosis designed to direct the inquiry tends, quickly and imperceptibly, to become a fixed conclusion, as all that confirms the diagnosis makes a strong imprint on the mind while all that runs counter to it is received with diverted attention.

An adversary presentation seems the only effective means for combating this natural human tendency to judge too swiftly in terms of the familiar which is not yet fully known. The arguments of counsel hold the case, as it were, in suspension between two opposing interpretations of it. While the proper classification of the case is thus kept unresolved, there is time to explore all its peculiarities and nuances.

These are the contributions made by partisan advocacy during the public hearing of the cause. When we take into account the preparations that must precede the hearing, the essential quality of the advocate's contribution become even more apparent. Preceding the hearing, inquiries must be instituted to determine what facts can be proved or seem sufficiently established to warrant formal test of their truth during the hearing. There must also be a preliminary analysis of the issues, so that the hearing may have form and direction. These preparatory measures are indispensable whether or not the parties involved in controversy are represented by advocates.

Where that representation is present there is an obvious advantage in the fact that the area of dispute may be greatly reduced by an exchange of written pleadings or by stipulations of counsel. Without the participation of someone who can act responsibly for each of the parties, this essential narrowing of issues becomes impossible. But here again the true significance of partisan advocacy lies deeper, touching once more the integrity of the adjudicative process itself. It is only through the advocate's participation that the hearing may remain in fact what it purports to be in theory: a public trial of the facts and issues. Each advocate comes to the hearing prepared to present his proofs and arguments, knowing at the same time that his arguments may fail to persuade and that his proofs may be rejected as inadequate. It is a part of his role to absorb these possible disappointments. The deciding tribunal, on the other hand, comes to the hearing uncommitted. It has not represented to the public that any fact can be proved, that any argument is sound, or that any particular way of stating a litigant's case is the most effective expression of its merits.

The matter assumes a very different aspect when the deciding tribunal is compelled to take into its own hands the preparations that must precede the hearing. In such a case the tribunal cannot truly be said to come to the hearing uncommitted, for it has itself appointed the channels along which the inquiry is to run. If an unexpected turn in the testimony reveals a miscalculation in the design of these channels, there is no advocate to absorb the blame. The deciding tribunal is under a strong temptation to keep the hearing moving within the boundaries originally set for it. The result may be that the hearing loses its character as an open trial of the facts and issues, and becomes a ritual designed to provide public confirmation for what the tribunal considers it has already established in private. When this occurs adjudication acquires the taint affecting all institutions that become subject to manipulation, presenting one aspect to the public, another to knowing participants.

These, then, are the reasons for believing that partisan advocacy plays a vital and essential role in one of the most fundamental procedures of a democratic society. But if we were to put all of these detailed considerations on one side, we should still be confronted by the fact that, in whatever form adjudication may appear, the experienced judge or arbitrator desires and actively seeks to obtain an adversary presentation of the issues. Only when he has had the benefit of intelligent and vigorous advocacy on both sides can he feel fully confident of his decision.

Viewed in this light, the role of the lawyer as a partisan advocate appears not as a regrettable necessity, but as an indispensable part of a larger ordering of affairs. The institution of advocacy is not a concession to the frailties of human nature, but an expression of human insight in the design of a social framework in which man's capacity for impartial judgment can attain its fullest realization.

When advocacy is thus viewed, it becomes clear by what principle limits must be set to partisanship. The advocate plays his role well when zeal for his client's cause promotes a wise and informed decision of the case. He plays his role badly, and trespasses against the obligations of professional responsibility, when his desire to win leads him to muddy the headwaters of decision, when, instead of lending a needed perspective to the controversy, he distorts and obscures its true nature.

The Lawyer's Role as Counselor

Vital as is the lawyer's role in adjudication, it should not be thought that it is only as an advocate pleading in open court that he contributes to the administration of the law. The most effective realization of the law's aims often takes place in the attorney's office, where litigation is forestalled by anticipating its outcome, where the lawyer's quiet counsel takes the place of public force. Contrary to popular belief, the compliance with the law thus brought about is not generally lip-serving and narrow, for by reminding him of its long-run costs the lawyer often deters his client from a course of conduct technically permissible under existing law, though inconsistent with its underlying spirit and purpose.

Although the lawyer serves the administration of justice indispensably both as advocate and as office counselor, the demands imposed on him by these two roles must be sharply distinguished. The man who has been called into court to answer for his own actions is entitled to a fair hearing. Partisan advocacy plays its essential part in such a hearing, and the lawyer pleading his client's case may properly present it in the most favorable light. A similar resolution of doubts in one direction becomes inappropriate when the lawyer acts as counselor. The reasons that justify and even require partisan advocacy in the trial of a cause do not grant any license to the lawyer to participate as legal adviser in a line of conduct that is immoral, unfair, or of doubtful legality. In saving himself from this unworthy involvement, the lawyer cannot be guided solely by an unreflective inner sense of good faith; he must be at pains to preserve a sufficient detachment from his client's interests so that he remains capable of a sound and objective appraisal of the propriety of what his client proposes to do.

The Lawyer as One Who Designs the Framework of Collaborative Effort

In our society the great bulk of human relations are set, not by government decree, but by the voluntary action of the affected parties. Men come together to collaborate and to arrange their relations in many ways: by forming corporations, partnerships, labor unions, clubs and churches; by concluding contracts and leases; by entering a hundred other large and small transactions by which their rights and duties toward one another are defined.

Successful voluntary collaboration usually requires for its guidance something equivalent to a formal charter, defining the terms of the collaboration anticipating and forfending against possible disputes, and generally providing a framework for the parties' future dealings. In our society the natural architect of this framework is the lawyer.

This is obvious where the transactions or relationship proposed must be fitted into existing law, either to insure legal enforcement or in order not to trespass against legal prohibitions. But the lawyer is also apt to be called to draft the bylaws of a social club or the terms of an agreement known to be unenforceable because cancelable by either party at any time. In these cases, the lawyer functions, not as an expert in the rules of an existing government, but as one who brings into existence a government for the regulation of the parties' own relations. The skill thus exercised is essentially the same as that involved in drafting constitutions and international treaties. The fruits of this skill enter in large measure into the drafting of ordinary legal documents, though this fact is obscured by the mistaken notion that the lawyer's only concern in such cases is with possible future litigation, it being forgotten that an important part of his task is to design a framework of collaboration that will function in such a way that litigation will not arise.

As the examples just given have suggested, in devising charters of collaborative effort the lawyer often acts where the affected parties are present as participants. But the lawyer also performs a similar function in situations where this is not so, as, for example, in planning estates and drafting wills. Here the instrument defining the terms of collaboration may affect persons not present and often not born. Yet here, too, the good lawyer does not serve merely as a legal conduit for his client's desires, but as a wise counselor, experienced in the art of devising arrangements that will put in workable order the entangled affairs and interests of human beings.

THE LAWYER'S OPPORTUNITIES AND OBLIGATIONS OF PUBLIC SERVICE

Private Practice as a Form of Public Service

There is a sense in which the lawyer must keep his obligations of public service distinct from the involvements of his private practice. This line of separation is aptly illustrated by an incident in the life of Thomas

Talfourd. As a barrister Talfourd had successfully represented a father in a suit over the custody of a child. Judgment for Talfourd's client was based on his superior legal right, though the court recognized in the case at bar that the mother had a stronger moral claim to custody than the father. Having thus encountered in the course of his practice an injustice in the law as then applied by the courts, Talfourd later as a member of Parliament secured the enactment of a statute that would make impossible a repetition of the result that his own advocacy had helped to bring about. Here the line is clearly drawn between the obligation of the advocate and the obligation of the public servant.

Yet in another case, Talfourd's devotion to public service grew out of his own enlightened view of his role as an advocate. It is impossible to imagine a lawyer who was narrow, crafty, quibbling, or ungenerous in his private practice having the conception of public responsibility displayed by Talfourd. A sure sense of the broader obligations of the legal profession must have its roots in the lawyer's own practice. His public service must begin at home.

Private practice is a form of public service when it is conducted with an appreciation of, and a respect for, the larger framework of government of which it forms a part, including under the term government those voluntary forms of self-regulation already discussed in this statement. It is within this larger framework that the lawyer must seek the answer to what he must do, the limits of what he may do.

Thus, partisan advocacy is a form of public service so long as it aids the process of adjudication; it ceases to be when it hinders that process, when it misleads, distorts and obfuscates, when it renders the task of the deciding tribunal not easier, but more difficult. Judges are inevitably the mirrors of the Bar practicing before them; they can with difficulty rise above the sources on which they must depend in reaching their decision. The primary responsibility for preserving adjudication as a meaningful and useful social institution rests ultimately with the practicing legal profession.

Where the lawyer serves as negotiator and draftsman, he advances public interest when he facilitates the processes of voluntary self-government; he works against the public interest when he obstructs the channels of collaborative effort, when he seeks petty advantages to the detriment of the larger processes in which he participates.

Private legal practice, properly pursued, is, then, itself a public service. This reflection should not induce a sense of complacency in the lawyer, nor lead him to disparage those forms of public service that fall outside the normal practice law. On the contrary, a proper sense of the significance of his role as the representative of private clients will almost inevitably lead the lawyer into broader fields of public service.

The Lawyer as a Guardian of Due Process

The lawyer's highest loyalty is at the same time the most intangible. It is a loyalty that runs, not to persons, but to procedures and institutions. The lawyer's role imposes on him a trusteeship for the integrity of those fundamental processes of government and self-government upon which the successful functioning of our society depends.

All institutions, however sound in purpose, present temptations to interested exploitation, to abusive short cuts, to corroding misinterpretations. The forms of democracy may be observed while means are found to circumvent inconvenient consequences resulting from a compliance with those forms. A lawyer recreant to his responsibilities can so disrupt the hearing of a cause as to undermine those rational foundations without which an adversary proceeding loses its meaning and its justification. Everywhere democratic and constitutional government is tragically dependent on voluntary and understanding cooperation in the maintenance of its fundamental processes and forms.

Without this essential leadership, there is an inevitable tendency for practice to drift downward to the level of those who have the least understanding of the issues at stake, whose experience of life has not taught them the vital importance of preserving just and proper forms of procedure. It is chiefly for the lawyer that the term "due process" takes on tangible meaning, for whom it indicates what is allowable and what is not, who realizes what a ruinous cost is incurred when its demands are disregarded. For the lawyer the insidious danger contained in the notion that "the end justifies the means" is not a matter of abstract philosophic conviction, but of direct professional experience. If the lawyer fails to do his part in educating the public to these dangers, he fails in one of his highest duties.

Making Legal Services Available to All

If there is any fundamental proposition of government on which all would agree, it is that one of the highest goals of society must be to achieve and maintain equality before the law. Yet this ideal remains an empty form of words, unless the legal profession is ready to provide adequate representation for those unable to pay the usual fees.

At present this representation is being supplied in some measure through the spontaneous generosity of individual lawyers, through legal aid societies, and—increasingly—through the organized efforts of the Bar. If those who stand in need of this service know of its availability, and their need is in fact adequately met, the precise mechanism by which this service is provided becomes of secondary importance. It is of great importance, however, that both the impulse to render this service, and the plan for making that impulse effective, should arise within the legal profession itself.

The moral position of the advocate is here at stake. Partisan advocacy finds justification in the contribution it makes to a sound and informed disposition of controversies. Where this contribution is lacking, the partisan position permitted to the advocate loses its reason for being. The legal profession has, therefore, a clear moral obligation to see to it that those already handicapped do not suffer the cumulative disadvantage of being without proper legal representation, for it is obvious that adjudication can neither be effective nor fair where only one side is represented by counsel.

In discharging this obligation, the legal profession can help to bring about a better understanding of the role of the advocate in our system of government. Popular misconceptions of the advocate's function disappear when the lawyer pleads without a fee, and the true value of his service to society is immediately perceived. The insight thus obtained by the public promotes a deeper understanding of the work of the legal profession as a whole.

The obligation to provide legal services for those actually caught up in litigation carries with it the obligation to make preventive legal advice accessible to all. It is among those unaccustomed to business affairs and fearful of the ways of the law that such advice is often most needed. If it is not received in time, the most valiant and skillful representation in court may come too late.

The Representation of Unpopular Causes

One of the highest services the lawyer can render to society is to appear in court on behalf of clients whose causes are in disfavor with the general public.

Under our system of government the process of adjudication is surrounded by safeguards evolved from centuries of experience. These safeguards are not designed merely to lend formality and decorum to the trial of causes. They are predicated on the assumption that to secure for any controversy a truly informed and dispassionate decision is a difficult thing, requiring for its achievement a special summoning and organization of human effort and the adoption of measures to exclude the biases and prejudgments that have free play outside the courtroom. All of this goes for naught if the man with an unpopular cause is unable to find a competent lawyer courageous enough to represent him. His chance to have his day in court loses much of its meaning if his case is handicapped from the outset by the very kind of prejudgment our rules of evidence and procedure are intended to prevent.

Where a cause is in disfavor because of a misunderstanding by the public, the service of the lawyer representing it is obvious, since he helps to remove an obloquy unjustly attaching to his client's position. But the lawyer renders an equally important, though less readily understood, service where the unfavorable public opinion of the client's cause is in fact justified. It is essential for a sound and wholesome development of public opinion that the disfavored cause have its full day in court, which includes, of necessity, representation by competent counsel. Where this does not occur, a fear arises that perhaps more might have been said for the losing side and suspicion is cast on the decision reached. Thus, confidence in the fundamental processes of government is diminished.

The extent to which the individual lawyer should feel himself bound to undertake the representation of unpopular causes must remain a matter for individual conscience. The legal profession as a whole, however, has a clear moral obligation to represent the client whose cause is in popular disfavor, the organized Bar can not only discharge an obligation incumbent on it, but at the same time relieve the individual lawyer of the stigma that might otherwise unjustly attach to his appearance on behalf of such a cause. If the courage and the initiative of the individual lawyer make this step unnecessary, the legal profession should in any event strive to promote and maintain a moral atmosphere in which he may render this service without ruinous cost to himself. No member of the Bar should indulge in public criticism of another lawyer because he has undertaken the representation of causes in general disfavor. Every member of the profession should, on the contrary, do what he can to promote a public understanding of the service rendered by the advocate in such situations.

The Lawyer and Legal Reform

There are few great figures in the history of the Bar who have not concerned themselves with the reform and improvement of the law. The special obligation of the profession with respect to legal reform rests on considerations too obvious to require enumeration. Certainly it is the lawyer who has both the best chance to know when the law is working badly and the special competence to put it in order.

When the lawyer fails to interest himself in the improvement of the law, the reason does not ordinarily lie in a lack of perception. It lies rather in a desire to retain the comfortable fit of accustomed ways, in a distaste for stirring controversy within the profession, or perhaps in a hope that if enough time is allowed to pass, the need for change will become so obvious that no special effort will be required to accomplish it.

The lawyer tempted by repose should recall the heavy costs paid by his profession when needed legal reform has to be accomplished through the initiative of public-spirited laymen. Where change must be thrust from without upon an unwilling Bar, the public's least flattering picture of the lawyer seems confirmed. The lawyer concerned for the standing of his profession will, therefore, interest himself actively in the improvement of the law. In doing so he will not only help to maintain confidence in the Bar, but will have the satisfaction of meeting a responsibility inhering in the nature of his calling.

The Lawyer as Citizen

Law should be so practiced that the lawyer remains free to make up his own mind how he will vote, what causes he will support, what economic and political philosophy he will espouse. It is one of the glories of the profession that it admits of this freedom. Distinguished examples can be cited of lawyers whose views were at variance from those of their clients, lawyers whose skill and wisdom made them valued advisers to those who had little sympathy with their views as citizens.

Broad issues of social policy can and should, therefore, be approached by the lawyer without the encumbrance of any special obligation derived from his profession. To this proposition there is, perhaps, one important qualification. Every calling owes to the public a duty of leadership in those matters where its training and experience give it a special competence and insight. The practice of his profession brings the lawyer in daily touch with a problem that is at best imperfectly understood by the general public. This is, broadly speaking, the problem of implementation as it arises in human affairs. Where an objective has been selected as desirable, it is generally the lawyer who is called upon to design the framework that will put human relations in such an order that the objective will be achieved. For that reason it is likely to be the lawyer who best understands the difficulties encountered in this task.

A dangerous unreal atmosphere surrounds much public discussion of economic and political issues. The electorate is addressed in terms implying that it has only to decide which among proffered objectives it considers most attractive. Little attention is paid to the question of the procedures and institutional arrangements which these objectives will require for their realization. Yet the lawyer knows that the most difficult problems are usually first encountered in giving workable legal form to an objective which all may consider desirable in itself. Not uncommonly at this stage the original objective must be modified, redefined, or even abandoned as not being attainable without undue cost.

Out of his professional experience the lawyer can draw the insight needed to improve public discussion of political and economic issues. Whether he considers himself a conservative or a liberal, the lawyer should do what he can to rescue that discussion from a world of unreality in which it is assumed that ends can be selected without any consideration of means. Obviously if he is to be effective in this respect, the lawyer cannot permit himself to become indifferent and uninformed concerning public issues.

Special Obligations Attaching to Particular Positions Held by the Lawyer

No general statement of the responsibilities of the legal profession can encompass all the situations in which the lawyer may be placed. Each position held by him makes its own peculiar demands. These demands the lawyer must clarify for himself in the light of the particular role in which he serves.

Two positions of public trust require special attention. The first of these is the office of public prosecutor. The manner in which the duties of this office are discharged is of prime importance, not only because the powers it confers are so readily subject to abuse, but also because in the public mind the whole administration of justice tends to be symbolized by its most dramatic branch, the criminal law.

The public prosecutor cannot take as a guide for the conduct of his office the standards of an attorney appearing on behalf of an individual client. The freedom elsewhere wisely granted to partisan advocacy must be severely curtailed if the prosecutor's duties are to be properly discharged. The public prosecutor must recall that he occupies a dual role, being obligated, on the one hand, to furnish that adversary element essential to the informed decision of any controversy, but being possessed, on the other, of important governmental powers that are pledged to the accomplishment of one objective only, that of impartial justice. Where the prosecutor is recreant to the trust implicit in his office, he undermines confidence, not only in his profession, but in government and the very ideal of justice itself.

Special fiduciary obligations are also incumbent on the lawyer who becomes a representative in the legislative branch of government, especially where he continues his private practice after assuming public office. Such a lawyer must be able to envisage the moral disaster that may result from a confusion of his role as legislator and his role as the representative of private clients. The fact that one in this position is sometimes faced with delicate issues difficult of resolution should not cause the lawyer to forget that a failure to face honestly and courageously the moral issues presented by his position may forfeit his integrity both as lawyer and as legislator and pervert the very meaning of representative government.

Mention of special positions of public trust should not be taken to imply that delicate moral issues are not confronted even in the course of the most humble private practice. The lawyer deciding whether to undertake a case must be able to judge objectively whether he is capable of handling it and whether he can assume its burdens without prejudice to previous commitments. In apportioning his time among cases already undertaken the lawyer must guard against the temptation to neglect clients whose needs are real but whose cases promise little financial reward. Even in meeting such everyday problems, good conscience must be fortified by reflection and a capacity to foresee the less immediate consequences of any contemplated course of action.

III

To meet the highest demands of professional responsibility the lawyer must not only have a clear understanding of his duties, but must also possess the resolution necessary to carry into effect what his intellect tells him ought to be done. For understanding is not of itself enough. Understanding may enable the lawyer to see the goal toward which he should strive, but it will not furnish the motive power that will impel him toward it. For this the lawyer requires a sense of attachment to something larger than himself.

For some this will be attainable only through religious faith. For others it may come from a feeling of identification with the legal profession and its great leaders of the past. Still others, looking to the future, may find it in the thought that they are applying their professional skills to help bring about a better life for all men.

These are problems each lawyer must solve in his own way. But in solving them he will remember, with Whitehead, that moral education cannot be complete without the habitual vision of greatness. And he will recall the concluding words of a famous essay by Holmes:

> Happiness, I am sure from having known many successful men, cannot be won simply by being counsel for great corporations and having an income of fifty thousand dollars. An intellect great enough to win the prize needs other foods besides success. The remoter and more general aspects of the law are those which give it universal interest. It is through them that you not only become a great master in your calling, but connect your subject with the universe and catch an echo of the infinite, a glimpse of its unfathomable process, a hint of the universal law.

Carrie Menkel-Meadow

THE TROUBLE WITH THE ADVERSARY SYSTEM IN A POSTMODERN, MULTICULTURAL WORLD

I. INTRODUCTION

In this essay I suggest the heretical notion that the adversary system may no longer be the best method for our legal system to deal with all of the matters that come within its purview. If late twentieth-century learning has taught us anything, it is that truth is illusive, partial, interpretable, dependent on the characteristics of the knowers as well as the known, and, most importantly, complex. In short, there may be more than just two sides to every story. The binary nature of the adversary system and its particular methods and tactics often may thwart some of the essential goals of any legal system. This essay argues that our epistemology has changed sufficiently in this era of poststructural, postmodern knowledge so that we need to reexamine the attributes of the adversary system as the "ideal type" of a legal system, and also reexamine the practice based on the premises of that system. Although some

From *William and Mary Law Review* 5 (1996). Reprinted with permission of the *William and Mary Law Review*.

scholars justify the adversary system on the grounds that it satisfies a variety of truth and justice criteria,[1] I believe that consideration of those criteria is, itself, contingent and must be historicized and reconsidered as our knowledge base changes.

In this essay I argue that the adversary system is inadequate, indeed dangerous, for satisfying a number of important goals of any legal or dispute resolution system. My critique operates at several different levels of the adversary system: epistemological, structural, remedial, and behavioral. I suggest that we should rethink both the goals our legal system should serve and the methods we use to achieve those goals. For those who cleave to the adversary system,[2] I want to shift the burden of proof to them to convince us that the adversary system continues to do its job better than other methods we might use.

My critiques, to be further elaborated below, are briefly as follows: Binary, oppositional presentations of facts in dispute are not the best way for us to learn the truth; polarized debate distorts the truth,[3] leaves out important information,[4] simplifies complexity, and obfuscates rather than clarifies.[5] More significantly, some cases mostly civil, but occasionally even criminal, are not susceptible to a binary (i.e., right/wrong, win/lose) conclusion or solution. The inability to reach a binary resolution of these disputes may result because in some cases we cannot determine the facts with any degree of accuracy. In other cases the law may bestow conflicting, though legitimate, legal rights giving some entitlements to both, or all, parties.[6] And, in yet another category of cases, human or emotional equities cannot be divided sharply.[7]

Modern life presents us with complex problems, often requiring complex and multifaceted solutions. Courts, with what I have called their "limited remedial imaginations," may not be the best institutional settings for resolving some of the disputes that we continue to put before them.

Even if some form of the adversary system was defensible in particular settings for purposes of adjudication, the "adversary" model employed in the courtroom has bled inappropriately into and infected other aspects of lawyering, including negotiations carried on both "in the shadow of the court" and outside of it in lawyers' transactional work.

Even in situations that call simply for factual determinations, the complexities of modern life—for example, the strong race issues implicated in several recent, notorious American cases—contribute to the problematic result that different people will interpret the same "fact" in different ways. Because of such interpretive differences, therefore, I find not only the structures of the adversary system wanting, but also how we think about the people within those structures.

Modern scholars outside of, as well as within, law have questioned each of the following assumptions underlying the use of the adversary system: objectivity, neutrality, argument by opposition and refutation, appeals to common and shared values, and fairness.[8] In my view, it is time for us to examine how these assumptions, which often are not "true," have affected our legal system. Lay people claim a crisis of legitimacy in the legal system, especially, for example, when the "race card" is deemed more important than any other factor in a trial, often not trusting jury verdicts. As scholars, we must take these criticisms seriously.

Multiculturalism, and all of the controversy that it has spawned in the universities, has at least reminded us that there is demographic, as well as epistemological, "positionality" and we do not all see things the same way.

With a healthy respect for the new knowledge about knowledge, we need to examine whether the adversary system helps or hinders the way we sort out disputes, differences, misunderstandings, and wrongdoings. Furthermore, the complexities of both modern life and modern lawsuits have shown us that disputes often have more than two sides in the sense that legal disputes and transactions involve many more than two parties. Procedures and forms like interpleader, joinder, consolidation, and class actions have attempted to allow more than just plaintiffs' and defendants' voices to be heard, all the while structuring the discourse so that parties ultimately must align themselves on one side of the adversarial line or another. Multiparty, multiplex suits or disputes may be distorted when only two sides are possible. Consider all of the multiparty and complex policy issues that courts contend with in environmental cleanup and siting, labor disputes in the public sector, consumer actions, antitrust actions, mass torts, school financing and desegregation, and other civil rights issues, to name a few examples.

Finally, scholars have criticized modern adversarialism for the ways it teaches people to act toward each other.[9] Although I share some of the critics' views regarding the incivility of lawyers, I am more concerned that the rhetoric and structure of adversarial discourse prevent not just better and nicer behavior, but more accurate and open thinking.

A culture of adversarialism, based on our legal system, has infected a wide variety of social institutions. Although I will focus primarily on the legal system and legal ethics here, consider how debate, argument, and adversarialism have, in recent years, dominated journalism, both print and electronic media, political campaigns, educational discourse, race relations, gender relations, and labor and management relations, to name only a few examples.

After I critique the adversary system, you will wonder what I would substitute for it. It should be obvious that as a postmodern, multicultural thinker I have no one panacea, solution, or process to offer. Instead, I think we should contemplate a variety of different ways to structure process in our legal system to reflect our multiple goals and objectives. For example, to achieve the goal of determining criminal guilt a different process may be required than is required for allocating money or human, parental, or civil rights. Sometimes other processes, such as mediation, inquisitorial-bureaucratic investigation, public forum or conversations, "intermediate sites of discourse," private problem-solving (negotiation) or group negotiation, and coalition and consensus building would resolve better the legal and other issues involved. I am thus suggesting variety and diversity for our legal process that will, in turn, require more diverse and complex thinking about which legal ethics would be appropriate in different settings. Some might prefer to reform the adversary system to keep it protean enough to remain inclusive, as a model, for our entire legal system. In my own view, this will not be adequate. We need to explore alternative models of legal process and ethics that will better meet the needs of more complex postmodern, multicultural disputes and issues.

II. THE PITFALLS OF ADVERSARIAL/BINARY THINKING IN A POSTMODERN WORLD

Although I cannot, in this limited time or space, review the full history and sources of this country's particular approach to adversarialism, I note that the Anglo-American legal system did not originate the idea of oppositional presentations of "facts." Both classical philosophical discourse and medieval scholastic disputations exhibit the belief that contested, oppositional presentations of "facts" will best reveal the truth. At this point we should note quickly one important error in the defense of the legal adversary system drawn from this tradition. Whatever the flaws of oppositional thinking discussed below, philosophers and others using this form of logic, at least, are committed theoretically to a genuine search for the truth. This is not the motivating ideal when an ethics regime that places duty to the client at least as high, if not higher than, the duty to truth harnesses the adversary system to the legal system. Although philosophers may seek the truth, lawyers seek to achieve their client's interests and to "win," which may entail simply obfuscating the other side's cases in the "creation" of reasonable doubt in the criminal cases leaving out important facts if they are deemed harmful. Even if the particular use of the oppositional/adversary model can be defended as a procedure of knowledge and truth-finding in other settings, as used in legal settings it lacks an important quality: the genuine search for truth.

Despite the longevity and robustness of adversarialism as a mode of human discourse, even some philosophers and epistemologists have questioned its value as the best way to understand the world. It is this feature of postmodernism that I want to apply critically to the adversary system as we know it in the legal system. In general terms, a variety of philosophers, literary critics, art and architecture critics, social scientists, and legal scholars have questioned whether any "truth" exists out there that is knowable and stable.[10] Postmodernism expresses some skepticism, if not cynicism, in the belief that there are immutable, universal, global, and discoverable facts or interpretations of facts. Whether by literary deconstruction, feminist epistemology, philosophical or linguistic decompositions of language, or in our own field, critical legal studies' exposure of the indeterminacies of our laws, the legacy of postmodernism is that truth is not fixed, meanings are "located" provisionally, not "discovered," and people who "find" truth, whether judges, juries, critics, or, yes, even scientists, have interests—social, economic, political, racial, gender—that affect how they see the world. In addition to interpretations of texts, meanings, and facts, postmodernists have questioned the very notion of a unified self having a stable set of characteristics, values, and attributes with which to process information.[11] Because we occupy multiple roles in modern society, being powerful in some—for example, the role of "father"—but subordinated in other—for example, the role of "worker"—the multiplicity of our social roles structures and filters our knowledge. Context—both present and our own personal and group histories—also deeply affects our knowledge. If we believe any of this (and I believe enough of it to consider the impact it might have on the finding of facts, the interpretation of law, and the production of "legal knowledge"), we must therefore ask how the legal system can assess truth and assign remedies confidently.

Let me illustrate the particular dilemma of oppositional, binary thinking at trial when linked with recent work in cognitive psychology and trial practice. If we take seriously the recent studies demonstrating that facts presented to fact finders are processed through "schemas," "filters," or common narratives,[12] then the presentation of two oppositional stories or conclusions may color how all of the facts are heard. Consider how the framing of a story by both sides then colors how each piece of evidence is interpreted. The oppositional story may work well when the fact finder has an off/on, guilt/innocence determination to make, though it still carries the danger that all the fact finders will process incremental facts through a preexisting frame, but will not work as well when polycentric factual findings, legal conclusions, and mixed fact/law questions are at issue: comparative negligence, business necessity defenses, excuse and justification in criminal law, and the best interest of the child, are a few examples. My argument here is that the "false" or "exaggerated" representation of oppositional stories may oversimplify the facts and not permit adequate consideration of fact interpretations or conclusions that either fall somewhere in between, or are totally outside of, the range of the lawyers' presentations. Indeed, one version of postmodernism could read the adversary system as totally and arbitrarily imposing order through its binary decision making process where no order exists, and where we cannot determine relevance rationally.

An implicit, but sometimes explicit, aspect of all postmodernism is a skepticism about both objectivity and neutrality. This has serious implications for our adversary system, not only for the advocate's role, but for the so-called neutral, passive judge as well. Critical legal scholars have advanced most explicitly the skeptical argument of postmodernism by demonstrating both the law's linguistic contingency—its indeterminance—and its manipulation by particularized interests, such as economic, or class (in critical legal theory), or race-based interests in critical race theory, and gender-based interests in feminist legal thought.[13] Most critical legal scholars' work has focused on the law and rules—the "texts" of the legal system.[14]

The attacks on certainty, legal knowledge, and neutrality, however, have clear and dangerous implications for legal process, and for the adversary system. A neutral judge, either as a passive umpire of a trial process or as a more active fact-finder, likely will be predisposed to favor one side of the story over the other or to favor his or her own interpretation of the story.

Party-initiated presentation of evidence might not uncover a judge's predisposition when the lawyers cannot learn the judge's own story. Some use this postmodern strategy to critique the false claims of objectivity and neutrality; others suggest that we simply should acknowledge the difference in values and accept that we may not have total unanimity over "fundamental interests."[15] The latter group of postmoderns argue that we should make explicit the appeal to fact finders' different values, beliefs, or emotions. More than "two stories" may thus exist in the courtroom if litigants attempt to deal with the variety of values or emotional "frames" that could influence a fact finder.[16] In my view, this reflects the reality of life in a postmodern, multicultural world—a recognition that if "truth" is to be arrived at, it is best done through multiple stories and deliberations rather than through only two. How this will be structured in a litigation system, which is still based on oppositional evidence presentation, remains to be seen.

Another common complaint about the adversary system demonstrates one of the claims made by deconstructionists. In litigation, the unequal resources of the parties will often determine the hierarchy of opposition. In an ideal and abstracted form, the adversary system clearly contemplates adversaries of equal skill and economic support; the result should not depend upon the resources or "skill" of the argument's representative, but on the merits of the argument. We all know, however, that "the 'haves' come out ahead."

III. THE LIMITED REMEDIAL POWER OF ADVERSARIALISM

I will heretically suggest that even some criminal matters, a category of cases most often understood as paradigmatically requiring binary solutions followed by punishment, might be susceptible to other processes and remedies such as Victim-Offender Mediation,[17] which attempts to create a guilt-imposing relationship between offenders and victims of some small crimes to encourage restitutionary remedies rather than punishment. If we are to defeat the hold that crime has on us then we must also broaden and increase our responses and searches for solutions, especially where there is not enough room for all at the inn—the prison.

In the civil arena, where I have focused my work, we must consider the cases that do not lend themselves easily to right or wrong answers or to more binary solutions. Often, third-party-imposed solutions, such as those imposed by courts, do not deal with causes underlying ongoing conflicts or disputes, especially if personal or relationship issues are at stake—this includes commercial as well as civil rights matters. Third-party-imposed solutions, therefore, may not endure. The courts, to their credit, have realized this, though not without a vast out-pouring of scholarship and criticism of the difficult road courts take when they attempt to order more complex remedial measures.[18] Most recently, courts have supervised other kinds of dispute resolution, particularly in class action settlements of consumer and antitrust cases[19] and mass torts.[20] We must look for ways to preserve limited funds so that they are fairly distributed to all deserving claimants as well as look for opportunities in which people may desire things other than, or in addition to, monetary relief. Greater possibilities of remedy and more creative "remedial" imaginations should thus affect the choices we make about what processes to use. Adversarialism may greatly restrict what can be accomplished.

IV. HOW MULTICULTURALISM (OR PLURALISM) CHALLENGES THE ADVERSARY SYSTEM

Recall that when we speak of the adversary system we say the "Anglo-American" adversary system.[21] "The inquisitorial system of civil law countries,"[22] "the mediation of Asian countries,"[23] "the dispute resolution processes of Native Americans,"[24] and the "moots" of some African cultures[25] remind us that legal processes are culturally specific and chosen, not given. With our increased participation in international treaties and tribunals such as the WTO[26] and the Law of the Sea Treaty,[27] experience of dealing with multiple parties having different cultures and legal regimes has revealed that we will have to participate in alternative (to us) forms of dispute resolution and culturally complex international cooperation.

Within our own borders multicultural concerns are revealed when immigrants from other systems either fear or will not use our system because they do not understand or trust it—or when it is alien to what they know. Although our dominant melting pot and assimilationist ideologies suggest that recent newcomers to our shores simply should acculturate themselves to our legal system as one of the few "all-

American" institutions, I, instead, posit that we might do well to take the opportunity of reexamining our system for ethnocentric bias and try to imagine creating and utilizing other dispute resolution institutions. The very premises of our system—that "winning" is all and that harms suffered are monetized—may not be culturally congruent with the belief systems of all members of our society.

I fear the adversary system and its contributions to the larger culture have hindered rather than helped race and ethnic relations by polarizing discussion and by continuing to perpetuate their own form of bi-polar thinking. Third-party-imposed solutions seldom get at root causes of conflicts or provide enduring solutions. Black/white race relations, as another binary construct, remain the paradigm for thinking about race, despite the growing multiplicity of race and ethnicities and diversification of our society and, slowly, of the legal profession itself. In my view, we need to rethink ways to permit more voices, more stories, more complex versions of reality to inform us and to allow all people to express views that are not determined entirely by their "given" cultural identities. To that end, let me turn to some proposals for reform of the adversary system.

V. REFORMING THE ADVERSARY SYSTEM

In what circumstances could we begin to experiment safely with other forms of process through which we could explore other forms of interaction and ethics? Many scholars in the dispute resolution field have called on us to provide both "thick description" and analysis of different modes of conflict resolution that have been successful, even in perceived intractable disputes. Mindful of the postmodern and multicultural critiques of legal knowledge, could we imagine a forum where more than two voices could be heard? Here I will sketch some possible alternate modes of dispute resolution to consider.

When a dispute involves more than two sides, one could imagine processes with more than just plaintiffs and defendants as parties. In a modification of old historical forms, one could imagine a tri-partite criminal proceeding with states' interests, victims' interests, and defendants' interests all represented. Or, as has occurred in a variety of environmental settings, community block-grants and other multiparty situations, one could utilize a multiparty mediation-like process in which a single dispute broadens community and democratic participation in a single issue that affects more than two parties and establishes a process for greater participation. "Reg-neg"—regulatory negotiation or negotiated rule-making—represents another example of current recognition that processes other than conventional adversarial ones may more effectively involve more than two parties and lend greater legitimacy to the result if people get involved in the construction of rules before they take effect.[28] We could further adapt our current forms of subclasses, multi-party, multidistrict litigation, and other forms of consolidation to allow for participation by more than "two sides" in civil cases having a variety of private and public issues at stake.[29]

[W]e might examine the circumstances under which some forms of the civil inquisitorial investigative procedures make sense—their major advantage being that a nonpartisan investigation leads to, at least in theory, a genuine search for truth. Purporting to engage in a genuine search for truth may be appropriate for some governmental and regulatory questions. Furthermore, as long as individual liberty is not at issue, even the most confirmed adversarialist might acknowledge that the proverbial quest for "truth" is, ultimately, likely to be both more effective and cheaper. Even the United Kingdom, with its commitment to the adversary system, employs governmental investigatory commissions and procedures far more often than we do.[30]

I strongly believe that we are on the right track in experimenting and using a variety of forms of "alternative dispute resolution" [ADR]—I prefer the new term "appropriate dispute resolution." Yet, I fear many of these forms (mediation, mini-trials, settlement conferences, early neutral evaluations, reg-neg) are becoming corrupted by the persistence of adversarial values.

Lawyers and third-party neutrals will clearly have to learn new roles to play in mediation. In recognition of this need, programs for teaching people to be effective problem solvers and, heaven forbid, advocates, within the ADR process are emerging. These fledgling programs are good, because dealing with the weaknesses of adversarialism necessitates new mindsets about law practice. Fact finding, third party neutraling, and judging might also deserve reconsideration. Some years ago, I suggested that if gender differences in judging and fact finding had any merit, the system might benefit if it considered using male-female judge teams, who had to decide together, instead of a single judge.[31]

Consider the changes required of both our judge and jury roles and selection processes if we are to reflect fully "multicultural" considerations in decision making and process facilitation. Close to my heart, and related to the concept of accounting for multicultural considerations, is my concern regarding whether different forms of process will require different ethical requirements. Should lawyers attending an in-office, Early Neutral Evaluation session with court-appointed volunteer lawyers have a duty of candor to the tribunal under *Model Rule of Professional Conduct* 3.3? What conflicts of interest rules should we apply to those who both mediate and litigate?

Although I would certainly like to see abuses of adversarial behavior curbed (and I still think professional reputation does more to police this than anything else, interspersed with a few very public scandals that cause us to reexamine our loyalties and rules once in a while), I am skeptical that ethics rules changes can really reform the adversary system. Adversarialism is so powerful a heuristic and organizing framework for our culture, that, much like a great whale, it seems to swallow up any effort to modify or transform it. Though some legal scholars have interpreted the *Model Rules'* language change from "zealous" advocacy to "diligence"[32] to mean that the ethics rules have shifted somewhat away from adversarialism, I still see the loophole in the language of the comments—where zeal continues to rear its dragon-like smoke. No one, however, can point to any change in lawyers' behavior that has resulted from that language change. (Remember the deconstructionists' view about indeterminate language with no meaning!)

VI. CONCLUSION

Although I am not happy with the structural, epistemological, remedial, and behavioral aspects of the adversarial system, I am skeptical
that we can reform it by changing some ethical or procedural rules. A
cultural change is required, and that is not easy to legislate. What I urge
instead is the cabining of the adversarial system to the situations where
it can do its best work, with all the limitations I have described. I would
prefer that we take the teachings of postmodernism and multiculturalism seriously enough to consider other forms and formats of conflict
and dispute resolution—such as employing many-personed and -sided
factual presentations and handling disputes with more deliberative and
participatory party and fact-finding processes—and begin to evaluate
their strengths and weaknesses as we come to develop something of a
typology for assessing which cases belong in which ADR process. I
believe that each process will need to carry its own ethics—the zeal of
the advocate does not play well in mediation and the mediator is both
a more active and more complex third-party neutral than the judge who
is governed by the Judicial Code of Conduct. To take up a more radical strain of postmodernism, our legal processes and ethics are "in
play" (or, in the French, "at play"). Our experimentation with ADR and
other forms of legal process reflects our collective dissatisfaction, for a
wide diversity of reasons, with the traditional adversary model and our
current postmodern penchant for "many methods," when one will not
suffice. I firmly believe that the only way to reform the adversary model
is to successfully "oppose" it with other modes and processes and see if
we can create a more varied legal system, one that is more sensitive to
the particular postmodern needs of parties and the particularities of
cases. I do not think that any one micro-reform or any single process
will successfully supplant and replace the adversary system. I hope,
however, that the post-postmodern legal system will give parties a
greater choice about how they want to resolve their disputes. Greater
choice in dispute resolution will allow lawyers who want to be "moral
activists," problem solvers, lawyers for the situation or the community,

discretionary lawyers, civic republicans, or statesmen to have greater flexibility in the models they choose. Not everyone will have to be a "hired gun" in an epistemological system that is crumbling as we speak.

NOTES

1. See generally David Luban, "The Adversary System Excuse," in *The Good Lawyer: Lawyers' Roles and Lawyers' Ethics*, ed. David Luban (1983), pp. 83, 93–111 [hereinafter *The Good Lawyer*] (describing various justifications for the adversary system).

2. See, e.g., Alan M. Dershowitz, *The Best Defense* (1982) (defining the lawyer's goals in competitive terms, such as winning); Monroe H. Freedman, *Lawyers' Ethics in an Adversary System* (1975) (exploring the impact of the conflict between moral obligations and duties to the client); Monroe H. Freedman, *Understanding Lawyers' Ethics* (1990) (expressing a traditional view of the lawyer's role in the adversary system).

3. See Marvin E. Frankel, *Partisan Justice* (1980); Marvin E. Frankel, "The Search for Truth: An Umpireal View," *University of Pennsylvania Law Review* 123 (1975): 1031 (hereinafter Frankel, "The Search for Truth"); Philip Shuchman, "The Question of Lawyers' Deceit," *Connecticut Bar Journal* 53 (1979): 101; Fred C. Zacharias, "Reconciling Professionalism and Client Interests," *William And Mary Law Review* 36 (1995): 1303.

4. See, e.g., A. Kenneth Pye, "The Role of Counsel in the Suppression of Truth," *Duke Law Journal* 921 (1978) (discussing how the defense counsel in criminal cases may suppress the truth).

5. Consider how the "evidence" emerged in the O. J. Simpson trial. See, e.g., Elizabeth Gleick, "Is the End Nigh? All Sides Take Lumps as the O. J. Case Wends Its Way toward the Jury," *Time*, September 18, 1995, p. 54 (discussing the presentation of evidence in the O. J. Simpson case).

6. See generally John E. Coons, "Approaches to Court Imposed Compromise—The Uses of Doubt and Reason," *Northwestern University Law Review* 58 (1964): 750, 753–54 (describing situations in which compromise is preferable to "winner-take-all" results); John E. Coons, "Compromise as Precise Justice," in *Compromise in Ethics, Law, and Politics*, ed. J. Roland Pennock and John

W. Chapman (1979): 190, 199 (explaining how a system of apportionment is preferable when conflicting policy values should be recognized in the outcome of litigation).

7. For example, in custody cases both parents may have equally valid legal and emotional claims.

8. See, e.g., Jerold S. Auerbach, *Justice without Law* (1983), pp. 144–46.

9. See Charles W. Wolfram, *Modern Legal Ethics* (1986), pp. 609–10 (discussing the relationship between adverse attorneys).

10. See generally *Discovering Reality: Feminist Perspectives on Epistemology, Metaphysics, Methodology, and Philosophy of Science*, ed. Sandra Harding and Merrill B. Hintikka (1983) (discussing feminist philosophical perspectives illustrating deconstructionism); Stanley Fish, *Doing What Comes Naturally: Change, Rhetoric, and the Practice of Theory in Literary and Legal Studies*, pp. 154–55 (1989) (noting the pervasiveness of deconstructionism).

11. See Mary Joe Frug, "Postmodern Legal Feminism," (1992); Naomi Scherman, "Individualism and the Objects of Psychology," in *Discovering Reality*, p. 225.

12. See, e.g., W. Lance Bennett and Martha S. Feldman, *Reconstructing Reality in the Courtroom: Justice and Judgment in American Culture* (1981) (describing the use of stories in legal judgments); John M. Conley and William M. O'Barr, *Rules versus Relationships: The Ethnography of Legal Discourse* (1990) (examining the tensions in the law with legal- (rule) and relationship-based "voices" of lay litigants).

13. In feminist epistemology more generally, philosophers of science have argued that even the construction of questions of "truth" in science have depended upon the "bias" of the masculinist view of reality. Consider the metaphors of "competition" and "survival of the fittest" and the struggle of the cell as examples. See Sandra Harding, *The Science Question in Feminism* (1986); Evelyn F. Kellar, *A Feeling for the Organism: The Life and Work of Barbara McClintock* (1983).

14. See, e.g., Mark Kelman, *A Guide to Critical Legal Studies* (1987) pp. 15–63 (chapter on rules and standards).

15. See generally *A Guide to Critical Legal Studies*, pp. 64–85 (discussing different critical legal studies approaches to the subjectivity of value).

16. Indeed, some have argued that the split between emotion and rationality is itself a "false dichotomy." See Joan Cocks, "Wordless Emotions: Some Critical Reflections on Radical Feminism," *Politics and Society* 13 (1984): 27;

Carrie Menkel-Meadow, "Women as Law Teachers: Toward the Feminization of Legal Education," in *Humanistic Education in Law: Essays on the Application of a Humanistic Perspective to Law Teaching*, ed. Columbia University (1981), p. 16.

17. See, e.g., Robert B. Coates and John Gehm, "Victim Meets Offender: An Evaluation of Victim-Offender Reconciliation Programs" (1985) (describing and evaluating victim-offender mediation); Jennifer G. Brown, "The Use of Mediation to Resolve Criminal Cases: A Procedural Critique," *Emory Law Journal* 43 (1994): 1247 (explaining the history and development of victim-offender mediation and criticizing it for placing excessive control in the victim's hands).

18. Abram Chayes, "The Role of the Judge in Public Law Litigation," *Harvard Law Review* 89 (1976): 1281, 1313–16 (stating that continual judicial oversight is necessary if justice is to be done in an increasingly regulated society); Stephen Yeazell and Theodore Eisenberg, "The Ordinary and the Extraordinary in Institutional Litigation," *Harvard Law Review* 93 (1980): 465, 474–94 (1980) (arguing that institutional litigation, in which courts are asked to oversee the operation of public institutions, has support from older judicial traditions).

19. Here, my personal favorite was when I received books from Harcourt, Brace, and Jovanovich, instead of cash, in settlement of an antitrust case involving overcharges in Bar Review courses. Such a settlement is not unlike the coupons for air fare discounts recently received in settlement of an airline antitrust action. See *In re Domestic Air Transp. Antitrust Litig.*, 148 F. R. D. 297 (N. D. Ga. 1993). These types of responses illustrate how "in-kind" or other forms of compensation are not zero-sum. The books and coupons give some benefit to the defendants, decreasing their cost for our recompense.

20. As in the Virginia bankruptcy court's supervision of the Dalkon Shield Claimants' Trust ADR program, see *Dalkon Shield Claimants' Trust v. Baker (In re A. H. Robins Co., Inc.)*, 197 B.R. 587 (Bankr. E. D. Va. 1995), and the now-rejected settlement of the breast implant litigation. See *Lindsey v. Dow Corning Corp. (In re Silicone Gel Breast Implant Product Liability Litigation)*, Civ. A. No. CV94-P-11558-5, 1994 WL 578353 (N. D. Ala. Sept. 1, 1994); Henry Weinstein, "New Terms Offered in Breast Implant Cases," *Los Angeles Times*, Oct. 3, 1995, at Dl.

21. See generally "Stephan Landsman, the Adversary System: A Description and Defense" (1984) (discussing the adversary system in terms of the Anglo-American legal tradition).

22. See ibid., p. 50.

23. See Jay Folberg, "A Mediation Overview: History and Dimensions of Practice," *Mediation Quarterly* (September 1983): 4.

24. See *Mediation Quarterly* (Summer 1993) (special issue on Native American Dispute Resolution).

25. See Folberg, "A Mediation Overview," pp. 4–5.

26. See Marrakesh Agreement Establishing the World Trade Organization (WTO), Pub. L. No. 103–465, 108 Stat. 4809 (1994).

27. See United Nations Convention on the Law of the Sea, July 29, 1994, 5. Treaty Doc. No. 103–39 (ratifying United Nations Convention of December 10, 1982).

28. See, e.g., Philip J. Harter, "Negotiating Regulations: A Cure for Malaise," *Georgetown Law Review* 71 (1982) (discussing the history, advantages, and function of negotiating regulations); Lawrence Susskind and Gerald McMahon, "The Theory and Practice of Negotiated Rulemaking," *Yale Journal on Regulation* 3 (1985): 133 (examining the results of Environmental Protection Agency evaluations of negotiated rulemaking).

29. For my argument that cases are not so easily denominated "public" or "private," see Carrie Menkel-Meadow, "Whose Dispute Is It, Anyway? A Democratic and Philosophical Defense of Settlement (In Some Cases)," *Georgetown Law Journal* 83 (1995): 2663.

30. See, e.g., The Royal Commission on Criminal Justice, 1993, CMND 2263 (following investigation of several cases of "miscarriages" and false convictions in political trials). White papers and green papers on important legal issues affecting public policy are also good sources.

31. See Carrie Menkel-Meadow, "Portia in a Different Voice: Speculations on a Women's Lawyering Process," *Berkeley Women's Law Journal* 1 "(1985): 39, 59; see also Judith Resnik, On the Bias: Feminist Reconsiderations of the Aspirations for Our Judges," *Southern California Law Review* 61 (1988).

32. *Model Rules of Professional Conduct, Rule* 1.3 (1983).

Elliot D. Cohen

LAWYERS' LIBERATION: MORAL AUTONOMY IN LEGAL PRACTICE

There is a movement in legal practice that has been brewing on a slow boil for the past two decades. This movement has been quietly advancing, almost imperceptibly, with occasional changes in the lawyers' code of ethics and professional ideology. The movement I speak of might appropriately be called *lawyers' liberation* since it seeks to make lawyers morally autonomous. This movement is heresy to lawyers shackled by professional faith in unfaltering devotion to clients' legal interests.

In its 1908 *Canons of Professional Ethics*, the ABA announced that the lawyer owes "'entire devotion to the interest of the client, warm zeal in the maintenance and defense of his rights and the exertion of his utmost learning and ability,' to the end that nothing be taken or be withheld from him, save by the rules of law, legally applied." This statement has, historically, capsulated the prevailing philosophy of legal practice in America. There are, doubtless, an abundance of lawyers steeped in this tradition who will look upon my plea for lawyers' liberation with incredulity, and even contempt. This tradition, with its professional shackles that constrain and keep lawyers from asserting their

---

Original essay included by permission of the author.

moral autonomy, has offered much resistance. In this paper, I will argue against this tradition.

AUTONOMY AND CODES OF ETHICS

Codes of ethics of lawyers have traditionally emphasized respect for *client* autonomy. Thus, according to EC 7-6 of the 1969 ABA *Code of Professional Responsibility*,

> In certain areas of legal representation not affecting the merits of the cause or substantially prejudicing the rights of a client, a lawyer is entitled to make decisions on his own. But otherwise the authority to make decisions is *exclusively* that of the client and if made within the framework of the law, such decisions are binding on his lawyer. [my italics].

Distinguishing between means and ends of legal representation, the Comment of *Rule* 1.2 of the 2009 ABA *Model Rules of Professional Conduct*[1] states that

> Paragraph (a) confers upon the client the *ultimate authority* to determine the purposes to be served by legal representation, within the limits imposed by law and the lawyer's professional obligations …With respect to the means by which the client's objectives are to be pursued, the lawyer shall consult with the client as required by *Rule* 1.4(a)(2) and may take such action as is impliedly authorized to carry out the representation. [my italics]

On the other hand, where the lawyer and client disagree on the means to be used to attain a legal end, this *Rule* is less definitive:

> Because of the varied nature of the matters about which a lawyer and client might disagree and because the actions in question may implicate the interests of a tribunal or other persons, *this Rule does not pre-*

scribe how such disagreements are to be resolved. Other law, however, may be applicable and should be consulted by the lawyer. The lawyer should also consult with the client and seek a mutually acceptable resolution of the disagreement. If such efforts are unavailing and the lawyer has a *fundamental disagreement* with the client, the lawyer may withdraw from the representation. See *Rule* 1.16(b)(4). Conversely, the client may resolve the disagreement by discharging the lawyer. *See Rule* 1.16(a)(3). [my italics]

Thus, there seems to be room for a lawyer's exercise of her own judgment in determining the means to client-determined legal ends. If there is a "fundamental disagreement," then the lawyer has the option of withdrawing. According to *Rule* 1.16(b)(4) referenced above, a lawyer *may* withdraw if "the client insists on taking action that the lawyer considers *repugnant* or with which the lawyer has a *fundamental disagreement*" [my italics].

By "fundamental disagreement," *Rule* 1.16(b)(4) presumably also refers to disagreement as to what means best conduce to the ends the client has decided to pursue. What is less clear is what is implied by the term "repugnant."

This term resurfaces in *Rule* 6.2(c) on public service acceptance of appointments as well as in its Comment, which states:

> "A lawyer ordinarily is not obliged to accept a client whose character or cause the lawyer regards as *repugnant* . . ."
>
> For good cause a lawyer may seek to decline an appointment to represent a person who cannot afford to retain counsel or whose cause is unpopular. Good cause exists ... if undertaking the representation would result in an improper conflict of interest, for example, when the client or the cause is so *repugnant* to the lawyer *as to be likely to impair the client-lawyer relationship or the lawyer's ability to represent the client.*[my italics]

The use of the term "repugnant" there seems to refer to character or cause of a client the lawyer deems to be morally unacceptable or inappropriate. But notice that it is not the lawyer's moral judgment that, in itself, constitutes good cause for declining an appointment to represent a client. Instead, it is the lawyer's inability to effectively represent the client, *as a result of this judgment*, that constitutes "good cause" for withdrawal. The fact that the lawyer considers what the client is trying to do immoral has no *intrinsic* merit. If such a lawyer could put his morals to the side, and put on a zealous representation of the client's legal interests, then the moral judgment in itself would not be a "good cause" to decline the appointment.

In contrast, what I want to argue is that the lawyer's moral judgment should matter; that lawyers should be encouraged to function as morally autonomous agents and not as mere conduits of clients. In the current system, it is the client who has "ultimate authority to determine the purposes of counseling" while the lawyer only retains autonomy to disagree with the client over what means best conduce to those purposes. This latter sort of autonomy, however, is not *moral* autonomy.

As I use the term, a lawyer exercises moral autonomy if she does her *own* moral reasoning—that is, comes to her decisions about moral issues by applying moral principles (to a given fact situation), and then, in turn, *acts* upon her considered judgment. The kind of discretion involved in this notion would include weighing and balancing conflicting moral principles, as, for example, when keeping a confidence is likely to cause serious third party harm. Such autonomy requires seeing these competing ethical principles as giving rise to *prima facie* duties wherein a lawyer's determination of her absolute duty is a function of the facts presented within the given situation.

The sort of autonomy afforded by the said ABA *Rules* does *not* grant a lawyer the power to do her own moral reasoning; she does not weigh and balance *prima facie* moral principles to determine her duty. Instead, she has but one primary (absolute) duty to further the client's legal interests within the bounds of the law. On this understanding, a lawyer can be said to exercise discretion in "determining the means by which a matter should be pursued" insofar as she exercises judgment in determining which means will, within legal limits, best advance the client's legal interests. But this is reasoning about cause and effect, not about morality. The "should" in the "should be pursued" is here a hypothetical imperative, not a categorical one. It states that, if you want to attain effect *y* then you should do *x*. This need carry no more moral implication than, "If you want to poison someone, then you should use a lethal dosage." This says nothing about the moral propriety of the end sought or of the means used to achieve it.

On the other hand, the Preamble of the *Model Rules* recognizes that, in order to resolve their difficult ethical problems, lawyers must exercise "moral judgment guided by the basic principles underlying the *Rules*."[2] The Preamble further states,

> ... The Rules do not, however, exhaust the *moral and ethical considerations* that should inform a lawyer, for no worthwhile human activity can be completely defined by legal rules. The Rules simply provide a framework for the ethical practice of law. [my italics][3]

Notice the explicit reference here to "moral considerations," "basic principles," and "moral judgment." If the ABA is to do more than pay lip service to the exercise of moral discretion in legal practice, then the bounds of discretion explicitly granted by the ABA *Model Rules* need to be broadened to include moral discretion in its own right, and the moral considerations or principles "not exhausted" by these rules need to be identified. Otherwise, the discretion alluded to in the Preamble is likely, in practice, to be restricted to what ultimately conduces to the interest of the client.

RULES, PRINCIPLES, AND REAL MORAL AUTONOMY

What can the ABA be taken to mean when it states that the *Rules* "do not exhaust the moral and ethical considerations that should inform a lawyer?" A suitable answer to this question appears to me to lie in the distinction, introduced by Ronald Dworkin, between a rule and a principle.[4] According to Dworkin, legal rules apply in an "all-or-nothing fashion." If the fact conditions that are stated in the rule's antecedent are true, then the rule *ipso facto* applies and its consequent must be accepted. It is, in other words, a logical deduction from the rule to the decision. If the rule's antecedent is not satisfied by the existing facts, then the rule does not apply and does not settle the case. For example, *Rule* 5.4(b) states that, "A lawyer shall not form a partnership with a non-lawyer if any of the activities of the partnership consist of the practice of law." If a lawyer is in partnership with a nonlawyer in the practice of law, then the unlawfulness of the partnership is, *ipso facto*, settled.

Rules can also include a finite range of explicit exceptions.[5] For example, 5.4(a) forbids a lawyer from sharing legal fees with a nonlawyer but makes explicit particular exceptions, which include complying with an agreement to make payments to a deceased lawyer's estate.

In contrast, legal principles do not apply in an all-or-nothing fashion and their range of exceptions is not finite and completely speci-fiable.[6] As an example of such a principle, Dworkin gives, "No person should be permitted to profit from his own wrongdoing," which was used by a New York court in 1889 in *Riggs v. Palmer* to prevent a grandson from collecting an inheritance from his grandfather after killing him to get it.[7]

Unlike rules, legal principles also have "weights" and one principle can outweigh another.[8] In this regard, they are *prima facie* in character. They apply, *ceteris paribus*, where this rider is not fully specifiable.

Further, according to Dworkin, some rules, which use terms like "reasonable," "negligent," "unjust," and "significant" are, to some extent, dependent upon principles that go beyond the rule.[9] For example, a legal rule, which proscribed "unreasonable" contracts, would require additional judgment in order to apply it. Or, for example, ABA *Rule* 3.2, which prescribes that "A lawyer shall make reasonable efforts to expedite litigation consistent with the interests of the client" would require additional criteria in order to decide what might consti-tute "reasonable effort" in a given situation.[10]

Another property of rules that can also provide occasion for additional judgment and discretion is afforded by the commonplace distinction between permissive rules and requirements. Whereas the latter prescribes what *must* be, the former neither requires nor forbids anything. For example, according to ABA *Rule* 3.3(a)(3), "A lawyer shall not knowingly offer evidence that the lawyer knows to be false." This is a requirement and there is no room for discretion. On the other hand, 6.1(b)(3) allows that, "A lawyer may reveal information relating to the representation of a client to the extent the lawyer believes necessary to establish a claim or defense on behalf of the lawyer in a controversy between the lawyer and the client." Here, there may be room for exercise of discretion (or judgment) as when a lawyer is faced with a decision whether or not to press for the collection of a fee.

The upshot here is that, in the aforementioned areas of discretion permitted by rules, an appeal to moral principles *in their own right* (and not merely as an unfortunate distraction from the primary duty of advancing clients' legal interests) is not only desirable, it should be part of what lawyers are expected to do. Similarly, where *Rule* 1.2 leaves open the basis of "fundamental disagreement" about the use of means to client's legal ends, lawyers should be encouraged to exercise such *intrinsic* moral judgment. And where lawyers find client's causes "morally repugnant" they should permit themselves to opt out on the moral issue, not merely on their ineffectiveness in advancing the cause in question.

As the Preamble of the *Model Rules* rightly recognizes, the rules "simply provide a framework for the practice of law." Within this framework, there is room for genuine moral discretion—"moral judgment guided by the basic [moral] principles underlying the Rules."

In my paper on "Pure Legal Advocates and Moral Agents: Two Concepts of Lawyer in an Adversary System,"[11] I provided a list of moral principles which I argued were fundamental to the moral practice of law. Within the latitude of discretion afforded by bar rules, the following *principles* can be important "moral considerations":[12]

- Treat others as ends in themselves and not as mere means to winning cases (Individual Justice).

- Treat clients and other persons affected by one's professional acts who are *relevantly* similar in a similar fashion (Distributive Justice).
- Do not deliberately engage in behavior apt to deceive the court as to the truth (Truthfulness).
- Be willing, if necessary, to make reasonable personal sacrifices— of time, money, popularity, and so on—for what you justifiably believe to be a morally good cause (Moral Courage).
- Do not give money to, or accept money from, clients for wrongful purposes or in wrongful amounts (Money Management).
- Avoid harming others in the process of representing your client (Nonmaleficence).
- Keep your commitments to your client, and do not betray his confidences (Trustworthiness).
- Make your own moral decisions to the best of your ability and act consistently upon them (Moral Autonomy).

The last of the above principles, that of Moral Autonomy, tells lawyers to follow their own ethical lights—to stand on principle— rather than to permit *themselves* to be reduced to *mere* means. In this respect, it is related to the first principle, that of Individual Justice. Whereas the latter prescribes treating *others* as ends and not as mere means, the former instructs lawyers to treat themselves the same.[13]

As principles, rather than rules, these moral considerations do not mechanically apply as a matter of deductive logic. Two or more of these principles can be in conflict in a given situation. For example, Truthfulness and Nonmaleficience can conflict with Trustworthiness when a lawyer learns in confidence from a client that evidence damaging to a third party but potentially favorable to the client is probably false.

Suppose the lawyer is representing a client to help him obtain custody of his six-year-old son, presently in the custody of the child's mother. Suppose the lawyer attains reasonable belief from discussions with his client, that the client is sexually attracted to children. Say the client admits enjoying child pornography depicting little boys, downloads it frequently from the Internet, but stops short of saying that he has sexually molested his own son. Suppose also that, as a result of such reasonable belief, the lawyer now also has reasonable belief that allegations of sexual abuse of the child, which had previously been investigated by the Department of Children and Families and deemed to be unfounded, were probably true; and that the timely complaint of the child that "Daddy touches my private parts" was also probably true; and not really the result of the mother's having coached the child—as the client consistently maintained. Suppose finally that the lawyer now has reasonable belief that evidence purporting to establish that the mother has been coaching the child to accuse the father of child abuse (for instance, the client's prospective testimony that his wife threatened to destroy him by fabricating sexual abuse) is probably false.

According to *Rule* 3.3(a)(3), "a lawyer shall not knowingly offer evidence that the lawyer *knows* to be false." On the other hand, "a lawyer may refuse [but is not required to refuse] to offer evidence ... that the lawyer *reasonably believes* is false." Insofar as the lawyer only has *reasonable belief* but not knowledge that the evidence in question is false, should the lawyer attempt to use it to establish that the mother has been coaching the child?

Conventional lawyer's wisdom would dictate that the lawyer present the evidence and let the adversarial process grind out its just verdict. It is, after all, up to the judge to decide the case, not the lawyer. The lawyer is an advocate, and not a judge. However, this is to ignore the Preamble of the Model rules, which recognizes lawyers' *moral* discretion. If this discretion is real and not merely apparent, the lawyer in such a case should go beyond the conventional model of legal practice to give substance to moral discretion by appealing to the relevant moral principles.

In this context, it is reasonable to argue that the Principle of Nonmaleficience (regarding harm to the child) and the Principle of Truthfulness (regarding honesty to the court) militate against presenting the evidence in question; and that these principles together *outweigh* the Principle of Trustworthiness (regarding client confidentiality and trust). Such a conclusion acted upon by the lawyer would provide a genuine example of lawyers' moral autonomy. It would be the act of a lawyer liberated from the shackles of being a "mere means." Yet it would arguably be autonomy exercised consistent with the requirements of bar rules. In fact, according to *Rule* 1.16(b)(4), it is (or should be) permissible for the lawyer to withdraw from the case if the client insists on presenting the evidence in question or otherwise "insists on taking action that the lawyer considers repugnant or with which the lawyer has a fundamental disagreement."

Thus, in light of the client's revelations about his sexual activities, it would also be permissible for such a lawyer to reassess the cause of helping such a parent obtain custody of his child. The lawyer could, within the latitude afforded by *Rule* 1.16(b)(4), invoke the principle of Nonmaleficience (and not merely his inability to do an effective job in representing the client) as an overriding *moral* basis for refusing to continue to represent the client.[14]

The client could get another lawyer to represent him. In this case, the client could withhold his sexual proclivities and activities from the new lawyer and eventually even gain custody of the child. Lawyers' liberation does not guarantee that clients will not successfully use the system to work moral iniquities. Nevertheless, if lawyers were generally guided by moral principles in the areas of discretion afforded by bar rules, and not by the conventional wisdom of amoral, zealous representation, it is unlikely that clients would get quite as much assistance from their attorneys in working misdeeds as they do at present. Further, lawyers would not have become accessories or "mere means" in the commission of such acts, which itself has considerable (intrinsic) moral worth.

SOME ARGUMENTS AGAINST LAWYERS' LIBERATION

It is sometimes suggested that encouraging lawyers to exercise moral autonomy would "reduce the ability of lawyers to prevent the oppression and exploitation of the powerless by the powerful."[15] Indeed, the arm of the law can be a formidable one for the poor defendant accused of a crime. Such individuals, it is argued, are best served when lawyers single-mindedly defend their clients zealously within the bounds of law.

This suggestion trades upon the assumption that morally autonomous lawyers are more likely to oppress and exploit those already oppressed and exploited. But is it true that a lawyer, who exercises moral discretion in the area of legal uncertainty, will act to undermine the very principles upon which she stands? The reverse may be more often the case than not. The lawyer who attains an acquittal for a psychopathic, persistent rapist by wittingly humiliating the truthful rape complainant; the lawyer who helps the wealthy, influential child abuser to gain custody of his child by casting aspersions on a protective mother; the corporate lawyer who helps a corporate client to persist in the manufacture of products that endanger thousands of lives; and the patent lawyer who helps a multinational corporation to "get around" a small inventor's rightful patent are instances of "oppression and exploitation of the powerless by the powerful." These miscarriages of justice arise when lawyers are compliant with a system that prescribes zealous defense of clients' legal interests without encouraging moral discretion. Such a system has serious potential for oppression and exploitation of the weaker, more vulnerable members of society.

A further objection to encouraging lawyers' exercise of moral autonomy lies in the view that moral principles and the value judgments derived from them are too subjective and variable to serve as reliable decisional bases.[16] What one lawyer might take to be morally compelling, another might dismiss as false. Accordingly, objectivity in legal representation would be jeopardized if lawyers were inclined toward exercising moral discretion. On the other hand, when lawyers are guided by bar rules, and a consistent regard for furthering clients' legal interests within the bounds of law, objective and reliable representation will prevail.

This argument might also be made, *mutatis mutandis*, against judges who invoke legal principles in cases that are not covered by legal rules. Inasmuch as legal principles are themselves moral principles, it would be hard to see how they could provide reliable standards for judges but not for lawyers. This is not to confuse the distinct roles of these authorities.

The present question is whether moral discretion is too subjective to be serviceable, not whether one official's use of it is more just than another.

Further, like legal reasoning, moral reasoning can attain greater rigor if guided by precedent. Lawyers are accustomed to arguing cases based on precedents established by prior legal decisions. It is feasible for lawyers to set precedents for other lawyers to follow in the weighing and balancing of moral principles. In addition to ethics opinions recorded by national, state, and local ethics committees and courts, it is also possible to establish legal resources that promulgate carefully constructed moral arguments advanced by lawyers in the exercise of moral discretion in their practices. These decisions could serve a similar function for lawyers in exercising their moral discretion, as do legal precedents in helping lawyers to develop cogent and convincing legal arguments.

Unfortunately, the failure to recognize lawyers' moral autonomy and the salient tradition of vehemently rejecting such a mode of practice may, arguably, have prevented serious consideration and development of such criteria. Lawyers' liberation would seek to remedy this deficit by recognizing moral reasoning as an integral part of what lawyers do in their professional practices.

It is sometimes argued that encouraging lawyers' moral autonomy would usurp the role of the judge. For example, Monroe Freedom quotes Samuel Johnson's famous expression of this argument:

> A lawyer has no business with the justice or injustice of the cause, which he undertakes, unless his client asks his opinion, and then he is bound to give it honestly. The justice or injustice of the cause which he undertakes is to be decided by the judge . . . If lawyers were to undertake no cause till they were sure they were just, a man might be precluded altogether from a trial of his claim, though, were it judicially examined, it might be found a very just claim.[17]

"No business with the justice or injustice of the cause?" Such lawyers would, like hired assassins, be required to submerge their humanity beneath a professional mask. I have argued elsewhere[18] that this mask is likely to become indelible, eventually becoming part of the lawyer's character, with habituation toward working misdeeds. On this view, the morally good person would have no reason to aspire to, and strong reason against, becoming an attorney.

Notice the categorical language in which this argument is cast: "If lawyers were to undertake *no* cause till they were *sure* they were just." Realistically, a liberated lawyer would not demand certainty about the justice of any cause before undertaking it. There is a difference between having reasonable assurance that a cause does not go against a basic moral principle and being sure that the cause is just. The latter is not even within the province of a judge or jury who must decide guilt not with certitude but at most avoiding reasonable doubt. In other words, this argument is a straw man.

A lawyer's moral autonomy is not absolute. Instead, it is circumscribed by bar rules. The argument that lawyers would usurp the role of the judge if afforded moral discretion would be as absurd as arguing that, because judges exercise moral discretion, they risk usurping the rule of law. The slide down this slippery slope need not occur where moral discretion is practiced within the parameters set by bar rules. On the other hand, arguing that lawyers can satisfactorily do without the exercise of moral discretion is to treat legal practice as though it were mechanical. This is the same fallacy as demanding that judges and juries stick to the rules without exercising moral discretion. As the Preamble of the *Model Rules* recognizes, legal practice is a human activity and "no worthwhile human activity can be completely defined by legal rules."[19] Exercise of moral judgment is inevitable. It should be cultivated in legal practice and education, and carefully studied.

SOME RECENT PROGRESS TOWARD LIBERATION

Lawyers' Liberation has made some codified inroads. One such change is in the 2002 revision of ABA *Model Rule* 1.6 on Confidentiality of Information. According to 1.6(b)(1), "a lawyer may reveal information related to the representation of a client to the extent the lawyer believes necessary to prevent reasonably certain death or substantial bodily harm." Previously, the rule had been restricted to imminent death or substantial bodily harm resulting from the commission of a *criminal* act. For example, this broader latitude for discretion empowers lawyers to weigh harm to others against client confidentiality when a client has accidentally discharged waste into a municipal water supply; or to disclose confidential information in order to prevent a state's execution of an innocent person. Such discretion represents *intrinsic* moral regard, not mere deference to the best interests of clients.

There has already been some progress toward including more emphasis on moral principles in legal education. For example, in 1997, the Florida Supreme Court amended continuing legal education (CLE) requirements to include five hours in legal ethics, professionalism, or substance abuse. According to the Florida Bar's Center for Professionalism, a salient distinction can be made between bar rules and professionalism:

> Truly ethical people measure their conduct not by rules but by basic moral principles such as honesty, integrity, and fairness. . . Professionalism discussions are too often framed as simple issues of rule-following or rule-violation. But the real issue facing lawyers as professionals is developing the capacity for critical and reflective judgment.[20]

Such capacity for "critical and reflective judgment" in the weighing and balancing of basic moral principles, within parameters set by bar rules, should be unequivocally recognized by the ABA in its code of ethics and standards of professionalism. Precedent should be set and promulgated to guide lawyers in the exercise of their moral discretion. Instead of indoctrinating lawyers into a culture of amoral representation, legal educators should scrupulously encourage and instruct prospective lawyers in autonomously, courageously, and responsibly confronting the inherent and unavoidable moral dimension of legal practice.

LAWYERS AS WILLING SLAVES: A MAJOR HURDLE FOR LIBERATION

All or most fruitful liberation movements have, in their histories, been opposed en masse with great fervor in part by those standing to benefit. For example, women's liberation in America met with strong resistance from the women oppressed as well as from their oppressors. Thus, Mill, in his famous treatise on the *Subjection of Women*, referred to the socialization women receive at the hands of an oppressive, patriarchal society as a kind of "willing slavery" in which the minds as well as the bodies of women are enslaved.[21] So, it was once considered an abomination for a woman to express herself as an independent, autonomous person, and this tradition has unfortunately still not been fully dislodged.

While I do not wish to overwork this analogy, the current state of professional servitude of lawyers to their clients bears some resemblance to such "willing slavery" in that lawyers are expected to *want* to relinquish their moral principles in zealously serving clients' legal interests. A lawyer who fails to meet this professional expectation is, like the noncompliant, "shrewish" woman, a social outcast. Further, the tenacity with which those socialized into this legal culture defend their amoral tradition has sometimes reached a pitch of antagonism not unlike that with which women's liberation has once—and for some, still is—denounced. As in the latter, the ferocity of the dissent may be inversely proportional to the likelihood of the dangers it seeks to prevent.[22]

CONCLUSION

Thus there is little wonder why the progress of lawyers' liberation has been slow. Like all legal reform, the success of this movement may ultimately depend on morally liberated lawyers with courage to challenge the prevailing tradition.

As I have suggested, while the *Model Rules*, in its present form, *can*, in principle, accommodate lawyers' moral judgment within the scope of its permissive bar rules and flexible language, the Comments annexed to these rules, which interpret them, tend to reflect a well entrenched tradition of legal practice which relegates moral considerations to impediments to zealous representation of clients' legal interests, and which treats non-moral deliberations about means-to-clients'-legal-ends as the primary locus of lawyers' autonomy.

On the other hand, what lawyers' liberation enjoins is consistent acknowledgment of the *intrinsic* merits of appealing *to moral* principles in the exercise of discretion. For example, instead of relegating the "repugnance" of a client's cause to an impediment to a legal defense, the Comment to 6.2(c) might state that lawyers have discretion to decline representing persons whose causes transgress basic moral principles. In such contexts, pertinent moral principles, such as those listed in this paper, should be identified. As discussed, resources should be developed that establish guidelines for identifying and weighing competing moral principles. Insofar as law schools define the culture of legal practice, legal education should include training in the exercise of moral judgment. With these changes will dawn a new culture of law in which legal practice is no longer severed from its moral roots.

NOTES

1. All subsequent references in this paper to bar rules are to ABA, *Model Rules of Professional Conduct* (2009) at http://www.abanet.org/cpr/mrpc/mrpc_toc.html.

2. Ibid., Preamble at ¶9.

3. Ibid., Preamble at ¶16.

4. Ronald Dworkin, "Taking Rights Seriously," in *The Philosophy of Law*, ed. Frederick Schauer and Walter Sinnott-Armstrong (1996), p. 76.

5. Ibid.

6. Ibid., pp. 76–77.

7. Ibid., p. 75.

8. Ibid., p. 78.

9. Ronald M. Dworkin, "The Model of Rules," in *Philosophy of Law*, ed. Joel Feinberg and Hyman Gross (1975), p. 82.

10. Nevertheless, Dworkin maintains that such principle-like rules are not themselves principles because, unlike principles, they could not be disregarded without having to change the law. In addition, rules are enacted whereas principles are not. Thus, the principle that "no one should be able to profit from his own wrong doings" was not enacted in 1889 when it was applied in *Riggs*, or at any time prior. On the other hand, the *Rules* providing for inherence were so enacted. Ibid., p. 82.

11. Elliot D. Cohen, "Pure Legal Advocates and Moral Agents: Two Concepts of a Lawyer in an Adversary System," *Criminal Justice Ethics* 1, no. 4 (1985): 38–59.

12. Ibid., p. 46.

13. These principles are effectually lawyers' versions of Kant's famous "Categorical Imperative." See generally Immanuel Kant, "The Categorical Imperative," in *Philosophers at Work: Issues and Practice of Philosophy*, ed. Elliot D. Cohen (2000) pp. 46–47.

14. While the cause in this case may be legal, it would still be immoral for the lawyer to assist the client in pursuing it. In this sense, a client should not, contrary to *Rule* 1.2, have "ultimate authority" over what legal remedies provided by the law to pursue.

15. John M. Memory and Charles H. Rose III, "The Attorney as Moral Agent: A Critique of Cohen," *Criminal Justice Ethics* 1, no. 21 (2002): 31.

16. Ibid., p. 34.

17. Monroe Freedman, *Lawyers' Ethics in an Adversary System* (1975), p. 51.

18. Cohen, "Pure Legal Advocates and Moral Agents."

19. ABA, Preamble at ¶16.

20. Florida Bar, CLE Guidelines at http://www.floridabar.org/tfb/TFB Profess.nsf/840090c16eedaf0085256b61000928dc/72e302f839a78f9d85256b2f 006ccdc1?OpenDocument.

21. John Stuart Mill, "The Subjection of Women," in *Philosophers at Work*, pp. 142–54.

22. See, for example, Memory and Rose, "The Attorney as Moral Agent," p. 28. Because my paper, "Pure legal Advocates and Moral Agents," was still being "frequently anthologized" even though it was originally published in 1985, these two lawyers stridently attacked it in 2003.

PROBLEM SET III

A DELAY THAT MAY KILL

Your clients are the parents of a child critically injured in an accident two days ago. The child needs an operation to live and blood transfusions to survive the operation. Your clients refused to authorize the transfusions because, according to their religion, taking the blood of another for any purpose is a grave sin. To use the blood of another is, they believe, to be damned. They refused the transfusions at the risk of their child's "earthly life" in order to save his "eternal life." That, anyway, is what they believe they are doing.

When you took the case yesterday, the child was in stable condition. The hospital had already filed a neglect petition. You had only to appear in court, ask for the statutory three-day delay, and set about preparing your case. The decision to give the transfusions or let the child die was to be the judge's, not yours. She would have the time she needed to make it. Your only responsibility was to present your clients' side. Everything was just as it should be.

Then, about 4:30 this afternoon, you received a call from opposing counsel. The child's condition was no longer stable. The doctors now believed that the child would be dead by tomorrow morning if he could not have the operation tonight. The child still could not be operated on without a blood transfusion. In two days there would be nothing for the hearing to decide. Opposing counsel wanted to know whether you would agree to move up the hearing to 5:00 this afternoon. He had found a judge who was willing to stay late.

You know the judge to be fair. You have just finished your preparations (except for a bit of double-checking) and so are just about as ready as you will be. Should you agree to move up the hearing date? Should you consult your clients or at least inform them of your intentions? If you do inform them, they may very well refuse the change of day. After all, if they refuse, their son will die but go to heaven. If they agree, he may survive and be damned. What should you do? Why?

You are now and always have been in favor of freedom of religion. You consider the present case to raise important questions and you believe your clients to have a good case, though you expect them to lose. You took the case because you thought they deserved to have their day in court.

THE SEX JACKET

It is your third year in practice as well as your third year working for the respected criminal-defense firm of Backpeddle, Backslyde, and Skemer. You are assisting Skemer in preparing an armed-robbery case for trial. The facts make it appear that the defense will have a hard time of it at trial:

Two females were involved in the robbery of a grocery store: your client, Jennifer McKinney, and Denise Tannery who is not your client. One of the females waited in the car; the other entered the store (wearing a bright yellow jacket with "sex" emblazoned in large black letters on the back), held up the grocer, ran back to the car, which was parked just down the street from the store (its motor running), and jumped in. The grocer followed the robber far enough to see the car, noted that there were two people in it, took down the license plate number, and immediately reported all he knew to the police.

The two occupants of the car were arrested on Jackson Boulevard about five minutes later "while fleeing south at about fifteen miles above the speed limit." In the car, the police found both a gun like that used in the robbery and the stolen money. At the time of arrest, Jennifer (your client) was sitting in the passenger's seat wearing the yellow jacket. Denise was in the driver's seat wearing a dark blue jacket. Jennifer, eighteen years old, was charged with armed robbery (an offence carrying a sentence of up to thirty years imprisonment). Denise, seventeen years old, was charged as an accomplice (an offence carrying a much lighter sentence). Jennifer was charged as an adult; Denise, as a juvenile. And, for that reason, Jennifer is to be tried alone.

Jennifer and Denise look enough alike to fool friends and relatives.

And, as teenage girls often do, they regularly wear each other's clothing. Neither has been arrested before.

During preparation for trial, this exchange occurred between Jennifer and attorney Skemer in his office with only the three of you present:

S: You claim you didn't do the job. You just went along for the ride. But the robber wore a "sex" jacket. Weren't you wearing such a jacket at the time of the arrest?

J: Yah. But I didn't wear it during the robbery. Denise did. We swopped jackets in the car as we drove down Jackson Boulevard.

S: No jury is going to believe that you managed to take off your jacket; Denise managed to take off hers; and that you exchanged jackets—Denise put on your jacket and you put on hers—all that with her driving down Jackson at fifty miles an hour! Now, if you had exchanged jackets before you pulled away from the curb, or while you waited at a stop light, or after the police pulled you over—then you might have a chance.

J: Oh, that's right. We swopped when Denise got into the car. She tore off the jacket as she got in, and said "Here, give me yours," which I did. It was her jacket anyway.

Is Skemer doing anything unethical? What would you do if he were? What part in your decision would be played by the *Model Rules*, by your general conception of professional responsibility, by moral considerations, and by prudence?

THE HELPLESS WITNESS

What should I do? I am a legal-aid attorney. My client, Bernie, was holding a gun when it went off and killed Alfie. There was just one witness, Carl. Both Bernie and Carl are juveniles. Bernie has not told the police anything about Carl and does not want Carl to get into trouble. Bernie has not yet been charged with any offense but is likely to be charged with delinquency (for having the gun) or homicide (manslaughter). Bernie admitted to the police that he was holding the gun when it went off but claimed the discharge was accidental. Bernie's statement may or may not be admissible in evidence against him. Carl could confirm Bernie's story or, by telling quite a different story, could make it possible to prosecute Bernie successfully. I believe (1) that I need to talk to Carl to prepare the case properly (2) that my connection with legal-aid would lead Carl and his parents to want to cooperate fully (unless I give full warning of the possible consequences) and (3) that, if what Bernie tells me is true, Carl could be charged in Juvenile court once he has testified on Bernie's behalf. (Just to put him at the site would, under the circumstances, probably constitute delinquency.)

SUGGESTED READINGS

Arthur Isak Applbaum, *Ethics for Adversaries* (Princeton, NJ: Princeton University Press, 2000).

Ronald Dworkin, "The Model of Rules," in *Taking Rights Seriously* (Cambridge, MA: Harvard University Press, 1977), chapter 2.

Marvin E. Frankel, "The Search for Truth: An Umpireal View," *University of Pennsylvania Law Review* 5, no. 123 (May 1975): 1060–66.

Monroe H. Freedman, *Lawyers' Ethics in an Adversary System* (Indianapolis: Bobbs-Merrill, 1975).

David Luban, "The Adversary System Excuse," in *Legal Ethics and Human Dignity* (Cambridge, MA: Cambridge University Press, 2007), chapter 1.

John T. Noonan Jr., "The Purposes of Advocacy and the Limits of Confidentiality," *Michigan Law Review* 8, no. 64 (June 1966): 1485–92.

PART IV:
CONFLICT OF INTEREST AND PROFESSIONAL JUDGMENT

INTRODUCTION TO
PART IV

The lawyer's role has built into it certain enduring tensions. The lawyer is, for example, supposed to be both "a zealous advocate" and "an officer of the court," to perform a public service and to serve a private client, to be relatively neutral concerning the client's ends and yet scrupulously moral concerning the means employed to achieve those ends. *The Model Rules of Professional Conduct* are certainly right to observe in the Preamble that "virtually all difficult ethical problems arise from conflict between a lawyer's responsibilities to clients, legal system, and to the lawyer's own interest in remaining an upright person while earning a satisfactory living." The first three sections of this book provided a framework for discussion of these general tensions. This section begins our discussion of particular problems.

We may be tempted to think of *all* the enduring tensions built into the lawyer's role as "conflicts of interest." Like most temptations, this one is better resisted. The more uses a term has, the less useful it is. "Conflict of interest" can be a very useful term but only if its use is limited to circumstances over which lawyers have some control. For lawyers, one has a conflict of interest when the circumstances in which one is called upon to exercise professional judgment tend to undermine the ability to exercise that judgment properly on behalf of clients (without making the lawyer's judgment incompetent). One's judgment, though still competent, is no longer "independent." Conflict of interest is a tension within the lawyer's role that is not supposed to be there. A conflict of interest is a threat to *ordinary* legal judgment.

Lawyers usually try to avoid conflict of interest. They sometimes fail. When a lawyer finds herself with a conflict, she may have three options. Some conflicts can be resolved simply by informing the client and giving him the opportunity to change lawyers or to change the terms of employment. This sort of resolution is often described as "consent after full disclosure." Some conflicts can be resolved only by withdrawing from the representation in question. Disclosure is not enough.

A few conflicts cannot be resolved at all. The lawyer may be unable to resolve the conflict by disclosure because the disclosure itself would require revealing something she should not reveal: for example, the confidences of another client. The lawyer may also be unable to withdraw without serious harm to the client's interests. Such a conflict of interest can only be "managed" (with risks both to the client's interests and the lawyer's integrity).

Conflicts of interest may be actual or potential. In an actual conflict of interest, the lawyer has a conflict of interest affecting a judgment he must make now. In a potential conflict of interest, the judgment in question is likely to have to be made but not immediately. Lawyers do not view potential conflicts of interest with the same trepidation with which they view actual ones—or all potential conflicts of interest with equal trepidation. A lawyer asked to represent codefendants in a criminal case will usually refuse unless there is some special reason for the joint representation (for example, the informed desire of all defendants to coordinate a political defense). When asked to advise a couple in an amicable divorce involving little property and no children, a lawyer often accepts, thinking that saving the couple money outweighs any potential conflict of interest. The lawyer is willing to risk the further breakdown in the couple's relationship that would make them adversaries, and leave him unable to serve either. But an attorney who has been invited to serve on the board of directors of a client corporation will ordinarily jump at the chance even though board membership means that he will have to be both active participant in deciding corporate policy and a detached judge of related legal matters.

Kenneth Kipnis is concerned to know what makes conflicts of interest "ethically interesting." He distinguishes two sorts of conflicts of interest: a) "conflict of obligation" (what others sometimes call "conflict of commitment") and b) "conflict of interest" proper. A conflict of obligation occurs when someone cannot satisfy one obligation without failing to satisfy another. The lawyer who is asked to represent codefendants in a criminal case may, for example, find that he cannot win acquittal for one defendant without implicating another. Unable to be loyal to both at once, he must give up representation of at least one. In contrast, a conflict of interest (proper) occurs when someone has an interest that he cannot satisfy without failing to satisfy obligations to those he is supposed to serve. His interest conflicts with his role. Thus, a lawyer who is asked to draft a will naming himself chief beneficiary suddenly has a pecuniary interest in drafting the will, an interest that is inconsistent with, for example, reminding the client of various alternative distributions. This second sort of conflict of interest might better be called "a conflicting interest."

Morally, this distinction between conflicts of obligations and conflicting interests does not seem important. Both are objectionable for much the same reason. For Kipnis, what is wrong with a conflict of obligation is that the lawyer involved is put into circumstances where he must betray the justified trust of a client, or at least appear to betray it. What is wrong with having a conflict of interest is that loyalty to one's client includes both exercising independent professional judgment on the client's behalf *and* giving the client no reason to believe the lawyer will do otherwise. A conflict of interest gives the client good reason to doubt the reliability of the lawyer's judgment whether or not the lawyer's judgment is in fact affected. While having a conflict of interest is not itself morally wrong, acting in a situation of conflict is wrong insofar as it betrays, or at least seems to betray, the client's proper reliance on the lawyer's judgment.

Kipnis's analysis seems to explain why certain conflicts can be resolved by disclosure while others must be resolved by withdrawal from representation. Under some circumstances, informed consent after disclosure redefines the lawyer-client relationship enough so that there is no longer a risk of betrayal (or the appearance of any). Under other circumstances, however, informed consent with disclosure is not enough to resolve the conflict because even informed consent cannot change the lawyer's obligations enough to eliminate risk of betrayal (or the appearance of it). A lawyer who is asked to advise a couple on their amicable divorce can, for example, define his relationship with them so they understand that he can help them only so long as they remain agreed and must withdraw as soon as there is a serious disagreement between them. He can manage the relation so that, in effect, they are a single client and thus avoid even the appearance of betrayal. But the lawyer who is asked to draft a will in which she is chief beneficiary cannot escape the appearance of betrayal ("overreaching"). However cautious her advice, the relation between lawyer and client is too intimate for any consent upon full disclosure to assure that the lawyer will avoid exercising undue influence upon the terms of the will. Even the lawyer herself is in no position to know that she has acted as she would have acted had she not had that conflict of interest.

Geoffrey Hazard connects Kipnis's discussion of conflicts of interest with preceding discussions of the adversarial style. Hazard's concern is that "lawyer for a situation" be a recognized role that lawyers can assume when necessary. A "lawyer for a situation" is a mediator or go-between, a common helper of parties who wish to cooperate even though they have (as people always do) at least potentially adverse interests. Though lawyers commonly call all that they do for a client "representing," being a lawyer for a situation does not look like representing. The lawyer does not "act for" either party, nor does he make either party "present" to the other. What the lawyer actually does is let the parties to the situation share his knowledge, skill, and judgment. For lawyers who are used to thinking in terms of "representing," "total loyalty," and "warm zeal" in defense of one client's interests against the rest of the world (that is, advocacy), lawyering for a situation seems strikingly like any other conflict of interest.

But, as Hazard points out, it looks that way only while we think of lawyering in adversarial terms. Once we stop looking at it that way, we can see that most American lawyers have in fact been doing such things for a century even though the bar's official policy seemed (and, to a substantial degree, still seems) to condemn it. Why then should lawyers not frankly permit themselves to be lawyers for a situation? Why indeed? Even Fuller and Randall (part III) seemed to allow for many roles in which lawyers act not as advocates but in what they identify as "non-adversarial roles."

David H. Taylor considers one such role, though one perhaps too close to traditional advocacy. Lawyers now help indigent clients in civil matters through organizations of lawyers, often state supported. For reasons of efficiency, most jurisdictions have only one such organization. Sometimes one lawyer in such an organization has a client whose interests are adverse to a client or former client of that organization. Under current ABA *Rules*, this situation is no different from that in which a private law firm (indeed, a single lawyer) stood in that relationship to the clients in question. While recognizing that there are good reasons for the general rule banning such conflict of interest, Taylor argues that there are reasons for making an exception for a non-profit practice serving indigent clients. In part, what justifies the exception is that the alternative seems to be no representation for some clients. This is a reason to "manage" the conflict. But, in part too, Taylor argues, the conflict is only apparent. Lawyers working in a public-assistance organization do not benefit financially from winning cases. Unlike lawyers in a private firm, they do not have a financial interest in their cases. They are therefore less likely to influence the judgment of other members of their firm.

Understanding conflict of interest helps us to see—argues Taylor in effect—that one of the traditional protections of the independence of a lawyer's judgment is not necessary here. How good a case has he made?

Ken Kipnis

CONFLICT of INTEREST AND CONFLICT of OBLIGATION

The term "conflict of interest" has its characteristic applications in settings in which formal responsibilities are assumed by individuals occupying certain more-or-less well-defined social roles. The notion is not well understood outside of the legal profession and inside of the legal profession it is probably not understood well enough. Part of the problem is that the expression itself is ambiguous, denoting at least two very different types of circumstance. Moreover, problems arising out of conflicts of interest are most easily understood in formal types of relationship, like those that obtain between lawyer and client. These have few counterparts in ordinary day-to-day life. Our purposes here will be twofold. First, we shall endeavor to distinguish among the different kinds of conflicts of interest. It is not only important for lawyers but for others as well—e.g., doctors, journalists, educators—to be sensitive to the possibility that they may be involved in a conflict of interest. For this reason our discussion in what follows will take examples, where possible, not only from law but from other areas as well. Second, we shall attempt—with respect to each of these types of con-

From *Legal Ethics* (Englewood Cliffs, NJ: Prentice-Hall, 1986), pp. 40–53. © 1986. Reprinted by permission of the author and of Prentice-Hall.

flict—to isolate what exactly makes the circumstance ethically interesting. Why should the ethically competent attorney be wary of conflict of interest? It is not enough to say, as many discussions of conflict of interest seem to, that you or your client may otherwise be sanctioned. That may be so, but one must still ask whether such penalties are deserved.

The two situations denoted by the term "conflict of interest" have very different ethical characteristics. Henceforth, we will use the term "conflict of obligation" to refer to the first type of situation and will reserve the term "conflict of interest" exclusively for the second type. It should be noted that there is a third concept of conflict of interest that has occasionally commanded the attention of philosophers. This type of conflict obtains whenever there are two interests such that the satisfaction of either precludes the satisfaction of the other. One person might want the air conditioner on and another might want the air conditioner off. Or a single person might want the air conditioner on but—equally—not want to have to pay a bigger electric bill. While it will be important at points to note conflicts falling under this concept—we can call them "interests that are in conflict"—this notion will not be a central topic of this chapter.

CONFLICTS OF OBLIGATION: ACTUAL AND POTENTIAL

Dexter, who used to box as a young man, has just started teaching his son and some other youngsters the elements of the sport. Working with heavily padded gloves, the boys have done well during practice sessions and seem to be ready for their first matches. With Dexter serving as referee, a bout begins with Dexter's son contending in the ring. Dexter tries to be fair as the two boys land punches on each other but feels uncomfortable struggling to suppress any suggestion of favoritism toward his son. The match is close and he wonders how the other boy will feel if he gives the bout to his son. He wonders how his son will feel if he gives the bout to the other boy.

At the core of Dexter's uneasiness is an ethical dilemma that he has unwittingly brought upon himself. For Dexter is a father and, on one common view of that role, he has an obligation to be a partisan supporter of his son. And yet Dexter is also the referee in a boxing match. As such his obligation is to be even-handed and fair. Clearly there is nothing wrong with being a father and clearly there is nothing wrong with being a referee. But there does seem to be something morally perilous about refereeing a match in which one's son is a contestant. With respect to one and the same youngster, Dexter must be both a partisan supporter and a disinterested judge. It seems impossible to meet either obligation without compromising one's ability to fulfill the other. It is of little solace that there may be a right or a best answer to the dilemma: "If you have to decide between being a bad referee and a bad father, always choose . . ." Regardless of the answer, Dexter is in the unenviable position of having to decide what kind of creep he is going to be. The situation Dexter has brought upon himself is one in which his obligations conflict with one another. Although the dilemma may be irresolvable once the bout has begun, had he been sufficiently attentive to the ethical implications of the roles of father and referee, Dexter could have prevented the problem from arising. For example he could have delayed the bouts until someone else could referee them. But conflicts of obligation are not always that simple.

Flynn is driving her car with her two friends, Chang and Ripley, and, out of nowhere, a bus collides with her vehicle. Chang and Ripley are injured and receive medical attention. While Flynn is not hurt, her car is damaged. A few weeks later the three meet with attorney Parker to discuss suing the bus company for damages. The evidence supports the bus driver's being at fault and Parker agrees to take the case. Chang's medical bills total $14,000 and Ripley's, $3,000. Flynn's car had $6,000 worth of repairs. Taking into account other costs to his clients, Parker files suit against the bus company for $30,000. As Parker anticipated it would, the bus company files a countersuit against Flynn, claiming that the accident was her fault. At trial, each side has the chance to present its case and the jury is asked to decide who is at fault and how much they have to pay and to whom. Horrified, Parker listens as the jury finds both Flynn and the bus company equally at fault and equally liable for $17,000 in medical bills.[1]

Why is Parker horrified? If Flynn, the driver of the car, had been Parker's sole client, Parker would have been obligated to discuss with her the option of filing an appeal. There is a chance that Flynn could escape the $8,500 judgment against her and perhaps even recover the costs of repairing the car. Filing an appeal might have been a very good idea. But if Chang and Ripley had been Parker's only clients, suggesting an appeal would have been absurd. They have essentially won their case. Merely to mention the word "appeal" to Flynn could be to betray Chang and Ripley. If Flynn decides to appeal, their award could be delayed for years. Conceivably, they might never receive payment. The authors of Canon 6 of the old ABA *Canons of Professional Ethics* (superseded in 1970) had this situation in mind when they wrote that "a lawyer represents conflicting interests when, in behalf of one client, it is his duty to contend for that which duty to another client requires him to oppose." Parker has an obligation, to Flynn, to discuss with her the advisability of an appeal. And simultaneously he has an obligation to Chang and Ripley not to discuss with Flynn the advisability of an appeal. Parker is caught in a classic conflict of obligations.

But where was it exactly that Parker went wrong? We can appreciate, perhaps, that fathers should not be referees in boxing matches where their sons are contenders. But what practical rule can attorneys adhere to that will serve to protect against having to decide which client they are going to betray?

Without doubt, the most commonly given reply to our question is the injunction to be found in Matthew: "No man can serve two masters: For either he will hate the one and love the other; or else he will hold to the one and despise the other." While there may be wisdom in this New Testament language, it seems unlikely that these words can illuminate professional responsibility in law. In the first place, lawyers do not serve their clients as servants do their masters. For while masters are owed obedience by those who serve them, lawyers only rarely have obligations to obey their clients. For the most part, their service is autonomous. They are paid in order that they may do their work. In the second place and more importantly, most practicing attorneys have no ethical problems in providing legal services for more than one client. If the Matthew rule is taken to be applicable to legal practice, it entails the preposterous conclusion that no lawyer can have more than one client! While this would clearly reduce the incidence of conflicts of obligation in legal practice, it is hardly a suggestion that any attorney would take seriously. On this account, Parker could not even decide to represent Chang and Ripley simultaneously. And indeed because Parker, like every attorney, is an "officer of the court," he is as beholden to the judicial system as he is to his client. He is in the service of both. A strict application of the Matthew Rule would thus preclude anyone from ever serving as anybody else's attorney.

A second more promising approach would require Parker to foresee that conflicting obligations are a possibility and to withdraw from such situations at once. When Flynn, Ripley, and Chang sit down to tell their problem to Parker (who has not yet agreed to be their attorney), Parker must anticipate that, given the occurrence of certain events, he will be faced with an actual conflict of obligation if he agrees to represent all three clients. The bus company may file a countersuit against Flynn and the jury may find Flynn liable for the injuries sustained by the two passengers. If those events occur—there is no way effectively to prevent them from occurring—Parker will be required to betray at least one of his clients. For that reason he may agree to represent Flynn or he may agree to represent Chang and Ripley. He may not agree to represent all three. The bare possibility that a conflict of obligation may arise would require the conscientious attorney, under this rule, to decline simultaneous representation of potentially conflicting interests. A responsible attorney must therefore be sensitive to the potential for conflict and be ready to step aside should a conflict of obligation be a possibility. On this account, the Matthew Rule should be modified to prohibit an attorney from agreeing to serve more than one client where there is any reason to believe that meeting professional obligations to one of the clients might require the lawyer to forbear meeting professional obligations to the other.

Like the original Matthew Rule, this version will effectively prevent the occurrence of actual conflicts of obligation. But also like the Matthew rule, it may be a more draconian measure than is justified by the problem it seeks to prevent. For one thing, it will mean that the general public will have to support many more attorneys than it would otherwise have to. If cases are not dropped, new lawyers will have to be employed whenever a potential conflict of obligation arises. While this may be financially beneficial for those in the legal profession, it may be that trust in lawyers will be eroded, especially if less drastic measures can do the job.[2]

The presence of multiple attorneys may also promote more litigiousness than there needs to be. Where Chang and Ripley might be able to reach agreement with Flynn in an informal setting, it may be that such agreement will be difficult where both sides are represented by attorneys *before* an actual conflict has arisen. Geoffrey C. Hazard has helpfully illuminated this point:

> In respect to these broader terms in which conflict of interest is defined, the culture of law itself is a contributing determinant. The point can be made more clearly by considering cultures that sharply contrast in this regard. In this country, the ideals of due process, private property, and formal equality (that is, equality in legal status) lead to the definition of human relationships in legal terms. They also imply that adjudication is a normal and in some sense an ideal form of resolving disputed relationships. A derivative of this premise is that the role of partisan advocate and counselor is a normal, primary, and perhaps idealized one for a lawyer to play. By way of sharp contrast, in Japanese culture the ideals of concord and deference to traditional authority predominate. The definition of human relationships in legal terms is regarded as the exhibition of something like anti-social tendencies. A derivative of this premise is that in Japan it is uncommon to resort to legal assistance and more uncommon still for lawyers to assume the role of partisan rather than neutral expositor of the law.

Within both countries, certainly this one, the degree of "legalism" in definition of relationships varies with specific context, as already suggested. But when an American lawyer is consulted, the client's orientation to the problem is usually adversarial, precisely because the lawyer's normal or expected role is that of partisan. Hence the fact that a client has consulted a lawyer can signify that the client contemplates a legally assertive course of action and itself is a step in the direction of defining a divergency of interest as a conflict of interest.[3]

If the potential for conflict of interest is well enough understood by the attorney and the prospective clients, it may be that agreement can be reached as to what the attorney's obligations will be in the event that events occur that would ordinarily give rise to an actual conflict of obligations. The obligations that Parker has to his clients, he has because they have delegated responsibilities to him. If the clients explicitly forbear delegating to Parker responsibilities that may give rise to a conflict of obligations, then, since Parker cannot then find himself in an actual conflict, he will have no reason to decline representation of all three. Let us see how this might work.

The scene is once again Parker's initial interview with Flynn, Chang, and Ripley. The subject of the conversation is whether Parker will agree to represent any or all of the three in their proposed lawsuit against the bus company. The three potential clients have just completed recounting to Parker their story of the mishap and its consequences. Parker speaks:

"Based on what you all tell me, the three of you appear to have a solid case against the bus company. You are all in agreement that the accident was caused by the bus driver. If the rest of the evidence holds up, I would expect that we would have a very good chance of prevailing at trial. But the bus company will not take this lying down. We can expect that they will file a countersuit against you, Ms. Flynn, and try to prove that the accident was your fault. From what you all tell me, it doesn't look like they will succeed. But they might. No one can be certain which way the jury will go. If the jury finds you to be at fault, you will be held liable for the injuries that your two friends have sustained. That will be a problem for you and it may be a problem for your two friends. But it will also be a problem for me.

As Ms. Flynn's attorney, it would ordinarily be my responsibility to advise her on whether she should file an appeal in the hope of getting a new trial and overturning the jury's judgment against her. The bus company will have won its lawsuit against you, Ms. Flynn, but there may be something we can do about it on appeal. If there is, while that will be a good thing for you, it may not be such a good thing for your two friends. An appeal and a new trial will take a great deal of time and, during that period, you will not have received money to pay your medical bills. The two of you will essentially have won your case and yet, because of my responsibilities to Ms. Flynn, I will be doing work that will delay your payment and possibly subject you to the difficulties of an appeal. If we are "successful" on appeal, there could be a second trial that will probably not net you one extra penny. Just as I would ordinarily have an obligation to advise and to represent Ms. Flynn in connection with her appeal, I would ordinarily have an obligation not to work to overturn any judgment in your favor. In short, I think that any responsible attorney should have some reservations about taking on all three of you as clients.

There may be, however, something that we can do now that will prevent such a conflict from arising later on. For example, if you, Ms. Flynn, were to stipulate now in our agreement that I am to have no responsibility to advise you and no responsibility to represent you concerning any matter that may arise subsequent to the jury's verdict in this case, then I believe that that would take care of my reservations. I will advise you now that if the jury should return a judgment against you it would be wise immediately to seek legal counsel on the question of appeal. I will be happy to suggest the names of several attorneys who would be able to help you to make your decision, should the need arise. On the other hand, if you two gentlemen were to stipulate now in our agreement that I am being retained, not merely to press the claims that you three have against the bus company, but equally to defend Ms. Flynn against any countersuit the company might file against her, at trial, on appeal, and, if necessary, at retrial, then it may be that we can reach agreement in that way. Perhaps we will want to discuss the responsibility for fees in the event it becomes necessary to file for an appeal. In any case, if we decide to go this second route, I would want to have it clearly stated in our agreement that the appeals process may delay and even jeopardize any payment to you that the courts may find owing.

There is possibly a third option which the three of you may wish to consider. We could agree that in the event that the jury returns a judgment against Ms. Flynn, I will neither have the responsibility to advise her nor the authority to represent her on appeal and thereafter unless the two of you explicitly consent to my doing so in full understanding of what the consequences might be.

I think that I can live quite comfortably with any of these three options. It will probably be less expensive and there will be less duplication of effort if the three of you proceed, for now, with one attorney. But you should consider carefully that your interests might diverge, now or later on, and that it may be better to bring in a second attorney or to accept that it may be costly to some of you if I work to meet all the responsibilities you have delegated to me. Why don't you talk these arrangements over among yourselves and if one of them seems suitable, I will be happy to draw up the appropriate agreement. On the other hand, if you feel it is better to go with separate attorneys, I will be happy to recommend several who can do the work."

Here, attorney Parker is treating a potential conflict of obligation not as a flashing red signal to stop, but, rather, as a problem that can be resolved to the advantage of his clients. When a potential conflict of obligation becomes apparent, it is clear that the first step ought to be disclosure. The lawyer-client relationship tends to be an unfamiliar one to many lay persons and explaining the problem can serve to clarify the nature of an attorney's obligation to a client. The second step, on this analysis, would be to set out ways in which the dilemma can be prevented from arising. Is it possible for clients to specify and limit the attorney's responsibility and authority so that the conflict cannot arise? Can clients explicitly waive certain rights or disavow expectations in order to consent to multiparty representation that would otherwise be ethically questionable? Is it possible adequately to advise clients in advance of those circumstances under which independent counsel should be sought? At the very minimum—and this may not be enough—the attorney should tell clients precisely what he or she will do in the event that a conflict of obligations arises and should secure from each client a consent that is informed by adequate knowledge of the consequences. What is suggested here is not so much a rule as a set of ethical strategies. To be sure, there will be many occasions in which a conscientious attorney, committed to doing the best for clients, can do nothing better than decline simultaneous representation. But it is often possible for an ethically competent lawyer to fashion a framework for cooperation that will serve all clients well.[4]

Our discussion of conflict of obligation has focused thus far on problems arising in simultaneous representation of divergent interests. But similar problems arise out of successive representations. While most of an attorney's obligations to a client end when the lawyer-client relationship is dissolved, there is one that does not. It is the obligation of confidentiality. It is typically involved in conflicts involving the former client.

For several years Mr. Gould refers legal questions arising in the course of his business to Mr. Kimura, his attorney. Eventually Gould's business grows and he begins to take his legal matters to another firm. Several years afterwards, Mrs. Gould shows up in Kimura's office to talk with him about getting a divorce from her husband. Because of Kimura's earlier relationship with Mr. Gould, Kimura knows a fair amount about the businessman's assets. He may have information that could be very useful to Mrs. Gould if there is litigation regarding a property settlement. But at the same time, Kimura is under an obligation not to disclose the information to anyone unless Mr. Gould's permission is obtained. If Kimura agrees to serve as Mrs. Gould's attorney in the divorce proceedings against the former client, he will have the obligation to serve as her "zealous advocate," using all the means at his disposal to prevail in the courts. If there is something Kimura has learned from his former client that is crucial or even helpful to his current client, Kimura will be caught in a second type of conflict of obligation. He must advise and represent his current client to the best of his ability and yet, at the same time, there may be information that he has that is essential to her welfare and that he is not at liberty to utilize or divulge. Once the actual conflict of obligations becomes apparent to Kimura, it becomes patently clear that he must withdraw immediately as Mrs. Gould's attorney. He must abandon her. Indeed, he is not even permitted to explain in any detail the reasons for his withdrawal: to do so may be to violate the confidences he is obligated to preserve.

Conflicts of obligations arising out of successive representation are not manageable in the same way as those arising out of simultaneous representation. There is no longer a continuing relationship with one of the parties and not always an opportunity to hammer out agreements to the advantage of all. It is also frequently a nice question whether, before exploring in detail the nuances of a new client's case, there is a potential conflict of obligation arising out of confidential communications from a prior client. Suppose Kimura only handled one or two minor matters twelve years ago. Suppose most of what Kimura learned while serving as Mr. Gould's attorney has since become generally known. Since it may be difficult if not impossible to know in advance whether one has confidential information from a prior client that could be helpful or even critical to a potential client whom one is interviewing for the first time, attorneys should probably err on the side of caution and decline representation when there is a possibility that zealous advocacy may be incompatible with the preservation of a former client's confidences.

One possible solution is to get the former client's consent. Waiving confidentiality, Mr. Gould can explicitly permit Kimura to represent his wife in the divorce action. A second solution might be to put the new client on notice that the attorney might withdraw at any moment without explanation. While there may be some clients who would accept representation under such conditions, the attorney also has an obligation to the court not to abandon clients in the midst of litigation. More to the point, the sudden decision to abandon a client can itself compromise the former client's confidences. Mr. Gould's wife can infer that the attorney knows something that would be useful to her that he cannot tell her. For this reason, unless there is consent from the former client, an attorney should disqualify himself or herself from representing any client where the matters under consideration are substantially related to matters considered in representing a former client.[5] Good judgment is called for in making this decision.

We are now brought to our final point in our discussion of conflicts of obligation. For if the evidence that a court is permitted to examine supports the conclusion that an attorney may have relied upon confidential information entrusted to him (or even to a partner) by his present adversary; if it appears that that there was an opportunity for the attorney to be entrusted with such information and that the information could have been utilized on behalf of a present client against the former client, then a court may well be inclined to disqualify the attorney and vacate a judgment gained on the client's behalf. As one court put it: "An attorney must avoid not only the fact, but even the appearance, of representing conflicting interests."[6] If the system of adjudication is to work, if it is to succeed in generating judicial decisions that are likely to be just and that the community *can accept* as just, it must preserve appearances. The trial may have been defective because one of the parties may have had improper or inadequate representation. Indeed, in *Jedwabney* v. *Philadelphia Transportation Co.* (upon which we loosely based our saga of Parker, Flynn, Chang, and Ripley), the attorney, whom we assume *was* horrified, stood by as the Company won a new trial because the driver of the automobile was inadequately informed of his attorney's potentially conflicting obligations. The judge felt that the driver had not been "given the chance to make an informed choice." In his dissenting opinion in the case, Justice Musmanno laments that the two injured passengers who had won their verdict must once again "be subjected to the turmoil, the expense, the loss of time, the worry and the agony which accompany a trial—with the possibility of drowning in a river they have already crossed."[7] But the community has a competing interest in ensuring that judicial proceedings preserve the appearance of propriety. Clients may indeed be ill-served if attorneys

neglect such conflicts. While this is not the whole reason for lawyer attention to the potential for conflict, it is certainly part of it.

CONFLICTS OF INTEREST: PERSONAL AND STRUCTURAL

In the preceding section we have seen how attorneys get into ethical
trouble if an obligation they have to one client is in potential or actual
conflict with an obligation they have to another client. A more frequent
type of conflict occurs where attorneys themselves have interests which
may incline them away from fulfillment of their obligations to clients.
Problems of this general type can arise wherever there are clear obligations associated with a social position. Consider the following:

> **Case 1: The Generous Defendant**. Big Jake, a reputed underworld
> kingpin, has a reputation for distributing extravagant gifts whenever
> things go well. After prevailing in a criminal case against him, Jake
> sends expensive presents to the prosecuting attorney on the other
> side, to the judge, and to all twelve of the jurors.

> **Case 2: The Will**. Three years ago, Scribner did some estate plan-
> ning and drafted a will for Whipple who was then 78 years old. Now
> Whipple has died and his Last Will and Testament are in probate.
> The will that Scribner earlier prepared for his client provides that
> one-third of the deceased's substantial estate is to go to his "good
> friend and faithful attorney, Scribner."

Suppose that, despite their expectation that they might receive expensive gifts from the overjoyed Jake, the prosecutor, the judge, and the
jurors do their very best not to let possible benefits for themselves affect
either their effort or their judgment. Even without Jake's reputation for
largesse, the outcome might have been the same. Let us also accept that
Scribner did not twist Whipple's arm in order to get him to sign the
will. It was Whipple's own idea to give a portion of the estate to

Scribner and, while Scribner did not object, other attorneys might well have found the bequest to Scribner to be unexceptional had they been drafting the will. Our concern here is not with the reasonableness or unreasonableness of the actions undertaken in behalf of the clients. It is rather with the gift and the bequest, each enriching fiduciaries who are beholden to clients.

It might be plausibly suggested that what is ethically perilous in these cases is the possibility that judgment might be affected despite the care taken to avoid influence. Subconsciously, the expectation that one has something to gain may play a hidden role in one's deliberations. To the extent that this is so (*ex hypothesi*, one cannot know it is not so), one may not be doing the most responsible work that can be done under the circumstances. While we might suppose in setting up our examples that other attorneys, judges, etc., might have acted similarly even without a comparable personal interest in the outcome, it may not be possible for one who is subject to a conflicting personal interest to be equally confident about what a disinterested judgment would look like. Without the attorney knowing about it, a personal interest in the matter may compromise an attorney's ability to exercise independent professional judgment on behalf of a client. Standing to benefit from specific advice or representation, the attorney also has an interest in underestimating the degree to which advantage to self may interfere with the fulfillment of obligations to the client. And so for many—perhaps for all—it may be ethically imprudent to trust one's own opinion that professional judgment will be unaffected by personal interest.

Still, an attorney might be confident—let us suppose for the sake of discussion, reasonably so—that her independent judgment will not be compromised by a personal interest. Is there reason still for the responsible attorney to be concerned about conflict of interest? Does "reasonable" confidence that independent judgment will not be affected suffice to satisfy an attorney's doubts about the propriety of proceeding in the face of a conflicting personal interest?

In a professionalized legal system such as ours, people are not expected to understand their legal situation without professional counsel nor are they expected to be able to secure that to which they are legally entitled unless they have access to professional services available only through a licensed attorney. Clients are thus sitting ducks for unscrupulous attorneys and, in general, they know it. Legal advice may further the attorney's interests more than the client's and legal action can benefit the attorney at the client's expense. For this reason loyalty to the client must be an overriding obligation of attorneys if the general public is to trust members of the legal profession. To the extent that lay persons believe that people generally pursue their own interests, attorneys must make a special effort to try to get it across to clients that it will be the client's interests that will be determinative of the lawyer's advice and representation, and that the lawyer's personal interests will not compromise that loyalty to the client. It is clearly part of the profession's responsibility that this be done. It is also in the profession's enlightened interest.

The duty of loyalty thus has two parts. There is a guarantee that the profession makes to clients on behalf of the attorney that he or she will exercise independent judgment on the client's behalf and will be a zealous advocate in representing the client's interests within the judicial system. That part is satisfied when the attorney is confident that significant personal interests will not interfere with independent judgment or zeal. But, additionally, there is a second guarantee: it is that the attorney will not give reason to believe that that loyalty has been compromised. A lawyer may be confident that potentially compromising influences are not having an effect. We may suppose that such confidence is reasonable in the light of the attorney's experience. But it is not possible to be equally confident that others, who believe that attorneys are as self-interested as anyone else, will be ready to accept the attorney's own assurances that personal interests played no role in professional judgment. In both cases, the existence of the conflicting personal interest *calls into question* the propriety of an action that might otherwise be unexceptional. It is that feature that evidences a conflict of interest.

It is not difficult to appreciate how the fairness of Big Jake's trial is called into question by his distribution of expensive gifts. Suppose a losing quarterback were to receive from the owner of the winning team $100,000 in a brown paper bag. Consider how the bare fact that the money had changed hands can compromise the integrity of the game. Apart from whether or not the quarterback deliberately shaved points or threw the game; apart from whether or not the payments were made in satisfaction of some agreement made earlier; in the light of the payment we have good reason to be uncertain whether what took place in the stadium was a genuine football game or an elaborate charade engineered to create the appearance of a fair contest. Likewise, if a trial is to serve as a social procedure for settling disputed questions, it is crucial that key participants in the transaction keep themselves above reproach. As with the role of quarterback, the positions of judge, prosecutor, and juror can create golden opportunities for self-enrichment at the expense of the apparent integrity of the process. The social positions themselves would lack point in the absence of a commitment not to benefit oneself in ways that *can be construed* as abusive of the privileges attaching to the roles. Thus, with only a few minor exceptions, the American Bar Association *Code of Judicial Conduct* (adopted in 1972) provides that "[n]either a judge nor a member of his family residing in his household should accept a gift, bequest, favor, or loan from anyone...." Specifically barred is the acceptance of gifts from donors whose interests have come or are likely to come before the judge.[8]

The Whipple will raises a different problem. Scribner drafted it making himself a beneficiary. Since Scribner *was* carrying out Whipple's instructions (and since Whipple is now dead), there is no occasion here for a client to lose trust. If eyebrows are raised at all, they will be those of the disinherited friends and relatives. Instead of decisively settling Whipple's intentions regarding the disposition of his estate, Scribner's document raises questions of undue influence and overreaching on the attorney's part, perhaps even questions of fraud arising out of the fiduciary relationship. In these ways Scribner's actions have compromised the integrity of the document. Roman law would not permit the individual drawing a will to receive a legacy under it and, today, the laws of some states provide that such a circumstance gives rise either to a presumption or an inference of undue influence.[9] Not only is it the case that Scribner may not receive the portion of the estate that Whipple wanted him to have: His interest as a beneficiary of the will he was drafting can suffice to void the entire document. As a beneficiary, Scribner's own testimony regarding the validity of the will can be called into question. Clearly, if Scribner wanted to do his best work for his client, he would have suggested, without recommending names, that Whipple retain some other attorney of his own choosing and ask that attorney to draft a codicil providing for the bequest.[10] In part, this is a matter of prudence and competence. To do any less is to do less than one's best work for one's client. But, in this case, the expected outcome of the shoddy legal workmanship involves a substantial benefit for the attorney. The conflict of interest could hardly be more glaring.

The conflicts of interest that are of most concern to the legal profession are those in which the attorney reaps a substantial financial benefit quite apart from payment for work done on the case. But as all of us value things other than money, the possibilities for conflicts of interest are perhaps as far-ranging as human desire itself. Service to a client can suffer if an attorney is uncomfortable unless in control of the client or, alternatively, uncomfortable unless the client is involved in the making of all decisions; if the attorney is worried about being too aggressive or not aggressive enough; or if the attorney is insufficiently concerned or excessively concerned about competency to handle a client's problem. Conflicts can arise as a consequence of assuming too many responsibilities. Which client's affairs can be put on a back burner? Which pressing problem am I going to neglect today?[11] The process of becoming a responsible attorney is in large measure a matter of coming to understand the personal tensions here and learning to manage and to avert the problems. Adaptation of one's self to the constraints of the professional role is often a difficult matter.

There are some conflicts of interest, however, that are neither personal in the sense just discussed nor the product of some special financial interest that the attorney has. These cannot be averted merely by referring the case to another attorney. Such conflicts are structural or systemic: rooted in the institutional context of the professional role. Attorneys are paid for their work and, under the hourly fee arrangements governing much attorney income, there is an ineradicable conflict of interest every time a lawyer advises a client to get legal help with a problem and that he or she is available to do the job. The conflict comes to the fore whenever a professional advises a client to purchase more professional services. The lawyer has a clear financial interest in the advice. Some might think that the problem could be ameliorated if attorneys were paid flat salaries in pre-paid legal services plans rather than on an hourly rate or a fee-for-service basis. But, instead of solving the problem, this arrangement merely changes its effect. The employee on a flat salary can be supposed to have an interest in working less for the same amount of money. Thus the incentive for a salaried attorney might be to say to prospective clients, not that they need professional services when they do not but, rather, that they do not need professional services when in fact they do. Conflicts of interest at this level require very careful specification of the concept of a need, and consideration of alternative incentive systems that can suffice to provide for those needs. The trick is to specify the details of a social structure that will make it reasonable for clients (or patients) to believe that the services they receive are services that they need, and the services they are denied are services they don't need. This is perhaps the most difficult question arising in the area of conflict of interest. At this writing, it cannot be said that there is a favored answer.

CONFLICTS AND THE CORPORATE CLIENT

Some of the most perplexing difficulties in legal ethics involve conflicts in the corporate setting. Often these are variations on the plight of Attorney Parker, considered earlier in this chapter. It will be recollected that Parker's "client" consisted of three people with potentially divergent interests. Likewise the corporation is a "complex" client. But unlike Chang, Ripley, and Flynn, a modern corporation has a legal, constitutional structure. In essence, the corporation is granted a legal recognition which has the effect of permitting its various agents to act in its name in the pursuit of lawful purposes. In addition to its agents, there are stockholders who nominally "own" the corporation and who are entitled to share in its profits.[12] Some may have purchased shares hoping for a prompt increase in the price of the stock while others may be looking for steady dividends in the long run; the owners may therefore have interests that are in conflict. In addition to the stockholders, there will be others with various legally secured rights to the corporation's assets: for example creditors (employees, suppliers, banks, etc.) and plaintiffs who have been awarded judgments against the corporation. There is a board of directors which is elected by the stockholders and which has formal responsibility for the corporation's policies. The board may be divided, with majority and minority members. And there is management which has responsibility for the day-to-day operation of the corporation. Heading management is the chief executive officer (CEO or president) who is appointed by the board of directors. Until recently most corporate law was practiced within law firms, private organizations (usually partnerships) with multiple clients. In a partnership, each partner can be held liable for the wrongful conduct of one. But in recent years the "in-house" corporate counsel has appeared. These attorneys are salaried employees of the corporation. The sole client is then, in a sense, the attorney's work environment.

Let us suppose that Baroni, Senior Partner of Baroni and Sells, receives an urgent call to meet with Mishkin, the CEO of Anodyne Pharmaceutical Corporation, B & S's biggest client. Mishkin and Baroni have worked together for twelve years on various corporate problems and, in fact, it was Mishkin who initially retained B & S on behalf of Anodyne. The men are friends. Mishkin takes a chair in Baroni's office and clears his throat: "It may be," he says, "that I have been involved in authorizing 'questionable payments' to foreign government officials in order to boost company sales. Of course there are no records of these expenditures on our books: all payments were laundered through multiple intermediaries."

As Mishkin pauses momentarily, Baroni is rapidly working out the implications. The Foreign Corrupt Practices Act makes it a crime for an American corporation to pay foreign government officials in order to obtain business. The corporation can be heavily fined and its officers jailed. Additionally, the Securities and Exchange Commission requires publicly owned companies, like Anodyne, periodically to issue accurate and complete financial statements as a condition for their stock to be bought and sold in the market. It is a requirement that questionable foreign payments be disclosed. What Mishkin is saying may mean that there is inaccuracy or incompleteness in some of the financial statements that Anodyne has filed with the SEC. Baroni immediately senses that things may become very messy for Mishkin and Anodyne.

But now a second more fundamental problem emerges. Baroni is *not* Mishkin's lawyer. Rather, Baroni's firm is in the service of Anodyne as its retained attorney. Even as Mishkin spoke, it dawned on Baroni that it was his job to further the interests of Anodyne and that what was good for Anodyne could conceivably be *very bad* for Mishkin.

But how is Baroni supposed to know what is good for Anodyne? There is no problem if, as far as Baroni is concerned, Anodyne *is* Mishkin. What is good for Anodyne is what Mishkin says is good for Anodyne. If Mishkin says that the best thing for Anodyne to do is to keep its Board of Directors in the dark about the problem, who is Baroni to disagree? Mishkin is the President of Anodyne, Chief Executive Officer, overseeing all of the operations of the company. The Board of Directors, in hiring Mishkin, has delegated to him the responsibility for day-to-day management of the corporation. And Mishkin can hire or fire Anodyne's lawyer. The man's opinion *surely* must be given weight.

But now Baroni considers that there must be *some limits* to Mishkin's authority to pursue what he says are the legitimate and proper purposes of Anodyne Pharmaceutical. If Mishkin had been channeling Anodyne's funds into his private accounts or if he had been ordering the assassinations of the competition's key personnel, surely then it would be clear that the boundaries of legitimacy and propriety had been overstepped. If there are discernible limits to the authority of a chief executive officer—limits to the authority granted to him by the board of directors that hired him—and if an attorney has good reason to believe that a CEO is acting beyond those limits, isn't the attorney for the corporation then accountable to the board rather than to the CEO? Since Anodyne's Board of Directors doesn't have the authority to permit Mishkin to act in violation of the law, Mishkin has clearly exceeded any authority the Board has to give *if* he has broken the law. Moreover, it may turn out that Anodyne's best move is to cooperate in the criminal conviction of their Chief Executive Officer. Since that course is pretty clearly not best for Mishkin, it can be supposed that in his Presidency of Anodyne he has an obvious conflict of interest. In acting as CEO, will Mishkin be wanting to protect the interests of the Corporation or his own? Perhaps, just for a moment, Baroni should consider that his primary obligation may be to the Board of Directors, which "personates" his client.

If, for the purposes of this matter, the Board of Directors is the client, then perhaps the attorney's duty is to apprise the Board, *if* that is what the Board would want the attorney to do. On the assumption that the Board consists of honorable men and women who would want to know if management had conducted unauthorized, illegal, and possibly economically imprudent activities, Baroni should convey the substance of his conversation to the Board as soon as possible. There may be a pressing need to map a corporate strategy well suited to the exigencies of the moment. Part of a corporate lawyer's job is to be a fire fighter, to prevent manageable blazes from erupting into conflagrations. Baroni's well-trained legal nose smells smoke.

But isn't Mishkin owed a duty of confidentiality? Didn't he call for Baroni's help when he needed legal advice? Hasn't Baroni worked for years to develop a relationship of trust and confidence with Mishkin, constantly stressing the importance of openness to the Corporation's counsel? But while Mishkin did call Baroni for help, Baroni did not answer the call as Mishkin's lawyer. Of all people, Mishkin should know that Baroni is the attorney for Anodyne Pharmaceutical; *he* was the one who hired Baroni for the job.

It begins to dawn on Baroni that the Chief Executive Officer thinks he is talking to *his* attorney. But if Anodyne, personated in its Board of Directors, is the real client, and if there is a strong possibility that Anodyne and Mishkin have interests that are in conflict (i.e., the satisfaction of the interests of one precludes the satisfaction of the interests of the other), then, even though Mishkin *thinks* he is talking to *his* lawyer, it may be that he is actually talking to his adversary's lawyer. It may be that everything he is saying to Baroni, his trusted friend, will be used by Anodyne to put him in jail.

Betrayal is only possible within a relationship of trust and confidence. It can occur when, on invitation, we make ourselves vulnerable to others in the hope that we will find counsel, compassion, and understanding and, instead, discover that our openness has become an avenue of attack. Betrayal breeds cynicism. Alan Dershowitz, in his *The Best Defense*,[12] recounts an interchange in an unnamed movie:

> First lawyer: Don't you trust me?
>
> Second lawyer: Absolutely.
>
> First lawyer: Me neither.

But surely, even if Mishkin is not Baroni's lawyer, he is at least Baroni's friend. And while Baroni may not have an obligation of confidentiality as Mishkin's lawyer, surely he has an obligation of confidentiality as his friend. Friends do not betray one another. Mishkin may expect that Baroni will not betray a friend. But if Baroni chooses to protect Mishkin by concealing his disclosures from the Board, he is going to have to trust Mishkin to conceal his own duplicity. For to the extent that Mishkin knows that Baroni understood what Mishkin said, Mishkin knows that Baroni will be concealing from the Board information that, perhaps, it ought to have. What the two *friends* need is a charade. They need to be able to "agree" on a common story without agreeing on a common story. Rising from the chair and walking toward the door, Baroni could say: "I am sure I didn't understand you. It sounds like you have some kind of personal problem that I can't help you with. Good day!" Following up on the hint, Mishkin can respond: "On second thought, Anodyne doesn't have a problem here. I apologize for taking your time." The two are now in agreement that Baroni never received the information from Mishkin. In their conspiracy against Anodyne, friendship is thus preserved and the corporate employer/client betrayed.

Baroni is in a classic conflict of obligation, much like the one that perplexed Dexter in the boxing ring with his son; he is going to have to choose between being a bad lawyer and a bad friend. Perhaps, being Anodyne's lawyer, it was unprofessional for him to befriend Mishkin. On the other hand, it was important for him, as an attorney, to invite a relationship of trust and confidence with the Chief Executive Officer. Mishkin can hardly be faulted for thinking of Baroni as more than simply Anodyne's attorney.

Baroni suddenly begins to think it is very wrong for him to sit there as Mishkin starts talking again. Mishkin has a *terrible* misapprehension about what is happening to him. Though he does not know it, he may be damaging himself horribly. Perhaps what Baroni ought to do is to warn Mishkin (out of friendship? out of fairness? out of decency?) as police do when, after an arrest, they give the suspect his "Miranda warning." "You have a right to an attorney. . . . Anything you say may be held against you." Baroni should read Mishkin his rights, admonishing him that anything the CEO says may have to be disclosed to the Board of Directors and possibly others as well. Perhaps Baroni should say something like this:

> As attorney for Anodyne, I must warn you that our conversations are not covered by the obligation of confidentiality. That obligation only protects my client, in this case Anodyne. Anything that you tell me may have to be revealed, at a minimum, to the Board of Directors. If you go on, it may be wise to assume that in talking to me you are disclosing to the Board.

But such a warning may not suffice. In the first place, the very words that created the occasion for this warning have also put Anodyne's attorney on notice that something may be seriously amiss with his client's legal affairs. If it is reasonable, on the basis of what has been said, to warn Mishkin—who is not the client—why is it not equally reasonable, on the same facts, to warn the client? Baroni cannot bring it about that the conversation did not occur nor can he deliberately forget the conversation took place. And it seems that it shouldn't be open to him to "wall off" a potentially valuable part of his consciousness, to ignore something he has reason to believe is true, if he is to discharge his responsibility to protect his client's interests. In its discussion of conflict of interest, the *Model Rules* holds that loyalty to a client is impaired "when a lawyer cannot consider, recommend or carry out an appropriate course of action for the client because of the lawyer's other responsibilities or interests. The conflict in effect forecloses alternatives that would otherwise be available to the client." Perhaps, as Anodyne's loyal attorney, Baroni should sit there quietly, listening attentively and drawing Mishkin out where appropriate. When the CEO has finished incriminating himself, Baroni should bring the matter to the Board at once. Unimpaired loyalty to the client would seem to require the betrayal of his friend.

But we have been assuming that the members of the Board of Directors would, if they had the choice, elect to be informed of their CEO's impropriety. This may not be so. Often board members will prefer to rely wholly on management, routinely ratifying its decisions and passively reviewing reports and statements. Even though the chances are slim that the directors themselves will be subject to a legal judgment against them personally, they may prefer not to become involved in litigation. Christopher Stone has written:

> In bending over backwards to protect the directors, top-level manage-
> ment is inclined to shield them from "bad news" of potential corpo-
> rate vulnerability.... This may seem odd to the layman, given ... the
> low risk that the directors, even if sued, will ultimately suffer any

out-of-pocket loss. But there is a special sort of conservatism that I have personally witnessed to operate in this setting. Everyone recognizes that the directors did not bargain even for the "hassle" of a lawsuit; no one wants to get them involved. What they don't know is often judged potentially less embarrassing than what they might discover.[13]

Suppose then that the Board will require an iron-clad case against Mishkin before it will entertain criticisms of him. Suppose they can be expected to fire attorneys who are foolish enough to do end runs around management, reporting their mere suspicions directly to the Board. If Baroni has good reason to believe that the members of the Board don't want to get involved—reason to believe that they would rather see the Corporation endure third-degree burns than be disturbed themselves by the sound of the fire alarm—then perhaps it is Mishkin who personates the corporation. In such cases it might seem that the Board has essentially delegated to the Chief Executive Officer, not only the responsibility for management, but the Board's responsibilities as well. If Anodyne's board is like this, then perhaps Baroni should simply roll up his sleeves and start protecting Mishkin's hide. It may be that Anodyne's interests can be served at the same time, provided they are not in conflict with Mishkin's. If the Board complains later on, Baroni can always say that while Mishkin clearly shouldn't have been given the authority he had—authority that he abused in directing the corporation's affairs illegally and in his own interests—the Board never acted to take that authority away from him. Though Baroni may end up assisting Mishkin in actions that turn out to be damaging to Anodyne, maybe he can defend himself later on by claiming that the blame belongs to the Board for appointing Mishkin in the first place.

But the legal profession's view has long been that a lawyer who is employed or retained by an organization owes loyalty *to the organization* "as distinct from its directors, officers, employees, members, shareholders or other constituents." The approach developed in the *Rules*— *Rule* 1.13(a)—applies to the situation in which the corporation's attorney "knows" that an officer is engaged in action that is either in violation of a legal obligation to the corporation or illegal in a way that could be imputed to the corporation, and that such action is likely to result in substantial injury to the organization. In such cases an attorney may be required to refer the matter to a higher authority in the organization or, if necessary, take further remedial action that the lawyer reasonably believes to be in the best interests of the organization. There is a requirement as well—in *Rule* 1.13(d)—that the attorney "in dealing with an organization's . . . officers, . . . shall explain the identity of the client when the lawyer believes that such explanation is necessary to avoid misunderstandings on their part." If Baroni gives Mishkin his Miranda Warning, Mishkin will then understand that it may be necessary to disclose the matter to the Board. (Does Baroni have to tell Mishkin about the five-year jail sentence for officers who violate the Foreign Corrupt Practices Act?) If, in spite of the warning, Mishkin tells all to Baroni, there may be no problem. Perhaps the matter can be competently cleared up without involving the Board or anyone else in the company. But if Mishkin balks, afraid of what the consequences might be if he confesses, the lawyer may find himself cut off from sources of information at the company.

At this point the *Model Rules* substitute an epistemological problem for an ethical one. The question is not whether to disclose. It is rather "What does the lawyer know?" As noted above, Baroni can be required to blow the whistle on Mishkin only if he *knows* that the officer has violated the law in acting for the corporation or has violated an obligation to the organization, and that what the officer has done is likely to result in a substantial injury to Anodyne. But what Mishkin said was "It *may* be that I have been involved . . . ." Baroni doesn't know, on the basis of what Mishkin told him, that there *has* been a violation. Moreover, the likelihood of substantial injury is impossible to discern without hearing what Mishkin has to say. And Mishkin has nothing to say to Baroni. In the absence of the required *knowledge*, the *Model Rules* does not seem to be of much help to an attorney caught between a suspiciously silent officer and a deliberately hard-of-hearing board of directors. How thick does the smoke have to get before we *know* there is a fire?

In fact, the real problem here is not an epistemological one at all. It is a structural one involving the constitution of the corporate client. What must be admitted at once is that, under the circumstances, it is impossible for Baroni to serve the interests of Anodyne. The officers of the organization appear to be abusing their authority and the directors appear to be neglecting their responsibilities. The President doesn't want to talk to Baroni and the Board doesn't want to listen to him. Baroni can pretend to be Anodyne's attorney—he may continue to be paid as such—but he is not helping the client to deal appropriately with its legal problems. Because of the way in which the organization is constituted, Anodyne's attorney is unable to speak with his client.

In the Comment to Rule 1.13, the *Model Rules* contains the following:

> Clear justification should exist for seeking review over the head of the officer or employee normally responsible for it. The stated policy of the organization may define circumstances and prescribe channels for such review, and a lawyer should encourage the formulation of such policy.

Corporations are, like virtually all organizations, social systems that formulate goals, gather information, make decisions, and act. Though more is required for organizational soundness, part of what is necessary is that relevant information make contact with the organization's decision procedure.[14] Good channels of communication are vital if a modern corporation is to be able to respond to its challenges. The *Model Rules* reflect an appreciation of this in the passage quoted above. For the organization effectively to pursue its purposes and avoid injury, sound legal advice must reach the appropriate level of decision-making. When the legal problem is potentially very serious, the appropriate level of decision-making is going to be very high. The problem with the approach of the *Model Rules* is that it requires the attorney to break down the door of a reluctant Board of Directors only when there is *knowledge* of seriously damaging wrongdoing. It is just the policy a deliberately negligent board would want: a board that would tell its employees to wait until they see the flames and feel the heat before ringing the fire alarm—*And make sure it is a serious fire!* In setting the standard of intellectual responsibility very high—knowledge—and in requiring warnings that will shut off the sources of information needed to meet that standard, the *Model Rules* does little to guarantee that the interests of the organization will be served by their attorneys.

What the example of Anodyne Pharmaceutical Corporation shows is that at a certain level of institutionalized thick-headedness, it is not possible for an organization to have an attorney. (Think of serving as an attorney for a crowd.) A lawyer who works for and is paid by such an organization may be defrauding the client. If what the organization wants (to the extent that it can formulate such an objective) are procedures that will ensure that legal advice makes contact with the appropriate level of decision-making, then perhaps attorneys can assist in crafting the required organizational arrangements for the corporate client. But in the absence of an acceptable corporate constitution, it would seem to be unethical for an attorney to represent himself or herself as corporate counsel.

In many cases it will not be enough for the profession merely to "encourage" the setting up of sound channels of corporate communication. One effective approach to the problems would be for the profession to set standards for contracts between attorneys and their corporate clients. Such contracts, mandated by the profession, would authorize and require the corporation's attorney to report to a specific member or members of the Board (or to a member of their staff) any substantive *evidence* that an agent of the corporation is engaged in action that is either in violation of a legal obligation to the corporation or illegal in a way that could be imputed to the corporation, where such action could result in substantial injury to the organization. The special director or directors designated for that purpose would have to be "outside directors"—ones who are not also employed officers of the corporation. Many corporate boards already have "audit committees" that could serve in this capacity. The Board of Directors would have to agree, as a condition for its receiving the services of an attorney, to review such reports as a regular part of its periodic meetings. Needless to say, the requirement that such terms be agreed to by corporations as a condition for the receipt of legal services would have to be set by the profession as a whole. Otherwise firms that did not require such agreements might have competitive advantages in the market against firms that did. In taking such a step, the profession would be asserting that it is unethical to take a position as a fire fighter if the employer doesn't provide a fire alarm.

The problems with Anodyne resemble those that arise in connection with incapacitated clients. The *Model Rules* specifies that a lawyer may "seek the appointment of a guardian, or take other protective action with respect to a client, only when the lawyer reasonably believes that the client cannot adequately act in the client's own interests." In medicine, patients are considered to be "decisionally incapacitated" when they are unable to appreciate their problem, the options that are open to them, and the probable and possible consequences of each option. Additionally, they must be able to express a decision and apply reasonably stable personal values to the pertinent medical facts. Unlike a patient, a corporation can only act through its agents. If its agents are unable or unwilling to act in the interests of the corporation, while the individual attorney may be unable to do anything to protect the client, the legal profession, acting collectively, may be able to do quite a bit.

Of course, where the Board of Directors is dominated by Board members who are also officers of the Corporation ("inside" directors) or if members of the Board are themselves the problem, pillaging the corporation's assets for their own benefit, these measures will not suffice. But others like them might.

NOTES

1. The facts here are adapted from *Jedwabney v. Philadelphia Transportation Company*, 390 PA 231, 135 A.2d 252, (1957).

2. See Thomas D. Morgan, "The Evolving Concept of Professional Responsibility," *Harvard Law Review* 90 (1977): 702, 727.

3. Geoffrey C. Hazard, *Ethics in the Practice of Law* (New Haven: Yale University Press, 1978), pp. 79–80.

4. One option that Parker does not discuss is the possibility of Chang and Ripley suing the bus company *and Flynn* for their injuries. It is useful to consider whether a conflict of obligations has prevented Parker from giving his best advice to two of his clients. Nor does Parker discuss with Flynn the possibility that Chang and Ripley caused the accident—and their own injuries—by interfering with Flynn's driving. Perhaps Ripley, but not Chang, interfered.

5. *Edelman v. Levy.* 346 N.Y.S. 2d 347 (1973).

6. *State v. Horan*, 21 Wis. 2d 66, 123 N.W.2d 488 (1963).

7. *Jedwabney v. Philadelphia Transportation Co.* It is a nice question, but one we will table, whether the Company ought to have had the standing to complain to the court and to win an appeal on the basis of the conflict of obligation on the part of the other side's attorney. The injured party—the driver of the car—never saw fit to protest that he had been unfairly treated. On the other hand, since the driver's attorney also represented the passengers, is it reasonable to expect that the court would hear of the driver's complaint against the attorney through that same attorney? How might a judge decide if a new trial is required because one of the parties was possibly not properly represented?

8. *State v. Horan*, 21 Wis. 2d 66, 123 N.W.2d 488 (1963).

9. This is the advice given by Henry Drinker, *Legal Ethics* (New York: Columbia University Press, 1953), p. 94.

10. Andrew S. Watson, "A Psychological Taxonomy of Lawyer Conflicts," in *The Lawyer in the Interviewing and Counseling Process* (Indianapolis: Bobbs-Merrrill Company, Inc., 1976), pp. 94–100.

11. On corporations as property, see Lawrence Becker, "Private Property and the Corporation," in *Proceedings of the Second National Conference on Business Ethics*, ed. W. Michael Hoffman (Washington, DC: University Press of America, 1979), pp. 257–67.

12. Alan M. Dershowitz, *The Best Defense* (New York: Random House, 1982), p. 358.

13. Christopher Stone, *Where the Law Ends* (New York: Harper & Row, 1975), p. 147.

14. On organizations as rational actors, see Amitai Etzioni *The Active Society* (New York: Harper & Row, 1975). Others who have written helpfully on the problem include Peter A. French, "The Corporation as a Moral Person," *American Philosophical Quarterly* 16 (1979): 207–15; and Christopher Stone, *Where the Law Ends*, p. 147.

Geoffrey C. Hazard Jr.

LAWYER FOR THE SITUATION

I. INTRODUCTION

In the confirmation hearings concerning Louis Brandeis before the United States Senate almost a century ago—hearings evaluating whether Brandeis was fit to be a Justice of the United States Supreme Court—Brandeis was challenged concerning his professional ethics as a lawyer. It was charged that he had involved himself in conflicts of interest, trying to assist conflicting parties in working out intense differences. When asked who he represented, he responded that he was a "lawyer for the situation."

That response, undoubtedly, was imprudent. Mr. Brandeis could have said that he represented multiple parties with conflicting interests but that he had done so with their informed consent. The standards of professional conduct of the time recognized the propriety of multiple representation under those conditions. Canon 6 of the American Bar Association's *Canons of Professional Ethics*, promulgated in 1908, provided: "It is unprofessional to represent conflicting interests, except by express consent of all concerned given after a full disclosure of the

From *Valparaiso University Law Review* 39 (Winter 2004). Reprinted with permission of the author.

facts." The standards of professional conduct still recognize the pro-priety of multiple representation in such circumstances.

However, the term "lawyer for the situation" took on a life of its own. The idea had and continues to have great appeal, in contrast to the concept of lawyer as advocate. The argument is that, in various sit-uations in practice, lawyers should consider the interests of others and moderate their conduct accordingly. My argument here is that the rules of ethics and the laws governing lawyers already require such moderation, to an extent perhaps not appreciated by either critics of the profession or zealous advocates of "zealous advocacy" within the profession.

Professional practice as conventionally understood requires a lawyer to advance the position and improve the situation of one party against the interests of an opposite party. Up to a point, that convention accurately describes the role of an advocate in litigation. Once a trial has started, an advocate is committed to almost unqualified loyalty to one client, pitted against an adverse party who, implicitly at least, is represented by an equally dedicated advocate. In this vision, the scene of the encounter is a courtroom and the lawyer is performing the role of barrister.

The scenario next dissolves into a conference room in which the lawyers are negotiators seated across the table from each other. In this setting the lawyers perform the role of solicitors with similarly coun-terposed orientations. On the logic of the adversary model, the solicitor has few if any obligations to the opposing party or its counsel. Much of law practice conforms to this model: trials, of course, and many negotiations. Perhaps more important, the legal profession's self-conception is based on that model. The classic formulation is that by Lord Brougham, in which he proclaimed:

> [A]n advocate, in discharge of his duty, knows but one person in all the world, and that person is his client. To save that client by all means and expedients, and at all hazards and costs to other persons, and, amongst them, to himself, is his first and only duty....

These strong words—"first and only duty" and "knows but one person in the world"—have become the credo of many lawyers, particularly when lawyers are called to account for injury to the interests of persons other than clients. The implications of the credo are found in judicial opinions that reject the possibility of imposing legal responsibility on a lawyer toward anyone other than a client.

However, in fact, law practice involves nearly infinite variations of "situation" in which lawyers have legal duties to persons other then their clients. Some of these duties are the minimal obligation to refrain from fraud, for example, or from counseling a client to commit perjury or to destroy evidentiary documents. Yet even the minimalist duty to avoid fraud contributes in a modest way to civilizing the relationship between a client and a third person. Other obligations to third persons are more exacting. Observance of these obligations reduces the transaction costs of total vigilance that an opposing party would otherwise be obliged to incur. By the same token, a duty to others imposes a limitation on a lawyer's duty to his client and therefore creates something of a conflict of interest on the part of the lawyer.

Thus, the scope of a lawyer's duties, according to the conventional advocacy model, is wholly oriented to the client, with a few exceptions dealing with extreme cases such as fraud. On the other hand, the rules of ethics can be differently understood, interpreted, and applied than according to that credo. The present analysis is an interpretation of the rules of ethics in those terms. Such an interpretation invites inquiry as to why the conventional advocacy model continues to have such attraction for the profession. That is, if we have been speaking prose all along, why do we insist that we are speaking otherwise?

Perhaps the precise focus of the analysis should be made even clearer. I am not suggesting that the rules of ethics should require wider scope in representation of multiple parties or necessarily that they should be changed to require lawyers to take greater account of the interests of parties other than clients. There is much to be said for such changes, and much has been said in support of them. The analysis here is based on the rules as they now are, including the rules of ethics and the rules of law. By rules of law, I refer to the complex general law that governs everyone, including lawyers, and specifically to application of that law to lawyers when representing clients.

II. THE "SITUATION" OF AN ADVOCATE

Even in the core function of advocacy in litigation, the lawyer has duties beyond those to clients. The rules of legal ethics that most sharply express the model of advocacy are those governing loyalty and the rule of confidentiality and its corollaries. The basic rule concerning loyalty is expressed negatively in terms of conflict of interest. *Model Rule* 1.7(1) (a) of the American Bar Association *Model Rules of Professional Conduct* prohibits a lawyer from undertaking a representation if:

> (1) the representation of one client will be directly adverse to another client; or (2) there is a significant risk that the representation of one or more clients will be materially limited by the lawyer's responsibilities to another client, a former client or a third person or by the personal interest of the lawyer.

The epitome of representation "directly adverse" to a client is litigation against the client. A lawyer is not permitted to sue a party that the lawyer concurrently is representing in the same or another matter. This rule is generally protective of the client, but it goes further, because a client cannot consent to such adverse representation. This limitation is explained in the *Restatement of the Law Governing Lawyers*: the rationale is not simply the interest of the clients involved, but it serves the interest of the judicial process in our adversary system. Its aim is that the court be presented with the strongest statements of the contending positions, so that the judge may more fully understand what is at issue. Thus, even the simplest rule of loyalty to the client—prohibiting the representation of opposing parties in litigation—is justified in part by reference to third party interests, in this case the interests of the court and its judges.

More fundamentally, our adversary system considers that litigation is not a street-fight. On the contrary, the system involves a complicated cooperative interaction between contending advocates. The interaction commences not later than the filing of the complaint and continues through the process of preliminary motions and discovery prior to possible trial. Indeed, in filing a complaint, the plaintiff's advocate is required to exercise some scrutiny of the substantiality of the claim being asserted for his client. Rule 11 of the *Federal Rules of Civil Procedure*, and its state law analogues, is not a very demanding standard, but it is not entirely empty.

Beyond the stage of filing the complaint, most litigation is terminated not by trial but by settlement. A settlement by definition requires the advocate to consider—that is, to think seriously—about the interests of the opposing party. Arriving at a settlement proposal that might be seriously considered requires an understanding of the case from the opponent's viewpoint. Moreover, there are decisions that have set aside settlements in which the advocate for one party failed to consider the interests of the opposing party in the course of supposedly providing adequate representation of the interests of his own client. Here I have in mind the now famous case of *Spaulding* v. *Zimmermann*.

If a case goes to trial, the competitive-cooperative interaction continues, in that the advocates are primarily responsible for presentation of evidence and legal contentions. The normal process of trial is a highly mannered but nevertheless cooperative portrayal of the competing versions of truth and the disputable issues of law. The judge is much more than an umpire, but the advocates have the laboring oars.

The procedure is intensely regulated. In this regulatory scheme the ethical rules are essentially secondary. The rules of ethics generally incorporate by reference the rules of criminal and civil procedure that directly govern the parties and, through them, the advocates. *Rule* 3.1, for example, prohibits frivolous legal contentions, but it does not define "frivolous." Instead, *Rule* 3.1 refers to the law of procedure for a definition. *Rule* 3.4 similarly has a catalogue of prohibitions cast in terms of the standing law of procedure; for example, *Rule* 3.4(a) states that a lawyer shall not "unlawfully obstruct another party's access to evidence or unlawfully alter, destroy or conceal a document. . . ."

These and similar rules obviously confer legal protection on persons other than the client. Immediate beneficiaries are opposing counsel and the opposing party, and secondary beneficiaries are the courts. The ultimate beneficiary is the public, which needs a law-abiding adjudicative system.

The law on this set of obligations is vacuous when stated in general terms but endlessly complex when examined in detail. Stated in general terms, the *Restatement of the Law Governing Lawyers § 105* says only that "[i]n representing a client in a matter before a tribunal, a lawyer must comply with applicable law, including rules of procedure and evidence and specific tribunal rulings."

At the same time, the "rules of procedure and evidence" constitute a huge compendium of duties and responsibilities, being entire legal subjects unto themselves. These rules typically are enforced through the old-fashioned technique of monitoring by opposing counsel, reciprocity among the advocates and remonstrance and, if necessary, by retribution by opposing counsel. The fact that the governing rules are typically enforced through informal mechanisms does not diminish their standing as rules. Indeed, one could say that the rules, as enforced through professional interaction of advocates, are the "situational" norms of advocacy itself.

However, the rules governing advocacy are also defined, and sometimes enforced, through formal process. A few examples will suffice. Rule 11 of the *Federal Rules of Civil Procedure* imposes an obligation of minimal integrity and diligence in making allegations against an opposing party. The rule is not very strict but it is not empty. *Rule 26,* governing discovery, imposes responsibility on the advocate to intercept discovery responses by his client that the lawyer knows to be false. There are decisions enforcing that obligation. *Rule* 16, dealing with pre-trial conferences, imposes a duty on counsel to attend and participate on pain of forfeiting the client's case. Concerning conduct in the trial itself, *Rule* 3.4(e) requires that a lawyer "not allude to any matter that . . . will not be supported by admissible evidence," a duty that has been sometimes enforced. The law of evidence imposes restrictions on the kind of proofs an advocate is permitted to present, for example, those governing expert testimony. And so on.

The point can be summarized in two propositions. First, as stated in Canon 7 of the ABA *Model Code of Professional Responsibility*, in representation of a client in litigation, "[a] lawyer should represent a client zealously" but "within the bounds of the law." And second, the limits imposed by law on zeal in advocacy are extensive and intensive. Furthermore, in my observation these limits are generally observed by lawyers in our system, even in an era of intense partisanship.

III. "SITUATIONS" IN TRANSACTION PRACTICE

The circumstances in which a lawyer has obligations to persons other than a client are far more extensive in transaction practice than in litigation. Partly this is because litigation, by definition, places other parties in a position adverse to the client and hence at an outer region of responsibility on the lawyer's part. In transaction practice, in contrast, the configuration of relationships covers a wide range. At one end of the range, the lawyer may, on the basis of informed consent, represent two or more clients whose interests conflict to some degree. That situation would have been an apt description by Mr. Brandeis of his role in at least some of the "situations" under discussion in his confirmation hearing. At the other end of the range, the lawyer may perform some incidental service for an opposing party that entails an arguable element of justifiable reliance giving rise to legal obligation.

A. Multiple Representation on the Basis of Informed Consent

The rules concerning conflicts of interest in transaction practice permit almost any multiple representation, if—and it is a strong "if" —

there is adequately informed consent of all affected clients. In formal terms, the rule prohibiting "direct adversity" can apply to transaction matters. That is, at least in principle some transaction matters present "nonconsentable" conflicts. Comment [7] to the Rule, as amended by the ABA in 2002, states that "[d]irectly adverse conflicts can also arise in transactional matters." No doubt this is true. However, no example of such a conflict is offered in the Comments. Rather, Comment [7] continues, "[f]or example, if a lawyer is asked to represent the seller of a business in negotiations with a buyer represented by the lawyer, not in the same transaction but in another, unrelated matter, the lawyer could not undertake the representation without the informed consent of each client."

The Comment therefore does not define or give examples of direct adversity in transaction matters. Instead, it specifies how such a conflict might be overcome, i.e., the familiar formula of informed consent. This suggests that the category of absolutely "nonconsentable conflicts" in transaction practice is very narrow indeed.[1]

Of course, a lawyer who proceeds with multiple representation on the basis of client consent takes a significant risk. The risk is that the relationship among the clients can undergo change, with resulting increased conflict in their positions. So also there is risk that an affected client will later become disaffected and assert that the consent was invalid. Typically, the claim will be that an inadequate disclosure was made concerning the implications of multiple representation. The risk to lawyers of client defection appears to be much greater these days than in the past, simply because clients are more willing to challenge lawyer probity and to obtain other legal assistance to do so. Nevertheless, lawyers every day undertake multiple representations on the basis of client consent.

Any case in which a lawyer properly obtains a conflicts consent or waiver can be viewed as a "situation" in the Brandeisian sense. A valid consent requires adequate disclosure of the existence and implications of the dual representation. Adequate disclosure of the implications requires attention to the reasonably possible "worst case" scenarios of mutual hostility. Consent by the clients reflects decisions on their part to forego extreme measures so that a single lawyer or law firm can carry on for the benefit of both. When the representations involve the same matter, the result is a "situation."

B. *The Confidentiality Rule*

At this point, it would be well to bring forward a second basic rule of responsibility to a client, the rule of confidentiality. The confidentiality rule is a basic support of the duty of loyalty, which has been addressed above in analysis of the advocate's role.

Fulfilling the duty of loyalty in a representation typically involves a measure of confidentiality, i.e., concealment of sensitive facts and strategic purposes. Hence, *prima facie* a lawyer keeps sensitive facts and strategic purposes from everyone but the client. By the same token, acting for the benefit of two or more people—which is what a multiple representation "situation" entails—requires a substantial measure of disclosure among the several intended clients. Such a disclosure is required in the predicate for consent, i.e., that the consent be "informed." Hence, the concept of lawyer for the situation entails a modification of the principle of confidentiality, as well as the principle of loyalty.

This modification of confidentiality is the predicate of the obligations imposed on a transaction lawyer who undertakes representation of multiple clients. On the one hand, the lawyer is required to maintain the confidences of each client, except as disclosure is necessary to obtain informed consent from the other client. On the other hand, an adequate disclosure is necessary to obtain valid consent. The definition of "adequate" is not simple. As formulated in the *Restatement of the Law Governing Lawyers § 202*, Comment c(i):

> [T]he information should normally address…contingent, optional, and tactical considerations and alternative courses of action that would be foreclosed…the effect of…the process of obtaining other clients'

informed consent upon confidential information...any material reservations that a disinterested lawyer might reasonably harbor ...if such a lawyer were representing only the client being advised; and the consequences and effects of a future withdrawal of consent by any client....

It is readily apparent that this formula affords opportunity for subsequent contentions that a disclosure was inadequate. As a precautionary matter, a lawyer ordinarily should obtain the consent in writing, even in jurisdictions where a writing is not required. Where the client is a corporation, or other organization with its own law department, the consent should be signed or countersigned by the company counsel. Even so, the standard for validity of consent is that the lawyer be able to provide each client the full measure of loyalty, competence, and diligence that is owed to a client represented alone. Such are the responsibilities of a lawyer for a "situation" in which the lawyer has undertaken representation of multiple clients on the basis of client consent.

Unfortunately, there are many decisions imposing liability on lawyers who have proceeded on the basis of supposed consent where it was subsequently disputed whether consent had been sought and obtained, or where the disclosure on which consent was based was determined to be inadequate. However, imposition of malpractice liability in such situations is consistent with the notion that a lawyer's duty runs exclusively to clients. In a multiple representation, the "relevant others" are indeed clients.

1. Responsibilities of Transaction Lawyers to Nonclients

Many lawyers seem to think that, when representation of only one client is involved, such is the end of the matter. But the rules of loyalty and confidentiality are, and always have been, subject to manifold exceptions and qualifications. Some of these exceptions and qualifications are directly referenced in the rules of ethics, but others are recognized by cross reference or by implication.

Taken together, these exceptions and qualifications permit or require a lawyer in various circumstances to make disclosures of information or take other action that would otherwise be covered by the primary duties to the client. These exceptions and qualifications, in other words, are recognitions that lawyers have obligations to nonclients. Assembling a complete catalogue of these "situations" would be difficult, if not impossible, but a substantial array can be readily brought into focus.

2. Impliedly Authorized Disclosures

An initial exception to the rule of confidentiality is the lawyer's right, prescribed in *Rule* 1.6(a), to make disclosures "impliedly authorized in order to carry out the representation." Of course, there is also an exception for expressly authorized disclosures, for example, where a client directs the lawyer to make a settlement offer in a negotiation. But the scope of implied authorization is functionally much broader. In the typical client-lawyer relationship, the details of the engagement are not explicated; rather, they are implied from the undertaking itself.

The undertaking in a client-lawyer relationship primarily concerns transmission of information—making contentions and proposals and supporting them with argument and information. Transmissions that would "reasonably" further the objectives of the representation are impliedly authorized, the "reasonably" concept referring to professionally recognized standards and professional judgment. Thus, a lawyer can disclose the availability of his client for an interview, or the acceptable scope of a due diligence visitation by an external auditor, or the status of client filings with a regulatory authority, and so on—all without express authorization of the client.

However, these disclosures are governed through regulation, rules of professional ethics, and legal obligations imposed by the general law. Under *Rule* 4.1 of the ABA *Model Rules*, a lawyer may not give false information in such a disclosure. Giving false information that is material would constitute fraud under general principles of law. As such, it would be a violation of *Rule* 1.2(d) of the professional rules, which forbids assisting in a crime or fraud, and would also be a basis for civil and possibly criminal liability on the part of the lawyer. Moreover, under tort law as it has evolved, fraud includes not only positive falsity but disclosures that are misleading because incomplete. As stated in Comment [1] to *Rule* 4.1, "Misrepresentations can also occur by partially true but misleading statements or omissions that are the equivalent of affirmative false statements."

In many circumstances, the lawyer's implied authority to make truthful disclosures becomes a mandatory duty to do so. A lawyer is always governed by the duty under *Rule* 1.3 to provide diligent representation. Diligent representation includes the obligation to transmit information to the extent reasonably expected under recognized standards of competence. Hence, lawyers have duties to convey information that is not misleading.

The term "not misleading" of course implicitly requires identification of those who might be misled. For example, a communication adequate to an experienced liability insurance executive ordinarily would not be adequate in a communication to an ordinary householder. Often communication must be made to several people or many. Gauging the circle of addressees and the terms of the communication must be based on assessment of the circumstances, i.e., the "situation."

3. "Blowing the Whistle"

The most intense debates about the rules of professional ethics in recent years have involved other exceptions to the rule of confidentiality. These exceptions were pejoratively characterized as "blowing the whistle" and understandably caused great concern within the bar. The professional debate began with the presentation of the Kutak Committee recommendations concerning *Rule* 1.6, which were largely rejected by the ABA House of Delegates in 1983. The debate at the national level more recently culminated in the adoption of the Cheek Report recommendations by the House of Delegates in 2003. The revisions of *Rule* 1.6(b) adopted in 2003 essentially corresponded to the revisions rejected twenty years earlier.

Rules 1.6(b)(1), (2), and (3) now would permit (but not require) a lawyer to disclose client confidences to prevent death or serious bodily harm or to prevent or mitigate financial fraud in which the lawyer's services have been exploited by a client. For legal, reputational, or moral reasons, a lawyer may feel required to make disclosures that these exceptions permit. Hence, in operative effect they can indeed involve "blowing the whistle." Accordingly, the question then becomes: When and to whom is a whistle to be blown?

The answer to the question of "when" is simply but opaquely "when the lawyer reasonably believes necessary," as stated in *Rule* 1.6(b). The obvious answer to the question "to whom" is the prospective victim, but, as noted in Comment [6] to *Rule* 1.6, there are instances when it would be appropriate to make disclosure "to the authorities." The more general point is that a lawyer can feel an unavoidable obligation to protect third parties from victimization by the lawyer's client. Lawyers only rarely have to deal with clients threatening victimization in the form of homicide or assault. But, given that much of law practice involves dealings with money and property, clients who may be committing fraud are more commonly encountered. Determining how to proceed often can be a "tough situation."

C. Escrows and Other Fiduciary Undertakings

Another kind of "situational" responsibility arises from various fiduciary undertakings to third parties that are designed to complete a transaction. A common type is acting as an escrow agent to assure proper transfer of money (or other property) to consummate an agreement. Examples include escrow of purchase money or title deeds in a real estate closing; filing of legal documents that regularize or officially record a transaction; after settlement of a litigation claim, the disbursement of funds among the client and other designated recipients such as health care providers; obtaining required verifications of corporate or government documents; and so on.

It is perfectly clear that in all such undertakings, the lawyer is undertaking obligations to third persons. The rules of ethics explicitly recognize some of these obligations, particularly those concerning the handling of money. *Rule* 1.15 treats money due to third persons on a par with money due to a client, so far as the lawyer is concerned. Accordingly, the lawyer is required to keep the funds in a trust account and to embargo a distribution if there is a dispute as to proper allocation of the funds. Parallel obligations can be derived from other ethical obligations, particularly the obligation to be truthful (*Rule* 4.1) and to avoid conduct involving dishonesty (*Rule* 8.4(c)).

Courts are coming to recognize that these ethical obligations should be reinforced by legal obligations in favor of third persons injured by their breach. However, many courts still resist this conclusion. There is understandable fear about putting lawyers in positions adverse to the immediate interest of clients, or in positions where the lawyer has to make a judgment call. There remains some resistance to the idea that a lawyer can ever be civilly liable to someone other than a client. Imposition of liability, in my opinion, could properly require a high standard of proof, based on the idea that a lawyer is an officer of the legal system and, as such, is entitled to a kind of *prima facie* immunity. But the evidence of breach can be quite plain. A common example is the improper distribution of settlement process in litigation. What possible social interest is furthered by exonerating a lawyer who gave all the settlement proceeds to the client (except, of course, the contingent fee!) and stiffed the hospital and the doctors?

D. Corporate Clients

Much, if not most, of modern law practice involves representation of corporations and other organizations. The basic rules are set forth in *Rule* 1.13 of the ABA Model. These rules apply in representing business corporations and nonprofit corporations, partnerships, unincorporated associations, and, with certain modifications, government agencies. All of these organizations can be regarded as "situations." That is, they involve interactions with persons who are not clients, who have interests of their own that may not be wholly consistent with the clients' interests, but whose aims and concerns have to be taken into account by the lawyer in the course of representing corporate clients.

The beginning point is stated in *Rule* 1.13(a), that the organizational client is "acting through its duly authorized constituents." Comment [1] to 1.13 recognizes the simple fact that the entity "cannot act except through its officers, directors, employees, shareholders and other constituents." *Rule* 1.13(b) recognizes that conflicting interests can be involved. Thus, the corporate constituents may be engaged in acts or have purposes that are "a violation of a legal obligation to the organization or a violation of law which reasonably might be imputed to the organization" with consequent "substantial injury to the organization." If so, the lawyer "shall proceed as is reasonably necessary in the best interest of the organization."

Rule 1.13(b) identifies various responses the lawyer may undertake to fulfill the responsibility to act in the best interests of the corporation. All of these responses in one way or another would interrupt or overrule the proposed course of action of the corporate operative. If necessary, what is called for is "referral to the highest authority that can act on behalf of the organization as determined by applicable law."

Rule 1.13(f) moves in a somewhat different direction. That rule requires the lawyer to explain the identity of the client (i.e., that it is the corporation) to a corporate constituent who does not seem to understand the direction of the lawyer's primary loyalties. This explanation is by hypothesis addressed to someone who is not the client, or at least not the only client. As recognized in *Rule* 1.13(g), a lawyer may represent both the organization and one of its constituents. But such a dual representation is governed by the conflict of interest standard in *Rule* 1.7 and the disclosure and consent provisions in that *Rule*. The newly adopted Sarbanes-Oxley statute and regulations appropriate these concepts into a federal regulation of companies whose shares are publicly traded.

The issues involved in representation of corporations and other organizations are almost endlessly complex. They certainly have evoked almost endless discussion—generally very serious discussion—

by members of the corporate bar. However, the point for present purposes is simple, even if, perhaps, not simply understood.

The people that a lawyer deals with in representing a corporate client are not clients. In legal contemplation, none of them are clients—the members of the board, the high level management, the corporate officials at intermediate levels, and the ordinary operatives at the bottom. Yet, their interests must be considered at every stage of a corporate representation. Indeed, a lawyer's representation of a corporation would be a practical impossibility except by consideration of the interests of the corporation's "constituents." From this viewpoint, representation of a corporation is yet another "situation."

IV. CONCLUSION

The idea of "lawyer for the situation" is nearly an anathema to lawyers who embrace the good old fashion religion uttered by Lord Brougham. They hold to the proposition that a lawyer "knows no other duty" than to a client. At the same time, the idea of "lawyer for the situation" is eagerly embraced by many critics of the profession, particularly those concerned with excessive partisanship on behalf of powerful clients. It is not always clear exactly what obligations these critics would impose—perhaps a responsibility always to be a mediator. However, as I hope the foregoing analysis has shown, the obligations of advocates and transaction lawyers in modern practice involve many and varied duties to third persons. Many of those duties are enforceable under the law of professional malpractice as it stands and is evolving. Whether some of those duties should be extended or more fully explicated is another question.

NOTE

1. A recent decision that suggests a "nonconsentable" conflict involved the pursuit of a patent on behalf of one client while also representing another client engaged in developing patentable compounds of a similar type. See *G. D. Searle & Co. v. Pennie & Edmonds LLP.*, 308 A.D.2d 404 (N.Y. App. Div. 2003).

David H. Taylor

LEGAL SERVICE FOR INDIGENTS

I n the world of legal services practice, the decision to decline or dis-continue representation due to a conflict of interest results in a con-sequence for the indigent client that is both extreme and unique. Unlike the client who has sufficient financial resources to retain other counsel, the indigent legal services client is unable to walk around the corner to the next available attorney when there is a disqualifying conflict. Thus, a conflict of interest can place the legal services client in the position that the only possible source of legal representation is unavailable due to the ethical constraints of the legal profession. In fact, the denial of represen-tation due to a conflict of interest most often results in a denial of any representation for the legal services client. No other client is placed in a similar position by a conflict of interest . . .. Therefore, this article makes specific proposals for approaching conflict situations in legal services and proposes a mechanism for making determinations of actual prejudice.

From *Arizona Law Review* 37 (Summer 1995). Reprinted with permission of the author and the *Arizona Law Review.*

WHY EVEN THINK ABOUT A DIFFERENT APPLICATION OF CONFLICTS OF INTEREST FOR LEGAL SERVICES?

At the outset, it should be considered what, if anything, would be gained by a different application of conflict principles in the legal services context so as to allow representation in situations where representation by the for-profit attorney would be prohibited. Though some indigent persons are denied the opportunity for legal services representation because of conflicts of interest, the demand for legal services for the indigent greatly exceeds the supply. Assuming present maximum utilization of resources, providing representation for the conflicted client merely would displace the representation of another client. Therefore, a different application of conflict principles for legal services, one that would allow for representation for an indigent client who would otherwise not be represented due to a conflict, would not result in a greater total number of indigent persons receiving representation. Why then should established principles of professional responsibility be applied differently if nothing is gained in terms of the number of persons who are able to obtain free legal services? Would applying conflict of interest principles in a different fashion for legal services be a compromise of the standards of the profession for a Pyrrhic Victory, if a victory at all? What would be gained is that decisions concerning who is the recipient of finite resources could be based entirely on the merit of the client's case and not upon a professional restriction of the attorney.

Because the demand for legal services for the indigent greatly exceeds the supply, most providers employ a case acceptance method that limits areas in which representation may be provided to certain substantive areas; most commonly, public benefits, housing, and family law. A client seeking representation is first screened for categorical eligibility in terms of income, assets, and citizenship. A client who is categorically eligible for services, and who is seeking representation in regard to a matter within a substantive area in which services are provided, has her case screened for merit. The relative strengths and merits of the numerous cases for which service is requested are weighed to determine which case will obtain the limited services available. The cases with the most merit have the greatest likelihood of being accepted by the office for representation.

A conflict of interest can cause a case of great merit to be declined by the office in favor of one with lesser substantive merit or lesser personal need. Therefore, a client in need of services will be denied them simply because she had the bad luck of seeking services from an office that is prevented from providing services to the client due to the rules of the profession. The consequence to the legal services client of this denial of services cannot be overstated. By far, the most frequent result is that the indigent client is left without any representation.

Certainly there are situations where the conflict presented is such that representation cannot be undertaken without a compromise to the interests of the client seeking services, or a compromise to the interests of a past or present client. Nevertheless, many conflict situations are based upon a presumption of prejudice to the interests involved, but not upon an actual prejudice. If a conflict of interest problem presents no actual risk of prejudice to the client, denying that client the only representation available makes little sense, particularly in light of the serious consequences for the indigent client. Therefore, an examination of the interests of the legal services attorney and client is warranted to determine whether the presumptions of prejudice reflected in conflict of interest principles as applied to for-profit practice are applicable to legal services practice. If a significant difference is present in the interests involved, a conflict of interest in for-profit practice may not pose an actual threat to the interests of the legal services client. Consequently, the difference in the nature of the interests involved would make the presumptions in for-profit conflicts of interest inapplicable to legal services and, therefore, warrant their abandonment. Case acceptance decisions would then be based solely on individual case merit, and the cases of greatest merit would receive the limited available resources and indigent persons would not be denied legal services from the only available source.

THE NATURE OF THE CONFLICTS OF INTEREST MOST FREQUENTLY ENCOUNTERED IN LEGAL SERVICES PRACTICE

…Two conflict situations were identified as those most frequently encountered by the legal services office. In the first, "simultaneous adverse representation," each opposing party seeks representation from the same legal services provider, most likely in the context of a husband and wife, each seeking representation in a family law matter. This situation involves the prohibition against representation that is directly adverse to another client contained in *Model Rule* 1.7(a) and the rule of vicarious, or imputed disqualification contained in *Model Rule* 1.10(a), thereby disqualifying all attorneys in the firm if one attorney has a conflict and prohibiting attorneys in the same legal services office or program from representing adverse parties. In the second, the "former client as adverse" party situation, the client seeks representation in a matter in which the adverse party had been previously represented by the office, and the previous matter is "substantially related" to the present matter in which the client now seeks representation, a situation prohibited by *Model Rule* 1.9(a). As with the simultaneous adverse representation situation, the former client as adverse party also involves the rule of imputed disqualification contained in *Model Rule* 1.10(a) disqualifying all attorneys in an office or program if one previously represented the former client.

These two situations certainly do not represent all of the conflict situations encountered in legal services. Nevertheless, both represent the use of a presumption of threat of compromise to the attorney-client relationship to find that representation is impermissible. *Model Rule* 1.10(a), a significant principle in both the simultaneous adverse representation and former client as adverse party situations, presumes that confidential client information will be exchanged between attorneys who practice in the same office, and that it could and will be used to compromise client interests. *Model Rule* 1.9(a), the crux of the former client as adverse party situation, presumes that confidential information was obtained from a former client, which is prejudicial and will be used to the detriment of the former client in representation of the present client in a substantially related matter.

It is these presumptions that serve to unnecessarily cause the denial of representation for the legal services client. A survey conducted in conjunction with this article revealed that, in both situations, the frequency that actual prejudice is involved in each conflict is less than the frequency of occurrence of the conflict itself.[1] Therefore, the presumptions that give rise to finding an impermissible conflict for the for-profit attorney operate to deny representation of the indigent client in situations where proceeding with representation would not pose actual prejudice to client interests. The heart of the question then is whether the presumption of prejudice involved in conflict of interest rules serves to unnecessarily foreclose the legal services client from the only available source of representation.

THE INTERESTS OF THE ATTORNEY SUBJECT TO CONFLICT—A DIFFERENT PROFESSIONAL STANDARD OR A DIFFERENT PROFESSION?

Arguably, the goal of accepting cases based entirely on considerations of merit and need does not alone justify rethinking the application of basic principles of conflicts of interest. In that those principles speak to the basic concepts of zealous representation and protection of client confidences that are at the essence of the attorney-client relationship, their application should not be altered if doing so degrades the basic nature of the attorney-client relationship. Much of the debate concerning conflicts of interest and legal services has centered on the question of whether, in light of legal services as the attorney of last resort, a different, and perhaps "lesser" standard of professional ethics is warranted. That posturing of the question has led critics of a different conflict of interest standard for legal services to a fairly obvious answer—no. Creating a different standard of professional ethics for legal services could lead to several undesirable results.

First, legal services clients deserve the same degree of loyalty, confidentiality, client autonomy, and zealous representation as do any other clients of an attorney. To conclude otherwise would create a client who receives representation that is second-rate due to that person's indigency. Not only would that run contrary to the purposes for which the legal services program was created, it simply is insulting to the population served by legal services to adopt a "you get what you pay for" mentality.

Second, creating a different standard of professional ethics for legal services could also serve to begin an ethical fragmentation of the profession. Many specialties, building upon the legal services model, could claim that the particular nature of their practice warrants a variation in ethical responsibilities.[2] Taken too far, the result becomes a multiplicity of ethical codes—something surely contrary to the intention of the organized profession that wrote the rules in the first place. One can only imagine the less scrupulous attorney, wishing to embark on a course of conduct generally prohibited by ethical standards, bringing a claim or defense that otherwise would not have been brought in order to raise the specter of practicing within a sub-specialty of the bar whose professional code allows that which is otherwise not permissible for the general practitioner. Therefore, in order for conflict principles to be given a different application, there must be something in the nature of legal services practice that makes it fundamentally different from the rest of the profession. Rather than focusing the debate on whether legal services attorneys should be held to a different set of professional standards, the debate instead should focus on whether existing professional ethical standards can be maintained while giving conflict of interest principles a different application in the legal services context. An examination of the interests involved in conflict of interest doctrine serves as the starting point for discussion of whether the nature of legal services practice warrants an application of conflict of interest principles that is different than that applied in for-profit practice.

By examining the interests of the legal services client and attorney that may be in conflict, it is seen that the threat of compromise to the legal services attorney-client relationship is not co-extensive with that in the for-profit attorney-client relationship. First, the legal services attorney does not have a pecuniary interest in the representation of a specific client. Second, the legal services attorney-client relationship is unique because of the serious result of a preclusion of representation due to a conflict of interest—the legal services client is left without any representation. It is only the legal services client who possesses this interest in procuring representation from one available source. For the indigent client, the legal services office is truly the "last lawyer in town." These fundamental differences in the interests of attorney and client set legal services apart from any other attorney-client relationship.

In light of these unique interests of the legal services attorney and client, conflict of interests principles are able to have a different application in the legal services context than in the context of for-profit practice without compromising established professional standards in terms of the duties and obligations owed to a client. This conclusion is reached by giving the interests of the legal services client and attorney the same effect that such interests are given when they occur in analogous situations in other aspects of regulation of the profession, such as the prohibitions against solicitation of clients and advancing financial support to clients. It is then seen that the presumptions of prejudice, based upon the model of for-profit practice, are both inappropriate and unnecessary in legal services practice. An argument by any other specialty area of the profession for a different application of conflict principles would fail, for it is only the unique nature of legal services as the "last lawyer in town" that warrants this different application.

The question of what constitutes a conflict of interest has been explained largely by the use of situational examples, or a listing of duties owed the client by the attorney. An impermissible conflict exists when an attorney's duties and obligations to her client are compromised. Nevertheless, guidance is lacking as to which attorney interests compromise which client interests, and when those interests are sufficiently in conflict so as to warrant representation not going forward.

Therefore, there is little definitional guidance for conflict situations that fall outside the situational examples that have been used to explain when an impermissible conflict of interest exists.

This lack of definitional guidance has served to lead astray the application of conflict of interest principles in the context of legal services representation. Conflicts of interest in legal services simply have been plugged into situational examples from the context of for-profit representation. The situations may be factually similar, and the duties of the attorney owed the client are the same. Nevertheless, the interests of attorney and client are different when representation is undertaken by a legal services attorney with no economic interest in the outcome of the case on behalf of a client who has limited opportunity, if any, due to indigency, to obtain representation from another source in the event that the legal services attorney has an impermissible conflict of interest. Therefore, an examination of the application of conflict principles to legal services practice must begin with an examination of the interests of the client sought to be protected and of the interests of the attorney that can be in conflict with those of the client. If the discussion does not take place in terms of the actual interests potentially in conflict, but rather is limited to hypothetically comparative situations or disembodied attorney duties, one does not appreciate the fundamental difference in the nature of legal services representation. The result then reached—prohibiting the conflict because of a falsely perceived "compromise" in the representation to the legal services client—is predictable, but wrong. When, however, the different interests at stake in legal services representation are appreciated, it is then seen that there is no compromise to the duties owed to the legal services client to obtain representation in a conflict situation that would preclude representation by the for-profit attorney.

A definition from an often cited article on conflicts of interest serves as a useful starting point:

> A conflict of interest exists whenever the attorney, or any person represented by the attorney, has interests adverse in any way to the advice

or course of action which should be available to the present client. A conflict exists whenever this tension exists—even if the attorney eventually takes the course of action most beneficial to the present client.[3]

For the definition to be fully understood, an explication of the respective "interests" of the attorney and the client is also necessary.

The "interests" of the client are commonly considered to be a preservation of confidentiality of information imparted to the attorney during the course of representation and the provision of zealous representation by an attorney whose loyalty to the client is undivided. The legal services client, however, has the additional interest of being able to secure representation from the only source available. This interest is unique and is not shared by clients in any other context.

The interests of the attorney that can come into conflict with those of the client, thus dividing the attorney's loyalty, are several. The attorney has personal financial interests and interests owed to third persons, such as other clients or the attorney's law partners. Here again, legal services practice varies from for-profit practice. The legal services attorney lacks both the personal economic interests and the economic interests owed to law partners that are present with the for-profit practitioner. The lack of economic interests by the attorney [is] not unique to legal services. Public defenders similarly have no pecuniary interests in their attorney-client relationships or practice relationships. Nevertheless, while courts have applied conflict principles differently to public defenders based upon the lack of attorney economic interests, they have not done so in legal services practice.

Though absent from the previous definition, another "interest" echoes throughout considerations of whether a conflict of interest is present—the interest of the legal profession in putting forth a good public face by seeking to have attorneys avoid the "appearance of impropriety." Though it could be argued that this interest of the profession is among the interests of the attorney, it is more appropriately considered an interest independent of either attorney or client because the interest of the profession in appearances can be in conflict with either attorney or client when it requires that representation must be declined. In such situations, the client is not able to receive representation by the attorney of choice, and the attorney is not able to receive the financial benefit of representation of the client. Again, when this interest of the profession is balanced against the interest of the legal services client in representation from the only source available, one must seriously question whether preserving the public face of the profession justifies a total denial of representation for the indigent client.

As for the interests of the attorney with which conflict principles are concerned, there are two fundamental differences in legal services practice that are at the heart of that which makes the world go around—money, or more appropriately, the lack thereof. First, the legal services attorney derives no economic benefit directly from her client, but rather is compensated on a salary basis by her program. The legal services attorney has no personal economic interest in the outcome of a particular case. Therefore, when confronted with a situation where the interests of two clients become adverse, there would not be an economic incentive to favor one client over another. Second, the nature of the legal services office is not a partnership where the attorneys in an office have a shared economic interest in the outcome of cases. Therefore, the underlying economic rationale is absent for imputing disqualification to all attorneys in an office if one attorney has a conflict.

The absence of these two economic interests, on its face, indicates that legal services practice is a different creature than private practice. The question then to be considered is whether these differences form a sufficient basis for rethinking when a conflict of interest is present that prevents representation of an indigent person who has no other opportunity to obtain representation.

In several areas of professional regulation the absence of economic incentives does allow the legal services attorney to be treated differently than the rest of the profession. Two exceptions to long established prohibitions against certain unprofessional conduct, the prohibition against solicitation of clients and the prohibition against providing financial assistance to a client, provide the strongest examples of how the lack of economic interests on the part on an attorney alters the application of a principle of professional conduct.

Solicitation of prospective clients has long been considered attorney conduct that is highly improper, and even illegal. Because of the opportunity for fraud, overreaching, and undue influence on the part of an attorney who seeks to solicit a client, solicitation is among the most mortal of sins the attorney can commit. Nevertheless, solicitation is not prohibited when it occurs in a situation where the attorney involved lacks the economic incentives that are feared to lead to the evils that the prohibition against solicitation seeks to prevent. Therefore, *Model Rule* 7.3(a) does not prohibit solicitation of a member of the attorney's family, and does not prohibit solicitation when the attorney's pecuniary gain is not the motive for the solicitation.

Similar to the exception to the solicitation prohibition is the exception to the prohibition against providing financial assistance to a client. Though *Model Rule* 1.8(e) "continues the general common law prohibition against advancing financial aid to a client in connection with pending or contemplated litigation" in order to prevent "encouraging a client to pursue lawsuits that might otherwise be forsaken," the rule contains an express exception for attorneys representing indigent clients. The exception of *Model Rule* 1.8(e)(2) recognizes that to continue the prohibition for indigent persons could operate to bar a client from pursuing litigation of her rights in a situation where "there will be little unseemly competition among lawyers to outbid each other for the right to represent parties." Therefore, in order to allow access to the judicial process, the exception is created because the indigency of the client may serve to lessen the economic incentives of the attorney to engage in unprofessional conduct.

The commentator who has written the most extensive work on the application of conflict of interest principles to legal services practice has sought to identify the non-economic interests of the legal services attorney that pose a sufficient threat to the "attorney's independent judgment" so as to warrant the finding of an impermissible conflict of interest even though pecuniary interests are not present. Those interests are identified as "ideological interests in the results obtained," "personal and emotional interests in the results of lawsuits they undertake," and "the fighting spirit required in zealous representation." It is difficult to see how those attorney interests serve to compromise the interests of the client in receiving zealous representation. Instead, it would seem that they would all indicate the converse, for they speak to an attorney's dedication to her client and to results obtained for her client, rather than to a compromise of dedication to one's client. That is, unless the attorney is opposed to the result which the client seeks—a situation not often present for ideologically oriented legal services attorneys. Additionally, those interests arguably are present in every attorney-client relationship. If those results-oriented interests were sufficient in and of themselves to create a conflict, representation would then be precluded in every situation where it is possible that they are present. Therefore, the exceptions for non-economic solicitation and financial assistance to the client could not be justified. An attorney could never be allowed to enter a contract with her client, for the attorney's contrary result-oriented interest apparently would be self-serving and, therefore, obviously detrimental to the client.

While it cannot be disputed that such influences on attorney interests might be present, it does not necessarily follow that those influences are always present to a degree that should give rise to an impermissible conflict of interest. The threat to confidentiality by joint supervision can be easily alleviated by adjusting supervisory responsibilities. The situation of pressure on the junior attorney is more accurately couched in terms, not of a conflict of interests of the adverse parties, but rather in terms of a limitation of the attorneys' ability to provide representation due to their personal interests. In such case, the disqualification is not required in every situation where adverse parties sought representation from the same legal services organization. In the event that the attorneys felt that their ability to provide representation would not be affected by the "subtle influences" involved, disqualification would not be necessary. Therefore, the disqualification would not be *per se*, with the result that she who gets to the legal services office first wins the prize of representation, while the runner up is foreclosed from the only available source of representation.

The lack of economic interests on the part of the legal services attorney should effect several ends. First, because the attorneys in an office have no shared economic interests, a legal services office should not be considered a "firm" for purposes of *Model Rule* 1.10(a). Whether a legal services office constitutes a "firm" within the meaning of the rule has been largely considered to be a question of proximity, in terms of offices and information. This view of the issue mostly addresses prevention of inadvertent disclosures of client confidences. In that such situations can be warded against by means of screening mechanisms, this is an unnecessarily onerous measure of whether an office constitutes a "firm," particularly when it is considered that indigent persons are denied access to their only source for legal representation.

Second, *Model Rule* 1.10(a) appears to speak to purposeful compromises of client confidences rather than inadvertent disclosures. The purpose could be either innocent sharing of information in furtherance of common enterprise or malevolent sharing for economic gain. Because physical separation would seem to be an ineffective impediment to attorneys bent on malevolent conduct, the physical separation test is considered superfluous in regard to for-profit practice. Therefore, *Model Rule* 1.10(a) utilizes the presumption of shared information to impute the disqualification of one attorney to all who might be predisposed to utilize that information. The existence of that predisposition is apparently measured by the "firm" concept, rooted in shared economic interests. Because the legal services attorney lacks shared economic interests, the presumption of shared information is inappropriate. Therefore, instead of basing imputation of conflict of interest on an inapplicable presumption that serves to deny the only source of services to indigent clients, imputation should be based on a standard of actual prejudice to client interest.

Arguably, the situation of the sharing of information for a common enterprise would seem to meet the test of a "firm," thereby imputing disqualification. Nevertheless, the use of the presumption to guard against the innocent sharing of information, particularly in the legal services context, seems unnecessary. If information had in fact been shared that would prejudice a client, the attorney who would be in a position to use that information to the detriment of a client should disqualify herself. But there is no reason for extending the disqualification beyond the attorney in actual possession of the information. Additionally, if the sharing had occurred for no improper purpose, must it be presumed that the attorney or attorneys involved would not disqualify themselves? The presumption upon which *Model Rule* 1.9(a) is based is similarly inapplicable to legal services practice. If an attorney is in possession of confidential information about a former client who is now an adverse party of a present client, that attorney should be relied upon to disqualify herself. Perhaps economic incentives make presumptions of prejudice necessary, but when those incentives are absent, the presumptions serve little purpose, particularly when balanced against client interests of securing representation.

NOTES

1. See, e.g., Stanley Sporkin, "The Need for Separate Codes of Professional Conduct for the Various Specialties," *Georgetown Journal of Legal Ethics* 7 (1993): 149 (arguing in the context of corporate and securities law that specialized areas of practice need separate standards of ethical conduct).

2 Robert H. Aronson, "Conflict of Interest," *Washington Law Review* 52 (1977): 807, 809, 856–57.

3. See Marshall J. Berger, "Disqualification for Conflicts of Interest and the Legal Aid Attorney," *Boston University Law Review* 62 (1982): 1115, 1123, 1130–31 (acknowledging that economic motivations that give rise to conflicts of interest are absent in legal services practice but arguing that other attorney interests are present that threaten client interests).

PROBLEM SET IV

MAINTAINING A LAWSUIT

Tam Wallach suffered whiplash when his 1961 Valiant was hit from behind by a city bus. He came to you, and you brought suit. The case has dragged on for a year (as such cases regularly do). Wallach has exhausted his unemployment benefits and savings; times are hard, and he has been unable to find work he can do given his injuries (which are substantial). He has been refused welfare. His medical expenses are covered by insurance he had before the accident, but his living expenses are not. He has no family, lives alone, and (while a pleasant enough person) has no close friends with money to loan.

You believe his injuries to be worth between $50,000 and $100,000 (supposing no good or bad surprises). You have taken the case on a contingent-fee basis (and so, if you settle now, you will receive 15 percent of the settlement; if you go to trial, your share will be 33 percent). The bus company is offering $3,000 (about what you expected at this point in negotiations). Wallach has come to your office today to tell you that he can't afford to wait any longer. You point out that $3,000 won't last him very long, to which he responds that it will last longer than nothing. You wonder whether you couldn't just write a check for $500 and ask him to hold out at least till that's gone. You would consider the $500 a loan. You recognize, of course, that you may have to write him several more such checks before the case is over. Such cases usually last several years. And you recognize as well that the more you loan him, the more you may want to settle just to get back what you invested in the case. What should you do?

SUING A FORMER CLIENT

You are an attorney for an automobile dealer who wants to bring suit against his manufacturer and an associated real estate corporation for breach of dealership lease. You were once an associate with a firm employing the attorneys, who represented the manufacturer during the period when the firm prepared the lease now in controversy. You have since joined another law firm. Your part in preparing that lease was limited to preparing briefs, informal discussions on procedural matters, and research into specific points of law. While much that you learned by such participation will be helpful now, you were not entrusted with any confidences that could be used against the manufacturer in this case. Would there be anything unethical about you representing the dealer in this case? Would there be anything unethical if some other member of your new firm represented the dealer instead?

THE BEST IN TOWN

Evelyn Grand, a senior partner in a major law firm, has informed her firm that she purchased stock in a certain company two years ago based upon what the Securities and Exchange Commission has now declared to be a fraudulent prospectus. Grand has decided to file a class action suit against the company on her own behalf and on behalf of all other stockholders similarly situated. The suit might well produce a judgment exceeding $25,000,000. Grand is willing to pay the "costs of litigation" herself but wants to employ the firm "because you're the best in town." The costs of litigation include the cost of notifying members of the class (amounting to perhaps $3000), filing fees (amounting at most to a few hundred dollars), and certain other minor expenses, but not the cost of the firm's time. The firm would be retained on contingency, as is customary in such cases. If the case were won, the firm would get between 10 and 25 percent of the judgment (depending on how long the case dragged on); the partner would get back whatever she paid in costs; and the remainder would be divided among the members of the class in proportion to their original investment in the stock (the partner taking her share just as the rest would). If the case were lost, the partner would be out her costs and the firm would be out its time. Is there anything unethical in the firm taking such employment? Would the answer be different if the partner proposed to resign from the firm?

SUGGESTED READINGS

Michael Davis and Andrew Stark, *Conflict of Interest in the Professions* (New York: Oxford University Press, 2001).

Janine Griffiths-Baker, *Serving Two Masters: Conflicts of Interest in the Modern Law Firm* (Oxford, UK: Hart Publishing, 2002).

Andrew Stark, *Conflict of Interest in American Public Life* (Cambridge, MA: Harvard University Press 2003).

Charles W. Wolfram, "Ethics 2000 and Conflicts of Interest: The More Things Change . . ." *Tennessee Law Review* 70 (Fall 2002): 27–62.

PART V:
PERJURY AND CONFIDENTIALITY

INTRODUCTION
TO PART V

W hat should a lawyer do when surprised by a client who knowingly gives false testimony in court? What should he do when a client merely announces an intention to give such testimony? What part, if any, may a lawyer have in the fabrication or presentation of false evidence?

Laypeople (and law students) are often surprised at the extent of the obligations lawyers suppose themselves to owe "the court." A lawyer should not (it is agreed) knowingly make a false statement of law or fact, fail to inform the court of controlling precedent even if to do so hurts the client's position, or offer evidence that the lawyer knows to be false. Indeed, lawyers are in general to avoid "fraud" in their dealings with the court (and with one another and the public), for example, by presenting as valid a will or contract she knows to be forged.

Were these the only obligations of a lawyer, none of the questions posed above would be a *problem* of legal ethics. The obligation of a lawyer (as lawyer) would be clear. It would be unprofessional to participate in the presentation of false evidence. A lawyer would have to dissuade his client from perjury or withdraw from the case. He would have to withdraw even if the client were already on the stand testifying (because continuing to help the client would then mean assisting the client in committing a "fraud upon the court"). The only ethical problem the lawyer could have is whether to honor his professional obligations or allow other considerations to overrule. The lawyer's professional concern would be for the court, not the client.

331

The "obligations of candor" are, however, not a lawyer's only obligations. Lawyers also suppose themselves to have extensive obligations to the client. Among them are "competence and diligence" in the pursuit of the client's cause, keeping confidential what is learned *from* the client (or about her) during the course of representation, and also keeping confidential any other "secrets" about the client. Lawyers also think that, in general, they should not use client confidences or secrets to the client's disadvantage.

Part IV of this volume was concerned with how far lawyers should go to preserve their professional judgment against threats from obligations and interests external to their role as lawyer for a particular client. This section addresses a conflict of obligations *internal* to the lawyer's role, that is, with how far a lawyer should go to avoid revealing or misusing confidences entrusted to her when doing so threatens (as Fuller and Randall put it in part III) to "muddy the headwaters of decision."

The obligation of confidentiality is, of course, not absolute. A lawyer may, for example, reveal to the police that a client has announced an intention to commit a violent crime if the client seems likely to do what he says. In this respect, lawyers are much like other professionals having an obligation of confidentiality. Physicians may also have a legal obligation to report a patient's bullet wound to the police; engineers, a professional obligation to report a threat to public safety to appropriate authority; and so on.

There is no agreement even about whether a lawyer should reveal a client's intention to commit a serious but nonviolent crime (for example, tax fraud or pollution) though the *Model Rules* now say that she "may." Much remains controversial. The questions discussed in this section belong to that controversy. The problem is not only how to design the lawyer's role but what the criteria for a good design should be. Though the discussion of confidentiality in lawyering has some analogy with the wider discussion of professional "whistleblowing," it differs insofar as confidentiality seems more important to lawyering than to most other professions, that is, professions in which the client has less control over the information provided (as in medicine), the information the client provides is less important (as in architecture), or the client has an independent lawyer to advise him (as in an audit).

Monroe H. Freedman began the modern discussion more than four decades ago (as he explains) by proposing what he described as a "trilemma," three uncontroversial obligations of lawyers: (a) learn everything he can about the client's case, (b) keep the information confidential, and (c) be candid with the court. Freedman argued, in effect, that in practice the three obligations are sometimes incompatible and, when they are, the one to abandon is candor to the court. A lawyer should present testimony known to be perjured just as he would any other. He should not do anything that might signal judge or jury that he does not believe the testimony he is presenting.

Freedman's argument for this conclusion seems to have two prongs. One is that the adversary system requires that lawyers so act. The argument appeals to consequences within a specific legal system. Justice would suffer if the client had to worry about the lawyer using what she learns against him. The other prong appeals to the logic of the lawyer-client relation. Without a strict obligation of confidentiality, one overruling candor to the court, the lawyer would be not the client's "legal friend" (in Fried's phrase) but a potential "snitch." The client should not have to face the legal system alone. True, we might respond, but does it follow that the client therefore has a moral right to an accomplice (rather than to a competent but honest legal assistant)?

The problem that Freedman raised seems much the same today as it did in 1966. That is not because of any lack of imagination in the development of alternatives. The two responses to Freedman included in this section give some idea of the variety of practical alternatives offered in the last four decades. The problem is that none of these alternatives seems clearly better than the rest. Underlying Freedman's trilemma may be a fundamental disagreement concerning what lawyers should, or can, be within an adversary system—or, at least, within something like this adversary system. That is why so much of Freedman's argument relies on his interpretation of constitutional law (cases concerned with the Fifth and Sixth Amendments).

Stephen Gillers argues, in effect, that there is no trilemma, only a number of difficult decisions. In part, what he offers is an empirical critique. Many of the consequences Freedman relies on to defend confidentiality are much more speculative than Freedman seems to appreciate. For example, lawyers may already have enough obligations to reveal some things learned from the client that one more is unlikely to change the relationship. In part, though, Gillers offers a legal critique. Freedman has, he argues, misinterpreted today's adversary system. The law neither recognizes a right to perjure oneself nor imposes on the lawyer an obligation to remain silent when she knows that her client will commit, or has committed, perjury with her help. There are, however, practical problems. Notifying a judge in advance of testimony in a criminal trial, for example, creates a problem for the judge without doing much to protect the court from fraud. The defendant has a right to testify as he thinks best. The lawyer can protect the integrity of the legal system by notifying an appropriate authority of the perjury after the trial. Of course, the lawyer should know—not just think—perjury was committed. She owes her client the benefit of the doubt. The obligation of confidentiality requires that much.

While Gillers denies that there is a trilemma, Daniel R. Fischel agrees with Freedman that at least one of the three obligations must sometimes go unsatisfied. But, unlike Freedman, he thinks that confidentiality is the obligation to sacrifice because both clients as a class and society as a whole would benefit. Like accountants (and most other professionals), lawyers supply their clients with "reputational goods." When, for example, a lawyer says he has produced all the documents called for in a discovery order, the judge and opposing counsel will ordinarily rely on that statement. That reliance will save the client the time and money it would otherwise take to prove the discovery order has been satisfied. The lawyer's reputation (or, if he is not known to the judge, his status as a lawyer) vouches for what he says. In the same way, if lawyers were understood to vouch for the testimony of their clients, the costs of litigation would be lower because there would be less false testimony. The stronger the obligation of confidentiality is (with its constraint on candor), the less the probative value of a client's testimony.

Why then do lawyers think the obligation of confidentiality so important? Fischel's answer is that the primary consideration seems to be the self-interest of lawyers themselves. They find it "demoralizing" to work in an environment in which they promise confidentiality in general but with express or tacit reservations for certain rare circumstances, such as perjury. Fischel seems to think that the feelings of lawyers (their "peace of mind") should not outweigh the general benefits of less confidentiality. He also denies that "it must be repugnant to any honorable man to feel that the confidences which his relation naturally invites are liable at the opponent's behest to be laid open through his own testimony." On the one hand, explaining to clients what they have a right to expect of him should dispose of any "natural invitation" to confide plans to commit perjury. On the other hand, should not "an honorable man" prefer to avoid complicity in wrongdoing?

This seems a long way from the assumptions on which Freedman rested his resolution of the "trilemma." Are we too far? If Fischel's arguments were as good as they seem, wouldn't we long ago have revised the confidentiality rules as he suggests? If his arguments are not as good as they seem, is the "discomfort" of lawyers with revealing confidence not only an empirical fact but also the relevant term in the justification of a position someplace between Freedman's and Gillers's?

Monroe H. Freedman

DISCLOSING THE TRUTH ABOUT CLIENT PERJURY

I. INTRODUCTION

Chief Justice Warren Burger and two other federal judges initiated disbarment proceedings against me in 1966.[1] The charge was that, in a lecture to a group of lawyers, I had expressed opinions that "appear to be in conflict with the *Canons of Professional Ethics* of the American Bar Association."[2] The offensive opinions related to the criminal defense lawyer's conflicting ethical obligations in dealing with client perjury, based on requirements in the *Canons of Professional Ethics*.[3]

While the disbarment proceedings were pending, the lecture became an article: "The Professional Responsibility of the Criminal Defense Lawyer: The Three Hardest Questions."[4] After four months of hearings and deliberations, the charges were dismissed. As shown below, however, the controversy continues four decades later, principally because of serious misunderstandings about the constitutional and policy issues involved.[5]

From *Georgetown Journal of Legal Ethics* 21 (2008). Reprinted by permission of the author.

II. THE BEGINNING OF THE CLIENT PERJURY CONTROVERSY

The question of how to deal with client perjury arose in the 1960s in informal discussions among a small group of young criminal defense lawyers in Washington, DC. These lawyers got together from time to time to discuss tactical problems like how to pick a jury or whether to defer an opening statement until after the prosecution's case-in-chief.[6] One day, a member of the group said, with considerable embarrassment, "My client is going to testify tomorrow, and he's going to lie, and I don't know what I'm supposed to do about it." To our surprise, we found that we all shared what we each considered to be a personal guilty secret. That is, each of us believed that he or she was unique in facing that and other serious ethical problems, and each assumed that he or she must have been doing something wrong or it would not have been happening. Certainly, such issues had never been recognized, much less discussed, either in our law school classes or in any professional conferences.[7]

As we explored the issue of client perjury, we found that the American Bar Association's *Canons of Professional Ethics* were internally contradictory.[8] A lawyer was required to "endeavor to obtain full knowledge of his client's cause before advising him."[9] As explained in an early ABA opinion: "[C]ounsel cannot properly perform their duties without knowing the truth."[10] In order to encourage clients to be candid with their lawyers, therefore, the *Canons* required lawyers to preserve their clients' confidences.[11] Nevertheless, the *Canons* also required lawyers to be candid with the court.[12] Thus, the trilemma: to know everything possible, and to keep it in confidence, but to divulge it to the court if candor to the court required it.

After the Supreme Court's decision in *Gideon v. Wainwright*,[13] holding that a criminal defendant facing imprisonment is constitutionally entitled to legal representation at trial, there was considerable concern about how enough lawyers would be found to handle the high number of cases. Accordingly, I obtained a grant to establish a Criminal Trial Institute, in which practicing lawyers who were not involved in criminal defense would be trained in how to represent a criminal defendant.[14]

In an introductory one-hour lecture, I discussed the ethical issues that my friends and I had found to be particularly troubling. With regard to client perjury, I noted that there are three ways to resolve the lawyer's problem. One possible resolution that I discussed is to caution the client against giving the lawyer incriminating information that might create ethical problems—what has since been called the "lawyer-client Miranda warning." This is the model of "intentional ignorance," which has been expressly condemned by the ABA; that is, "[d]efense counsel should not . . . intimate to the client in any way that the client should not be candid in revealing facts. . . ."[15] Another solution I discussed is to promise the client confidentiality, but to break that promise if the client later proposes to give false testimony in his defense. The third solution, which I have favored, is to make good faith efforts to dissuade the client from committing the perjury, but, if the lawyer is unsuccessful in those efforts, to present the client's false testimony to the court in the ordinary way.

The lecture was reported the next day in the *Washington Post* and, the day after that, the United States District Court Committee on Professional Admissions and Grievances sent me the letter saying that I was subject to disbarment proceedings because of the opinions that I had expressed in the lecture. After four months, which included a hearing and considerable public controversy, the charges were dropped....

Ironically, the controversy over the lecture and the article stimulated my interest and involvement in lawyers' ethics, a subject which, at that time, was not even recognized as an acceptable "field of law" by the American Bar Association.[16]

II. THE ABA'S SOLUTIONS TO THE PERJURY TRILEMMA

A. The Canons of Professional Ethics (1908–1969)—Protecting Clients' Confidences Given Primacy Over Candor to the Court

At the time of the 1966 lecture and article, there was significant support for the resolution that I favored. For example, in its Formal Opinion 268 (1945), the ABA Standing Committee on Ethics and Professional Responsibility recognized the conflict within the *Canons of Professional Ethics* regarding client perjury. Resolving the conflict in favor of confidentiality, the committee stated: "While ordinarily it is the duty of a lawyer, as an officer of the court, to disclose to the court any fraud that he believes is being practiced on the court [*Canon* 22], this duty does not transcend that to preserve the client's confidences [*Canon* 37]."

Eight years later, Formal Opinion 287 (1953) dealt with two situations. In one a lawyer who had obtained a divorce for a client learned from the client that the client had committed perjury in the divorce proceedings. In the other, a judge was about to impose sentence upon the client based upon misinformation that the client had no previous criminal record, while the lawyer knew from the client that he did have a criminal record. The Committee determined that in both those cases, the lawyer's obligation was to urge the client to disclose the truth, but to remain silent if the client did not do so....

B. The Model Code of Professional Responsibility (1969–1983) Disclosing Client Perjury Continues to Be "Unthinkable"

The Model Code, as originally promulgated in 1969, appeared to revive the ambiguities regarding confidentiality that had existed under the *Canons* prior to Formal Opinions 268 and 287. The *Model Code* recognizes that full knowledge of the facts by the lawyer is "essential to proper representation," and that such knowledge is facilitated by the "observance of the ethical obligation of the lawyer to hold inviolate the confidences and secrets of his client."[17] Nevertheless, the original version of DR 7-102(B)(1) of the *Model Code* also appeared to require the lawyer to reveal a fraud by the client upon a tribunal or a third party, just as some provisions of the *Canons* had appeared to do prior to Opinions 268 and 287.[18]

DR 7-102(B)(1) had two operative clauses in the event of client fraud. The first required that the lawyer "promptly call upon the client to rectify the [fraud]."[19] The second clause—the "and if" clause—provided: "and if his client refuses or is unable to do so, [the lawyer] shall reveal the fraud to the affected person or tribunal."[20] That appeared to reverse the policy under the 1908 *Canons*, and to make candor to the court superior to client confidentiality in both criminal and civil cases.

However, the ABA acted promptly to exclude criminal defense lawyers from the disclosure obligation of DR 7-102(B)(1). In 1971, the House of Delegates approved the *ABA Standards Relating to the Defense Function*, in which the ABA explained that the lawyer's obligation to reveal client fraud under the "and if" clause of DR 7-102(B)(1) did not relate to false testimony in a criminal case.[21]

Then, in 1974, the ABA added a new clause, following the "and if" clause of DR 7-102(B)(1). As a result of that amendment, the attorney was required to reveal the client's fraud on a court or a third party, "except when the information [was] protected as a privileged communication."

On a plain-meaning reading, the phrase "privileged communication" appeared to mean only "confidences," a term of art that referred only to information that is protected by the lawyer-client evidentiary privilege.[22] If construed broadly, however, the phrase "privileged communication" could have included "secrets." The definition of "secrets" included all information gained in the representation, and went so far as to protect information that would be embarrassing to the client.[23] Read that way, the "except" clause (forbidding disclosure) would have swallowed up the "and if" clause (which appeared to require disclosure). That is, the ABA's amendment to DR 7-102(B)(1) could have been understood to nullify the clause that says, "and if his client refuses or is unable to do so, [the lawyer] shall reveal the fraud to the affected person or tribunal." Interpreted in such a way, DR 7-102(B)(1) would have completely restored the primacy of confidentiality over candor to the court.

That is what happened. In Formal Opinion 341 (1975), the ABA Committee on Professional Ethics considered whether the phrase "privileged communication" in the new "except" clause referred only to clients' "confidences" or, more broadly, to clients' "secrets" as well. The committee determined that the "except" clause includes secrets, which means that a lawyer is forbidden to reveal a client's fraud on a tribunal or third party if doing so would be "embarrassing" to the client.[24] As Professor Geoffrey Hazard has wryly remarked, "fraud is always embarrassing," and the ABA's amendment to DR 7-102(B)(1) therefore "eviscerated the duty to report fraud."[25]

Opinion 341 condemned the apparent requirement of unamended DR 7-102(B)(1), that a lawyer disclose client fraud on the court or third parties, as "unthinkable" and dismissed it as the result of an oversight in drafting. Instead, Opinion 341 construed DR 7-102(B)(1) to "reinstate the essence of Opinion 287," and held that client confidentiality is "so important that it should take precedence in all but the most serious cases." Acknowledging that "the conflicting duties to reveal fraud and to preserve confidences [had] existed side-by-side for some time," Opinion 341 added that "it is clear that there has long been an accommodation in favor of preserving confidences either through practice or interpretation." On the basis of "tradition . . . backed by substantial policy considerations," therefore, Opinion 341 reaffirmed the traditional model in which client confidentiality takes precedence over candor to the court.

C. *The Model Rules of Professional Conduct (1983)—*
The Apparent Change in Policy in Rule 3.3 Has Been Virtually
Nullified by Interpretation of "Knowing"

The ABA's *Model Rules of Professional Conduct* appear to reject those substantial policy considerations and to reverse the long-standing tradition of upholding client confidentiality in cases of client perjury. If so, it would indeed be "a major policy change" from earlier ethical obligations regarding client perjury.[26] The change, however, is more apparent than real.

Under *Model Rule* 3.3(a)(3), a lawyer is forbidden to offer evidence that the lawyer knows to be false. Also, under the same provision, if the lawyer offers material evidence that the lawyer later learns to be false, the lawyer is required to "take reasonable remedial measures." As explained in the comment to *Rule* 3.3, "remedial measures" include the obligation to inform the court of the client's perjury.[27]

The reason the rule change is more apparent than real is that the lawyer has no obligation either to prevent client perjury or to report it to the court unless the lawyer "knows" that the client's testimony will be or has been perjurious.[28] Moreover, the words "know" and "knowledge" have been defined in the Terminology section of the *Model Rules* in the most restrictive terms. Thus, "knowing" means "actual knowledge," and the ABA, the American Law Institute, and the courts have all made it clear that a lawyer will rarely "know" about client perjury.[29]

For example, in the words of ABA Formal Opinion 87-353, it will be "the unusual case" where the lawyer "does know" that a client intends to commit perjury. That opinion states that knowing can be established only by the client's "clearly stated intention" to perjure himself at trial....

III. MODEL RULE 3.3 UNFAIRLY PREJUDICES DEFENDANTS WHO ARE POOR AND MEMBERS OF MINORITY GROUPS

One might conclude that the issue of client perjury no longer warrants discussion because, as a practical matter, virtually all authorities agree on the end result—that is, that the lawyer should present the client's perjury in the ordinary way.

Nevertheless, there remains a critical policy issue under *Model Rule* 3.3, because there are still some cases in which lawyers conclude that their clients are lying and then betray their clients' confidences. Unfortunately, those lawyers are almost always court-appointed attorneys representing indigent criminal defendants, most of whom are members of minority groups.[30] This has produced a race- and class-based double standard, creating a de facto denial of equal protection of the laws.[31]...

IV. MODEL RULE 3.3 VIOLATES THE PRIVILEGE AGAINST SELF-INCRIMINATION AND THE RIGHT TO COUNSEL

An essential part of a defense lawyer's job in providing effective assistance of counsel is to advise the accused about the privilege against self-incrimination and whether it should be invoked in a particular situation.[32] The obvious reason is that "[a] layman may not be aware of the precise scope, the nuances, and boundaries of his Fifth Amendment privilege," and the assertion of that right therefore "often depends upon legal advice from someone who is trained and skilled in the subject matter."[33] Thus, as reiterated by the Supreme Court, the Fifth Amendment protects an accused from being made "the deluded instrument of his own conviction."[34]

Accordingly, there is a crucial relationship between the Sixth Amendment right to counsel and the Fifth Amendment privilege against self-incrimination.[35] It is the lawyer's cautionary counseling of the client that gives meaningful effect to the privilege.[36] Thus, the Sixth and Fifth Amendments work in tandem to forbid a lawyer from eliciting incriminating information from a client who has not been warned of the consequences and then revealing the elicited information to the court.

The way in which the right to counsel and the privilege against self-incrimination are inextricably interrelated was made clear in *Massiah v. United States*.[37] In *Massiah*, the defendant was indicted, retained a lawyer, and was released on bail. While Massiah was free on bail, his friend and co-defendant, Colson, agreed to cooperate with the government. Colson allowed an agent to install a transmitter in his car, and then had a lengthy conversation with Massiah in the car while the agent listened in. In the course of that conversation, Massiah made several incriminating statements that were used against him at trial.

The Supreme Court held that Massiah's self-incriminating statements had to be suppressed because they had been "deliberately elicited by the police after the defendant had been indicted, and therefore at a time when he was clearly entitled to a lawyer's help."[38] The Court went on to hold that the Constitution must protect the defendant's right to counsel in that extrajudicial setting, because otherwise the defendant might be denied "effective representation by counsel at the only stage when legal aid and advice would help him."[39]

Accordingly, Massiah's Fifth and Sixth Amendment rights were jointly violated "when there was used against him at his trial evidence of his own incriminating words, which federal agents had deliberately elicited from him after he had been indicted and in the absence of his counsel."[40] Moreover, the fact that the damaging testimony was not elicited from Massiah in a police station, but when he was free on bail, meant that Massiah was "more seriously imposed upon . . . because he did not even know that he was under interrogation by a government agent."[41] In short, the Supreme Court has recognized that a pretended friend creates a more serious constitutional problem than a known agent of one's adversary. As the Court has said, "An open foe may prove a curse / But a pretended friend is worse."[42]

Massiah was followed by *United States v. Henry*.[43] There, a government informer who had been placed in the cell with Henry established a relationship of trust and confidence with him. As a result, Henry revealed incriminating information to the informer. Chief Justice Burger wrote the opinion for the Court, vacating Henry's conviction because it had been based in part on the admissions elicited through a false relationship of trust and confidence.

The Court decided *Henry* under the Sixth Amendment right to counsel, but *Henry*'s relevance to the Fifth Amendment aspect of client perjury is plain. The Chief Justice's statement of the issue, and the emphasis throughout the opinion, was on the "admission at trial of *incriminating statements* made by [the defendant] to his cellmate."[44] As Justice Powell expressed it, the government, through the cellmate, had engaged in "the functional equivalent of interrogation."[45]

In addition, Justice Rehnquist, dissenting in *Henry*, linked the Fifth and Sixth Amendments together, noting that they reflect the Framers' intent to establish an accusatory rather than an inquisitorial system of justice."[46] Rehnquist added that "the Sixth Amendment, of course, protects the confidentiality of communications between the accused and his attorney,"[47] and "[a]ny dealings that an accused may have with his attorney are of course confidential, and anything the accused says to his attorney is beyond the reach of the prosecution."[48]

Moreover, both the majority and dissenting Justices recognized that a statement can be "involuntary" for Sixth Amendment purposes if it has been "deliberately elicited" by a covert government agent in the absence of counsel.[49] The exclusionary rule of *Massiah*, the Court said, is expressly designed to counter "'deliberat[e]' interference with an indicted suspect's right to counsel."[50] The Court also held that because Henry had not known that his cellmate intended to relate his admissions to the government, "the concept of a knowing and voluntary waiver of Sixth Amendment rights does not apply," and Henry "cannot be held to have waived his right to the assistance of counsel."[51] Again, therefore, the Supreme Court gave particular constitutional significance to admissions made to a pretended friend.

Henry also demonstrates that the future crime exception to the lawyer-client evidentiary privilege is not relevant to the present analysis of client perjury. The defendant's *constitutional* privilege against self-incrimination, safeguarded by his *constitutional* right to counsel, is not dependent on his lawyer-client *evidentiary* privilege, so exceptions to the evidentiary privilege are irrelevant. In *Henry,* the defendant had no lawyer-client privilege (or any other evidentiary privilege) with his cell-mate. Nevertheless, the incriminating statements that the defendant had made to the cellmate were excluded under the Sixth Amendment because he was entitled to have his lawyer available to warn him when he was making the self-incriminating statements to his cellmate. Thus, what is important for constitutional purposes is not whether there is an evidentiary privilege regarding the lawyer-client communications, but whether unwarned admissions have been elicited from the defendant by an agent of the state who then uses those admissions against him in court.[52]

Accordingly, even if the future crime exception to the lawyer-client privilege would apply to false testimony regarding the past crime which is the subject of the representation,[53] that would not affect the present constitutional analysis of the Fifth and Sixth Amendments.

The recognition in *United States v. Henry* of the interrelationship between the Sixth and Fifth Amendments was again applied in *Estelle v. Smith.*[54] In that case, a psychiatrist examined defendant Smith to determine his competence to stand trial. Subsequently, based on what he had learned in the competency examination, the psychiatrist testified in the penalty phase of the trial that Smith was a future danger to society.[55]

The trial judge had ordered the State's attorney to arrange the psychiatric examination regarding Smith's competence to stand trial, but apparently had neither ordered Smith to cooperate with the psychiatrist nor advised him that he did not have to do so.[56] Also, defense counsel were not notified in advance that the examination would encompass the issue of future dangerousness, and so did not advise Smith about his Fifth Amendment privilege.[57]

Again writing the opinion for the Court, Chief Justice Burger reversed, holding that the psychiatrist's testimony could not be used against the defendant in the sentencing phase because "the psychiatric examination on which [the psychiatrist] testified at the penalty phase proceeded in violation of [Smith's] Sixth Amendment right to the assistance of counsel."[58] The Court also held that a waiver of the assistance of counsel "must not only be voluntary, but must also constitute a knowing and intelligent relinquishment or abandonment of a known right or privilege...."[59]

Estelle v. Smith is particularly important to the present analysis because the defense lawyer who elicits a client's incriminating information does not do so initially for purposes of prosecution. Similarly, the purpose of the psychiatrist's examination in *Estelle* was not initially prosecutorial.[60] Rather, the trial judge, sua sponte, had ordered the psychiatric evaluation of Smith for the neutral purpose of determining his competency to stand trial.[61] Indeed, as the Court recognized, the doctor's diagnosis might well have benefitted the defendant by helping him to escape the death penalty.[62] Only at the sentencing hearing did the psychiatrist's "role change[]," and only then did he become essentially "an agent of the state recounting unwarned statements made in a post-arrest custodial setting."[63] Accordingly, the defendant's Fifth and Sixth Amendment rights had been violated, and Smith's sentence was vacated.

The Supreme Court recently reiterated the vitality of *Massiah* and *Henry* in *Fellers v. United States* even as it noted a difference between the Fifth and Sixth Amendment standards for exclusion of self-incriminatory statements.[64] Under the Fifth Amendment alone, exclusion depends upon whether there is in-custody interrogation.[65] However, "an accused is denied 'the basic protections' of the Sixth Amendment 'when there [is] used against him at his trial evidence of his own incriminating words which federal agents ... deliberately elicited from him after he had been indicted and in the absence of his counsel."[66] The Court added that it has "consistently applied this deliberate-elicitation standard in subsequent Sixth Amendment cases,"[67] "even when there is no interrogation and no Fifth Amendment applicability."[68]

Moreover, as *Massiah*, *Henry*, and *Estelle* make clear, the "basic protection[]" that is specifically at issue in these Sixth Amendment cases is the lawyer's advice to the client regarding the Fifth Amendment privilege against self-incrimination. Thus, the privilege against self-incrimination takes on a broader constitutional significance once the accused has a lawyer.

Surely a defendant's own lawyer cannot do what the pretended friend in *Massiah*, the psychiatrist in *Estelle*, or the cellmate in *Henry* could not do—that is, establish a relationship of trust and confidence and then "become an agent of the State recounting unwarned statements." In fact, the role of the lawyer is a more serious one in this regard than that of a cellmate. The Supreme Court has never described trust and confidence between cellmates as "imperative," but it has used that word in describing the relationship of trust and confidence between lawyer and client.[69] Moreover, as Chief Justice Rehnquist noted in *Henry*, "the Sixth Amendment, of course, protects the confidentiality of communications between the accused and his attorney."[70] There is no such protection for communications between the accused and his pretended friend, his cellmate, or his court-appointed psychiatrist.

If, then, the lawyer's responsibility is to provide the basic protection of warning her client about the risks of incriminating himself to other persons who might later reveal his confidences, who has the responsibility of warning the defendant about the risk of confiding incriminating information to his lawyer?

The difficulty is that the lawyer is forbidden to engage in "intentional ignorance" by giving the client a "lawyer-client Miranda warning." That is, the lawyer is forbidden to "intimate to the client in any way" that the client should withhold information "so as to afford defense counsel free rein to take action which would be precluded by counsel's knowing of such facts."[71] This is an elaboration on *Model Rule* 1.6, comment [1], which explains that a purpose of lawyer-client confidentiality is that the client is "thereby encouraged . . . to communicate fully and frankly with the lawyer even as to . . . legally damaging subject matter." Beyond that, the lawyer must impress upon the client "the imperative need [that the lawyer] know all aspects of the case."[72]

In addition, under *Model Rule* 3.3(a)(3), the lawyer is forbidden to "offer evidence that the lawyer knows to be false," and is required to "take reasonable remedial measures, including if necessary, disclosure to the tribunal" with respect to evidence that the lawyer has offered and that she comes to know is false. Of course, in those jurisdictions in which the lawyer employs the narrative method as a remedial measure, the lawyer effectively discloses the client's confidences to the jury (the finder of fact) as well as to the judge (the sentencer).

This means that the lawyer, in preparing for trial, is required to deliberately elicit incriminating information from the client without first warning the client that, if the client later testifies falsely, the lawyer will reveal the client's incriminating confidences at trial.[73]

Therefore, just like the pretended friend in *Massiah*, the cellmate in *Henry*, and the psychiatrist in *Estelle*, the lawyer elicits unwarned admissions from the defendant and then becomes "an agent of the state recounting unwarned admissions" at trial. Indeed, the lawyer is more clearly an "agent of the state" than the other three, because only the lawyer is threatened with punishment by the state for failing to report the defendant's damaging admissions. Ironically, the Sixth Amendment "guarantees the accused . . . the right to rely on counsel as a 'medium' between him and the State,"[74] warning the defendant about potential self-incrimination, but there is no one to serve as a medium between the accused and his counsel. On the contrary, the defendant is denied "effective representation by counsel [i.e., a warning to the defendant about the potential loss of his Fifth Amendment privilege] at the only stage when legal aid and advice would help him."[75] . . .

It has also been suggested that the defense lawyer can properly reveal the client's perjury because statements elicited by agents of the state and revealed by them to the prosecutor can be used by the prosecutor for impeachment.[76] This is a non-sequitur. The fact that a prosecutor might be able to use such information for impeachment purposes[77] does not mean that defense counsel can be the agent of the state who is required to do the revealing or the advocate who is required to do the impeaching. As stated by Chief Justice Rehnquist, "[a]ny dealings that an accused may have with his attorney are of course confidential, and anything the accused says to his attorney is *beyond the reach of the prosecution*."[78]

None of this means that a defendant has a "right to lie" with impunity. One immediate penalty is that the defendant's sentence may be enhanced if the judge concludes that he has committed perjury in his defense.[79] Another penalty is that the defendant who testifies falsely can thereafter be prosecuted for perjury.[80] However, the penalties for perjury do not include a waiver of the defendant's Sixth and Fifth Amendment rights to be warned by his lawyer of the potentially harmful consequences before he unwittingly makes incriminating statements to his lawyer. That can be done only by a knowing and voluntary relinquishment of a known right, which is not possible when the defendant is unaware of the consequences at the time he incriminates himself.

Nor is denial of the right to counsel in presenting his testimony a penalty for a defendant's perjury.[81] In *New Jersey v. Portash*,[82] defendant Portash had been granted use immunity for earlier grand jury testimony. When he was subsequently prosecuted based on other evidence, the trial court ruled *in limine* that if Portash testified to an alibi that contradicted his grand jury testimony, the prosecution would be able to use the grand jury testimony to impeach him. Accordingly, Portash did not testify at his trial. He was convicted.

On appeal, the Supreme Court assumed that Portash's immunized grand jury testimony had been truthful and that his trial testimony would have been perjurious.[83] Nevertheless, the Court held that Portash had a constitutional right to present his alibi without being impeached with his grand jury testimony. Portash's conviction was therefore reversed by the Supreme Court in order to allow him to present the alibi on retrial. Moreover, there was no suggestion that Portash's lawyer had acted improperly in attempting to present the perjurious alibi; on the contrary, the appeal could not even have been taken if the lawyer had not assisted Portash in that effort.[84]

Furthermore, the decision in *Portash* was based on the Fifth Amendment alone. The case is that much stronger when the incriminating evidence has been obtained in violation of the Sixth Amendment—that is, when it has been deliberately elicited from the defendant by his own lawyer, acting as an agent of the state, and forbidden to warn him in advance of the consequences. In that event, the evidence cannot be used against the defendant at trial with respect to either guilt or sentencing.

V. CONCLUSION

In formal opinions under its 1908 *Canons of Professional Ethics*, the ABA recognized that a lawyer's duty to disclose fraud on the court is subordinate to the obligation to preserve a client's confidences. The ABA explained that because the lawyer is an officer of the court, she is required to maintain her client's confidences even in cases of client perjury. Thereafter, in a formal opinion interpreting its *Model Rules of Professional Responsibility*, the ABA expressly relied on tradition as well as substantial policy considerations in stating that for a lawyer to disclose her client's fraud on the court was "unthinkable."[85]

The traditional view that was recognized in those formal opinions appeared to have been reversed in 1983, when the ABA adopted *Model Rule* 3.3 requiring lawyers to take remedial action in cases of known perjury. In some jurisdictions, remedial action has meant that a trial lawyer must distance herself from her client by requiring the client to testify in narrative and then to omit any reference to the client's false testimony in closing argument. The result of the narrative method is that the lawyer effectively communicates to the jury as well as to the judge that the lawyer believes that the client is guilty.

However, the appearance that *Model Rule* 3.3 brought about a major policy change from the traditional view has been rendered practically meaningless by the requirement that a lawyer have "actual knowledge" before taking any remedial action. The result is that a defense lawyer may refrain from concluding that her client's testimony is perjurious, despite the fact that the client has told the lawyer inconsistent versions of the truth, and despite the fact that the client's testimony is far-fetched or preposterous, unsupported by other evidence, and dramatically contradicted by credible evidence. Through the disingenuous use of the "knowing" requirement, therefore, the courts and the ABA have effectively maintained the result of the traditional view.

Nevertheless, there remains a critical policy issue under *Model Rule* 3.3 because there are still some occasions when lawyers conclude that their clients are lying and then betray their clients' confidences. Unfortunately, those lawyers are almost always court-appointed attorneys representing criminal defendants who are poor and members of minority groups. This has produced a race- and class-based double standard, resulting in a de facto denial of equal protection of the laws.

It is therefore important to consider the point that *Model Rule* 3.3 violates the Fifth and Sixth Amendments to the Constitution. This is an issue that no court has yet ruled upon. However, analogous authorities strongly support the conclusion that a lawyer violates the Constitution by deliberately eliciting unwarned admissions from a client and then revealing those admissions to a court.

The Supreme Court has held that the Sixth Amendment forbids an agent of the state to reveal at trial admissions that have been elicited from a defendant who has not first been advised by his lawyer about his privilege against self-incrimination. Nevertheless, ethical rules require the lawyer to deliberately elicit incriminating information from the client without warning the client of the consequences in advance. In addition, the ethical rules require the lawyer to reveal the client's incriminating confidences at trial if the client should testify falsely. Thus, the lawyer, as an officer of the court, acts under state compulsion, subject to state sanctions including loss of a state-issued license to practice law, if the lawyer should fail to comply with the state's ethical requirements.

Ironically, therefore, the Sixth Amendment guarantees the defendant the right to have counsel advise him about his Fifth Amendment privilege before the client incriminates himself to a third-party agent of the state. However, there is no one to advise the defendant about his Fifth Amendment privilege before he is induced by his lawyer to incriminate himself. Accordingly, the client is unable to make an informed and voluntary waiver of a known right before giving the lawyer incriminating information. Therefore, when a lawyer later

reveals at trial the incriminating information that the lawyer has deliberately elicited from the client, the lawyer violates the client's Fifth and
Sixth Amendment rights.

Linking the Fifth and Sixth Amendments together, Chief Justice
Rehnquist noted that they reflect the Framers' intent to establish an
accusatory rather than an inquisitorial system of justice. He added that
the Sixth Amendment protects the confidentiality of communications
between the accused and his attorney, and that anything the accused says
to his attorney is beyond the reach of the prosecution. It is particularly
ironic, therefore, that *Model Rule* 3.3 turns the criminal defense lawyer
into the functional equivalent of the prosecutor of her own client,
charged with disclosing her client's incriminating confidences at trial.

NOTES

1. The letter from the grievance committee initiating the proceedings
referred to communications to the committee from "[s]everal judges." Letter to
Monroe H. Freedman, Esq., from Ralph A. Curtin, Secretary to the US District
Court for the District of Columbia Committee on Admissions and Grievances,
January 12, 1966 (on file with author). The judges proved to be Warren Burger,
who, at the time, was a judge in the US Court of Appeals for the DC Circuit,
and US District Judges Alexander Holtzoff and George Hart. See, e.g., "Court
Clears Attorney In Client-Lie Furor," *Sunday Star* (May 15, 1966), p. A14.

2. Letter to Monroe H. Freedman, Esq., from Ralph A. Curtin, Secretary
to the US District Court for the District of Columbia Committee on Admissions and Grievances, January 12, 1966 (on file with author).

3. See "Canons of Professional Ethics," *Canon* 6 (1908) [hereinafter 1908
Canons]; 1908 *Canons* 8; 1908 *Canons* 22; 1908 *Canons* 37.

4. Monroe Freedman, "The Professional Responsibility of the Criminal
Defense Lawyer: The Three Hardest Questions," *Michigan Law Review* 64
(1966): 1469. The article has been expanded and updated in Freedman and
Smith, ch. 6 ("The Perjury Trilemma"). Yale Kamisar, then the junior author
of Hall and Kamisar, *Modern Criminal Procedure* (1966), included the article in
the book. This was the first time that ethics materials were incorporated into

another course, in what has come to be called the "pervasive method" of teaching lawyers' ethics.

5. See, e.g., Stephen Gillers, "Monroe Freedman's Solution to the Criminal Defense Lawyer's Trilemma Is Wrong as a Matter of Policy and Constitutional Law," *Hofstra Law Review* 34 (2006): 821. Gillers's original title, announced at a Hofstra Law School conference on lawyers' ethics, was "The Perjurious Criminal Defendant: A Critique of Freedman's Critique and All Other Solutions (or Why Do We Keep Talking about This?)." The answer to Gillers's parenthetic question in his original title is this: We keep talking about the issue of the perjurious client because commenters like Gillers persist in getting it wrong by not recognizing how *Model Rule* 3.3 works in practice, by ignoring the most important policy issue under that rule, and by misreading the relevant constitutional cases.

6. The group included, from time to time, Barbara Babcock, Gary Bellow, Sam Dash, A. Kenneth Pye, Florence Roisman, Ralph Temple, and Jonathan Weiss.

7. Other issues included whether it is proper to give a client legal advice when the client might use the advice to concoct a perjurious alibi or to commit other wrongs, and whether it is proper to cross-examine a prosecution witness who the lawyer knows is testifying accurately and truthfully in order to make the witness appear to be mistaken or lying. These issues are discussed in Freedman and Smith, "Counseling Clients and Preparing Witnesses," ch. 7; and "Cross-Examining to Discredit the Truthful Witness," ch. 8.

8. The *Canons* had been promulgated by the ABA in 1908, and governed the conduct of lawyers at the time.

9. 1908 *Canons* 8.

10. ABA Committee on Professional Ethics and Grievances, *Formal Opinion* 23 (1930).

11. 1908 *Canons* 37. See 1908 *Canons* 6.

12. 1908 *Canons* 22.

13. *Gideon v. Wainwright*, 372 U.S. 335 (1963).

14. The funding organizations were the National Legal Aid and Defender Association and the United Planning Organization. The Institute used techniques that have subsequently been used in the National Institute for Trial Advocacy and similar programs.

15. American Bar Association, "Standards for Criminal Justice, The Defense Function," *Standard* 4-3.2(b) (1993). See also ibid., *Standard* 3.2, cmt.

(warning that advising the client at the outset not to admit anything that might handicap the lawyer's freedom in calling witnesses or in otherwise making a defense is "most egregious" and is advocated only by "unscrupulous" lawyers); ibid. (describing such conduct as a "flagrant" impropriety).

16. Eleven years later, in 1977, I succeeded in persuading a reluctant ABA Standing Committee on Law Lists that legal ethics and professional responsibility should be recognized as an acceptable "field of law." Thus, lawyers' ethics joined 155 previously recognized fields of law, including cemetery law and drainage and levee law. See Monroe Freedman, "Crusading for Legal Ethics," *Legal Times* (July 10, 1995), p. 25.

17. *Model Code* EC 4-1.

18. 1908 *Canons* 22 ("Candor and Fairness"); 1908 *Canons* 15 ("How Far a Lawyer May Go in Supporting a Client's Cause").

19. *Model Code* DR 7-102(B)(1).

20. At the same time, *Model Code* EC 8-5 said that the lawyer should reveal any knowledge of "[f]raudulent, deceptive, or otherwise illegal conduct by a participant in a proceeding before a tribunal ... *[u]nless constrained by his obligation to preserve the confidences and secrets of his client*" (*Model Code* EC 8-5; emphasis added).

21 American Bar Association, "Standards Relating to the Prosecution and Defense Function," *Supplement* 18 (1971).

22. *Model Code* DR 4-101(a) distinguished between "confidences" and "secrets." "Confidences" referred narrowly to information protected by the attorney-client privilege, that is, information that cannot be used as evidence in a judicial proceeding. The elements of the privilege vary somewhat from state to state, but basically they require that the information be in a communication between a client and lawyer that is made in confidence for the purpose of obtaining or providing legal assistance.

23. *Model Code* DR 4-101(a).

24. Ibid.

25. Geoffrey C. Hazard Jr., *Ethics in the Practice of Law* (1978), p. 27.

26. ABA *Formal Opinion* 87-353 (1987).

27. See *Model Rules* R. 3.3, Comment on *Remedial Measures*. If perjured testimony or false evidence has been offered, the advocates's proper course ordinarily is to remonstrate with the client confidentially. If that fails, the advocate should seek to withdraw if that will remedy the situation. If withdrawal will

not remedy the situation or is impossible, the advocate should make disclosure to the court.... .

28. *Model Rules* R. 3.3(a).

29. The way in which standards of "knowing" have been manipulated in rules of lawyers' ethics was first recognized and analyzed in Monroe H. Freedman, "Lawyers' Ethics in an Adversary System," *What Does a Lawyer Really "Know": The Epistemology of Legal Ethics* (1975).

30. Jay Sterling Silver, "Truth, Justice, and the American Way: The Case against Client Perjury Rules," *Vanderbilt Law Review* 47 (1994): 339.

31. Ibid., p. 359. Oddly, Professor Gillers deliberately ignored this issue in contending that "Freedman's Solution... Is Wrong as a Matter of Policy." See *Hofstra Law Review* 34 (2006): 821. I had specifically asked Gillers in advance of the Hofstra conference to address this issue. See ibid., p. 841. When I raised it with Gillers again during the question-and-answer session following his presentation at the conference, he responded: "So now we got a little too complicated, because we are forced to look at the rules. All right. Well, then there are—that would be part of the record and, you know, it depends upon the conversation." Ibid., see also *Professional Lawyer* 17 (2006): 25 (letters from Freedman and Gillers confirming the previous exchanges regarding the issue).

32. "Our Constitution... strikes the balance in favor of the right of the accused to be advised by his lawyer of his privilege against self-incrimination" (*Escobedo v. Illinois*, 378 U.S. p. 488; citing note, "An Historical Argument for the Right to Counsel during Police Interrogation," *Yale Law Journal* 73 (1964): 1000, 1048–51).

33. *Estelle v. Smith*, 451 U.S. 454, 471, 101 S. Ct. 1866, 1877 (1981) (Burger, C.J., quoting *Maness v. Meyers*, 419 U.S. pp. 449, 466 [1975]). As Justice Robert Jackson more pungently expressed it: "[A]ny lawyer worth his salt will tell the suspect in no uncertain terms to make no statement to police under any circumstances" (*Watts v. Indiana*, 338 U.S. pp. 49, 59 (1949); Jackson, J., concurring in part and dissenting in part).

34. *Estelle*, 451 U.S. pp. 454, 462 (1981); Burger, C.J. (quoting *Culombe v. Connecticut*, 367 U.S. pp. 568, 581 (1961); (quoting William Hawkins, *Pleas of the Crown* 8th ed. (1824)). See also *Bram v. United States*, 168 U.S. pp. 532, 547 (1897), quoting William Hawkins, *Pleas of the Crown* 6th ed. (1787); *Mitchell v. United States*, 526 U.S. pp. 314, 325 (1999) (the defendant should not be enlisted as "an instrument in his or her own condemnation").

35. The defendant's Sixth and Fifth Amendment "right...to be advised by his lawyer of his privilege against self-incrimination" was neither argued to the Court nor discussed in *Nix v. Whiteside*.

36. "Cases in this court, to say the least, have never placed a premium on ignorance of constitutional rights." *Escobedo v. Illinois*, 378 U.S. pp. 478, 499 (1964) (White, J., dissenting).

37. 377 U.S. p. 201 (1964).

38. Ibid., p. 204, quoting *Spano v. New York*, 360 U.S. pp. 315, 327 (1959) (Stewart, J., concurring). *Spano* had involved a confession in a state court. Chief Justice Warren's opinion for the Court, requiring exclusion of the confession as involuntary, was based on the totality of the circumstances under the due process clause of the Fourteenth Amendment. Although *Massiah* was a federal prosecution, the holding applies as well to state prosecutions. See *Brewer v. Williams*, 430 U.S. pp. 387, 401 (1977).

39. *Massiah*, 377 U.S. p. 204 (quoting 360 U.S. p. 326; Douglas, J., concurring).

40. *Massiah*, 377 U.S. p. 206.

41. Ibid., quoting *United States v. Massiah*, 307 F.2d pp. 62, 72–73 (2d Cir. 1962); Hays, J., dissenting, rev., 377 U.S. p. 201. The present analysis does not rely on the Fourth Amendment "false friend" cases. However, the language of those cases is consistent with the Fifth and Sixth Amendment analysis. See, e.g., *Hoffa v. United States*, 385 U.S. p. 293 (1966). When a pretended friend, who was acting as a government informant, obtained incriminatory statements from Hoffa in a conversation in Hoffa's hotel room, there was no violation of the Fourth Amendment because the risk that a friend will betray a confidence is "the kind of risk we necessarily assume whenever we speak." 385 U.S. p. 303, quoting *Lopez v. United States*, 373 U.S. pp. 427, 465 (1963). *Hoffa* was reaffirmed in *United States v. White*, 401 U.S. p. 745 (1971), which established that "a person confiding in another takes the risk that the confidence may be misplaced and that the confidant may memorize or record the statements and repeat them at trial." *United States v. White*, 405 F.2d p. 838, 846 (1969). When a client speaks to a lawyer, of course, he does not assume the risk inherent in ordinary conversation with a friend; rather, the client has a reasonable expectation that the lawyer will protect his confidences, and does not assume the risk either that the lawyer will reveal confidences without the client's consent or that there are exceptions to confidentiality that have not been explained to him. See, e.g., *Model Rules* R. 1.6, cmt. [2] ("A fundamental principle in the client-lawyer relationship is that, in the absence of the client's informed consent, the lawyer

must not reveal information relating to the representation."); *Model Rules* R. 1.4 ("A lawyer shall explain a matter to the extent reasonably necessary to permit the client to make informed decisions regarding the representation.").

42. *Spano*, 360 U.S. p. 323 (1959), quoting John Gay, "The Shepherd's Dog and the Wolf," in *The Poetical Works of John Gay*, vol. 337, photo reprint 2001 (1787).

43. 447 U.S. p. 264 (1980).

44. Ibid., p. 265 (emphasis added).

45. Ibid., p. 277 (Powell, J., concurring).

46. Ibid., p. 295 (Rehnquist, J., dissenting).

47. Ibid.

48. Ibid., p. 293 n.4.

49. See ibid., p. 269 (Burger, C. J., for the Court), 281, 2192 (Blackmun, J., dissenting).

50. Ibid., p. 282 n. 6.

51. Ibid., p. 273.

52. For further discussion, see Freedman and Smith, pp. 176–77, 186–88.

53. But see ibid.

54. *Estelle v. Smith*, 451 U.S. p. 454 (1981).

55. Ibid., pp. 459–60.

56. Ibid., pp. 456–57.

57. Ibid., n.15. Indeed, it appears that defense counsel were not even informed in advance that any psychiatric examination would take place.

58. Ibid.

59. Ibid., n. 16.

60. Ibid., p. 465. See also ibid., p. 476 (Rehnquist, J., concurring) ("Unlike the police officers in *Miranda*, Dr. Grigson was not questioning respondent in order to ascertain his guilt or innocence.").

61. Ibid., p. 465.

62. Ibid., p. 472.

63. Ibid., p. 467. In a similar case, *Satterwhite v. Texas*, 486 U.S. p. 249 (1988), the Court applied the harmless error doctrine to the Sixth Amendment right, but found that the psychiatrist's testimony had not been harmless.

64. *Fellers v. United States*, 540 U.S. p. 519 (2004).

65. Ibid., p. 524.

66. Ibid., p. 523, citing *Massiah v. United States*, 377 U.S. pp. 201, 206 (1964).

67. Ibid., p. 524, citing *United States v. Henry*, 447 U.S. pp. 267, 270, (1980).

68. Ibid., citing *Rhode Island v. Innis*, 446 U.S. pp. 291, 300 n.4 (1980).

69. *Trammel v. United States*, 445 U.S. pp. 40, 51 (1980).

70. *Henry*, 447 U.S. p. 295.

71. American Bar Association, "Standards for Criminal Justice, The Defense Function," *Standard* 4-3.2(b) (1993). The purpose of the Standards is to elaborate on the *Model Rules of Professional Conduct* by providing a "consensus view of all segments of the criminal justice community about what good, professional practice is and should be." American Bar Association, "Standards for Criminal Justice," *Introduction* (1993). Thus, *Standard* 4-3.2 is an elaboration on *Model Rule* 1.1 ("Competence") and *Model Rule* 1.6 ("Confidentiality of Information").

72. American Bar Association, "Standards for Criminal Justice, The Defense Function," *Standard* 4-3.2 cmt. (1993). *Model Rule* 1.4(a)(5) is not material to this discussion because it says that the lawyer "shall consult with the client about the limitations" on confidentiality only after the lawyer "knows that the client expects assistance not permitted by the Rules." *Model Rules* R. 1.4(a)(5). Even setting aside the "knowing" problem, the rule is clear that this cannot happen until it is already too late for the lawyer to give fair warning to the client. That is, before the lawyer informs the client of the risk that his confidences will be revealed, the client must have given the lawyer knowledge of an intention to commit perjury.

When the Massachusetts Supreme Judicial Court adopted its version of *Model Rule* 3.3, the Court invited me to address it in a formal hearing. Making the constitutional argument, I suggested that the *Rule* say expressly in the comment that anything the lawyer learns before the warning should not be relied upon in making a decision to reveal the client's perjury. The Court clearly understood the argument, but chose not to address the issue in promulgating the rules. On the Court at the time was Charles Fried, author of "The Lawyer as Friend: The Moral Foundations of the Lawyer-Client Relation," *Yale Law Journal* 85 (1976): 1060.

73. Even under the due process "totality of the circumstances" test, government agents are forbidden to use this kind of trickery. *State v. Nash*, 421 N.W.2d pp. 41, 43–44 (Neb. 1988) (defendant's reasonable understanding that admissions would be confidential made them involuntary); *State v. McDermott*, 554 A.2d p. 1302 (N.H. 1989) (confession was not "voluntary," but "coerced," because it was given under the promise of confidentiality, and "to allow the government to revoke its promise after obtaining incriminating information obtained in reliance on that promise would be to sanction governmental

deception in a manner violating due process."); *People v. Easley*, 592 N.E.2d pp. 1036, 1051 (Ill. 1992) (violation of due process where fellow inmate obtained admissions by saying information was for defendant's lawyer); *United States v. Goldstein*, 611 F. Supp. 626, 632 (N.D. Ill. 1985) (implied assurance that defendant's statements would not be used against him in a criminal prosecution made admissions involuntary); *United States v. Wolf*, 601 F. Supp. 435, 441–43 (N.D. Ill. 1984) (defendant's statements were involuntary because they were made to Canadian agents in reliance upon promise not to give them to IRS).

74. *Michigan v. Jackson*, 475 U.S. pp. 625, 632 (1986); quoting *Maine v. Moulton*, 474 U.S. pp. 159, 176 (1985), quoting *Brewer v. Williams*, 430 U.S. pp. 387, 415 (1977) (Stevens, J., concurring).

75. *Massiah v. United States*, 377 U.S. pp. 201, 204 (1964); quoting *Spano v. New York*, 360 U.S. pp. 315, 326 (1959) (Douglas, J., concurring).

76. Gillers, "Monroe Freedman's Solution to the Criminal Defense Lawyer's Trilemma Is Wrong as a Matter of Policy and Constitutional Law," p. 836.

77. But see *Michigan v. Harvey*, 494 U.S. pp. 344, 354 (1990).

78. *United States v. Henry*, 447 U.S., pp. 264, 293, n.4 (1980) (emphasis added).

79. *United States v. Grayson*, 438 U.S. p. 41 (1978).

80. See *United States v. Apfelbaum*, 445 U.S. p. 115 (1980).

81. *Nix v. Whiteside* noted the repudiation of the narrative method. *Nix v. Whiteside*, 475 U.S. pp. 157, 170 n.6 (1986).

82. *New Jersey v. Portash*, 440 U.S. p. 450 (1979).

83. See ibid., pp. 452–53.

84. See also *United States v. Midgett*, 342 F.3d p. 321 (4th Cir. 2003). In response to appointed defense counsel's motion for leave to withdraw on ethical grounds, the trial judge told the defendant that if he chose to take the stand and present what his lawyer and the judge believed to be perjury, the lawyer's motion would be granted. The Fourth Circuit reversed, explaining: "The defendant was told to waive either his right to counsel or his right to testify, because neither his counsel nor the court was satisfied that his testimony would be truthful. In so doing, the court leveled an ultimatum upon Midgett which, of necessity, deprived him of his constitutional right to testify on his own behalf" (ibid., p. 327, quoting United States *ex rel. Wilcox v. Johnson*, 555 F.2d pp. 115, 120–21, 3d Cir. 1977) ("A defendant in a criminal proceeding is entitled to certain rights. . . . He is entitled to all of them; he cannot be forced

to barter one for another. When the exercise of one right is made contingent upon the forbearance of another, both rights are corrupted."). The Fourth Circuit added: "[T]he court impermissibly forced the defendant to choose between two constitutionally protected rights: the right to testify on his own behalf and the right to counsel" (ibid.).

85. ABA Committee on Ethics and Professional Responsibility, *Formal Opinion* 341 (1975).

Stephen Gillers

MONROE FREEDMAN'S SOLUTION TO THE CRIMINAL DEFENSE LAWYER'S TRILEMMA IS WRONG AS A MATTER OF POLICY AND CONSTITUTIONAL LAW

I. INTRODUCTION

Monroe Freedman has argued ... that criminal defense lawyers have a "trilemma" because the rules of their profession give them potentially contradictory instructions. First, competence requires lawyers to seek all information that can aid a client's matter. Second, lawyers have a duty of confidentiality that generally forbids them to use a client's information except for the client's benefit. Third, lawyers have a duty of candor to the court that may require them to reveal a client's confidential information in order to prevent or correct fraud on the court (which perjury would be).

All in all . . . Freedman argues, one of the duties in the trilemma will sometimes have to yield to another duty in the trilemma, and it is best as a matter of policy (and sometimes required as a matter of law) that it be the duty of candor where the lawyer is defending a person charged with a crime. But the qualification on the duty of candor goes no further than allowing the lawyer, who can neither dissuade the client nor withdraw without prejudicing the client, to introduce false testimony of an (uncoached) client or the client's parent, spouse, or partner and then to argue the truth of that testimony to the jury.

Analysis of these issues must begin with temporal snapshots of when they may arise. Three situations are possible. First, the perjury can be anticipated. For example, a client may say she wants to testify to a false alibi and insist on her right to be called. Second, the perjury may occur by surprise. The lawyer may call the client anticipating truthful testimony (or at least testimony the lawyer does not know is false), but the client then lies while testifying, and the lawyer knows it. Third, the perjury may be concluded. The lawyer may learn only after the testimony has been given but before the conclusion of the representation that the client lied. The second situation (surprise perjury) and the third (concluded perjury) are the same insofar as the lawyer knows of the perjury only after it is committed. In either situation, a rule may require the lawyer to reveal confidential information to correct the perjury and forbid the lawyer to argue it in summation. In the case of concluded perjury, the lawyer has finished his questioning when he learns the client lied, while surprise perjury envisions that the client is still on the stand when the perjury occurs, but these differences are not significant for purposes of the policy or constitutional analysis. However, surprise and concluded perjury differ from anticipated perjury in a critical way. If the perjury is anticipated, no crime has yet been committed. If the lawyer is permitted to refuse to call the client to testify before the perjury occurs, no crime will ever be committed. By definition, perjury has already occurred in the case of surprise perjury and completed perjury, and the lawyer's knowledge of it may then impose a duty of candor to the court, one prong in the trilemma.

Because the analysis partly differs depending on whether the perjury is anticipated or concluded, I will discuss the two situations separately.

II. ANTICIPATED PERJURY

As stated, Freedman's solution to his trilemma in the case of anticipated perjury is to permit the criminal defense lawyer to elicit perjury from the defendant and certain persons close to the defendant if the lawyer is unable to change the client's mind or perhaps withdraw. Doing so, he argues, helps insure that the client will be candid with counsel and that the lawyer will avoid intentional ignorance. Freedman's purpose here appears to be more utilitarian than normative. That is, he seems to assume that under his solution the amount and value of the information that is not lost will result in more accurate verdicts or resolutions than would result from threats to accuracy created by the perjury he would allow. Of course, we can never know.

I do not accept these policy arguments for relieving the lawyer of candor to the court and allowing him to call the defendant (or certain witnesses) he knows will lie, and then to argue their testimony. I do not believe that the failure to permit a lawyer to engage in this activity will dissuade clients from being candid with their lawyers (in order to deny them knowledge that their possible testimony will be false). There are many things lawyers cannot do if they have knowledge, and that is true even under Freedman's proposal. The surmise that the limitation on calling the defendant to testify increases clients' recalcitrance above what it would be absent that limitation is not an acceptable basis for authorizing lawyers to assist perjury. I have no qualm about saying that clients who hold back so that they can commit perjury by keeping their lawyers in ignorance take their chances that the withheld information might have helped them. If the tactic enables perjury to get by on occasion, so be it. The client may also be worse off for it.

Of course, we can also reject the proposition that absent Freedman's solution a lawyer is, in all fairness, required to alert his client to the fact that if the client says he "did it," the lawyer will not be allowed to let him testify that he did not do it. In short, we can accept that clients understand that lawyers cannot break the law. There should be and is no need to warn them. Although Freedman's solution to his trilemma does not go so far as to let a lawyer knowingly introduce a forged document or the testimony of a bribed witness—not even where the lawyer's knowledge is based on a client interview—he does not require the lawyer to warn the client of these limits beforehand. Nor does Freedman warn the client that in the event the client decides to commit perjury, the lawyer will not help prepare the false testimony.

Elsewhere, Freedman acknowledges that there are three circumstances in which even he would violate confidentiality, although he would not tell the client about them in advance.[1] These include to protect human life, "to avoid having to go to trial before a corrupted judge or jury," and "to defend [himself] against formalized charges of unlawful or unprofessional conduct," though he recognizes that the last exception "is more difficult to defend than the first two."[2] Freedman would not warn the client about these exceptions to the confidentiality pledge because "the likelihood of these contingencies occurring is so slight that the harm that would be done to the lawyer-client relationship by a "*Miranda* warning" on these particular issues far outweighs the marginal value of fairness to the exceptional client to whom the warning would be relevant."[3] Freedman is thus drawing an empirical inference. But one might ask why the empirical balance does not come out the same way for a fourth exception—that a lawyer will reveal confidential information to prevent or correct perjury.

I am also unpersuaded by Freedman's focus on the second leg of the trilemma—the pressure that candor to the court puts on a lawyer's willingness to learn as much information as possible, with the prospect of a lawyer's intentional ignorance as one consequence. Certainly, intentional ignorance will hurt clients. Lawyers who indulge in it should be disciplined where the proof is available. Their representations may also be viewed as constitutionally ineffective. But it is a non-sequitur, and akin to blackmail to my mind, to say that in order to keep lawyers doing their jobs properly and ethically, we must let them assist perjury. To put it another way, the prospect that some lawyers will seek to avoid candor to the court by avoiding knowledge, even at the expense of staying ignorant of their clients' stories, is a problem, however rare. But the problem is about these lawyers. I am not prepared to make so fundamental a change in the rules of criminal law and ethics in order to accommodate lawyers who would engage in the tactic.

Let me offer another argument in favor of Freedman's proposal with regard to anticipated perjury. Assume that a criminal defense lawyer may refuse to call a defendant if the lawyer knows that the defendant will commit perjury. A strong belief is not enough. Now imagine that a defense lawyer refuses to let a client testify because of what the lawyer thinks he knows. The defendant protests the lawyer's decision. He tells the court that the lawyer is wrong, that the lawyer does not know what he thinks he knows, and that the lawyer's mere belief that the client will lie cannot override his constitutional right to testify. What should the judge do?

The dilemma this presents for a judge is difficult. If the judge simply accepts the lawyer's conclusion, she makes the lawyer the judge of the client's credibility. Doing so on evidence short of a direct statement by the client to the lawyer that he will lie is not a comfortable solution. If the judge insists that the lawyer tell her the basis for his conclusion that the client will lie, the lawyer will likely have to reveal confidential information. That may not unduly concern us if the information the lawyer reveals is the client's express intention to lie, and the client has insisted on doing so after the lawyer warns of his obligation to the court. But rarely will that be the lawyer's evidence. Rather, the evidence will be circumstantial, with the lawyer drawing a particular inference, though we can assume a strong one. If the judge agrees with the lawyer's inference, she is also displacing the jury's credibility role. If the judge disagrees with the lawyer, concluding that the lawyer does not know what he thinks he knows, the case continues but at a price to the professional relationship. And if a judge is presented with this issue, what process should she employ to resolve the competing claims? Does the defendant have a right to be heard? Have we not created the need for some kind of satellite proceeding? Should it be before the trial judge? Another judge? Does the defendant have a right to (different) counsel in that proceeding? These are messy questions. We should not be surprised, therefore, that to avoid them some courts have set a rather high standard for what constitutes "knowledge" in this situation.

Other courts have chosen a compromise that I find unsatisfactory. It is to permit the lawyer to call the client and have him provide in narrative fashion the testimony that the lawyer presumably "knows" is false. The lawyer then ignores the testimony in summation. In this way, the lawyer does not assist perjury.

This solution has superficial appeal, but on closer examination it makes no sense. If the lawyer really does know that the client will lie, the client should not be allowed to testify in any fashion, at least not to the lies. But perhaps the narrative solution is meant to recognize that the lawyer may be wrong, and so, as a precaution, the defendant is permitted to give the jury her story. But if we set a standard of knowledge, we should be prepared to say that the lawyer either has it or does not have it. If we are tempted to allow the narrative because (or when) we do not have the necessary confidence to say that the lawyer knows the client will lie, then we do not have knowledge. As a result, we would be cheating the client of her right to testify in the usual fashion, with counsel's preparation, and have her testimony argued in summation. It has to be one or the other. The compromise of narrative slights both values—the value of avoiding perjury and the value inherent in the constitutional right to testify with the aid of counsel.

Furthermore, the narrative solution is also plagued by the prospect of a client who challenges a lawyer's prediction that the client will lie. She demands to testify in the usual way, pointing out, quite accurately, that a narrative is no substitute for the question and answer format in which the lawyer will question the other witnesses, and that she will suffer the additional harm of having her testimony ignored on summation. This demand puts the problem back in the lap of the judge, with the same process questions identified earlier.

Permitting lawyers to introduce and argue perjury is an extreme price to pay to avoid the dilemma created for a court when a lawyer concludes that he knows his client will lie but the client denies it. For one thing, that situation should be extraordinarily rare. We can expect that lawyers will give clients the benefit of the doubt, as they should. At other times, the lawyer really will know and the client will not claim otherwise, eliminating the need for a trip to the judge. If the lawyer does know of intended perjury, the lawyer will often be able to discourage the client from asking to testify. This may be accomplished by warning the client about cross-examination, telling the client that he will not prepare her to give the false testimony, and informing the client that the judge might use the client's false testimony against her at sentencing. In the unusual circumstance where the client is adamant and the disagreement does surface and is then presented to the judge, a high threshold for knowledge should insure against the risk of false positives (which would occur if the judge sides with the lawyer erroneously).

III. CONCLUDED OR SURPRISE PERJURY

While solutions to the prospect of anticipated perjury turn on policy considerations rather than legal ones—because no client has a legal right to commit perjury or to a lawyer's help in doing so (and Freedman does not argue otherwise)—the situation is said to be different where the client has already committed perjury. That may happen in the middle of the client's testimony, as where the lawyer has called the client to offer legitimate testimony and is then surprised when the client interjects a fact, perhaps gratuitously, that is knowingly false. Or a lawyer may first learn after the client testifies and before the conclusion of the matter that some of the testimony was perjurious. I am going to focus on concluded perjury, but I think the legal issues are the same for surprise perjury because it is also concluded—i.e., already committed—when the lawyer must decide whether to take action. In addition to policy arguments, Freedman claims that revealing completed perjury (again assuming knowledge) violates the client's constitutional rights. He cites a number of cases in support of this claim, which he finds grounded in the Fifth Amendment's privilege against self-incrimination and the right to counsel guaranteed in the Sixth Amendment. But the cited cases and constitutional provisions do not in fact give the client a right to a lawyer's silence. Consequently, a jurisdiction may properly require the lawyer to correct the perjury even if it means implicit or explicit revelation of the client's confidential information.

Before coming to the constitutional analysis, I want to say a word about the policy considerations when dealing with completed perjury. They are in fact weaker than when perjury is only a future possibility. This is because the burden on the two values Freedman wishes to protect—encouraging clients to be candid with counsel and discouraging a lawyer's intentional ignorance—are less threatened in the case of completed perjury. Freedman's argument when dealing with anticipated perjury is that either or both values will suffer because the client who intends to commit perjury will not want to be stopped by a rule that forbids the lawyer to assist that goal. The client will not be candid and the lawyer may try to remain ignorant of information that will limit his options. When dealing with completed perjury, this argument is attenuated to the point of being an indefensible basis on which to build policy. The argument would be: In the lawyer's investigation of the case, including conversations with the client, the lawyer will think this way: It may happen that my client testifies and I will not then know that the testimony is false. But I may later learn that the testimony was false and if I do, I will have a duty to inform the court. I want to be sure that I will not have this duty to the court when and if I learn that testimony I have already introduced is false. So anticipating that possibility, I will not ask certain questions.

The client would supposedly go through an analogous reasoning process when deciding whether or not to be candid with the lawyer. I reject these predictions for the same reason I rejected them in the case of anticipated perjury but more emphatically now because of the greater attenuation.

I now turn to Freedman's claim that the Fifth and Sixth Amendments do not allow a jurisdiction to require lawyers to remedy completed client perjury. Freedman assumes, and I agree, that any remedy will generally require the lawyer, directly or indirectly, to reveal client confidential information or to use confidential information to the client's disadvantage (whether or not the client is the source of the information). It seems to me impossible to think of even a remotely realistic situation where a lawyer will know of a client's perjury except, at least in substantial part if not exclusively, based on client confidential information even if the information does not come exclusively from the client. However, the constitutional argument is not based solely on the use or revelation of confidential information. Information aside, we have the prospect of the lawyer doing something that harms his own client in the very matter in which he represents the client. I conclude, however, that constitutional jurisprudence does not support the argument Freedman makes. Requiring a defense lawyer to remedy client perjury, even through the use or revelation of confidential information, violates no constitutional rights of the accused as these are understood. Time and space do not permit a detailed examination of all cases Freedman cites in support of a contrary argument. I will here focus on three cases, from which I think he mainly claims support, and a fourth case he does not cite but which I believe undermines his interpretation of the cases he does cite.

The three cases Freedman mainly cites in support of his argument and which I will address are *New Jersey v. Portash*,[4] *United States v. Henry*,[5] and *Estelle v. Smith*.[6] In *Portash*, the defendant was granted use immunity for grand jury testimony. He was indicted and his lawyer asked for a ruling that if Portash testified, his grand jury testimony could not be used to impeach his credibility. The trial judge declined and Portash did not testify. On appeal, the state court held that the trial court had erred. The grand jury testimony could not have been used to impeach Portash's testimony. The Supreme Court agreed. It distinguished a separate line of cases in which the Court had upheld the use of statements taken in violation of *Miranda v. Arizona* to impeach the accused if he testified. Those cases differed, the Court said, because the statements there were not involuntary. The fact that they were elicited in violation of *Miranda* meant they could not be used to build the state's case, but because they were not involuntary, they could be used to impeach if the accused testified inconsistently with them. By contrast, Portash's immunized testimony was involuntary because a refusal to testify would have put him in contempt of court and subjected him to incarceration. The Court did not address where the truth might lie between the defendant's grand jury and proposed trial testimony.

United States v. Henry and *Estelle v. Smith* can be discussed together. In both cases, the Sixth Amendment right to counsel of the accused had already attached. In *Henry*, "incriminating statements [were] made by the accused to an . . . undercover Government informant while in custody and after indictment."[7] The informant was a fellow prisoner whose assistance the government had secured. The informant testified to the defendant's incriminating statements.[8] The Court held that Henry's right to counsel had been violated, citing *Massiah v. United States*.[9] The statements of the defendant in *Estelle v. Smith* were also made to a government agent, but here the agent was a government psychiatrist, who ostensibly examined the defendant only to determine if he was competent to stand trial. Unlike the witness in *Henry*, the defendant knew that he was speaking to a person working with the prosecutor. The defendant did not challenge the state's right to have its psychiatrist examine him for competency. But the trial court then admitted the psychiatrist's testimony at the penalty phase of Smith's capital trial on a separate issue— Smith's future dangerousness. The Texas capital statute made future dangerousness a factor for the jury to evaluate in deciding whether the defendant should be sentenced to death, which Smith was. The Court held that the psychiatrist's testimony violated *Miranda*, explaining:

> When Dr. Grigson went beyond simply reporting to the court on the issue of competence and testified for the prosecution at the penalty phase on the crucial issue of respondent's future dangerousness, his role changed and became essentially like that of an agent of the State recounting unwarned statements made in a post-arrest custodial setting.[10]

In addition, citing *Henry* and *Massiah*, the Court held that the interview with Dr. Grigson was a "'critical stage' of the aggregate proceedings against respondent."[11] Accordingly, the right to counsel had attached, yet:

> Defense counsel . . . were not notified in advance that the psychiatric examination would encompass the issue of their client's future dangerousness, and respondent was denied the assistance of his attorneys in making the significant decision of whether to submit to the examination and to what end the psychiatrist's findings could be employed.[12]

None of these decisions bears on the distinctly different claim Freedman advances. In *Portash*, the statement the Court excluded was made on threat of imprisonment. The state compelled the statement; it was involuntary. However, a defendant's statements to counsel are neither involuntary nor compelled by the state. The fact that the client has a motive to be candid with his lawyer and the fact that the lawyer has a professional duty to encourage candor does not make the statement involuntary in the Fifth Amendment sense. Portash would go to jail if he refused to talk after receiving immunity. The state does not imprison a defendant who refuses to talk to his lawyer. Furthermore, Freedman's argument cannot be limited to the criminal defendant. All individual litigants are protected by the Fifth Amendment. So if it violates the Fifth Amendment to require counsel to reveal an accused client's confidence in order to correct client perjury, that would also be so for civil litigants. In fact, I wonder how we could then distinguish transactional work. Wouldn't it follow that a state could not, consistent with the Fifth Amendment, require (or perhaps even authorize) a lawyer who has unwittingly helped a client commit criminal fraud, reveal client confidences in order to prevent harm from the fraud? But we need not go down that road because *Portash* simply does not support Freedman's argument. In the different situation under discussion, unlike *Portash*, we have no use of officially compelled statements.

Nor are *United States v. Henry* and *Estelle v. Smith* of any use to Freedman's argument. In each case, after the right to counsel had attached and without *Miranda* warnings, a state agent elicited incriminatory statements from the accused which the Court held could not then be used against him. The fact that the jailhouse informant and the psychiatrist were state agents was central to the Courts' *Miranda* analyses. In the situation here, however, a lawyer for an accused is not a state agent, not even if the lawyer is appointed. Appointed or retained, the state is not sending the lawyer to talk to the accused to obtain incriminating statements that it can then use in building its case. Furthermore, neither case would exclude use of the evidence to impeach. Statements obtained in violation of *Miranda* can be used to impeach, as can statements taken in violation of the Sixth Amendment right to counsel. In any event, in addition to not being an agent of the state, the lawyer who remedies completed perjury by revealing client confidences is not offering evidence at all, not even to impeach. He is simply undoing a fraud on the court, which he unwittingly aided, by revealing information to the court.

The weaknesses of the cases Freedman cites in support of his conclusion are underscored by a case he does not cite, namely, *United States v. Apfelbaum*.[13] The issue it resolved is expressly reserved in *Portash*.[14] As described in *Portash*, the reserved issue is this: "[W]hether possibly . . . immunized testimony may be used in a subsequent false declarations prosecution premised on an inconsistency between that testimony and later, nonimmunized testimony."[15] Recall that in *Portash* the Court held that compelled testimony (given under a grant of immunity) could be used neither as evidence in chief nor to impeach in a later prosecution. The issue the Court preserved was whether such testimony could be used as part of the government's case in chief if the later prosecution is for making a false statement. *Apfelbaum* was a prosecution for making false statements to a grand jury. The government introduced the portions of the defendant's immunized grand jury testimony it claimed were false. There was no challenge to its right to do so. The grant of immunity did not entitle the defendant to lie under oath and the government was free to introduce the testimony it alleged was false. But the government also sought to introduce other testimony the defendant had given before the same grand jury. The government did not claim that the other testimony was false. Rather, it offered this testimony "to put the charged statements in context and to show that respondent knew they were false."[16] The question before the Court was whether the government could introduce this other testimony or whether the grant of immunity, which meant (as in *Portash*) that the testimony was involuntary, prevented the government from using the testimony for that purpose. The defendant claimed that both the immunity statute and the Fifth Amendment prevented introduction of any portion of the immunized testimony that the government did not allege was false.

The Court unanimously rejected both arguments. The majority opinion held that the grant of immunity was meant to prevent use of the immunized testimony in a prosecution for the crimes the grand jury was then investigating (extortion, mail fraud, racketeering), not for the perjury that the defendant, once immunized, might thereafter commit. The Court held that "in our jurisprudence there . . . is no doctrine of 'anticipatory perjury.'"[17] While it was logically true that the grant of immunity resulted in testimony that the government would not have had absent the grant (because the defendant would then have been able to remain silent), and that therefore the defendant was not in precisely the same position as he would have been in had he remained silent, the defendant had no Fifth Amendment right to be put in the same position as if he had remained silent. That was, of course, true with regard to that part of the testimony alleged to be false and which was the basis for the perjury prosecution. Absent immunity, there would be no false statement to prosecute. But the Court held that it was also true with regard to use of the defendant's other testimony to the grand jury. Neither the immunity statute nor the Fifth Amendment protected the defendant from use of this testimony, if otherwise admissible and relevant, to prove the perjury.

Apfelbaum undermines Freedman's reliance on *Portash* because it reaches a contrary result where the crime on trial is false statement or perjury, the very subject of Freedman's trilemma. Even testimony that is truly compelled by the state, on pain of incarceration, is admissible in a trial alleging that other testimony given during the same grand jury appearance was false. And here we are dealing only with a *charge*, and therefore only a determination of probable cause to believe that perjury was committed, not a lawyer's knowledge that it was committed. Nonetheless, the immunized testimony is admissible. Further, unlike a rule requiring a lawyer to remedy completed perjury only by communication with the court, *Apfelbaum* admitted the immunized testimony in evidence as part of the government's case in chief.

I am prepared to entertain (though I have not seen and have a difficult time imagining) a non-frivolous argument for the proposition that the Fifth or Sixth Amendments should be read to invalidate a rule that requires criminal defense lawyers to remedy completed client perjury, including by revealing confidential information. It is an argument, however, that has many problems, not least of all describing its limitations and the absence of authority or constitutional policy that can by any careful reading support it.

IV. CONCLUSION

Let me end with these words. I believe Professor Freedman's solution to the trilemma he describes is wrong. But I know to a moral certainty that he performed a valuable service forty years ago in identifying this issue (as well as many others then and thereafter) clearly and forcefully. At a time when legal ethics was a remote and largely unexamined backwater in legal scholarship and in the minds of lawyers and judges, Professor Freedman was one of a very few scholars to identify serious issues in the field and to subject them to critical inquiry. That is work for which the legal profession and academy will forever be in his debt.

NOTES

1. Monroe H. Freedman and Abbe Smith, *Understanding Lawyers' Ethics*, 3d ed. (2004), p. 187

2. Ibid., pp. 171–72.

3. Ibid.

4. 440 US 450 (1979).

5. 447 US 264 (1980).

6. 451 US 454 (1981).

7. 384 US 436 (1966).

8. 447 US at 269.

9. Ibid., p. 273, citing *Massiah* v. *United States*, 377 US 201 (1964).

10. 451 US at 467.

11. Ibid., p. 470.

12. Ibid., pp. 470–71.

13. 445 US 115 (1980).

14. 440 US 450, 459 n.9 (1979).

15. Ibid.

16. US 445 at 119.

17. Ibid. p. 131 (Brennan, J. concurring); see also *Brogan* v. *United States*, 522 US 398, 404 (1998) ("[N]either the text nor the spirit of the Fifth Amendment confers a privilege to lie.").

Daniel R. Fischel

LAWYERS AND CONFIDENTIALITY

CONFIDENTIALITY AND THE ADVERSARY IDEAL

Confidentiality frequently is viewed as a necessary corollary of the adversary ideal. No client would want a lawyer who is anything less than a vigorous advocate on his behalf. Being a vigorous advocate means doing everything possible to advance the client's cause (subject to the prohibition against fraud), regardless of the attorney's personal knowledge or beliefs. Any obligation to reveal information inimical to the client's interests is obviously inconsistent with the zealous advocate's objective to cast his client's position in the best possible light and therefore evidences disloyalty to the client. As a leading authority on the rules of evidence has stated:

> Our adversary system of litigation casts the lawyer in the role of fighter for the party whom he represents. A strong sentiment of loyalty attaches to the relationship, and this sentiment would be outraged by an attempt to change our customs so as to make the lawyer

From *University of Chicago Law Review* 65 (Winter 1998). Reprinted with permission of the publisher.

amenable to routine examination upon the client's confidential disclosures regarding professional business.[1]

Equating confidentiality with zealous advocacy, however, confuses means with ends. Clients value winning, not zealous advocacy for its own sake. If confidentiality does not increase the probability of winning, it has no independent value. And, at least in the context of civil litigation . . . there is no reason to believe that confidentiality rules increase the probability of winning because the benefit of confidentiality in any particular case is offset by the cost in another. Clients as a class gain nothing.

But there is a more fundamental point. Proponents of confidentiality as a necessary attribute of vigorous advocacy ignore its effect on the decision maker. Simply stated, an argument made by someone known to be an advocate is less credible than the same argument made by someone who is expressing his own beliefs after independent investigation. Anyone who is being paid by a party in a legal dispute likely will have his views discounted somewhat. And if the person is known to be acting as an advocate, the discount is greater still. No matter how compelling the claim being made, the rational response of the listener will be skepticism (what does the speaker, whom I know to be a paid advocate, know that he is not telling me?).

For this reason, confidentiality penalizes clients with nothing to hide. Such clients would like their attorneys to communicate credibly that nothing is being hidden from the decision maker but confidentiality makes this impossible. Civil litigants with competing claims have to convince the uninformed decision maker to believe them over their adversaries. The result resembles a lemons market, where clients with nothing to hide attempt to signal the merit of their case by using attorneys as reputational intermediaries to overcome informational asymmetries between themselves and the decision maker. Confidentiality, however, weakens the ability of these high-quality clients to distinguish themselves through their attorneys from low-quality clients with something to hide (the lemons). Attorneys of low-quality clients rely on confidentiality to mimic the claims made by attorneys of high-quality clients, making it more difficult for the decisionmaker to distinguish between the two.

The reputational issues surrounding the attorney-client privilege also influence those fields in which attorneys compete with other professionals. It is interesting to compare the Supreme Court's recognition of broad confidentiality privileges for attorneys with its rejection of any analogous privilege for accountants.

In *United States* v. *Arthur Young & Co.*,[2] the Court refused to extend to accountants the work product protection earlier recognized for attorneys in *Hickman* v. *Taylor*.[3] The Court based its holding on the difference between the role of attorneys as zealous advocates and the role of accountants who serve as "public watchdog"[4]:

> The *Hickman* work-product doctrine was founded upon the private attorney's role as the client's confidential adviser and advocate, a loyal representative whose duty it is to present the client's case in the most favorable possible light. An independent certified public accountant performs a different role. By certifying the public reports that collectively depict a corporation's financial status, the independent auditor assumes a public responsibility transcending any employment relationship with the client. The independent public accountant performing this special function owes ultimate allegiance to the corporation's creditors and stockholders, as well as to the investing public. This "public watchdog" function demands that the accountant maintain total independence from the client at all times and requires complete fidelity to the public trust. To insulate from disclosure a certified public accountant's interpretations of the client's financial statements would be to ignore the significance of the accountant's role as a disinterested analyst charged with public obligation.[5]

The Court's analysis is fundamentally flawed. The Court simply assumes, without explanation, that it is preferable for attorneys retained by clients to be "advocates" while accountants retained by the same clients should be "public watchdogs." Based on this assumed premise, the Court then concludes that confidentiality is necessary for attorneys to present clients' cases "in the most favorable light," but not for "independent" accountants who "certify" the accuracy of clients' communications to the investing public.

In reality, the economic function of attorneys and accountants is far closer than the Court's analysis suggests. Accountants are reputational intermediaries who help to overcome information asymmetries between firms and outside investors. By certifying firms' financial statements, accountants make the financial disclosures in those statements more credible. For this reason, firms have strong private incentives to hire independent accountants, even in the absence of any regulatory requirement to do so. Firms hire independent accountants, particularly large accounting firms with strong incentives to preserve a reputation for independence, in order to reduce information asymmetries between themselves and investors that, in turn, lowers their cost of capital relative to firms that prepare their financial disclosures internally. The public/private distinction drawn by the Court in *Arthur Young* is illusory. Attorneys are also reputational intermediaries. And just as clients (at least those with nothing to hide) benefit from hiring "independent" accountants because their communications become more credible when "certified," they could benefit from hiring "independent" attorneys to act as informational intermediaries. Such clients are harmed, therefore, by legal rules that make this more difficult.

The analogy between lawyers and accountants is not perfect. Accountants have strong incentives to develop reputations for honesty and independence because many market participants, such as institutional investors, analysts, ratings services, and investment bankers that take firms public, are repeat players. An accountant who aids a fraudulent scheme will suffer a heavy reputational penalty with these groups. The legal system is different. Jurors are not repeat players, which makes it more difficult for clients to signal quality by hiring brand name attorneys. On the other hand, lawyers must interact with judges (who are repeat players) even in cases that are ultimately decided by juries. Moreover, judges communicate with each other either formally through published opinions or informally through conversation.

Lawyers who mislead the court or the fact finder will suffer damage to their reputation. But confidentiality makes it harder to discern when lawyers are being candid.

THE IMPEDIMENTS TO WAIVING CONFIDENTIALITY RULES

Clients who have nothing to hide are harmed by confidentiality rules because they are less able to distinguish themselves from clients who do. The force of this claim would be substantially weakened if clients, the supposed beneficiaries of confidentiality rules, could waive confidentiality rules to communicate credibly that they have nothing to hide. Because the legal profession benefits from confidentiality, however, we can predict that the applicable rules would make waiver difficult. This is exactly what has occurred.

The witness-advocate rule generally prohibits attorneys from testifying in the same case in which they serve as advocate. The antivouching rule goes further and prohibits attorneys from expressing their personal beliefs about their client's cause.

These rules effectively prevent attorneys from performing the same certification function as other informational intermediaries such as independent accountants.

The witness-advocate and antivouching rules focus on the different roles played by partisan advocates and objective reporters of facts. Combining the two roles—as occurs when an attorney acting as advocate communicates his own knowledge and beliefs in argument or as a witness—is thought to be unacceptable. But why?

Maintaining this separation has been defended from the clients' perspective. Attorneys who undermine their clients' positions, even if indirectly by not certifying their belief in those positions, cannot be effective advocates. Once separation is compromised, therefore, certain clients (those with something to hide) will be unable to secure effective representation. But, to paraphrase Jeremy Bentham, this is a benefit, not a cost.[6] Why clients should be entitled automatically to "effective representation," if what that means is the ability to assert frivolous claims, is far from obvious. This justification for separation, to put the point differently, confuses the interests of those clients with something to hide with the interests of clients as a whole. Not surprisingly, the rationales given for maintaining separation focus primarily on its importance to the legal profession. Concerns expressed range from the need to protect attorneys from the awkward and "unseemly" situation of arguing their own credibility to maintaining the attorneys' ability to get business.

If separation is preserved, attorneys could represent all clients, regardless of their personal beliefs. If separation is blurred, however, attorneys who did not believe in their clients' causes would have a hard time getting hired because their lack of belief would be revealed to the fact finder.

JEREMY BENTHAM AND THE PRIVILEGE

More than 150 years ago, Jeremy Bentham attacked the attorney-client privilege as benefiting the guilty.[7] Bentham mocked the traditional justification of the privilege as necessary to foster candid communications between clients and their attorneys:

> "A counsel, solicitor, or attorney, cannot conduct the cause of his client" (it has been observed) "if he is not fully instructed in the circumstances attending it: but the client" (it is added) "could not give the instructions with safety, if the facts confided to his advocate were to be disclosed." Not with safety? So much the better. To what object is the whole system of penal law directed, if it be not that no man shall have it in his power to flatter himself with the hope of safety, in the event of his engaging in the commission of an act which the law, on account of its supposed mischievousness, has thought fit to pro-

hibit? The argument employed as a reason against the compelling of such disclosure, is the very argument that pleads in favour of it.[8]

Bentham thought it was a benefit, in other words, for the guilty to withhold information from their attorneys. They would then receive lower quality legal advice and be more likely to be convicted. My argument is similar to Bentham's but goes further. Whereas Bentham argued the privilege benefited the guilty but was of no value to the innocent, I argue that the privilege in fact harms the innocent. The harm exists because the privilege makes it more difficult for the innocent credibly to communicate that they have nothing to hide. Modern commentators, however, for the most part simply take the privilege as given[9] and therefore do not consider the possibility that Bentham did not go far enough. Because the argument developed here is an extension of Bentham's, it is useful to examine the claims made by those few commentators who have addressed his argument.[10]

First, Bentham's view of the world as consisting of the guilty who benefit from the privilege and the innocent who do not has been criticized as oversimplified, particularly in civil cases.[11] In the typical contested civil case, both parties will attempt to use the privilege to prevent certain information from reaching the tribunal. But this point, even if conceded, does not weaken Bentham's argument. That both parties may have something to hide in particular cases is not a justification for their being able to do so. Moreover, one party typically will benefit more from being able to withhold information than the other. Bentham's basic point—that the privilege benefits those with the most to hide— still holds in the civil context.

Second, recent commentators have criticized Bentham for failing to consider the situation where a party thinks he has something to hide but in fact does not.[12] The example given is a party who behaves negligently, but is unaware that he has a defense of contributory negligence. If confidentiality is not absolute, such an individual would be less likely to disclose the truth to his attorney because of the mistaken belief that truthful disclosure would result in liability. Under a rule of absolute confidentiality, by contrast, the party will disclose everything and learn about the contributory negligence defense. According to this argument, what Bentham ignored is that confidentiality benefits the innocent who think they are guilty as well as the guilty themselves.

This critique of Bentham is very much overstated. Why isn't the problem solved by the attorney explaining to the client that he can prevail if either he was not negligent or the other party was contributorily negligent? So informed, the client would behave the same as under a confidentiality rule. Moreover, as a practical matter, parties are most likely to be ignorant of the law in the context of highly technical regulatory offenses where there is no necessary relationship between moral intuition and legal requirements. But even here, parties can obtain effective advice without confidentiality simply by learning from their advisor what the governing legal rules are, just as parties learn from their accountants what tax deductions they can take or how transactions should be treated in financial statements. And if a lack of complete confidentiality results in less effective legal advice relating to complex regulatory requirements, so what? It is precisely in this context where the presumption that improved legal advice will result in socially desirable behavior (as opposed to, say, increased rent-seeking activity) is the weakest.

Third, Bentham's attack on confidentiality has been criticized as insensitive to the effect of compelled disclosure on the morale of the legal profession.[13] Wigmore [in his classic work on evidence] makes the following claim in response to Bentham:

> If the counsellor were compellable to disclose . . . the position of the legal adviser would be a delicate and disagreeable one; for it must be repugnant to any honorable man to feel that the confidences which his relation naturally invites are liable at the opponent's behest to be laid open through his own testimony. He cannot but feel the disagreeable inconsistency of being at the same time the solicitor and the revealer of the secrets of the cause. This double-minded attitude would create an unhealthy moral state in the practitioner. Its concrete impropriety could not be overbalanced by the recollection of its abstract desirability. If only for the sake of the peace of mind of the counsellor, it is better that the privilege should exist.[14]

The Supreme Court has relied on similar reasoning in justifying confidentiality rules. In *Hickman v. Taylor*, the Court stressed how any weakening of confidentiality rules would be "demoralizing" to the legal profession.[15] Justice Jackson in his concurring opinion echoed the same theme, stating that the "primary effect" of disclosure "would be on the legal profession itself."[16] He continued: "I can conceive of no practice more demoralizing to the Bar than to require a lawyer to write out and deliver to his adversary an account of what witnesses have told him."[17]

Why legal rules should depend on the "morale" of the legal profession, however, is nowhere explained. In any event, compromising confidentiality would almost certainly not be "demoralizing" for the legal profession (except to the extent that it would result in less business). The accounting profession, for example, seems to have survived legal rules that require disclosure of work papers, including notes of client interviews. And non-lawyer confidants such as close friends and business partners are to disclose communications, whether or not made in confidence. Compelled disclosure is probably more "demoralizing" in these situations than in the legal context because the parties are more likely to have a continued course of dealing. Finally, the effect of disclosure on morale is a function of the existing legal rule. If everyone understands at the outset that confidentiality is not absolute, no feeling of betrayal will result from disclosure.

But convincing or not, the Supreme Court's justification for confidentiality rules in *Hickman*, like Wigmore's earlier defense, at least puts all the cards on the table—the legal profession is the primary beneficiary of confidentiality. What is important to recognize, however, is that the benefits identified are not shared by clients or society as a whole.

NOTES

1. Edward W. Cleary, ed., *McCormick's Handbook of the Law of Evidence* (West: 2nd ed.,1972), p. 176 § 87.

2. *United States* v. *Arthur Young & Co.*, n54 465 US 805, 817–18 (1984).

3. *Hickman* v. *Taylor*, n55 329 US 495, 508–14 (1947).

4. n56 465 US pp. 817–18

5. Ibid., n57.

6. See Jeremy Bentham, *Rationale of Judicial Evidence* 5, bk IX, pt IV, ch. V, p. 304 (Garland: 1978) (originally published in 1827) ("The argument employed as a reason against the compelling disclosure, is the very argument that pleads in favor of it.").

7. Ibid.

8. Ibid., pp. 309–10, quoting Thomas Peake, *A Compendium of the Law of Evidence,* ch. III § IV (Abraham Small: 5th ed., 1824), pp. 250–51 (emphasis omitted). Edmund Morgan has voiced a similar critique of the privilege—that it facilitates perjury. Morgan described the effect of the privilege on clients who testify at trial as follows: "If he told his lawyer the truth, he must now tell the same thing from the witness box. If he told his lawyer a lie and sticks to it, he will tell the same story at the trial or hearing. If he told his lawyer the truth and now tells a lie, why should he be protected from exposure? Is the privilege retained in order to protect perjurers? How can that either directly or indirectly further the administration of justice?" Edmund M. Morgan, foreword, *Model Code of Evidence* 26–27 (1942).

9. Summarizing modern developments, one commentator has stated: "There is no responsible opinion suggesting that the privilege be completely abolished." Geoffrey C. Hazard, "An Historical Perspective on the Attorney Client Privilege," *California Law Review* 66 (1978): 1061, 1062. See also "Developments in the Law—Privileged Communications," *Harvard Law Review* 98 (1985): 1450, 1473 ("Society would surely suffer greatly if the lack of a privilege discouraged clients from conferring with their lawyers.").

10. For a sympathetic discussion of Bentham's analysis of the privilege relative to arguments advanced by Bentham's critics, see Louis Kaplow and Steven Shavell, "Legal Advice about Information to Present in Litigation: Its Effects and Social Desirability," *Harvard Law Review* (1989): 102, 605–608.

11. See John Henry Wigmore, *A Treatise on the System of Evidence in Trials at Common Law* 4 (Little, Brown: 1905), pp. 3203–3204 § 2292.

12. See Ronald J. Allen et al., "A Positive Theory of the Attorney-Client Privilege and the Work Product Doctrine," *Journal of Legal Studies* 19 (1990): 359, 371.

13. See Wigmore, *Evidence* 4 § 2291, p. 3202 ("There is in civil cases often

no hard-and-fast line between guilt and innocence, which will justify us as stigmatizing one or the other party and banning him from our sympathy.... We are therefore not necessarily abetting crime or other moral delinquency when we permit the concealment of the party's admissions to his attorney.") (emphasis omitted).

14. Ibid.
15. 329 US p. 511.
16. Ibid., p. 514 (Jackson concurring).
17. Ibid., p. 516.

PROBLEM SET V

GUARDING THE GUARDIAN

Your client, a court-appointed guardian of the person and property of a minor, has informed you, his attorney, that he (the guardian) has misappropriated a considerable amount of his ward's estate. The information was more or less unintended although it was the obvious conclusion from what your client had to tell you to receive legal advice. Upon hearing of the misappropriation, you immediately arrange to deny the guardian further access to the deposited funds in the ward's estate. The guardian is not a lawyer. You were employed by him rather than imposed by the court, but the guardianship is your only connection with him. The guardian is bonded; so it is the bonding company and not the ward who will suffer ultimate loss. So far as you know, the guardian has not yet had to file an accounting of the estate's assets either with the court or the bonding company. But he will have to file such an accounting eventually. So, while there has been no perjury yet, it may not be far off. Should you report the misappropriation to the court? Should you seek removal of the guardian? Should you resign as his attorney if he does not agree to make restitution? Or should you do something else? Indeed, should you have arranged to deny your client further access to the ward's estate in the first place? Your client is your client, after all.

LOOKING OUT FOR NUMBER ONE

As an oil business expert, you were employed as attorney to help Company X, a corporation organized to engage in wildcat drilling, to obtain leases for drilling on certain federal lands. Your fee was to include part of the proceeds of oil or gas discovered on the land. Company X obtained the leases by acting as you advised, found oil, and has now tendered you $130,000 as your fee for services rendered under the agreement. Based on information you received from Company X in the course of your employment, you have good reason to believe that your fee should be at least $150,000 and that Company X has on deposit in the state funds sufficient to pay everything owed to you. May you use this information obtained from Company X to support your suit to compel payment of the full sum owed? May you use the information to attach (that is, have a court seize and hold) the assets that X has in the state until the suit is tried? Without attaching X's assets in the state, you may have trouble collecting on the judgment even if you win. X is a "foreign" corporation that would be hard and expensive to collect from but for its deposits in this state. Would it be professionally proper to do these things? The suit will cost X a good deal of money. Attaching X's funds will be a substantial inconvenience for X. And, of course, there is always the possibility that you may not prevail in court.

DOING JUSTICE AGAINST THE CLIENT'S WISHES

You are an attorney for C, who was convicted of rape. His case is now on appeal. One day during the trial you had lunch with attorney L, a member of your firm. The conversation naturally turned to the trial. When you described the rape in question, he remarked that he had a client two years ago who had been accused of three similar rapes. That client had been convicted largely on the identification of several witnesses even though he had taken the stand to deny the charges. He had continued to deny them even when to admit the rapes might have helped him get a lower sentence. More discussion revealed that L's client looked very much like yours. After the trial you ask your client about the other rapes. He admitted committing all of them, giving details only the actual rapist could have known. But he refused to admit them to anyone else: "One rape conviction is enough for me. I want to get out while I'm still young enough to have some fun."

You could take your information to the district attorney. You could tell her what you know without revealing your client's name. The district attorney might take you at your word, investigate on her own, and perhaps do something to get lawyer L's client out of prison. But would she agree to leave your client alone if the trail of evidence led back to him? You believe she would. Your client will be in prison for a long time no matter what.

May you—against your client's wishes and without his knowledge—reveal your information (minus your client's name) to the district attorney (a) if the she agrees not to prosecute your client for the three rapes in question or (b) even if she refuses to agree? *Should* you reveal that information under either condition?

SUGGESTED READINGS

Michael D. Bayles, "Obligations of Trustworthiness," in *Professional Ethics* (Belmont, CA: Wadsworth Publishing Co., 1981), pp. 79–99.

Jeremy Bentham, "Rationale of Judicial Evidence," bk 9 ch 5, John Bowring, ed., in *The Works of Jeremy Bentham*, vol. vii (London: Simkin, Marshall, & Co., 1843).

Michael Davis, "Some Paradoxes of Whisteblowing," *Business and Professional Ethics Journal* 15 (Spring 1996): 3–19.

Monroe H. Freedman, "Professional Responsibility of the Criminal Defense Lawyer: The Three Hardest Questions," *Michigan Law Review* 64, no. 8 (June, 1966): 1469–84.

"A Lawyer Who Justifies Perjury: The Bizarre View of Legal Ethics Taken by Morris Salem in His 'Reflections,'" *New York Times*, November 19, 1911. Available online at http://query.nytimes.com/gst/abstract.html?res =9801EFDE123AE633A2575AC1A9679D946096D6CF.

Timothy L. Perrin, "The Perplexing Problem of Client Perjury," *Fordham Law Review* 76 (2007) (symposium issue). Available online at http://law .fordham.edu/publications/articles/500flspub9779.pdf.

Lloyd B. Snyder, "Is Attorney-Client Confidentiality Necessary?" *Georgetown Journal of Legal Ethics* 25 (Spring 2002): 477, 480. Available online at http://findarticles.com/p/articles/mi_qa3975/is_200204/ai_n9066428.

PART VI:
MAKING LEGAL
ASSISTANCE AVAILABLE

INTRODUCTION
TO PART VI

Lawyers have organized as a profession, they tell us, in part to make competent legal help available to those who need it. But having so organized does not mean that any particular lawyer has an obligation to do anything, much less that he has an obligation to help prospective clients in any general or specific way. Someone needs to decide what part each lawyer is to have in providing legal services, what those legal services are, and how they are to be provided. The options are many: The profession could, for example, decide that providing legal services to whomever one chooses is all a lawyer need do to contribute to the goal of making such services available to all who need it. The marketplace and government money can do the rest. Charles Fried seems to take such a view in "The Lawyer as Friend." Or, instead, the profession could decide that a lawyer must accept any person who seeks help, whether or not the prospective client is able to pay. In some states, lawyers still take an oath in which (among other things) they undertake "never to reject the cause of the defenseless." The profession could require lawyers to practice only alone, or in partnerships, or allow lawyers to practice as corporations.

The essays in this part are concerned with defining the lawyer's obligation to help make legal services available in three strikingly different contexts: (a) unpaid legal assistance between neighbors, (b) writing "cover memos" to insulate agents of a large organization from legal liability, and (c) providing legal advice in an international practice. These contexts have been chosen more or less at random. They are representative of the range of context in which providing legal assistance is in one respect or another now problematic. What is important about the three discussions presented here is not so much the specific problems discussed (though those are important) as understanding what providing legal assistance is, or should be, an understanding that should underwrite as well the identification of other problems and the design of their solutions.

Debra Moss Curtis begins her paper with two police cars and an ambulance outside her house. A neighbor has been the victim of "domestic violence" and Curtis, a teacher of law, had practiced family law until a few years before. She knew what her neighbor needed to know to protect herself from a dangerous husband. Curtis was competent to provide the legal assistance her neighbor needed and—unlike Laura Eagle (part II)—had no interest in having her neighbor as a paying client. Yet, *Model Rule* 6.1 was no help. It spoke of clients "unable to pay." Her neighbor could afford a good lawyer and needed one. The problem was that she might not understand how much a lawyer could do for her—or how little adequate legal assistance would cost.

Having reached the conclusion that she could be a "Good Samaritan" to her neighbor, Curtis meditates—as lawyers will—on the legal risks involved in making her services available. Good Samaritan laws protect physicians and others who render physical assistance to an injured or endangered person, but do not seem designed to protect lawyers from suit for free but poor advice. Is Curtis now in an "emergency" situation? Her neighbor's husband will be locked up for a few days at least. Curtis also wonders whether she is a lawyer, with the professional obligations of a lawyer (whatever they are), since she no longer practices law but only teaches it. If she is a lawyer, when does talking to a neighbor become a lawyer-client relationship—with the accompanying obligations and rights? Curtis gives her questions what she explicitly says is an unsatisfactory answer, leaving readers to think further about the questions raised.

David Luban seems to be concerned with the opposite of Curtis's subject, lawyers doing "too much" for their clients. Between 2001 and

2003, a small number of US government lawyers wrote a series of memos on torture (and other forms of extreme mistreatment) of "unlawful enemy combatants." The purpose of these memos does not seem to have been to advise the government how to avoid breaking the law but to provide "legal cover" for individual acts even the lawyers recognized to be illegal. The memos resemble courtroom argument in which the lawyer resolves reasonable doubt about legality in favor of the client's position. The lawyers' hope was that the memos would allow government agents involved in torture to defend themselves from criminal liability by claiming they acted on the advice of government lawyers (as evidenced by the memos). The "torture lawyers" (as Luban calls them) were definitely providing the government agents with legal assistance. Whether they were doing what they should is the question Luban poses. Before that question can be answered, two others need to be considered.

The first question is whether the lawyers were serving their client. Who was their client? Not any of the government agents who asked for the memo. Not the Executive Branch or the President of the United States. Their client was, it seems, the US government (or perhaps the People of the United States). Lawyers in large organizations have a tendency to confuse superiors with clients. They need to decide who their client is before they can decide whether they are serving it. Protecting government agents from having to answer to laws they are violating does not seem to serve the government (whose job it is to enforce the laws, not break them) or the people (whose laws they are).

Luban's focus is not on that first question but on the second. What standards apply to what the lawyers were doing? The courtroom has one set of standards for legal work, for example, resolving all reasonable doubts about legality in favor of the client's side. Advising one's client has another set of standards, in particular, telling the client what the law (probably) requires whether she wants to hear it or not. A lawyer's memo can properly provide legal cover if written as advisory memos customarily are. However, if written with the intention of providing cover for conduct already chosen, the memo is not an advisory memo but its counterfeit and the lawyer is involved in a conspiracy to fabricate a defense. A "cover memo" is never legitimate legal assistance even if the client (rather than just some of its agents or employees) would benefit.

These first two selections concern practice within the United States. In the last paper, Ethan S. Burger and Carol M. Langford consider ethical issues likely to arise because of radical economic, technological, and political changes already taking place. Because the world is increasingly a global market, because electronics have made communication to almost anywhere fast and cheap, and because a complex system of treaties makes many more legal questions at least in part questions of international or foreign law, lawyers increasingly face questions about where they are practicing law, whether they are competent to practice there, and whether what they are doing is even legal to practice there.

American lawyers have always faced a tension between the way they are licensed, by state, and the way they practice. The problem is not serious for litigators. They cannot practice before a court without the court accepting them—with most states having a simple procedure for temporary or quick admission of a lawyer licensed in another state. The problem of licensure is more serious for legal advice. For example, a New Jersey manufacturer may consult a New Jersey lawyer about sale of goods to a retailer in New York City. (The goods will travel five miles.) The retailer uses a standard contract specifying that the commercial law of New York is to apply. The client wants to know of any risks involved in signing. The lawyer is not licensed to practice in New York. May he explain the legal consequences of that specific provision? Is providing such advice practicing law in New York (or just practicing New York law)? Is the problem here competence rather than licensure? (See *Model Rule* 5.5.)

In some respects, international practice is not that different. For example, a lawyer with offices in Chicago may receive a phone call from a client in London who asks about a complicated deal involving property located in Australia, Malaysia, and Brazil. Even if the lawyer is licensed to practice law in Australia, Malaysia, and Brazil (itself unlikely), she will be giving advice to someone in London. Should she be licensed in the UK? Should she be licensed in Chicago when her clients are all foreign? What if the client calling from London is a large corporation registered in Delaware—but with only a part-time agent there and plants and offices in thirty countries? What if the lawyer advises the London office almost every day—without leaving Chicago? The client served in the global economy may be even harder to identify than in more traditional large organizations and so may the location of practice.

The "lawyer" serving the client may also be harder to identify. Law firms have grown enormously in size in the last fifty years. In 1960, a law firm with two hundred lawyers (partners and associates) would be one of the largest in the world, would have been headquartered in New York, and would have had a small satellite office in Washington, DC, and one or two more other cities. Today, a firm that size is not unusual. The large firms have several thousand lawyers—with large offices in many of the world's capitals—all linked by phone, fax, email, and teleconferencing. Where does a lawyer in such a firm practice? Should such large law firms have their own ethics programs—as many large corporations now have?

There is certainly a need to change the way lawyers are licensed (or, at least, what forms of practice constitute "the unauthorized practice of law"). How that should be done is a question about which the legal profession will have considerable say even though the ultimate decision-makers will be courts, legislatures, and international standard-setting bodies. There may also be a need to change the way legal ethics is taught. Lawyers working anywhere in the United States (except Louisiana) are working in a common law jurisdiction. The same is true if they work in Australia, Malaysia, or most other former colonies of Britain. But if they work in Europe, Latin America, or China, they will be working within a civil law system, a system that has a different understanding of "the adversary system" and of how lawyers should act. Should lawyers seek to develop an international code of ethics? Can lawyering be an international profession? Should it be?

Lawyers will doubtless continue to be the primary means by which legal assistance is made available to those who need it (though computer programs, legal assistants, and other alternatives to lawyers may become more important). But both what will count as a lawyer and what standards will apply seem likely to change radically in the next few decades. Now is a good time to start thinking about such changes.

Debra Moss Curtis

DOMESTIC VIOLENCE AND THE LAWYER AS GOOD SAMARITAN

I t is 8:30 p.m. and the telephone rings. My two children are in bed, and I am cooking for a holiday dinner the next night. On the other end of the receiver is my neighbor, who greets me with a panicked question that changes life in my neighborhood: "Why are there two police cars and an ambulance in front of your house?"

The answer, it turns out, has nothing to do with my home. A neighbor has attempted to strangle his wife, in front of her three children. They have lived in their house only a few months and have been married for less than a year. She is treated for injuries; he is arrested for battery and taken away in the squad car.

As a lawyer formerly practicing in domestic relations, I am not shocked by this type of scenario. I am, however, taken aback as a neighbor, one whose children have played with this woman's children nearly daily for several months. The question for me then becomes, "how do I help?" I know more about what she is likely to face than perhaps any other neighbor on our street, from restraining orders and marriage dissolution to asset division and child custody. Should this enhanced knowledge and legal training automatically imbue me with a responsibility that other well-meaning neighbors may not have?

From *Whittier Journal of Child and Family Advocacy* 6 (Fall 2006). Reprinted with permission of the publisher.

Were I a physician with special training in medical care, I might be obligated to run across the street and utilize my unique knowledge, experience, and abilities to treat my neighbor. And if I did, it is likely that the statutory framework regarding medical treatment could offer legal protection if I did step into such an emergency situation and offered treatment. However, the issue is not so certain for attorneys, for whom the code of ethics is unclear as to such "Good Samaritan" actions and for whom the law does not specifically offer any legal protections.

So what should I do with my neighbor? I am hardly alone in questioning the manner in which I, as an attorney, should act, for attorneys consistently are challenged as to how to get involved in such situations.

On [the] one hand is the mantra, "first, do no harm," which notes that wrong legal advice can, for example, endanger victims of domestic violence. The American Bar Association's Commission on Domestic Violence contends that knowing how to handle domestic violence matters should be basic to professional competency, but many lawyers may not be so trained. An attorney who steps in with bad advice for a battered woman may do more harm than good.

On the other hand, what if the problem is not attorney incompetence, but rather competence coupled with a crippling fear of using it?

THE LAWYER AS "GOOD SAMARITAN"?

In the United States, "Good Samaritan" laws are designed to protect from liability—in case things go wrong—those who choose to aid an injured stranger. The idea is to "reduce bystander's hesitation to assist" those in distress. Good Samaritan laws are clearly intended to cover immediate physical harm, as they tend to include the provision of first aid and the relief of the responsibility when trained assistance arrives. In other countries, Good Samaritan laws actually may require citizens to assist people, as long as it would not cause harm to the helper. These legal requirements were famously put into play recently in France, when the photographers at the scene of Princess Diana's car accident were investigated for a possible violation of these laws. While the US versions of such laws tend to focus only on relief of personal liability, the non-American versions often put that direct responsibility on its citizens.

Could the spirit of these laws—protecting from liability those who, in good-faith, assist people in need—translate to a professional responsibility for lawyers? The main focus of many Good Samaritan laws in the United States is protection of the "rescuer." Lawyers may hesitate to give advice because they do not want to create situations in which they may be held liable for giving legal assistance to strangers. If the impetus for some Good Samaritan laws is to reduce hesitation by bystanders in intervening in medical scenarios, should there be similar inducement for attorneys to get involved in legal situations?

Rule 6.1 of the *Model Rules of Professional Conduct* is an oft-discussed place to start: "Every lawyer has a professional responsibility to provide legal services to persons unable to pay." This Rule carries no enforcement power in the licensing of any individual attorney, as each state Bar sets rules for the attorneys it licenses. The rule is not intended to be "enforceable" with discipline; rather it is a goal for lawyers.[1] Is this "aspirational" rule the equivalent of the non-American Good Samaritan law, thereby placing some type of direct responsibility on lawyers to get involved in situations where people need legal advice?

To be sure, although lawyers have long resisted the idea of mandatory pro bono service,[2] it has been formally encouraged in the legal profession since 1969. In recent years, academic arguments have been proposed in favor of mandatory pro bono. But ideologically, should a lawyer have an obligation to use specialized knowledge to assist someone in an emergency situation? Some would say that to turn from assisting in domestic violence is "morally indefensible and ethically and legally unreasonable." Failure to get involved can hurt more than just the parties involved—it may hurt an entire community. In domestic abuse cases, nosy neighbors often ask, "why doesn't she leave?" What if the answer is, "because her neighbors didn't help her?" It is clear that ignoring the problem does not make it go away on a particular street, a whole neighborhood, or an entire community.

It has been suggested that lawyers are "trustees" of the law, setting them apart from vendors of other non-legal commodities due to the relationship between dates, producer, and beneficiaries.[3] In other words, if lawyers have an "oligopoly" on the law, then lawyers have a responsibility to help certain in-need people to access the law. In addition, lawyers have been considered "public citizens" with obligations to assist society by seeking improvement in the law, administration of justice and access to the law. It has been clearly stated that the duty to act pro bono as a lawyer exists not because lawyers could be disciplined if they do not, but because of the larger responsibility of lawyers.

MORE QUESTIONS THAN ANSWERS?

Even if we decide that attorneys with specialized knowledge should step into emergency situations and provide legal assistance, a number of questions remain.

(1) Definition of "lawyer." First, who is to be considered a lawyer in this analysis? Is it a licensed lawyer? A person with a J.D. degree? A lawyer actively practicing? A lawyer who did actively practice but is now not? And what about law school faculty? Luban points out that although the concepts of "professionalism" taught by law school faculty include a commitment to pro bono, most law schools do not encourage pro bono practice by the faculty. On the flip side, he points out that non-clinical law teachers have purposefully chosen teaching over practice, and thus have transformed their professional identities from lawyers to teachers.[4] In addition, Luban notes that some faculty believe the law teaching field is already public service, presumably eliminating the obligation to perform pro bono.

(2) Definition of "specialized knowledge." Next is the question of what is to be considered "specialized knowledge" in this analysis? Should only those who actively studied or practice in an area of

law be inclined to intervene, or should every attorney be presupposed to have specialized knowledge in every area of the law?

While lawyers may not consider themselves to be in the practice of dealing with domestic violence, any lawyer may encounter persons dealing with it in her practice, whether that includes estate planning, tax preparation, or criminal matters. A reasonable attorney must be prepared to ask about these matters and handle them in a wide variety of areas. As such, all lawyers are thus imputed to have domestic violence knowledge, and so the burden should not fall only to those "practicing" in that area.

Therefore, law schools also must educate students about domestic violence and assist students in understanding how to integrate the watch for this widespread problem into any kind of practice. While the need to teach such competence may be obvious in clinical settings, the legal issues should be part of the core curriculum courses, such as civil procedure, contracts, property, torts, constitutional law, and criminal law. Graduates who go on to be uninformed legal professionals can endanger victims or contribute to the problem being unrecognized communitywide. All law students can be taught to screen for abuse and make a positive impact on the professionalism and expertise of the future of the legal profession. It has even been suggested that law students themselves could benefit from mandatory pro bono programs.[5]

(3) Definition of "emergency." Third, what is an emergency? Certainly, a life-threatening situation, such as domestic violence—which has been asserted to be "the leading cause of injury to women in America between the ages of fifteen and forty-four"—fits the bill. Surgeon General statistics and ABA reports have estimated that as many as four million American women are battered and up to 10 million children have witnessed violence. Some research holds that a woman is beat every nine seconds. Despite the morning-after disbelief of my neighbors, domestic violence can and does happen in all kinds of house-

holds, in all kinds of communities. It reaches all races, religious backgrounds, and socio-economic groups and must be responded to immediately.

But what other kinds of legal problems should be considered an "emergency"? What about time-sensitive situations that require immediate advice? How about issues that can wait until tomorrow, but which nevertheless may result in dire, bank-breaking financial straits? Such situations may prove to create a non-navigable slippery ethical slope.

(4) Definition of "legal assistance." What actually constitutes giving legal assistance? Is there a solid middle ground between taking a case and turning one's back? Any neighbor, friend, or family member should be bringing a battered woman into one's home, giving her a cup of coffee, and lending her a sensitive ear. But what happens when the discussion turns to questions of basic legal information such as explaining the concept of "equitable distribution" or the basics of the dissolution of marriage process? Giving this information, calmly explaining the process to the woman, helping her "get prepared" to see a lawyer by getting financial information in place is not "taking the case," but rather contributes to helping a person in need, without crossing that line into a formal attorney-client relationship.

Such a definition of "legal assistance" may prove to be a fair middle ground, the safe harbor upon which well-meaning attorneys could remain. But what if the information went further? What if the "legal assistance" were more than explanations, and were really advice upon which the woman relied? What if some type of attorney-client relationship were formed? Is this so terrible? Those without malpractice insurance might say "yes" until a solid legal base for "Good Samaritan" lawyering is built. Others would say "no" —that ethically, the lawyer was doing the right thing, as set out by that aspirational pro bono goal of the American Bar Association.

Where does this leave me—a law professor, licensed by my state Bar but who is out of the practice of law—when faced with an issue of domestic violence that permeates my own neighborhood? I may not take my neighbor's case, but I am morally obligated not to turn away. I listen and offer support. I give information. I give advice, though making clear that the advice is in preparation for her meeting with an attorney that she should call first thing in the morning. Clearly I am directed by the moral compass instilled through the legal profession— the one that directs us to assist those in need, even without encouragement by model rules, protection by state statutes, or reward by employment compensation. *Model Rule* 6.1 has had some effect, although perhaps not the one intended by its drafters. Authors often discuss many options for those unwilling to take on direct cases, such as funding others who represent clients or educational programs. But sending a check to a formal program may not help the person across the street when she knocks on your door.

A few days after that awful phone call, I sat in my living room with my neighbor and—between the tears—gave her some legal information and guidance. When she walked back across the street to her own home, I stood on my porch knowing that I had done all I could for her—short of taking her on as a client—but wondered if that was nearly enough. Did I fail her? Did the profession fail her? Did the profession fail me? Are we, as attorneys and as a legal community, doing all that we can? Answers are needed soon.

NOTES

1. Irma S. Russell, "The Lawyer as Public Citizen: Meeting the Pro Bono Challenge," *University of Missouri Kansas City Law Review* 72 (2003): 439.

2. David Luban, "Faculty Pro Bono and the Question of Identity," *Journal of Legal Education* 49 (1999): 58; Kellie Isbell and Sarah Sawle, "Pro Bono Publico: Voluntary Service and Mandatory Reporting," *Georgetown Journal of Legal Ethics* 15 (2002): 845, 856. (Only New Jersey currently requires pro bono service.)

3. Luban, "Faculty Pro Bono and the Question of Identity," p. 63.

4. Ibid., pp. 66–67.

5. Christina M. Rosas, "Mandatory Pro Bono Publico for Law Students: The Right Place to Start," *Hofstra Law Review* 30 (2002): 1069, 1071.

David Luban

SELLING INDULGENCES

Lynne Stewart has been convicted of material support for terrorism in assisting her client, Egyptian Sheik Omar Abdel Rahman, now serving a life sentence for conspiring to commit acts of terrorism in New York City in the months after the 1993 World Trade Center bombings. If her conviction "stands for" any basic proposition, it's that there is no such thing as lawyer's immunity—either legal or moral (though many people, including myself, have sympathy with Stewart's fervent belief that she is morally blameless). Stewart, a lifelong radical, was on the same wavelength as her terrorist client in his desire to launch revolutionary struggle. She insists, however (and there's no reason to doubt her), that she never sympathized with his anti-Semitic or fascist agenda, and that she never sought to facilitate actual violence. The jury concluded she was deceiving herself and that she had crossed the line from zealous advocacy to criminal conduct. Ironically, one could offer the same assessment for the "torture lawyers"—the cabal of attorneys advising the Bush administration on the legality of U.S. interrogation policies—including former White House counsel Alberto Gonzales, vice presidential counsel David Addington, Justice Department lawyers Jay Bybee and John Yoo, and Pentagon counsel William Haynes. For the torture lawyers, the political polarities are reversed, but their gut-level affinity with the client's politics is the same, as is their willingness to bend (or break) the law to make their client's wishes come true. The torture lawyers' protestations that they never sympathized with a pro-cruelty agenda, or with abuses like those at Abu Ghraib, sound very much like Stewart's defense. Both believe that being a lawyer conveys a certain moral immunity. Fortunately for us all, it doesn't.

As I've learned from teaching professional responsibility for twenty-five years, the non-immunity message is a hard one for lawyers to understand and accept. After all, the most basic proposition about advocacy, endorsed by ABA *Model Rule* 1.2, is that lawyers should not be held accountable for their clients. The lawyer makes the client's arguments, not her own, and her job is to make them as persuasively as possible. In court, lawyers are allowed to make any argument that is not frivolous, and they may assert anything not positively known to be false. These rules permit lawyers to say a great deal that they themselves privately disbelieve or dislike—and, as zealous advocates, they often do.

Criminal defenders like Stewart embrace the role of fighting like hell for people they may know to be guilty. Some take this even further, believing that to fight like hell you must see the world through your client's eyes. With a client like Rahman—confined for life and forbidden to communicate with the outside world—building this personal rapport can involve bucking the rules the government lays down to limit your advocacy. Even though the ABA formally removed the "zealous advocacy" standard from its professional code, the ideal remains intact in the commentary to the rule—and, more important, it remains central to the folklore of the profession. Lawyers who will never set foot in a courtroom make "zealous advocacy" their mantra and accept the lawyer's moral immunity as an article of faith.

Even within this ethos, however, there are lines that may not be crossed: *Model Rule* 1.2(d) holds that "[a] lawyer shall not counsel a client to engage, or assist a client, in conduct that the lawyer knows is criminal or fraudulent." The jury concluded that Stewart crossed that line—not just in terms of the ethical standard, but in terms of the federal statute prohibiting material support to terrorism as well. Business lawyers have occasionally found themselves convicted as accomplices for papering crooked deals. Wrongly supposing they were immune, they went down with their clients. Some who cross the line have sterling reputations, such as Michael Abbell, a State Department extradition scholar who went into private practice, only to represent the Cali drug cartel so aggressively that he was tried and convicted for money laundering.

Many of my legal-ethics colleagues think the torture lawyers crossed *Rule* 1.2(d)'s line regarding criminal conduct with their torture memoranda, but I don't agree. It's unlikely these lawyers knew they were facilitating illegal conduct. After all, the whole point of their elaborate sophisms was that the intended conduct was perfectly legal for US soldiers and intelligence officers to engage in. Bad as their arguments were, the torture lawyers may have actually believed them—in which case they didn't "know" the conduct was criminal. Besides, the torture lawyers didn't tell President Bush what to do; they merely advised him on the legal consequences of an interrogation policy, should he choose to adopt it.

However, Gonzales, Bybee, and their crew crossed a different ethical line. They were not acting as courtroom advocates but as legal advisers, with a different professional standard to which they needed to adhere. *Model Rule* 2.1, titled "Advisor," provides that "a lawyer shall exercise independent professional judgment and render candid advice." Legal advisers must play it straight, even where the "[l]egal advice [may] involve[...] unpleasant facts and alternatives that a client may be disinclined to confront." Independence means saying what the law *is*—as mainstream lawyers and judges understand it—regardless of what the client *wishes it to be*. Candor requires lawyers with eccentric theories to warn their clients whenever their legal advice veers away from the mainstream. The torture lawyers betrayed both these principles with the advice they gave the White House.

In the "Bybee Memo," for example, candid advice demands that when you discuss the "necessity defense" to the crime of torture, you mention that the defense has always been a loser in federal court. In the case of a later OLC memo by now-Harvard law professor Jack Goldsmith on the Geneva Conventions, candor means forthrightly reminding your client that Geneva forbids coercive interrogations— not burying this unwelcome point in a vaguely worded footnote.

To be sure, no lawyer has ever been disciplined for violating the ethical rule on candid advice-giving. But that has nothing to do with the validity of the standard and everything to do with the secrecy that usually cloaks attorney-client advice. Clients are seldom in a position to know when their lawyer's advice has *not* been candid; aggrieved clients are more interested in obtaining malpractice damages than in filing grievances. And in the rare case when a lawyer's bad advice becomes an issue—for example, when a receiver takes over a bankrupt corporation and goes after the lawyers that colluded with the old management— there are almost always easier to prove and more serious charges to file.

But that doesn't mean that the "independent and candid advice" standard is unimportant. The entire theory of the attorney-client privilege rests on the notion that lawyers must be able to hear and keep their clients' secrets in order to offer good advice. Obviously, the privilege comes at a cost to truth, as when big-tobacco lawyers abused the privilege for decades to bury scientific studies on the addictiveness of smoking. For more than a century, critics have charged that the cost to society of the privilege is too great. The organized bar responds by insisting that the privilege actually enhances compliance with the law, rather than undermining it.

Confidentiality encourages lawyers to give their clients unvarnished advice—and, in the ABA's words, "almost all clients follow the advice given, and the law is upheld." But if the lawyer doesn't give independent, candid advice, this entire argument, and indeed the whole edifice of confidentiality, comes tumbling down.

But what happens when the client doesn't want candid advice? When the client says, in effect, "give me a legal opinion saying I can do what I want to do?" Lawyers confront such requests every day—but if the lawyer does the client's bidding, she has crossed the fatal line from adviser to accomplice. No longer an adviser or advocate, the lawyer now becomes an absolver or indulgence-seller. There is some historical precedent here—Martin Luther launched the Reformation because early-Renaissance popes were selling papal dispensations to sin along with indulgences sparing sinners the flames of hell or a few years of purgatory. Rodrigo Borgia once arranged a papal dispensation for a French count to sleep with his own sister. It was a good career move: Borgia later became Pope Alexander VI, while Jay Bybee merely ended up on the Ninth Circuit Court of Appeals.

The important thing to note is that the role of absolver—unlike the roles of advocate or adviser—is totally illegitimate. The advocate is supposed to—in the words of the old ABA *Code of Professional Responsibility*—"resolve in favor of his client doubts as to the bounds of the law." The adviser, by contrast, owes the client independent and candid advice, even if it's "unpalatable to the client." The advocate's arguments follow only the permissive non-frivolity standard; the adviser must honor the more demanding candid, best-judgment standard. The advocate's biased presentation will get countered by the adversary in a public hearing. The adviser's presentation will not—and unless it's leaked, it will in fact be shielded by the attorney-client privilege. That's why it's disastrous when the adviser loopholes the law like an advocate. Conflating these two roles moves the lawyer out of the limited role-based immunity that advocates enjoy (although I think that the profession exaggerates the immunity there, too) and into the world of the indulgence-seller. Dante consigned the indulgence-selling popes to hell. Maybe Canto VII of [Dante's] "Inferno" belongs as an appendix to the *Rules of Professional Conduct.*

Ethan S. Burger and Carol M. Langford

GLOBALIZATION AND THE FUTURE OF LEGAL ETHICS

I. INTRODUCTION

To many observers it seems that the basic ethical principles underpinning the practice of law in America are not likely to undergo significant change in the foreseeable future. Nonetheless, lawyers are increasingly confronting novel issues arising from the globalization of their clients' activities. In addition, changes in technology have both altered the manner in which their clients operate, and also the nature of law firm practice.

These developments might suggest that in light of these changes there should be concomitant changes in the ethical rules governing how lawyers practice. Changes in this area, however, have been limited. Perhaps this reflects the attitude that if it isn't broken, don't fix it; or to borrow from the medical profession's ethical norms—first do no harm. This may also explain why there have been surprisingly few changes to the ABA *Model Rules of Professional Responsibility* after the completion of the ABA's extensive work on Ethics 2000 that significantly reflects issues arising from the globalization of the practice of law. This raises questions as to whether the ABA's International Law Section's Transna-

From *Widener Law Journal* 15 (2006).

tional Legal Practice Committee exercised their expertise in the changes. Indeed, most lawyers are vaguely aware of the potential problems inherent in the current situation. This is not a matter affecting only specialists engaged in transnational legal practice. Unfortunately, few ethics lawyers concerned with transnational law have devoted considerable effort to promote a thorough examination of how globalization may have created a need for refining existing ethical rules.

Legal ethics is frequently taught, rules developed, and resource materials prepared in isolation from non-lawyers who are likely to play an increasingly important role in the development of legal practices, and hence legal ethics. In the United States, the roles played by regulatory bodies such as the Securities and Exchange Commission, the US Department of the Treasury, and the US Patent Office cannot be ignored.

While there is an intellectual awareness of the challenges of domestic inter-jurisdictional and transnational practice, including the need for new rules regarding the unauthorized practice of law, enforcement of existing rules often seems anachronistic. Furthermore, given that they seem out of date and hence irrelevant to practitioners, there may be a tendency to ignore them entirely. For example, some lawyers engaged in the practice of law in a jurisdiction in which they are not licensed are not competent to do so. Lawyers observing the mishandling of legal matters having international elements have an ethical obligation to report professional misconduct [*Rule* 8.3]. This situation conflicts with the human tendency not to get involved if the rewards are intangible and the potential downside great.

At the heart of the matter is that compared to law firm profitability legal ethics is frequently a minor concern, despite speeches given by prominent lawyers and academics to the contrary. So long as a law firm or corporation is making money, the hurdles that must be overcome to properly ensure the ethical conduct of lawyers working in domestic multi-office or international law firms are sometimes mentioned but not addressed until a problem arises. It is difficult enough to confront issues having potential ethical implications, like client conflicts, where the persons involved know one another; it is far more difficult to do so if one does not know the attorneys in other offices involved. Therefore, there is less likelihood of knowing of or investigating the relevant facts.

In the United States, the appearance of "International Legal Consultants" is becoming more prevalent—but little attention is being paid to what they are doing on a day-to-day basis. In theory, such individuals may only deal with legal matters arising from the application of the law of the jurisdiction in which they are licensed to practice. Can they merely opine on questions of foreign law, or "international" law? May they participate in the entire transaction (e.g., review all the documents connected with due diligence)? Are law firms using them as if they were members of the local bar? Circumstances vary not only by law firm, but may change from matter to matter.

Regulators of the legal profession in foreign countries are likely to become increasingly assertive as foreign lawyers play a growing role in the provision of legal services in their countries. US and foreign insurance companies and stock exchanges establish their own rules that have implications with respect to the standards of care and fiduciary duties of lawyers. For example, will lawyers who in the United States have fiduciary duties to the corporation (and its shareholders) change their ethical conduct if their clients are organized in countries where a corporation must consider the interest of all its stakeholders (including potentially a governmental body)? Will courts and bar regulatory authorities abdicate their authority over lawyers when the relevant events largely occur abroad and the principal actors are foreign parties and their local lawyers?

Eventually, the World Trade Organization may resolve some of these issues through negotiation, but it will not be easy. Not only are the issues complex, but lawyers, like farmers, are notorious for their protectionist tendencies. While they may lack societal support in justifying the need to protect national culture, lawyers abroad no doubt will emphasize the importance of understanding local legal practice and the importance of human relationships in resolving disputes.

Moreover, while English has become the *lingua franca* of business for purposes of cross-border commerce, there is always the risk that a particular term possesses a particular meaning in a different country's legal system. The French have a term describing this problem—"*faux amis*"—false friends. This raises the issue of whether law will always retain a local component.

II. THE NEED FOR CHANGE IN LAW PRACTICE MANAGEMENT AND LEGAL ETHICS

The practice of law has been rapidly adapting to the demands of business clients operating in a global economy.[1] Regulation and law enforcement tend to have national bases, but both transactions and disputes are increasingly taking on transnational (cross-border) features. At the same time, regional legal regimes are becoming more prevalent and cannot be overlooked. It is difficult enough to get political units within the same country or agencies at a particular level to cooperate. It is exceedingly more difficult to develop effective cooperation across national borders where linguistic, cultural, and other differences exist.

Presently, Anglo-American legal concepts (including the role of lawyers) dominate international commerce, though this is moderated to some extent by various international trade agreements. This situation exists even though a majority of the world's population operates under other legal systems. For example, most of Europe, South America, and Francophone Africa generally have their own civil law systems. China follows different legal precepts. And some Islamic countries integrate civil, religious, and tribal law.

In some respects, Anglo-American lawyers are frequently propagators of a legal culture to societies very different from their own. It should come as no surprise that a US or English lawyer may feel more comfortable discussing questions of law with Indian or Zambian counterparts than with Dutch or French citizens since lawyers who have worked in common systems may have similar expectations of how to approach legal issues.

While the use of the term "globalization" has become commonplace, the consequences of practicing law in a global environment are difficult to fully comprehend. Indeed, globalization can make it difficult to establish the nationality of a product, legal entity, or individual. It is beyond dispute that globalization has had a real impact on international business and international organizations. Globalization forces lawyers to determine what set of rules should govern their conduct in particular circumstances. What factors should be used to determine the proper range of activities a lawyer may engage in on behalf of clients in a foreign jurisdiction; that is, one in which the lawyer lacks the relevant license or is not a member of the bar? Must a lawyer comply with regulatory and ethical norms promulgated by foreign authorities or international organizations, if the relevant authorities only rarely enforce them?

III. COMPLEXITIES ARISING FROM TECHNOLOGICAL CHANGE

Innovation in computer technology and communication has impacted change in the law, but not fast enough. The rate of technological change and capacity frequently outpaces the ability of organizations and individuals to assimilate it. Yet as corporate business practices change, the lawyers servicing those clients must change as well. The acceleration of the pace of business planning and operations often defy careful planning. Are lawyers capable of meeting their demands or are they likely to be bypassed? Do lawyers have the ability to work with business to ensure compliance with applicable regulatory norms, particularly where there are multiple norm-promulgating entities in more than one country? Are law firms as organizations capable of managing the information their clients may potentially have a need to know? Adding to the mix is that information formerly accessible only to lawyers is frequently available to clients independently.

As many companies seek to contain operating costs and increasingly pursue export markets abroad, lawyers will have to be more sensitive to the international implications of their activities. This is a change in the traditional lawyer paradigm, exacerbated by the fact that the scope and depth of issues with which lawyers must be familiar are increasing exponentially.[2] Though the law is becoming more specialized, it is often the case that lawyers simply cannot be current in all areas. Technology has frequently raised many clients' expectations of their lawyers' ability to respond to their demands in increasingly short periods of time and at lower costs. This has occurred despite the growing complexity of governmental and international regulation in many areas. Instantaneous communications (e.g., telephone, telefax, or e-mail) means that clients can in theory obtain information from their outside counsel in lightning speed. The impact on the quality of lawyers' work product if clients expect responses in increasingly unrealistic short times is rarely thoroughly discussed in law firms prior to taking on a new client.

What new pressures may arise if the information that formerly was available only to lawyers who practiced in narrow fields becomes readily available using services like Lexis and Westlaw, or is even available on the Internet? Will lawyers be willing to explain to their clients that it takes billable time to verify that one's first impressions are indeed correct? Since many law firms' institutional clients can no longer be taken for granted, there is a tendency to try to meet deadlines, often at the cost of quality and ethics.

IV. LAWYERS AS ENTREPRENEURS

In recent years, the manner in which lawyers are organized in the United States, and to a lesser extent in other countries, has also changed. Though many lawyers continue to work as solo practitioners and for small firms, those serving larger corporate clients are increasingly, at least in Canada, Germany, and the United States, taking on the characteristics of their corporate clients. Many law firms are becoming more bureaucratized, impersonal, and focused on shareholder profits.

Nonetheless, law remains a "people" business where human relations (with client personnel, government officials, and colleagues) will always play a critical role in one's ability to succeed. It is not sufficient to be a technically competent lawyer. Successful lawyers working within large law firms are usually expected to be marketers and effective communicators (with respect to clients, colleagues, counterparts, governmental bodies, and regulators). One's technical competence is often no longer sufficient to become and remain a partner or shareholder in a law firm. Lawyers are also discovering that the individuals to whom they are marketing are becoming increasingly diverse. They are no longer only dealing with other Americans with whom they are likely to share common expectations, backgrounds, and manner of professional interaction.

Although law has increasingly taken on characteristics of a business, the paradigm of law as a profession, the conduct of which is governed by generally accepted norms, persists. That is because unlike most other businesses, lawyers are usually not just hired to produce a product or render a generic service. Rather they are hired due to their judgment and experience in dealing with particular types of matters.

To date, ethical rules governing lawyers (particularly the conflict rules) still work better for lawyers that practice in the United States for clients that are small and medium private entities, and are more likely to be engaged in litigation than counseling. These assumptions are almost certainly not the case. As noted above, lawyers are typically involved in a broad range of activities.

To complicate the situation, today's lawyers are increasingly expected to take into account their obligations with respect to other stakeholders, including the public. Regulators, legislators, reporters, and the public are increasingly questioning certain fundamental assumptions underlying the lawyers' professional conduct. This dynamic situation has and will continue to generate novel legal and ethical issues for lawyers serving corporate clients.

V. THE AMERICAN BAR ASSOCIATION, LEGAL ETHICS, AND LEGAL MALPRACTICE

The revolution in corporate governance in America, which has forced the recognition that in a corporate setting US lawyers represent interests of the corporation, and not those of corporate management, have significant implications for lawyers seeking to conduct themselves in an ethical manner. Abuses in this area may arise from the fact that corporate management pays for legal services with someone else's money (i.e., the legal entity and ultimately the owners), which produces a different dynamic than when an individual is the client. The American Bar Association's *Model Rules of Professional Conduct* cannot alone provide US-qualified lawyers engaged in an international/transnational (principally transactional) practice sufficient guidance as to how to uphold their ethical obligations in a manner protecting both their client's, and if relevant, their employers' interests.[3]

The potential risks of violating the ethical rules are huge though often underestimated. When companies pursue business abroad, the relevant transactions are typically larger than the average purely domestic deals. While to some extent such risk is insurable, not all forms of risk are. These risks come in many forms and may involve the failure to manage differences in legal systems, differing expectations of the parties, and miscommunication.

Ethical problems exacerbated by the above factors likely correlate with an increased risk of legal malpractice. Data in this area, however, is limited. It is interesting to note that despite the increase in international trade and investment in connection with the globalization of the world economy, the data collected by the ABA on the number of malpractice claims in recent years that are classified as "international" has been declining. This may be because the insurance companies included in the ABA sample were not representative of the carriers writing the policies for law firms engaged in international matters. Alternatively, law firms may be settling claims without informing their professional liability carrier. Many instances of malpractice are settled quietly, sometimes without the involvement of third parties. Public companies may fear triggering shareholder lawsuits. They know that if a company terminated its own employees involved in a failed project, it is impossible to predict how they will testify.

The human component of international malpractice must not be ignored. As mentioned above, it is difficult to manage from afar. In many markets, senior attorneys lack the language skills to properly render legal services to clients. Expatriate lawyers become increasingly dependent on the judgment of junior, inexperienced local attorneys. While many law firms do an excellent job training and assimilating local lawyers, this is not always the case.

Another factor is that many international law firms often find that the use of expatriate lawyers presents special problems. While it is usually easy to find qualified individuals to live and work in Berlin, Hong Kong, London, and Paris, this is less true in locations where the standard of living is low, western goods are in short supply, and good medical care is not accessible. The result is high turnover among expatriate lawyers. These factors accelerate the process of American firms relying prematurely on local lawyers in various less developed countries.

Lawyers (particularly partners) whose firms maintain offices abroad need to be vigilant in exercising quality control over the work produced for clients. Otherwise, they may find themselves directly liable for malpractice under theories of the failure to supervise, or for not having in place an adequate mechanism for other attorneys to articulate their concerns about the unsatisfactory manner in which particular matters are being handled. Often lawyers who are inclined to be "whistleblowers" but see that their firm's management is nonresponsive usually will stop expressing their views and may ultimately leave the firm. The result is that an overseas office will be staffed and overseen by attorneys who are less sensitive to potential legal malpractice risks or the requirements of professional conduct.

VI. CAN IT BE FIXED? WHAT CAN WE DO?

We have described a picture of a situation that badly needs fixing. But where to start? If lawyers are to adequately conform in order to serve their clients in an increasingly complex world, it may first be necessary to reduce billable hours so that they can have a few extra hours a week to at least contemplate the international or foreign implications of the ethical issues they encounter. Many corporations have found that relying less on outside counsel and expanding the corporate legal department is better because it reduces the divergence in interests between their interests in keeping down fees and their lawyers' interest in making their billable hours. Many law firms advocate billing clients in a manner other than charging by the hour, such as the use of value billing or success fees. This has the additional arguable benefit of bringing the interests of the outside lawyer more in line with the client. It is difficult to exaggerate the interrelationship between conduct (including its ethical component) and the manner in which lawyers are compensated.

Lawyers could increase their billable rates while at the same time reducing billable hour targets so that lawyers can keep abreast with legal developments, chat with a colleague about a legal issue where the client would not regard the activity as billable, or inform themselves of events that could have an impact on how they would counsel an overseas client.

Lawyers may also have to increasingly become self-regulated gatekeepers. Governments at all levels and international bodies seldom have the personnel or other resources to properly monitor corporations and enforce the laws/rules for which they were established. This creates a temptation to increase the gatekeeper role of lawyers. This has received the greatest level of attention in the areas of securities regulation (e.g., the Sarbanes-Oxley Act of 2002, and foreign counterparts), and combating money laundering (e.g., the Bank Secrecy Act as amended by the USA PATRIOT Act of 2001, and their foreign counterparts). Indeed these laws are a harbinger of increased federal regulation of lawyers.

The training of young lawyers in the future thus cannot be conducted in isolation from the practice of law in today's increasingly global society. A lawyer's familiarity with legal ethics, which consists of taking one two-credit course for one semester and reviewing the local rules of professional responsibility during the first week of their first job, will not be adequate. A large organization should not assume that having a single legal ethics counsel is sufficient to prevent and resolve ethical issues, particularly conflict of interest issues.

Ethics should be integrated into substantive areas of the law during law school, particularly in courses dealing with areas of law likely to have international complexities, such as intellectual property law. But even more important is that law schools have a course in international ethics so that students, particularly those who plan on practicing in a large firm environment, are at least made aware of the international implications of their matters. There are currently few law schools that have an ethics course that focuses even partly on international issues. Professors are reluctant to teach it, there are few if any texts that address the issues, and law schools are by nature wary of change. Law schools that don't adopt such a course, however, will soon be held accountable by students and alumni who demand a more relevant ethics course.

Law schools are not the only organizations that must make some changes. Lawyers in firms with multiple and international offices will have to have specialized ongoing training in the area of legal ethics that goes beyond that which is usually provided by one-office firms. Those engaged in an international practice will have to be able to spot a legal matter having implications for the ethical practice of the law, both under the rules of their own jurisdictions and under the norm-promulgating bodies in other states and international organizations, or risk discipline and/or a legal malpractice suit.

How lawyers are to respond to such situations is likely to be a fertile field for legal ethics and hence legal malpractice lawsuits. There is likely to be a great debate within the American Bar Association about some of the fundamental premises upon which the practice of law is based such as attorney-client privilege, conflicts of interests, and other areas. As long as life continues, the ethical questions lawyers face will change and the less likely there will be appropriate guidance formally established and universally accepted. The American Bar Association must take the lead in this change, as it is the sole organization that has the clout to make national legal ethics policy.

With globalization comes greater responsibility to clients that can no longer be ignored.

NOTES

1. Peter J. Gardner, "A Role for the Business Attorney in the Twenty-first Century: Adding Value to the Client's Enterprise in the Knowledge Economy," *Marquette Intellectual Property Law Review* 7: 17 (identifying and evaluating the effect of globalization on the practice of law).

2. See "Introduction and Overview," *American Bar Association Report of the Commission on Multijurisdictional Practice* (August 2002), available at http://www.abanet.org/cpr/mjp/intro-over.doc (accessed March 16, 2006).

3. *Model Rules of Professional Conduct* (2003) R. 1.0. Terminology does not explicitly define "lawyer"—the meaning of which can be gleaned from the *Model Rules'* Preamble—A Lawyer's Responsibilities and other provisions. In contrast, a "firm" or "law firm" is defined as "a lawyer or lawyers in a law partnership, professional corporation, sole proprietorship or other association authorized to practice law; or lawyers employed in a legal services organization or the legal department of a corporation or other organization." See also "Public Company Accounting Reform and Investor Protection (Sarbanes-Oxley) Act" (West: 2005) § 307, *U.S.C.A.* 15 § 7254; *Model Rules of Professional Conduct* (2003) R. 1.5, 1.13 (Confidentiality of Information; Organization as Clients).

PROBLEM SET VI

HELPING MURDERERS GO FREE

You are an attorney in a small city, one of only twenty who do criminal trials on a regular basis. Mr. Debachnik has sought your services. He turned to you only after every other attorney turned him down. Although not an indigent, Mr. Debachnik cannot afford your usual fee.

Based on what he has already admitted to you, Mr. Debachnik is guilty of the charges against him. However, he has a good chance of getting off on a technicality. The police force, while honest and good at catching criminals, suffers from small-town nonchalance: The police did not exactly read Mr. Debachnik his rights before questioning him. They just asked him whether he knew his rights and, when he responded that he had watched a lot of TV, they started their questioning. Mr. Debachnik gave them a good deal of damaging information without asking for an attorney (though he offered nothing that resembled a confession). The state will not have much of a case if all the evidence resulting from these damaging statements is thrown out, and a good attorney would certainly have a good chance of getting them thrown out.

Mr. Debachnik is accused of torturing and then killing six children during the last year. The oldest child was fifteen; the youngest, ten. Mr. Debachnik is not, as far as you can tell, legally insane. May you refuse to take the case? Should you refuse? If you refuse, the court will appoint an attorney fresh out of law school who will most likely not be equipped to make the full defense Mr. Debachnik needs to get off. Is the fact that the court will probably appoint an inexperienced attorney reason enough not to refuse the case? Is it a reason to refuse?

SPREADING DEVASTATION

Your client, a large coal company, owns the mineral rights to tens of thousands of acres of Illinois farmland. The company bought those rights during the Great Depression for a few cents an acre. The deeds permit the company to do whatever is necessary (and legal) to mine the minerals (in this case, coal) under the land. The mining will be done by stripping off the buildings, topsoil, and anything else lying on the surface; digging down until there is no coal left; and then filling the huge hole with whatever fill is available. When the company is done with the land, even grass will have trouble growing there. No one knows how to make such strip-mined land good for much of anything,

Because of the high price of oil, the price of coal has risen sharply. Your client can now make a substantial profit mining the coal it bought during the 1930s. The company has also become concerned that if it sits on the coal too long, the state will make strip-mining of good farmland too expensive or impossible. Thus, your client has asked you to begin eviction proceedings against one hundred families to make room for a huge mining operation. Even given the recent changes in state law, your client will probably prevail if the evictions are contested in court. If you proceed as planned, one hundred wealthy Illinois farming families will suddenly be transformed into paupers. Farms worth almost a million dollars each will be reduced to worthless desert. Society will lose but your client stands to make a good profit.

May you refuse to do as your client asked? Should you? If you were to decline, some other attorney would, you are sure, do what you have refused to do, and he would do it citing the duty of attorneys to make legal counsel available.

HELPING THE ALMOST POOR

Uchettle Omoz has an eight-unit apartment building about two blocks from his home. He is an aging factory worker who invested his savings in "income-producing property." The neighborhood in which the building is located, while not "changing," is a rough mixture of hardworking Mexicans, heavy-drinking Irish, and the poor residue of several Eastern European nationalities who once dominated the neighborhood. Omoz belongs to one of those nationalities and does not trust the

Irish or the Mexican residents. His building, unfortunately, is filled entirely with those he generally distrusts. "I can't rent to nobody else," he says. Most of his tenants are "exceptions" about whom he has no complaints. But he has had trouble now and then with nonpayment of rent, belligerence, and noise. "I try to run a good building. I keep the building good and don't want no trouble."

Until now he has rented without leases, since he thought he could just throw out anyone he wanted to evict. But recently he read in a consumer newsletter that a tenant could hold out, even without a lease, for at least ninety days and maybe not even have to pay the rent for that period. The possibility made him look for a new way to avoid trouble, a new tactic to protect his property. His idea is to make each tenant sign a lease that says in effect, "If you don't pay the rent or if you cause trouble, you have to leave the day I tell you to, no delay, no courts, no nothing." He wants the eviction provision in "bold print, simple English, so that I can show it in their faces when I want them out." He wants a lease prepared with blanks he can fill in for the particular tenant at the time he rents an apartment. He would have copies run off at the local print shop and use the lease for years to come.

Omoz has (quite rightly) a suspicion that the lease he wants would not stand up in court: "They don't care about the little property anymore." But he is not worried by this suspicion. He does not believe his tenants would go to court: "They are working people, like myself. They have too much money, too much pride, to go to legal aid. But they don't have enough money to feel they can go to attorneys, not when the lease says plain 'you lose.' Ah, even I can barely afford an attorney." The lease is to be a shortcut to save both money and trouble.

Should you prepare the lease? If not, what should you do instead?

SUGGESTED READINGS

Michael Bayles, "A Problem of Clean Hands: Refusal to Provide Professional Services," *Social Theory and Practice* 5 (Spring 1979): 165–81.

James Fallow, "Sheepskins Are for Sheep," *Washington Monthly* (1980): 9–17.

Robert W. Gordon, "A New Role for Lawyers?: The Corporate Counselor After Enron," *Connecticut Law Review* 35 (Spring 2003): 1185–1210.

Robert R. Kuehn, "Undermining Justice: The Legal Profession's Role in Restricting Access to Legal Representation," *Utah Law Review* (2006): 1039.

Michael W. Loudenslager, "E-Lawyering, The ABA's Current Choice of Ethics Law Rule & the Dormant Commerce Clause: Why the Dormant Commerce Clause Invalidates Model Rule 8.5(B)(2) When Applied to Attorney Internet Representations of Clients," *William & Mary Bill of Rights Journal* 15 (December 2006): 587.

David Luban, "Washington's Torture Lawyers," *Legal Ethics and Human Dignity* (Cambridge, UK: Cambridge University Press, 2007), chapter 5.

APPENDIX

—

MISCELLANEOUS PROBLEMS

ADDITIONAL PROBLEMS

IS HONESTY THE BEST POLICY?

You recently advised J. J. Cantilever concerning his nonresidential $500,000 mortgage with the Minimal Mortgage Company, which was threatening foreclosure. You informed him as gently as you could that there was no legal way to prevent the foreclosure, and you explained why. Cantilever said, "I see" and left.

Two days later Cantilever kidnapped Mr. Heindricks, the president of Minimal Mortgage, and hid Heindricks in his apartment. According to police, Cantilever claims to have wired the apartment so that it will explode if anyone opens the front door. Cantilever is known to have received extensive demolition training in the Army and is believed to be technically capable of carrying out his threat. The police are afraid to storm the building for just that reason.

Cantilever also strapped a shotgun to Heindricks's neck and threatened to kill him if the mortgage company did not cancel the obligation and apologize publicly for the terrible way he had been treated. Minimal Mortgage met both demands quickly.

You had followed these events with considerable interest over the two days they unfolded but as no more than an interested bystander. Now you are no longer a bystander. Cantilever has also demanded total immunity from criminal or civil prosecution or psychiatric confinement arising out of his acts during the last two days. He demanded that the immunity be in writing and signed by the county prosecutor. The county prosecutor has provided such a guarantee and publicly said he intended to honor it. But Cantilever was not satisfied. He thought there might be some legal trick. So, he has asked you to review the grant of immunity and give him your professional opinion on its completeness and effectiveness. The police transmitted his request to you.

Though you had previously advised Cantilever on business matters only, you are qualified to answer the questions he is asking. Your research has convinced you that the prosecutor is probably not legally bound by his grant of immunity, especially under the circumstances. You therefore wonder what to tell Cantilever. You have every reason to believe that he will kill Heindricks if he believes the prosecutor's offer is not good. Should you advise Cantilever at all in this matter? If so, how should you advise him?

Suppose again the facts of the previous problem, except that you are now the prosecutor rather than Cantilever's adviser. You know you cannot make a (legally) effective offer of immunity under these extraordinary circumstances. But you are morally certain that if you do not appear to make such an offer, Cantilever will kill his hostage. You cannot appear to make such an offer without publicly making false or misleading statements. Should you, as an attorney and a public prosecutor, make such statements?

YOUR CLIENT WANTS TO BLAB

Your client is one of four persons indicted in a narcotics conspiracy case. Each of those indicted has his own attorney. To avoid having the government play them off one against the other, you all agreed to meet in your conference room to coordinate strategy.

During the meeting, the defendants discussed their roles in the conspiracy, each making damaging admissions. The conspiracy was a complex affair. As it turned out, your client had no idea how complex it really was. He had thought himself a crucial figure linked to the others in a single chain. He was both disappointed and relieved to find out that he was only an expendable part in a series of interlocking wheels.

Before the meeting, your client wanted to fight the case every inch of the way. But now he wants to go to the district attorney and tell everything he knows. Most of what he knows, it turns out, is what he picked up at the meeting. There is no doubt that the DA would be willing to drop most or all of the charges against your client in return for his information—provided the information includes admissions made in your conference room.

What should you do if your client persists in his plan to tell all? May you continue to represent him? Or must you withdraw? Should you do everything you can to assist him? May you—must you—inform counsel for the co-defendants of what your client is about to do? What do you owe those who trusted your client and you? What do you owe your client now?

FINDING A WAY TO HELP YOUR CLIENT

An attorney in a sensational robbery case entered into an agreement with his client taking as his fee (a) a lien on the defendant's home, (b) assignment of the defendant's right to money seized by police (not all of which may be provably part of the loot), and (c) all publication rights to the story of the defendant's life. The agreement was entered into before the case was tried. Did the attorney do anything unethical? Does the answer to this question depend upon how much the attorney told his client about the legal consequences of his agreement? Does it matter that the client could not otherwise have paid the attorney anything approaching his usual fee?

WHAT IF ERNEST ISN'T EARNEST

You are an assistant district attorney in a big city. Most of the cases you deal with are simple misdemeanors (for example, shoplifting or carrying a concealed weapon), and most are settled by plea-bargaining between you and the accused's attorney after the usual (brief) negotiation. Most attorneys with whom you deal are long-time members of the "lower" criminal bar, plodding but hard-nosed, businesslike, and skilled in making a deal. Most days there is nothing memorable about what you do or whom you talk to.

Today, however, is different. You have before you one Frank Lee Ernest, Esq., a recent graduate of a local law school and an even more recent admittee to the bar. A solo practitioner, he has come to you to plea-bargain for a client accused of shoplifting. In the course of a three-minute conversation with you, he has revealed (quite unintentionally, of course) that all he knows of his client's record is what he learned from his client (an experienced shoplifter and confidence man for whom, it seems, most of his past is a closed book). He has also made it pretty clear that he does not have a firm grasp of the law of shoplifting and is depending on you to tell him what he needs to know to make a good deal. Because you are a decent sort, you tell him (and otherwise help him to make a fair deal for his client).

But you find the whole experience troubling. At best, Ernest has been gullible and lazy. He has believed his client without checking the public record and has not bothered to learn the law relevant to the case because he assumed you would be fair with him. At worst, he is an incompetent attorney, whom his client, however unsavory himself, has relied on to present his case in the best light so that he can make the best deal. The deal you have made with Ernest, though fair, probably is not the deal an experienced attorney would have wrung from you.

Has Ernest done anything ethically wrong? Should he be disciplined in some way? How and why? Do you have a professional obligation to say anything to him about what he has done? Do you have a professional obligation to report him to the local Grievance Committee?

USING WHAT ONE LEARNED IN GOVERNMENT SERVICE

An attorney worked for the federal government in the antitrust division for six years during which he spent almost one year helping to prepare a case against a certain company for conspiring to fix prices for police mobile computers. Although never in charge of the case, the attorney did much to give it its final shape. The case was settled by a consent decree in 2006, three years after the attorney left government service. Suppose the attorney, now in private practice in Chicago, were to be offered employment by the City of Chicago to sue the very same company for recovery of monies the city paid in excess of the fair market value of the mobile computers it purchased. Chicago intends to bring a class action on behalf of all cities similarly situated and proposes to retain the attorney on a contingency basis. Would it be unethical for the attorney to accept the proffered employment? Would your answer be any different if the city had (a) offered to pay the attorney on an hourly basis instead of on a contingency basis or (b) if it asked the attorney to join the city's legal office part-time for the duration of the case?

USING YOUR WITS

An attorney in Idaho has been retained to file suit against a California company for unfair business practices and violation of trademark rights. It would be more convenient for the client if the suit could be filed in a federal court in Idaho rather than in a federal court in California. If the California company does substantial business in Idaho, it can be sued there. Otherwise it cannot be. Information will be needed to establish such substantial business before the attorney can make use of discovery and other means of forcing the California company to reveal the extent of its business dealings in Idaho. The information can probably be obtained simply by phoning the company's main office and asking for the names of its outlets in Idaho. Is there anything unethical about an attorney getting the information in this way? You may suppose (1) that the person giving the information will be a low-level clerk, (2) that any person wishing to buy the company's product could do the same thing, (3) that the reason the clerk will give out the information is that he supposes the person requesting such information to be a potential customer, (4) that the California company has permanent counsel the name of which the company would happily reveal if the attorney were to ask for it, and (5) that the company's counsel would not reveal the information in question unless a court ordered it. Would your answer be different if the information were available on the company's Web site?